FIFTY KEY VIDEO GAMES

This volume examines fifty of the most important video games that have contributed significantly to the history, development, or culture of the medium, providing an overview of video games from their beginning to the present day.

This volume covers a variety of historical periods and platforms, genres, commercial impact, artistic choices, contexts of play, typical and atypical representations, uses of games for specific purposes, uses of materials or techniques, specific subcultures, repurposing, transgressive aesthetics, interfaces, moral or ethical impact, and more. Key video games featured include *Animal Crossing*, *Call of Duty*, *Grand Theft Auto*, *The Legend of Zelda*, *Minecraft*, *PONG*, *Super Mario Bros.*, *Tetris*, and *World of Warcraft*. Each game is closely analyzed in order to properly contextualize it, to emphasize its prominent features, to show how it creates a unique experience of gameplay, and to outline the ways it might speak about society and culture. The book also acts as a highly accessible showcase to a range of disciplinary perspectives that are found and practiced in the field of game studies.

With each entry supplemented by references and suggestions for further reading, *Fifty Key Video Games* is an indispensable reference for anyone interested in video games.

Bernard Perron is a Full Professor of Film and Game Studies at Université de Montréal. He co-edited, among others, *The Video Game Theory Reader 1* and *2* (2003; 2009), *The Routledge Companion to Video Game Studies* (2014), and *Video Games and the Mind: Essays on Cognition, Affect and Emotion* (2016) and edited *Horror Video Games: Essays on the Fusion of Fear and Play* (2009). He is the author of *Silent Hill: The Terror Engine* (2012) and *The World of Scary Video Games: A Study in Videoludic Horror* (2018). His research concentrates on video games, interactive cinema, the horror genre, and on narration, cognition, and the ludic dimension of narrative cinema.

Kelly Boudreau is an Associate Professor of Interactive Media Theory and Design at Harrisburg University of Science and Technology. With a background in sociology, film studies, and games studies, she has published on topics ranging from player/avatar relationships in the networked process of video game play, different forms of sociality in and mediated by digital games, to toxic and problematic player behavior in different player communities.

Mark J. P. Wolf is a Professor in the Communication Department at Concordia University Wisconsin whose books include *The Video Game Theory Reader 1* and *2* (2003; 2009), *The Routledge Companion to Video Game Studies* (2014), *Building Imaginary Worlds* (2012), *The Routledge Companion to Imaginary Worlds* (2017), *The Routledge Companion to Media Technology and Obsolescence* (2018), and *Encyclopedia of Video Games* (2nd Edition, 2021).

Dominic Arsenault is an Associate Professor of Film and Game Studies at Université de Montréal. His main publications revolve around narrative and narration in games, genre, and video game history, notably with his recent *Super Power, Spoony Bards, and Silverware: The Super Nintendo Entertainment System* in the MIT Press platform studies series. He teaches on narratology for film, games and literature, video game screenwriting, and animation film history and theory. He also explores the links between video games and heavy metal music through research and creation with his solo chipmetal project *Multi-Memory Controller*.

FIFTY KEY VIDEO GAMES

Edited by
Bernard Perron, Kelly Boudreau, Mark J.P. Wolf
and Dominic Arsenault

NEW YORK AND LONDON

Cover image: © Mickey Lam

First published 2023
by Routledge
605 Third Avenue, New York, NY 10158

and by Routledge
4 Park Square, Milton Park, Abingdon, Oxon, OX14 4RN

Routledge is an imprint of the Taylor & Francis Group, an informa business

© 2023 selection and editorial matter, Bernard Perron, Kelly Boudreau, Mark J. P. Wolf, and Dominic Arsenault; individual chapters, the contributors

The right of Bernard Perron, Kelly Boudreau, Mark J. P. Wolf, and Dominic Arsenault to be identified as the authors of the editorial material, and of the authors for their individual chapters, has been asserted in accordance with sections 77 and 78 of the Copyright, Designs and Patents Act 1988.

All rights reserved. No part of this book may be reprinted or reproduced or utilised in any form or by any electronic, mechanical, or other means, now known or hereafter invented, including photocopying and recording, or in any information storage or retrieval system, without permission in writing from the publishers.

Trademark notice: Product or corporate names may be trademarks or registered trademarks, and are used only for identification and explanation without intent to infringe.

Library of Congress Cataloging-in-Publication Data
Names: Perron, Bernard, editor. | Boudreau, Kelly, editor. | Wolf, Mark J. P., editor. | Arsenault, Dominic, editor.
Title: Fifty key video games / edited by Bernard Perron, Kelly Boudreau, Mark J.P. Wolf, and Dominic Arsenault.
Description: New York, NY : Routledge, 2022. | Includes bibliographic references and index.
Identifiers: LCCN 2022005203 (print) | LCCN 2022005204 (ebook) | ISBN 9781032057989 (hardback) | ISBN 9781032053608 (paperback) | ISBN 9781003199205 (ebook)
Subjects: LCSH: Video games--History. | Video games--Reviews.
Classification: LCC GV1469.3 .F55 2022 (print) | LCC GV1469.3 (ebook) | DDC 794.8--dc23/eng/20220421
LC record available at https://lccn.loc.gov/2022005203
LC ebook record available at https://lccn.loc.gov/2022005204

ISBN: 978-1-032-05798-9 (hbk)
ISBN: 978-1-032-05360-8 (pbk)
ISBN: 978-1-003-19920-5 (ebk)

DOI: 10.4324/9781003199205

Typeset in Bembo
by SPi Technologies India Pvt Ltd (Straive)

CONTENTS

Alphabetical List of Contents	vi
Chronological List of Contents	viii
Contributors	x
Introduction	1
Fifty Key Video Games	7
Index	313

ALPHABETICAL LIST OF CONTENTS

Adventure (1979)	9
Angry Birds (2009)	15
Animal Crossing (2001)	21
Assassin's Creed Origins (2017)	26
Bejeweled (2001)	32
BRAID (2008)	38
Call of Duty: Modern Warfare 2 (2009)	44
Dance Dance Revolution (1998)	50
Diablo (1996)	56
Donkey Kong (1981)	63
DOOM (1993)	69
Dragon's Lair (1983)	75
The Elder Scrolls II: Daggerfall (1996)	81
Elite (1984)	88
EVE Online (2003)	93
FarmVille (2009)	98
FIFA 14 (2013)	104
Final Fantasy VII (1997)	110
Fortnite Battle Royale (2017)	116
Grand Theft Auto III (2001)	123
Guitar Hero (2005)	129
Half-Life (1998)	135
Journey (2012)	141
King's Quest (1984)	148
The Legend of Zelda (1986)	153
Minecraft (2009)	159
Mortal Kombat (1992)	166
Need for Speed III: Hot Pursuit (1998)	172
No Man's Sky (2016)	178
The Oregon Trail (1971)	184
Pac-Man (1980)	190

ALPHABETICAL LIST OF CONTENTS

Pokémon Go (2016)	196
PONG (1972)	202
Portal (2007)	209
Resident Evil (1996)	216
Riven (1997)	222
Sid Meier's Civilization (1991)	227
SimCity (1989)	233
The Sims 4 (2014)	239
Space Invaders (1978)	245
StarCraft (1998)	251
Super Mario 64 (1996)	257
Super Mario Bros. (1985)	262
Tetris (1984)	268
This War of Mine (2014)	274
Ultima IV: Quest of the Avatar (1985)	280
Wii Sports (2006)	286
Wing Commander III: Heart of the Tiger (1994)	293
World of Warcraft (2004)	299
Zork (1980)	305

CHRONOLOGICAL LIST OF CONTENTS

The Oregon Trail (1971)	184
PONG (1972)	202
Space Invaders (1978)	245
Adventure (1979)	9
Pac-Man (1980)	190
Zork (1980)	305
Donkey Kong (1981)	63
Dragon's Lair (1983)	75
Elite (1984)	88
King's Quest (1984)	148
Tetris (1984)	268
Super Mario Bros. (1985)	262
Ultima IV: Quest of the Avatar (1985)	280
The Legend of Zelda (1986)	153
SimCity (1989)	233
Sid Meier's Civilization (1991)	227
Mortal Kombat (1992)	166
DOOM (1993)	69
Wing Commander III: Heart of the Tiger (1994)	293
Diablo (1996)	56
The Elder Scrolls II: Daggerfall (1996)	81
Resident Evil (1996)	216
Super Mario 64 (1996)	257
Final Fantasy VII (1997)	110
Riven (1997)	222
Dance Dance Revolution (1998)	50
Half-Life (1998)	135
Need for Speed III: Hot Pursuit (1998)	172
StarCraft (1998)	251
The Sims 4 (2014)	239
Animal Crossing (2001)	21

CHRONOLOGICAL LIST OF CONTENTS

Bejeweled (2001) 32
Grand Theft Auto III (2001) 123
EVE Online (2003) 93
World of Warcraft (2004) 299
Guitar Hero (2005) 129
Wii Sports (2006) 286
Portal (2007) 209
BRAID (2008) 38
Angry Birds (2009) 15
Call of Duty: Modern Warfare 2 (2009) 44
FarmVille (2009) 98
Minecraft (2009) 159
Journey (2012) 141
FIFA 14 (2013) 104
This War of Mine (2014) 274
No Man's Sky (2016) 178
Pokémon Go (2016) 196
Assassin's Creed Origins (2017) 26
Fortnite Battle Royale (2017) 116

CONTRIBUTORS

Espen Aarseth is Professor of game studies at the IT University of Copenhagen, and a member of the Royal Danish Academy of Sciences and Letters. He is the founding editor of *Game Studies*, and directs the European Research Council's Advanced Grant project MSG – Making Sense of Games.

Kati Alha is a researcher and a university lecturer, teaching game studies in Tampere University, Finland. She has been a part of Tampere University Game Research Lab since 2009 and has studied games from multiple perspectives, with expertise in free-to-play games, location-based games, and player experiences. In her dissertation, she focused on how the free-to-play model has changed games and playing.

Dominic Arsenault is Associate Professor of film and game studies at Université de Montréal. His main publications revolve around narrative and narration in games, genre, and video game history, notably with his recent *Super Power, Spoony Bards, and Silverware: The Super Nintendo Entertainment System* in the MIT Press platform studies series. He teaches on narratology for film, games and literature, video game screenwriting, and animation film history and theory. He also explores the links between video games and heavy metal music through research and creation with his solo chipmetal project *Multi-Memory Controller*.

Kelly Bergstrom is Assistant Professor in the Department of Communication and Media Studies at York University. Her research examines drop out and disengagement from digital cultures, with a focus on digital games and social media. She is co-editor of *Internet Spaceships are Serious Business: An EVE Online Reader* (University of Minnesota Press, 2016) and her work has been published in journals such as *Feminist Media Studies*, *Critical Studies in Media Communication*, and *Games & Culture*.

CONTRIBUTORS

Kelly Boudreau is Associate Professor of Interactive Media Theory and Design at Harrisburg University of Science and Technology. With a background in sociology, film studies, and games studies, she has published on topics ranging from player/avatar relationships in the networked process of video game play, different forms of sociality in and mediated by digital games, to toxic and problematic player behavior in different player communities.

Nicholas David Bowman (PhD, Michigan State University) is Associate Professor in the College of Media and Communication at Texas Tech University. His primary research examines the uses and effects of interactive media technologies, such as video games, virtual/augmented/mixed reality, and social media. His most recent work focuses on the cognitive, emotional, physical, and social demands of interactivity. He has extensive teaching and research experience in the United States, Germany, and Taiwan, and prior editorial experience with *Communication Research Reports* and *Journal of Media Psychology*. Most recently, he was named the Fulbright Taiwan Wu Jing-Jyi Arts and Culture Fellow at the National Chengchi University in Taipei.

Shira Chess is Associate Professor of Entertainment and Media Studies at the University of Georgia. Her research explores how video games are designed and advertised to women audiences, often de-prioritizing leisure. She is the author of *Ready Player Two: Women Gamers and Designed Identity* (University of Minnesota Press, 2017) and *Play Like a Feminist* (MIT Press, 2020).

David Church is a film and media scholar who specializes in genre studies, taste cultures, and histories of film circulation. He is the author of *Grindhouse Nostalgia: Memory, Home Video, and Exploitation Film Fandom* (Edinburgh University Press, 2015); *Disposable Passions: Vintage Pornography and the Material Legacies of Adult Cinema* (Bloomsbury Academic, 2016); *Post-Horror: Art, Genre, and Cultural Elevation* (Edinburgh University Press, 2021); and *Mortal Kombat: Games of Death* (University of Michigan Press, 2022).

Michael J. Clarke is Associate Professor of TV, Film, and Media Studies at California State University, Los Angeles. His work has appeared in *Television and New Media*, *Games and Culture*, and *Journal of Graphic Novels and Comics*. His book, *Transmedia Television*, is available from Bloomsbury Press. He is currently completing a book-length manuscript on *Dragon's Lair* to be published in 2022.

CONTRIBUTORS

Hilde G. Corneliussen is a Research Professor in Technology and Society at Western Norway Research Institute. She has a doctoral degree (2003) in Humanistic Informatics from University of Bergen, where she was a lecturer and researcher between 1998 and 2016. Her main field of research relates to gender, diversity, and technology in a variety of arenas including leisure activities, education, and work. She is one of the principal researchers in Nordwit, a Nordic Centre of Excellence on Women in Technology Driven Careers, and she has been a project leader for several research projects on gender cultures of computing. Her publications include the monograph *Gender-Technology Relations: Exploring Stability and Change* (2012, Palgrave Macmillan), and the anthology *Digital Culture, Play, and Identity: A World of Warcraft® Reader* (2008, MIT Press) co-edited with Jill Walker Rettberg.

Angela R. Cox was most recently an Assistant Teaching Professor at Ball State University in Muncie, Indiana, USA, where she taught first-year composition courses. Her interest in game studies and research is deeply rooted in childhood memories of playing Sierra adventure games. She earned her PhD in 2016 from the University of Arkansas in English Rhetoric and Composition; her current research interests include genre, nostalgia, and retrograming.

Maxime Deslongchamps-Gagnon has a PhD in cinema and video game studies from Université de Montréal, where he is a lecturer. His thesis project concerns the role of emotions in the ethics of narrative video games. He is a research assistant for the Video Games Observation and Documentation University Lab (LUDOV). He has published on the emotional experience of video games and its connection to aesthetics and virtue ethics, on the walking simulator genre, and on the relation between cinema and video games. In collaboration with Hugo Montembeault, he co-hosted Profil Ludique, an academic podcast dedicated to the walking simulator genre.

Simon Dor is Assistant Professor at Université du Québec en Abitibi-Témiscamingue (UQAT). His research mainly focuses on strategy and management games, whether from a gameplay or representational point of view, with a competitive or narrative lens, or using a cognitive, philosophical, or historical approach. His teaching and research has also led him to work on e-sports, immersion, ethics, emulators, and game design. He also writes on a personal research blog (http://www.simondor.com) and often uses Twitch and YouTube to understand their impact on gaming culture and to share his work.

CONTRIBUTORS

Marc-André Éthier is Professor of History Didactics (Université de Montréal, Québec, Canada). The major Canadian research councils have funded his work on teaching materials and curricula, the teaching, learning, and assessment of skills related to historical and critical thinking. With Lefrançois and others, he is conducting research on how teachers and students use teaching materials (including video games), and the effects of this use in the development of the agency and historical thinking. He serves as a spokesperson of the Association Québécoise pour la didactique de l'histoire et de la géographie, and as editor-in-chief of the *Revue des sciences de l'éducation*.

Manuel Garin is Senior Lecturer in Film and Media Studies at Universitat Pompeu Fabra, Barcelona, where he teaches and develops research on cinema, art history, and comparative media.

Harrison Gish is a doctoral candidate in UCLA's Cinema and Media Studies program. His work appears in the recent edited collections *How to Play Video Games* and the *Encyclopedia of Video Games*, as well as the journals *eLudamos*, *Mediascape*, and *CineAction*. He is a member of the Society for Cinema and Media Studies Video Game Studies Scholarly Interest Group, of which he was the co-chair from 2014 to 2017, and the Learning Games Initiative.

Paweł Grabarczyk is Associate Professor at the IT University of Copenhagen. He is an analytic philosopher and a game scholar who studies the boundaries between philosophy and technology. His work covers philosophy of language and mind, game ontology, and the history of computing. He is the editor-in-chief of *Replay. The Polish Journal of Game Studies*.

Julianne Grasso is a Visiting Assistant Professor of Music at the Butler School of Music at the University of Texas at Austin. She earned her PhD in Music History and Theory in 2020 from the University of Chicago, where her dissertation explored musical meaning and experience in video games.

Ashley Guajardo (formerly Brown) is Associate Professor (Lecturing) at Entertainment Arts and Engineering, University of Utah. She teaches game user research and design as well as runs a games user research lab. Her research interests include gaming and sexuality, Twitch, and gaming and pedagogy. She has been a fan of *Animal Crossing* ever since it came out on the GameCube, even going so far as to name her yellow rescue mutt Isabelle after the infamous assistant.

CONTRIBUTORS

Mark Hayse is Director of the Mabee Library and Director of the undergraduate Honors Program at MidAmerica Nazarene University in Olathe, KS. His research and writing interests include digital and tabletop games, curriculum theory and design, and the interdisciplinarity of religion, philosophy, technology, and education. He has published over twenty book chapters, journal articles, or essays about video games and tabletop games, primarily focused upon their religious, spiritual, ethical, and educational dimensions.

Adam Hunter spent the first dozen years of his career in the video game industry as a narrative director, writer, and designer. He now works at the University of Utah's top-ranked Entertainment Arts and Engineering (EAE) program, where he has the privilege of helping teach and guide the next generation of game developers.

Andra Ivănescu is Senior Lecturer in game studies and ludomusicology at Brunel University London. Her primary area of research lies at the intersection of nostalgia, musicology, and video games. She has published work in the fields of ludomusicology and game studies in journals including *The Soundtrack* and *The Computer Games Journal* as well as a number of edited collections, most recently *The Cambridge Companion to Video Game Music* (2021). She is the author of *Popular Music in the Nostalgia Video Game: The Way It Never Sounded* (2019).

Alexandre Joly-Lavoie (PhD) is a pedagogical counselor specializing in the use and implementation of technology in teaching practices. He is also a part-time lecturer in various teacher training courses, specifically on the different uses of media such as video games, comics, etc. as didactic tools. For his doctoral thesis, he analyzed the representation of agency in various historical games. Recent research interests focus on the integration of video games and the use of virtual reality in teaching practices.

Jesper Juul is a Copenhagen-based video game theorist interested in how video games are meaningful to players. He has published on the interaction between rules and fiction in video games (*Half-Real*, 2005), on the design of casual games for a broad audience (*A Casual Revolution*, 2009), on the aesthetics of failure (*The Art of Failure*, 2013), and most recently *Handmade Pixels* on the rise of smaller and more experimental video games. He also co-edits the Playful Thinking Series for MIT Press. https://www.jesperjuul.net@jesperjuul

CONTRIBUTORS

Brendan Keogh is a researcher of video game culture at Queensland University of Technology in the Digital Media Research Centre. He is the author of *A Play of Bodies: How We Perceive Videogames*; *Killing is Harmless*; and *The Unity Game Engine and the Circuits of Cultural Software* (co-authored with Benjamin Nicoll).

Jessica Kizzire earned her Ph.D. in musicology at the university of Iowa and studies music in popular media, including film and video games. Her research has included explorations of the intersection between video game music and player nostalgia in *Final Fantasy IX*, as well as her most recent research exploring the interrelation of multiple villains' themes across several games in the *Final Fantasy* franchise. Jessica also studies the role of music in multimedia adaptations, and she is currently working on her first book, which analyzes the narrative implications of musical adaptations of Lewis Carroll's *Alice's Adventures in Wonderland*.

Jens Kjeldgaard-Christiansen is a postdoctoral researcher at the Department of English, Aarhus University. His research explores the nature of villainous characters in popular culture as well as ethical issues surrounding video games. His work appears in journals such as *Poetics, Projections*, and *The Journal of Popular Culture*.

Peter Krapp is Professor of Film and Media Studies at the University of California, Irvine, and also affiliated with the Departments of English, Music (Claire Trevor School of the Arts), and Informatics (Donald Bren School of Information and Computer Science). He taught at the University of Minnesota and at Bard College before coming to UC Irvine; he has since held visiting positions in Taiwan, South Africa, Germany, and Brazil. Among his main publications are *Deja Vu: Aberrations of Cultural Memory* (2004), and *Noise Channels: Glitch and Error in Digital Culture* (2011), both with the University of Minnesota Press; he was also an editor of *Medium Cool* (Duke UP, 2002) as well as of the *Handbook Language-Culture-Communication* (DeGruyter, 2013). His main research interests include digital culture, media history, secret communications, and cultural memory.

Mark Kretzschmar is a video game researcher and holds a PhD in Texts and Technology from the University of Central Florida. His research emphasizes games studies, including control, commodification, consumerism, and creation in video games, and how these terms intersect in emergent media to impact storytelling and gamer experience. He also studies the history of video games, modifications, and the roles video game genres play in discussions about gamer culture, gamer perceptions of control, philosophy, and game design.

Selim Krichane is a scientific collaborator at EPFL and Université de Lausanne, Switzerland. His doctoral thesis deals with the relationship between cinema and video games, focusing on the history of the "camera" in videogames. An augmented version of his PhD has been published in French (*La Caméra imaginaire*, Georg, 2018). Co-founder of the GameLab UNIL-EPFL, he has published several articles on cinema and video games in scientific journals (*Game Studies, Cahiers de Narratologie, Décadrages, Archipel*) and frequently contributes to joint publications (*Genre et jeux vidéo / Gender and Videogames*, PUL, 2015; *Christian Metz and the Codes of Cinema*, AUP, 2018).

Lori Landay (PhD) is an interdisciplinary teacher, scholar, and artist whose creative and critical work explores themes of transformation in audiovisual cultural forms, technology, and perception. She is Professor of Visual Culture and New Media at Berklee College of Music (Boston), and authored the Berklee Online courses, Game Design Principles and The Language of Film and TV. Dr. Landay is the author of two books, *I Love Lucy* and *Madcaps, Screwballs, and Con Women: The Female Trickster in American Culture*, and publications on commodification, subjectivity, and innovation in media. Lori's award-winning new media art has exhibited internationally. Lori is the Creative Director of *Dream Machine*, rock legend Nona Hendryx's multimedia immersive, interactive performance platform for VR and web. As Vice Chairperson of the Board of Directors of Brookline Interactive Group/Public VR Lab, she advocates for public access to media. She lives in Boston with her spouse, twin sons, and forest cat.

David Lefrançois is Professor of Education Sciences (Univerité du Québec en Outaouais, Canada). His research and publications examine school program content and methods used to teach and assess learning in elementary and secondary social sciences. His work focuses on: (1) the critical analysis of the Québec curricula in social studies; and (2) the development of critical thinking in history and financial education. He participates as a researcher in the Centre de recherche interuniversitaire sur la formation et la profession enseignante, and the partnership Accès au droit et à la justice, through the legal education project, in collaboration with Éthier.

CONTRIBUTORS

David J. Leonard is a writer, teacher, and scholar. He is the author of several books, including *Playing While White: Privilege and Power on and off the Field* (University of Washington Press, 2017) and *After Artest: The NBA and the Assault on Blackness* (SUNY Press, 2012). With C. Richard King, he is co-author of *Beyond Hate: White Power and Popular Culture* (Routledge, 2014).

Neil Lerner is a scholar of music and screen media. He has written about music in a wide variety of films, television shows, and video games. His work as an editor includes *Music in Video Games: Studying Play* (with K.J. Donnelly and William Gibbons), *The Oxford Handbook of Music and Disability Studies* (with Blake Howe, Stephanie Jensen-Moulton, and Joseph N. Straus), and *Music in the Horror Film: Listening to Fear*.

Jonathan Lessard is Associate Professor of game design and virtual worlds in the Design and Computation Arts Department of Concordia University, Montréal. He has published multiple game history papers, particularly from the perspective of game design. He is also a long-time game designer, developer, and research-creator. He leads the LabLabLab research group on interactive conversations and emergent storytelling.

Corrinne Lewis (MFA) is Assistant Professor (Lecturer) and the Undergraduate Director for the top-ranked Entertainment Arts and Engineering (EAE) program at the University of Utah. She has taught a variety of game-oriented classes for over a decade, is the co-host of the game developer podcast, *Building 72*, and her area of research is video game storytelling and narrative.

Henry Lowood is the Harold C. Hohbach Curator at Stanford University, responsible for history of science and technology collections, and film and media collections in the Stanford Libraries. With combined interests in history, technological innovation and the history of digital games and simulations, he heads several long-term projects at Stanford, including *How They Got Game: The History and Culture of Interactive Simulations and Videogames* in the Stanford Humanities Lab and Stanford Libraries, the Silicon Valley Archives in the Stanford Libraries and the Machinima Archives and Archiving Virtual Worlds collections hosted by the Internet Archive. He led Stanford's work on game and virtual world preservation in the Preserving Virtual Worlds project funded by the U.S. Library of Congress and the Institute for Museum and Library services and the Game Citation Project also funded by IMLS. He is also the author of numerous articles and essays on the history of Silicon Valley and the development of digital game technology and culture. With Michael Nitsche, he co-edited *The Machinima Reader* (2011) and, with Raiford Guins, *Debugging Game History: A Critical Lexicon* (2016), both for MIT Press. With Guins, he also co-edits the book series, *Game Histories*, for MIT Press.

Martin Lüthe is currently Assistant Professor at the John F. Kennedy Institute for North American Studies at Freie Universitaet Berlin and Einstein Junior Fellow. Lüthe published the monographs *"We Missed a Lot of Church, So the Music Is Our Confessional": Rap and Religion* (Lit Verlag, 2008) and *Color-Line and Crossing-Over: Motown and Performances of Blackness in 1960s American Culture* (WVT, 2011). He also co-edited a volume on *Unpopular Culture* (Amsterdam UP, 2016) with Sascha Pöhlmann, and is on the editorial board of *Eludamos: Journal for Computer Game Culture*.

Rosa Mikeal Martey is a Professor in the Department of Journalism and Media Communication at Colorado State University. She holds a PhD from the Annenberg School for Communication at the University of Pennsylvania. Her research focuses on identity and social interaction in digital contexts, including single- and multi-player games, virtual worlds, and social media. She examines the impact of visual and technical design features on interaction, identity, and self-expressions in games and other digital platforms, including for employment and health information. She focuses on ways that specific identities emerge and change in such spaces, including gender, race, and sexual identities.

Victoria McArthur is a Professor in the School of Journalism and Communication at Carleton University in Ottawa, Canada where she teaches courses on game design and augmented reality. Her primary research interests include human-computer interaction (HCI), narrative affordances of digital media, and storytelling in virtual and augmented reality.

Mario Michaelides is Reader (Professor) in Games Design and the Director of Teaching and Learning for Arts and Humanities at Brunel University London. For over nineteen years, Mario has dedicated his career to academia, teaching a range of subjects encompassing games design and development. His achievements have led Mario to be awarded Senior Fellow of the Higher Education Academy (SFHEA) and Fellow of the Royal Society of Arts (FRSA). Like his famous namesake, both were born in 1981—it truly was destiny! As a lifelong gamer, Mario over the years has developed an encyclopedic knowledge of the subject and is more than happy to talk trivia to anyone who cares to listen! Mario enjoys prototyping games, experimenting with software and hardware, and spending time in Hyrule.

Hugo Montembeault has a PhD from the Department of Film Studies of the University of Montreal where he is also a lecturer in game studies. He teaches courses on game aesthetic, immersion, gaming culture, and methodology. His main work studies the transgressive nature of glitches from a media archeological perspective to criticize their noisy participation in the political economy of game design and gaming culture. Throughout his collaboration with the Video Games Observation and Documentation University Lab, he took part in two funded research projects, one on video game genres and the other on game criticism. His other contributions touch on the areas of narratology, game historiography, discourse of the gaming press, and the walking simulator. In 2020, he started a two-year postdoctoral research-creation project at TAG (Concordia University). Through the design of a glitch-based experimental game, he explores, tinkers, and maps out glitches' poetry and politics.

Torill Elvira Mortensen is Associate Professor at the Department of Digital Design, IT University of Copenhagen, and the Faculty of Social Sciences at Nord University, Bodø. Torill was a member of the board for Norsk Tipping 2011–2015, she served on the board of DiGRA, Digital Games Researchers Association from 2006 to 2010, and she was a founding member of the journal *Gamestudies*. She is active in several research communities, and has chaired conferences for the Association of Internet Research (AoIR) and Digital Games Research Association (DiGRA). She is a DiGRA Distinguished Scholar and a Fellow of the Higher Education Video Games Alliance (HEVGA). She published *Perceiving Play: The Art and Study of Computer Games* (2009), was main editor of the anthology *The Dark Side of Gameplay: Controversial Issues in Playful Environments* (2015) and co-author of *The Paradox of Transgression in Games: Games and Transgressive Aesthetics* (2020). Transgressive, provocative, and controversial online aesthetics and challenging uses of games is her current research focus.

Sheila C. Murphy is Associate Professor of Film, Television and Media and Digital Studies at the University of Michigan. She is the author of *How Television Invented New Media* (2011), as well as several essays on popular digital culture and the history of video games. Her forthcoming book is a history of the legacies of technological innovation in California. She teaches courses on Internet history, intersectional online cultures, cyborg media, and digital media theory. She is a founding member of the Digital Studies Institute at the University of Michigan.

James Newman (PhD) is Research Professor in Digital Media and University Teaching Fellow at Bath Spa University in the UK. Over the past twenty years, he has written widely on aspects of video games, players and fans, game preservation, exhibition, and interpretation. He has spoken across the world at events for academics, policy makers, game developers and players. His books include *Videogames*; *Playing with Videogames*; and *Best Before: Videogames, Supersession and Obsolescence* (for Routledge); and *100 Videogames* and *Teaching Videogames* (for BFI Publishing). Most recently, James co-authored *A History of Videogames* (Carlton Books) which is the first volume to explore and draw on the collections of the UK's National Videogame Museum where James also works as Research Lead and Curator. As outputs of projects funded by the British Academy/Leverhulme Trust (2018–19) and ESRC (2020–2021), James has authored two White Papers on video game history and preservation and, in 2020, co-founded the Videogame Heritage Society which is the first Subject Specialist Network (SSN) dedicated to digital media. James currently has contracts for monographs on video game spectatorship and the histories of early video game music and sound.

Bernard Perron is Full Professor of Film and Games Studies at Université de Montréal. He has co-edited *The Video Game Theory Reader 1* (2003), *The Video Game Theory Reader 2* (2008), *The Routledge Companion to Video Games Studies* (2014), as well as *Figures de violence* (2012), *The Archives: Post-Cinema and Video Game Between Memory and the Image of the Present* (2014), *Z pour Zombies* (2015), and *Video Games and the Mind. Essays on Cognition, Affect and Emotion* (2016). He has edited *Horror Video Games: Essays on the Fusion of Fear and Play* (2009). He has also written *Silent Hill: The Terror Engine* (2012) in The Landmark Video Games book series he is co-editing and *The World of Scary Video Games: A Study in Videoludic Horror* (2018). His research and writing concentrate on video games, interactive cinema, the horror genre, and on narration, cognition, and the ludic dimension of narrative cinema. More information can be found at his research team website: http://www.ludov.ca/.

CONTRIBUTORS

Dana Plank (@Musicologess) holds a PhD in historical musicology from Ohio State University, with a dissertation on representations of disability in 8- and 16-bit video game soundscapes. She has published on the music of *Tetris*; 8-bit uses of BWV 565; Mario Paint Composer and participatory culture on YouTube; Nobuo Uematsu's score for *Cleopatra no Ma Takara* (1987); and cognitive, physiological, and emotional effects of game sound on the player. She serves on the boards for Game Sound Con, the North American Conference on Video Game Music, and the *Journal of Sound and Music in Games*, and previously served as a co-chair for the American Musicological Society's Ludomusicology Study Group. In addition to her scholarship, she remains active as a violinist, chamber musician, and professional arranger, and she co-hosts a weekly stream on video game music with Ryan Thompson, Julianne Grasso, and Karen Cook on Thursdays at 9 p.m. EST at twitch.tv/bardicknowledge.

Cindy Poremba is a digital media researcher, gamemaker and curator. They are Associate Professor (Digital Entertainment) at OCAD University (Toronto, CA) and Co-Director of OCAD's game:play Lab. Dr. Poremba has presented internationally at conferences, festivals, and invited lectures, on topics relating to game art and curation, capture in postmedia practices, and interactive documentary. Their research and critical writing has been published in journals such as *Eludamos*, *Loading*, *Game Studies*, and *Games & Culture*, as well as edited collections, art catalogs and magazines. Cindy has held positions on award juries including the Independent Game Festival (Design and Nuovo), served as Co-Chair for the IndieCade: International Festival of Independent Games, and is a past Board member of the Hand Eye Society, North America's oldest video game arts non-profit. They currently sit on the Board of the Game Arts International Network (GAIN). Cindy also organizes non-traditional exhibitions as an independent curator, including Joue le jeu/Play Along (FR), and XYZ: Alternative Voices in Game Design (US). Their award-winning game and "New Arcade" work as a member of the Kokoromi experimental video-game collective has been featured in both international game and digital art exhibitions.

Yannick Rochat is Assistant Professor of game studies at Université de Lausanne, Switzerland, and a co-founder of the GameLab UNIL-EPFL. He holds a MSc in Mathematics (EPFL, 2007) and a PhD in Mathematics applied to Humanities and Social Sciences (SSP UNIL, 2014). His research activities dedicated to video games focus on digital humanities (analysis of large corpora of game magazines), the documentation and preservation of video game and computer heritage in Switzerland, research creation, and education with video games.

Anastasia Salter is the Director of Graduate Programs and Associate Professor of English for the College of Arts and Humanities, including the innovative interdisciplinary doctoral program in Texts and Technology. They have authored seven books that draw on humanities methods alongside computational discourse and subjects, including most recently *Twining: Critical and Creative Approaches to Hypertext Narratives* (Amherst College Press, 2021, w/ Stuart Moulthrop), *Portrait of the Auteur as Fanboy* (University of Mississippi Press, 2020, w/ Mel Stanfill), and *Adventure Games: Playing the Outsider* (Bloomsbury 2020, w/ Aaron Reed and John Murray).

Kevin Schut is Chair and Professor of the Media + Communication Department, and founder and Program Lead of the Game Development program at Trinity Western University in Langley, BC, Canada. He is the author of the book *Of Games & God: A Christian Exploration of Video Games*, and has researched and published on a variety of video-game-related topics, including religion, masculinity, narrative, and history. His current work focuses on moral and ethical decision-making in video games and the role of interpretation in gameplay.

Michael Thomasson is one of the most widely respected video game historians in the field today. He currently teaches college-level video game history, design, and graphics courses. For television, Michael conducted research for MTV's video game-related program *Video MODS*. In print, he authored *Downright Bizarre Games*, and has contributed to over a dozen textbooks. Michael's historical columns have been distributed in newspapers and magazines worldwide. He has written business plans for several vendors and managed a dozen game-related retail stores spanning three decades. Michael consults for multiple video game and computer museums and has worked on nearly a hundred titles on Atari, Coleco, Sega, and other console platforms. In 2014, *The Guinness Book of World Records* declared that Thomasson had "The Largest Videogame Collection" in the world. His organizations sponsor gaming tradeshows and expos across the US and Canada. Visit www.GoodDealGames.com.

CONTRIBUTORS

Hanna Wirman is Associate Professor of Games and Play Design at the Center for Computer Games Research of the IT University of Copenhagen. She writes about game fandom, game design, serious games, and marginal ways of playing and making games. She currently serves as the Vice President of DiGRA.

Mark J. P. Wolf is Professor in the Communication Department at Concordia University Wisconsin. His twenty-three books include *The Video Game Theory Reader 1* and *2* (2003, 2008), *The Video Game Explosion* (2007), *Myst & Riven: The World of the D'ni* (2011), *Before the Crash: An Anthology of Early Video Game History* (2012), *Encyclopedia of Video Games* (2012), *Building Imaginary Worlds* (First Edition, 2012; Second Edition, 2021), *The Routledge Companion to Video Game Studies* (2014), *LEGO Studies* (2014), *Video Games Around the World* (2015), *Revisiting Imaginary Worlds* (2016), *Video Games FAQ* (2017), *The World of Mister Rogers' Neighborhood* (2017), *The Routledge Companion to Imaginary Worlds* (2017), and *The Routledge Companion to Media Technology and Obsolescence* (2018) which won the SCMS 2020 award for best edited collection, *World-Builders on World-Building: An Exploration of Subcreation* (2020), *Exploring Imaginary Worlds: Essays on Media, Structure, and Subcreation* (2020), and more; *Fifty Key Video Games* is his thirteenth book for Routledge alone.

Bryan-Mitchell Young received his PhD in 2014 from Indiana University, where he researched LAN parties. He is currently an Assistant Professor in Communication at Ivy Tech Community College in Terre Haute, Indiana. Despite hours of trying, he has never beaten *Super Mario Bros*.

INTRODUCTION

Video games continue to mature as a medium, as evidenced by the increasing number of entire museums dedicated to games curation, collection, and education such as *The National Videogame Museum* in Sheffield, England; the *Computerspiele Museum* in Berlin, Germany; and the *Strong National Museum of Play* in Rochester, New York, USA. These collections clearly demonstrate that individual games deserve to be viewed, played, and studied for their uniqueness. The Library of Congress already has thousands of games preserved for its archives, following the establishment of a "game canon" selected by a small committee of academics, designers, and journalists (Chaplin, 2007). The LoC's "game canon", though, is only a list of ten games said to have started genres that are still important today (see Chaplin, 2007); such a list is obviously too short and too limited to represent the medium as a whole. The World Video Game Hall of Fame of the *Strong National Museum of Play* is already more varied with its 32 inducted games.[1] From this perspective, we agreed that it is not enough to simply select and feature important games (however that is defined by individuals), but that there is a need for a reasonable, yet scholarly collection that situates a curated selection of games based on a range of criteria surrounding each title's contribution, contextualized within the broader social, technical, and cultural history of video games.

When we began to work on this collection, we were aware of the challenges we faced in editing a book of fifty key games without aiming to formally establish some kind of video game canon. We did not let ourselves be lulled by what Janet Staiger described in her foundational essay "The Politics of Film Canons" as "the illusion of consensus" (1985, p. 10). Neither did we indulge in the idea of neutrality, another illusion which Staiger discusses. Our aim was to collect a series of essays that focus on a wide range of contributions to game design, culture, aesthetics, and production. But in order to do so, we had to make conscious decisions as to what to include and examine what was being excluded in consequence. In "The Politics of Game Canonization: Tales from the Frontlines of Creating a National History of Games", Glas and van Vught summarize Staiger's argument very well:

> During all the different steps in the process from admission to selection and reflection, different values, different motifs, and different arguments are at play, steering the final selection of works into a specific direction. This selection often reinforces dominant social, political, economic and cultural ideologies and has the potential to marginalize others.
>
> (2019, p. 2)

It is indeed useful to reflect on the process through Staiger's three types of politics.

Staiger states that "[c]ompetition in academics and the film [or, in our case, video game] industry reinforces canons and canon-making", and that consequently an escape from canon formation is difficult to achieve. Identifying specific works brings attention and advantage to them. In our situation, we were mindful of the third kind of politics she mentions: the one of the Academy. Publishers wish to position themselves in the market of game studies publications and to have a canon of literature regarding video games. For us, admittedly, "academic reputations and economic rewards are also at stake" (Staiger, 1985, p. 19). The fact that the press is now publishing a book on key video games sheds light on the first kind of politics, namely the politics of admission. Whereas many of the early writings about cinema were "involved in proving film was an art" (1985, p. 4), the video game's current situation is very different.

The video game has become one of the main forms of cultural expression of the twenty-first century and was named the 10th Art in France in the mid-1990s. The discourses about it in the public sphere are numerous. Since the advent of the field of research called Game Studies, they have been examined from a variety of theories and disciplines, with colleges and universities dedicating whole programs to game design, game studies, and videoludic literacy. There is no longer the need to single out some strategically chosen games as objects worthy of admission into the realm of artworks, and art is not the only frame to be considered for inclusion.

Rather than the prescriptive politics of canon-making as a legitimizing strategy for video games in general, it is the second kind

INTRODUCTION

of politics distinguished by Staiger that remains at the core of the discussion around canonization: the politics of selection.

> In purely practical terms, a scholar of cinema [*or of video games*] cannot study every film [*or game*] ever made. Selection becomes a necessity and with selection usually comes a politics of inclusion and exclusion. Some films [*or games*] are moved to the center of attention; others, to the margins.
>
> (1985, p. 8)

These movements have important impacts on the appraisal of the works and are the ones that are scrutinized as well as questioned. Paring down the thousands of published video games and the hundreds of candidates that could be considered "key video games" to a mere fifty was nothing short of difficult. We would have been much happier to be able to include more games, a luxury had by a book like *1001 Video Games You Must Play Before You Die* (Mott, 2010) – but with only 300-word essays on each game, the book would not have delved into the games and would have remained largely just an annotated list. While the chapters in this collection were substantially longer, 2,500 words still greatly limits how deep we can delve into each game.

Of course, we are not the first to attempt such an exercise. Our colleagues behind *Fifty Key British Films* have eased our minds by expressing what we wished to propose. According to John White and Sarah Barrow (2008, p. xv), "the suggestion [*we really like this choice of word*] is more simply that this selection of [*games*] operates to provide an initial appreciation" of different aspects of the video game since its advent. We do not intend to assert that the video games we have chosen are the greatest. Similar to White and Barrow, our purpose is not to promote a particular canon of video games.

> The very nature of a 'canon' is that it is exclusive and this list is not designed to be that (other than in the sense that we only have room for 50 essays in this book). Nor is this list ranked in order of merit; there are two contents lists, one in date order and the other in alphabetical order, and both of these structures leave a virtually infinite space for your own additions.
>
> (2008, p. xv)

From the start, we envisioned this book as *Fifty Key Video Games* – not THE *Fifty Key Video Games*. There are dozens or even hundreds of key games (depending on how one defines "key"), and they vary according to individual tastes, interests, histories, and framings; but here are fifty of them, as a start. Rather than thinking in terms of "masterpieces", we worked around the idea of "key", taken as something that opens doors for the understanding of the games, and through these games, of the medium itself. Each author, then, situates the game they wrote about within the broader video game landscape, referencing other games within their historical, technological, cultural, and aesthetic context, essentially paying homage to those that came before them, and fundamentally opening the door for the reader to explore beyond the pages of the book.

While it was not easy to come up with this list of *Fifty Key Video Games*, we each nominated 50 games, explaining the rationale for inclusion. Our separate selections amounted to twice as much as required. Selections were then voted on and then further discussed to balance the many different factors under consideration, until we all agreed on a list that represented the diverse range of contributions that video games have to offer. Interestingly, only 20 games are part of the "games studies canon" identified by Jonathan Frome and Paul Martin (2019. p. 6), who wrote, "A content analysis of over 580 articles from the field's two main journals is used to identify the currently-invisible canon of most-frequently cited games in game scholarship" (Abstract). Our aim was not to develop a canon based on a citation count, or any other single criterion of success. We wanted to create a list of interesting games that perhaps were not always the top selling or most critically acclaimed, but were ones that contributed to several different aspects of video game history and culture. It is also important to understand that any individual reading of a game, even when the focus is on its key elements and contributions, will always be reductive and situated within the context and disciplinary frame of the author.

Our rationale in creating this list of fifty games is no exception. The selections are, of course, made from our own socio-cultural positions, as White North Americans, in our 40s and 50s, all working within games academia. Many nominations were informed, to some capacity, by our firsthand experiences with the games either as players, community members, or within our specific scholarly contexts. That being said, we also made sure not to privilege our personal favorite games or genres. In addition, we also considered the state of game studies scholarship; we sometimes avoided obvious choices to go for more interesting ones, or looked for contributors to explore novel, original facets of them. The final selection covers a range of historical periods and platforms, genres, commercial impact, artistic choices, contexts of play, representations, uses of games for specific purposes, uses of materials or techniques, specific subcultures, repurposing, transgressive aesthetics, interfaces, moral or ethical impact and more. Thus, serious discussion went into the selection of the games; the list is not merely the whim of a single author, but one in which each entry's merit had to be debated and accepted by the four of us.

Coming from different backgrounds and selected for their knowledge of the work analyzed, the various contributors were invited to frame the games discussed in their essays as keys that open ideas that they are researching. The chapters thus provide a glimpse into fifty doors, opened to areas of further research into the many disciplines that are practiced by the diverse cast of authors. The study of individual games through such a range of perspectives offers a broader understanding of games in general, as an important phenomenon.

Though the task of reducing our list of video games down to a mere fifty turned out to be quite the challenge, it was nonetheless a fun one. Our main wish is not different from the one of White and Barrow (2008, p. xv):

> Therefore, beyond the theoretical seriousness of discussions about the potential elitism, exclusivity and political manoeuvrings associated with the notion of canons, hopefully you will also simply enjoy agreeing and disagreeing with the inclusions and exclusions you find here.

The ludic dimension of the exercise should not be forgotten.

Note

1. 19 of its 32 inducted games are on our list: https://www.museumofplay.org/exhibits/world-video-game-hall-of-fame/inducted-games/

References

Chaplin, H. (2007, March 12). Is That Just Some Game? No, It's a Cultural Artifact. *New York Times*. Retrieved November 26, 2021, from https://www.nytimes.com/2007/03/12/arts/design/12vide.html

Frome, J. & Martin, J. (2019). Describing the game studies canon: A game citation analysis. *DiGRA '19 - Proceedings of the 2019 DiGRA International Conference: Game, Play and the Emerging Ludo-Mix*. Retrieved October 11, 2021, http://www.digra.org/wp-content/uploads/digital-library/DiGRA_2019_paper_283.pdf

Glas, R. & van Vught, J. (2019). The politics of game canonization: Tales from the frontlines of creating a national history of games. *DiGRA '19 - Proceedings of the 2019 DiGRA International Conference: Game, Play and the Emerging Ludo-Mix*. Retrieved October 11, 2021, from http://www.digra.org/wp-content/uploads/digital-library/DiGRA_2019_paper_339.pdf

Mott, T. (2010). *1001 Video Games You Must Play Before You Die*. London: Quintessence.

Staiger, J. (1985, Spring). The Politics of Film Canons. *Cinema Journal*, 24(3), 4–23.

White, J. & Barrow S. (2008). *Fifty Key British Films*. New York: Routledge.

FIFTY KEY VIDEO GAMES

ADVENTURE (1979)

Adventure is an Atari VCS (or Atari 2600) game cartridge published in 1979,[1] designed and developed by Warren Robinett. The gameplay consists in navigating a labyrinth, evading dragons and finding keys to retrieve the enchanted chalice. It sold over a million units and regularly ranks among significant historical games for the numerous "firsts"[2] often put to its credit: first action-adventure game, first game to cut between multiple screens, first fantasy-themed video game,[3] first Easter egg,[4] and first fog-of-war representation. Such a high level of innovation for a single game is remarkable even for a time in which genres were not as deeply entrenched. This radical departure from existing contemporary video games finds an explanation in Robinett's efforts to adapt a game from a very different platform to the Atari VCS (Robinett, 2005).

A Platform Adaptation

In 1979, Robinett had finished work on his first video game for the Atari company: *Slot Racers*, a more conventional two-player, single-screen chase and shoot game. He was beginning to think of his next title when a friend introduced him to a program called *Adventure*,[5] playable on a Stanford University mainframe computer. This text-only game, developed by William Crowther in 1976 and refined by Don Woods in 1977, was the sensation in computer labs across the United States. It is now considered as having initiated the adventure-game genre on computer platforms. Beyond the purely textual representation, *Adventure* (which itself had been inspired by Gygax and Arneson's *Dungeons & Dragons*, 1974) was radically different from the arcade and home video games Robinett was familiar with: it featured a vast world to be explored, treasures to be collected, puzzles to be solved, enemies to be vanquished and a quest to be accomplished. Robinett's ambition was to adapt *Adventure* to his employer's platform: the Atari VCS.

Jesper Juul distinguishes two extremes when adapting a game to a different context (2005). On one end, the "port" is a quasi-identical reimplementation of an existing game to a new platform. On the other, an "adaptation" *per se* entails a significant divergence in experience between the two versions. A typical example is the sports adaptation: although playing the *NHL Hockey* franchise (Electronic Arts) on a video-game console evokes many aspects of the original game, there is obviously an immense gap between the embodied feeling of skating on ice and pushing buttons on a gamepad. In a game adaptation, something new is created.

Although the PDP-10 mainframe on which the original *Adventure* ran and the Atari VCS were both technically computers, the differences between the two were far from trivial. First, the home console was comparatively a very underpowered machine. The Atari VCS cartridges could store no more than 4kB of information whereas the original text game required over 100kB. The two platforms also had very different interaction modalities. *Adventure* was designed assuming a keyboard as input device and a text-focused output device (either a printer or a screen). On the other hand, the Atari VCS had been engineered to play *PONG* (Atari, 1972) or *Combat* (Atari, 1977) (Montfort & Bogost, 2009) and relied on joystick input and the display of simple moving objects. It had no native text display support; any characters on screen implied the manual repurposing of visual elements. Robinett's project would entail significant creativity and his adaptation would highlight the differences between computers and consoles as gaming platforms at the time.

Extending the Playfield

The world of the original *Adventure* is modeled as an arbitrary network of discrete nodes ("rooms") represented as textual descriptions (Lessard, 2013) such as: "You are standing at the end of a road before a small brick building." Moving from one place to the other entailed typing simple instructions such as "go north" or "enter house" which would take the player to a new location. In contrast, all home console and arcade games of the time took place on a single-screen "playfield" (as per VCS terminology). However, dynamic objects could move *within* this playfield whereas in *Adventure*, one is either in a room or not, and movement happens *in-between* places.

Robinett's proposition would be to do both things at once: combining continuous *and* discrete space. In Atari's *Adventure*, a single room is represented on the screen as a maze of walls. The player can navigate this space by maneuvering a representation of themselves (a square) with the joystick, as was typical in Atari games at that time. When coming in contact with an opening on the sides of the screen, the player-character is transported to another room (understood as being adjacent). This division of game space across multiple discrete screens combining both *within* and *in-between* movements would become a staple of action-adventure games as later seen in the early *Ultima* (Origin Systems, 1981) or *Zelda* (Nintendo, 1986) series.

Interacting with Objects

A key element of the original *Adventure*'s gameplay is solving problems by using objects. For example, one needs to fill a bottle and water a plant so that a beanstalk can grow. These operations are also undertaken via textual commands such as: "take bottle", "fill bottle" and "water plant". In Atari games, player input takes the form of either directions (moving the joystick) or pressing a button. Typically, these translate to moving some objects on the screen and firing missiles. The main modality through which video-game objects interact is through collision detection (Montfort & Bogost, 2009): hitting the ball in *PONG* boils down to making sure your paddle touches the ball; you score a point in *Combat* when your bullet touches the opponent's tank. The importance of this modality is evidenced by the specific programming affordances provided by the Atari VCS hardware to identify these collisions.

In the Atari *Adventure*, the player takes an object (visually represented on screen) by touching it with the player-character. Although Robinett toyed with the idea of allowing an inventory with multiple objects (as is the case in his model game), he decided to keep things simple and allowed only one item to be held at a time (Robinett, 2015), something he could clearly convey by displaying the object next to the player-character as it moves around. Object-to-object interaction is triggered by colliding with a second visual element while holding an object. The typical example of this is colliding with a closed door while holding the right key. This simple interaction scheme will also be widely imitated. One still picks up a gun by running into it in modern Triple-A first-person shooter games.

Putting the Action in *Adventure*

The treatment of enemies is a main point of divergence between the two *Adventures*. While the original model did feature evil dwarves, a bear, a dragon, and a pirate, these were approached with the usual turn-by-turn textual commands and did not lead to high-intensity confrontations. The dragon, for instance, is dealt with in this incongruous manner:

> \> kill dragon
> With what? Your bare hands?
> \> yes
> Congratulations! You have just vanquished a dragon with your bare hands!
>
> (Unbelievable, isn't it?)

The real-time and direct manipulation regime of Atari games changed things drastically. Robinett introduced a dragon who would kill the player after two contacts in a row—creating an incentive to actively avoid the creature. To balance things, he introduced the sword object that the player could use to vanquish the dragon by bringing both objects into precise contact. These design decisions brought about challenges of dexterity and timing entirely absent from the original *Adventure*. It was no longer sufficient to simply find out what to do, one also needed to deliver a performance. Robinett added two more dragons, considering these fights to be one of the most exciting aspects of his game. This combination of quest elements with twitch gameplay would become a signature of action-adventure games, the genre that would be retroactively traced back to Atari's *Adventure*.

The Problem of Replayability

According to Juul, the adventure-game genre (as exemplified by Crowther and Woods's *Adventure*) represents the introduction of a new structure he calls "games of progression" in which "the player has to perform a predefined set of actions in order to complete the game" (2005, p. 5). This allowed new elements of world building and narrative development that would become key features in games to come, but also introduced a new problem: once you have discovered the whole world and performed all the steps, there is nothing left to do. This was a minor issue for the original *Adventure*; with nearly 140 locations and over fifty interactive objects, it was so large and complicated that it could take weeks, months or even years for a player to solve (if ever). Because of technical constraints, however, the *Atari* version only had thirty rooms and twelve objects. This meant that the possible combinations could be mapped relatively quickly.

One of Robinett's strategies to extend the game's longevity was to augment the role of dragons and increase their number. The real-time fighting added some uncertainty even for players knowing their way around the maze and the location of objects. To complicate things further, he took inspiration from the pirate character in the original *Adventure* which steals random objects from the player and brings them to a hiding place. In the Atari game, this took the form of an autonomous bat which roams the game world to pick up objects and drop them in random locations (even when off-screen). This meant that players could not rely on following a series of instructions to win the game. Again, we see Robinett finding strategies to balance static quest features with the more dynamic elements typical of action games of his time.

Auteur Politics

Early Atari developers were responsible for every aspect of the game they were making; taking care of game design, programming, as well as audio-visual content. Yet, Atari's policy was to not publicly associate the makers with their work, presenting all titles simply under the company's banner. Developers were salaried employees and did not maintain any rights to their games. According to Robinett, the company wanted to avoid any of them leveraging their fame to negotiate better conditions (Robinett, 2015).

This was frustrating to Robinett who was proud of a title which was not only original but also represented a significant technical feat. He even had to secretly develop a prototype when his superior had refused his project, considering that adapting the original *Adventure* represented an impossible task and a waste of resources. In the same way, he proceeded to disregard Atari's authority by secretly embedding credits in the game. He used the little space left on the cartridge memory to introduce an extra room containing large, vertically aligned letters reading "created by Warren Robinett". One had to find a hidden object and use it on a specific part of a wall to open access to this room. The cartridge was published without anyone being aware of this and the room was only discovered accidentally months later by a young player. By then, Robinett had already left the company. Atari chose to not remove it both because of the costs of modifying the cartridge master and also because they realized players enjoyed looking for secret content. The concept was entirely appropriated when the company announced that all its future games would contain what they named "Easter eggs", evoking the traditional treasure hunt.

Robinett was not the only developer frustrated by the lack of recognition. Four Atari employees left the company as early as 1979 to found Activision whose policy would be, at least in the beginning, to give full public credit to the game makers. However, while these creators wanted their names associated with their work, none questioned the copyright assumptions of their previous employer.

Robinett wanted full credit for his game *Adventure*, somewhat obscuring the important debt owed to the model game which existed in a very different intellectual property regime. The original *Adventure* was a public-domain, collaborative work for which none of the authors received any significant salary or royalties. Robinett never hid his inspiration, but did not shy away from reusing the exact same title, therefore overwriting the reference for a large portion of the public. For video-game players from then on, *Adventure* would mean Atari's *Adventure* (and designate, by extension, action-adventure games), whereas for computer-game players, the label would continue to refer to the genre initiated by Crowther and Woods's program.

Jonathan Lessard

Notes

1. In interviews and in his unpublished book, Warren Robinett evokes a 1979 Christmas release. However, no documentary evidence of the availability of the game before 1980 has yet been produced (Derboo 2012).
2. Such attributions depend on specific definitions and are always debated. Whether or not *Adventure* is the actual first occurrence of these features does not alter the recognition that the game was original and innovative.
3. "Video game" being understood here as arcade and console games—there were precedents on computers, as we'll see.
4. An earlier example was recently identified in *Video Whizball* (Fairchild, 1978), but *Adventure*'s is the one that led to the construction of the "Easter egg" label.
5. The program did not have an official title and was sometimes called *ADVENT*, referring to the executable name, *Adventure* or *Colossal Cave Adventure*.
6. It is worth noting that most of the existing scholarship on this game relies on its author's own testimonials.

References[6]

Derboo, S. (2012, July 7). Adventure, a game released in the year of wedontknow. *Hardcore Gaming 101*. Retrieved August 27, 2021, from http://blog.hardcoregaming101.net/2012/07/adventure-game-released-in-year-of.html

Juul, J. (2005). *Half-real: Video games between real rules and fictional worlds*. Cambridge, MA: MIT Press.

Lessard, J. (2013). Adventure before adventure games: A new look at Crowther and Woods's seminal program. *Games and Culture*, 8(3), 119–135.

Montfort, N., & Bogost, I. (2009). *Racing the beam: The Atari video computer system*. Cambridge, MA: MIT Press.

Robinett, W. (2005). Adventure as a video game: Adventure for the Atari 2600. In K. S. Tekinbas & E. Zimmerman (Eds), *The game design reader: A rules of play anthology* (p. 690–713). Cambridge, MA: MIT Press.

Robinett, W. (2015). Classic Game Postmortem: Adventure. Game Developers Conference 2015, San Francisco. Retrieved August 27, 2021, from https://www.gdcvault.com/play/1021860/Classic-Game-Postmortem

Further Reading

Smith, A. (2019). *They create worlds: The story of the people and companies that shaped the video game industry, Vol. I: 1971–1982*. Boca Raton, FL: CRC Press.

DOI: 10.4324/9781003199205-2

ANGRY BIRDS (2009)

While there are many popular video games, few reach the level of cultural ubiquity of *Angry Birds*. In the decade after the first game's release in December 2009, the dozens of games in the franchise were downloaded over 4.5 billion times (*Angry Birds*, 2019). Other blockbuster media franchises like *Star Wars* and *Transformers* rely on *Angry Birds* crossovers to market their new releases. There's an *Angry Birds* movie (Clay Kaytis and Fergal Reilly, 2016). Regardless of where in the world you live, you've seen children and middle-aged men alike wearing knock-off *Angry Birds* clothing.

Angry Birds is more than a popular game franchise. Its immediate, massive success in late 2009, sustained for the following decade, echoes broader, seismic shifts in video game culture, and in how video games fit within broader popular culture. The rise of casual games and mobile games alongside the breakdown of a monolithic and hegemonic hardcore-gamer culture pivots on *Angry Birds* and its contemporaries. The importance of *Angry Birds* cannot be appreciated apart from this context.

How to Play

The game itself is a straightforward, colorful experience in which the player shoots the titular angry birds out of a giant slingshot to destroy their green pig enemies by causing their buildings to collapse. Different birds have different skills and strengths: the small blue bird splits into three, creating more widespread damage; the large black bird creates a secondary explosion after landing, useful for taking out strong concrete supports; the white bird drops an egg bomb straight down, useful for getting into hard-to-reach spots. For each level, the player is provided with a specific line-up of birds to be used in a specific order, forcing them to think strategically about what sort of damage needs to be caused to the structure and in what order to take out all of the pigs with the birds available.

Points are awarded for simply causing damage to the structures and for actually destroying the evil pigs. Crucially, players also gain significant bonus points for any birds left unused after the pigs are destroyed, and so are encouraged to complete a level efficiently and accurately with as few birds as possible. This becomes particularly important when one considers the game's three-star rating system, with stars awarded for the total points scored on a level. To get a three-star rating on any one level will almost certainly require the player to have at least one bird left over at the end. For advanced players, *Angry Birds* becomes like golf, where they try to finish the level in the lowest number of shots possible.

While *Angry Birds* has since been ported to all sorts of platforms with different input affordances, the success of its design is in how its original release took advantage of the technological and social affordances of smartphone devices, such as Apple's iPhone. To look around the entire level, the player uses pinch-and-grab gestures, which are now common throughout touchscreen applications but were still novel at the time of the game's release. To fire a bird out of the slingshot, the player directly touches the bird in the slingshot on the left of the screen and physically pulls it back to determine the angle and power of the shot. When the player removes their finger from the screen, the slingshot snaps back and flings the bird forward in a satisfying, heavy-feeling parabola. The game uses basic physics simulation to ensure nearly every shot causes some level of spectacular damage, no matter how accurate it was.

The Rise of Casual Mobile Games

At a cursory glance, there is little that is uniquely remarkable about *Angry Birds* that explains its sustained cultural ubiquity. The core mechanics of destroying structures by flinging things at them had already been achieved by browser-based Flash games such as Joey Betz and Chris Condon's *Crush the Castle* (2009). Nor was *Angry Birds* the first smartphone game. Critically and commercially successful smartphone games such as Lima Sky's *Doodle Jump*, Firemint's *Flight Control*, and Area/Code's *Drop7* were all released in 2009 before the first *Angry Birds* game. Nevertheless, the design and persistence of *Angry Birds* provide insights into how smartphone devices radically altered how video games are designed, and how they fit within broader culture.

For the first couple of years of its existence, very few people—including those at Apple—considered the iPhone as a serious platform for video games. It had no buttons, and no ability to engage with physical media—two attributes that at the time still seemed crucial for any video game platform. As a device, it offered the antithesis of what video games had traditionally required. Yet, what the iPhone did offer, and what *Angry Birds* made exceptionally clear to a generation of mobile game developers to follow in its wake, was a golden opportunity for game designers to reimagine the context and value of "casual" games and the broader demographics that would play them.

"Casual games" is a highly contested term. It can imply that games under such a label aren't "serious" or "important", or that their players do not actually care about them. Scholars have shown how the label has long been used detrimentally to marginalize video game titles with more feminized communities (Hjorth and Richardson, 2009; Chess, 2017). The explosion in popularity of casual games through the 2000s, even before the release of the iPhone, was beginning to challenge the hardcore gamer's dominance of video game culture. It denaturalized what had come to be accepted as what video games simply were and who had come to be accepted as video games' audience. It opened a space of alternatives.

Around the same time as *Angry Birds*' initial release, what games scholar Jesper Juul dubbed *The Casual Revolution* (2009) was well underway. Drawing inspiration from the success of Nintendo's Wii console, as well as the growing trend of browser-based casual and social games, Juul theorized just what sort of aesthetic experience casual games offer, and how they challenge traditional understandings of video games. These casual games, and their casual players, Juul argues, are not just "more simple" or "less complex" than so-called hardcore games. Rather, they offer different, no less valid, experiences and aesthetics than traditional games for hardcore gamers.

Hardcore-gamer culture, since at least the 1980s, has privileged video games that offer systemic complexity, technological superiority, and extensive narrative content—all while cultivating a field of primarily young male players (Kirkpatrick, 2015; Arsenault, 2017). In casual games, however, Juul (2010, p. 50) identifies five design aspects that contrast with these traditional values. The design of casual games typically (1) presents a pleasant fictional framing; (2) is highly accessible even if one has little pre-existing knowledge or experience of video game conventions; (3) is highly interruptible, designed to be played in brief bursts rather than sustained periods; (4) is difficult but rarely punishing; and (5) provides excessive and "juicy" audio-visual feedback, ensuring maximum spectacular reward in response to minimal input.

In *Angry Birds*' deceptively simple and straightforward design, we can see all five of Juul's casual game design conventions. The cartoony visual style is immediately recognizable and inoffensive, far removed from the gritty machismo of console games at the time.

The touch controls, simply requiring the player to touch and pull back a slingshot, make immediate sense and do not require any familiarity with a complex gamepad controller or keyboard. Individual levels are short, able to be completed in a few minutes, and the style of play permits the player to look away from the screen at any time without fear of consequence. *Angry Birds* is easy to play, to just fling a few birds and see what happens, but the three-star rating system also provides a level of heightened difficulty for those players that want it. Finally, the exaggerated spectacle of the building collapses is nothing if not juicy.

Of all these aspects of casual game design that *Angry Birds* exemplifies, however, it is Juul's point that casual games are typically "highly interruptible" that best explains *Angry Birds*' explosive success and ability to penetrate all sorts of audiences that would typically not think twice about committing the time required to play a video game. Ultimately, as a video game that had to adapt to both the technological affordances and social contexts of a smartphone device, *Angry Birds* made it possible to play video games without committing to them as a dedicated activity or hobby. They made video games normal.

Video Games as Everyday Media

With *Angry Birds* and its contemporaries, video games stopped being something players had to commit to; they stopped being a sealed-off world one committed to wholly, both in terms of embodiment and identity. Instead, playing *Angry Birds* was something players could do almost unthinkingly, no different than looking at Facebook or checking the time. Traditionally, playing a video game on a console has required the player to insert the correct disc, wait for it to load, sit down on a couch with a fourteen-button controller, and wait for various copyright and health warnings before the game can be loaded and, finally, played. *Angry Birds*, meanwhile, could be opened in a matter of seconds while one is waiting at a bus stop, sitting on the toilet, or lying in bed. One simply unlocks the phone, taps the icon, and will be flinging birds within a few seconds.

But even once the game starts, *Angry Birds* does not require the player's full attention. Where traditional video games have fixated on the player's "immersion" in the virtual world, with *Angry Birds* the player can fling and forget. The player can look up between shots to check if they are at their train station yet, or because the commercial break is over. There is no risk of missing important narrative beats or being attacked by a monster in the split second one is distracted. There is no need to play for another fifteen minutes to get to the next save point when a level can easily be finished in a minute or two.

Where video games for hardcore gamers had, traditionally, required the gamer's life to fit around the video game, *Angry Birds*, and casual smartphone games more broadly, fit around our busy lives. With the smartphone, video games become easy to access. Players no longer have to wait, either to start or to finish. Furthermore, players no longer need to commit dedicated chunks of time in order to play a video game. And, crucially, they no longer need to commit financially and subjectively to a video game-playing hobby or identity, buying dedicated hardware and keeping up with enthusiast discourses—one just uses the phone one already owns.

Casual mobile games like *Angry Birds* are not simply "easy" games, but they make video games, as a cultural form, easy to engage with. One no longer has to care about video games to play them. One no longer has to invest (physically, emotionally, financially) in video games to play them. In the 2010s, starting with *Angry Birds* and its contemporaries, the video game industry figured out how to make games for everyone else, everyone except the gamers that had been their stable consumer demographic for two decades, and in doing so figured out how to break out of the second-class citizen cultural mold it had developed for itself. *Angry Birds* is so culturally ubiquitous explicitly because it was designed for everyone but traditional gamers.

Conclusion

Over a decade later, the smartphone game world looks very different than when *Angry Birds* first came out. The push to capture video game players who did not want to commit to playing video games pushed prices lower and lower, first to $1, and then lower still to no upfront cost, with games instead demanding in-game purchases, or forcing the player to watch advertisements. While some games and companies still make a lot of money on the App Store, the gold rush is over.

The original *Angry Birds* has received countless updates over the years to bring it in line with these monetization models, and to work on current devices. The original *Angry Birds* that made history in 2009 is now almost impossible to access. Many of its contemporaries, like *Flight Control* (Firemint Pty, 2009), are no longer accessible in any form, with constant operating system updates rendering them unplayable until their developer decides to invest the time and effort required to update them. As video games have become normalized, their preservation as cultural artifacts has become almost impossible.

But even as the smartphone game space that *Angry Birds* ushered in no longer exists in the same way, its legacy now pervades all aspects of game design and business. Home consoles now have standby modes and autosave functions, making it somewhat easier to stop and start games at any point. Free-to-play and games-as-a-service business models now find themselves on all devices. *Angry Birds*—or some version of it—has been released over and over again on any platform that will have it.

Angry Birds is a small, simple, casual smartphone game made by a tiny Finnish company about flinging cartoon birds at cartoon pigs out of a giant slingshot. It was released on a device with no buttons, created by a tech company with no interest in video games. Yet in the years that followed, it would come to be found in hundreds of millions of pockets around the world and ushered in a period of seismic change for both the business and culture of video games.

Brendan Keogh

References

Arsenault, D. (2017). *Super power, spoony bards, and silverware: The Super Nintendo entertainment system*. Cambridge, MA: MIT Press.
Chess, S. (2017). *Ready Player Two: Women gamers and designed identity*. Minneapolis: University of Minnesota Press.
Hjorth, L., & I. Richardson (2009). The waiting game: Complicating notions of (tele)presence and gendered distraction in casual mobile gaming. *Australian Journal of Communication* 36 (1), 23–35.
Juul, J. (2010). *A casual revolution: Reinventing video games and their players*. Cambridge, MA: MIT Press.
Kirkpatrick, G. (2015). *The formation of gaming culture: UK gaming magazines, 1981–1995*. London: Palgrave Macmillan.

Further Reading

Hjorth, L., J. Burgess, & I. Richardson, eds 2012. *Studying mobile media: Cultural technologies, mobile communication, and the iPhone*. New York: Routledge.
Keogh, B. (2014). Paying attention to *Angry Birds*: Rearticulating hybrid worlds and embodied play through casual iPhone games. In Goggin, Gerard & Hjorth, Larissa (Eds) *The Routledge companion to mobile media* (pp. 267–275). Routledge: New York.
McCrea, C. (2011). We play in public: The nature and context of portable gaming systems. *Convergence* 17 (4), 389–403.

DOI: 10.4324/9781003199205-3

ANIMAL CROSSING (2001)

Nintendo GameCube's *Animal Crossing* (2001) is cute. Seriously cute. Overwhelmingly cute. It is a game in which you play a stylized human with a giant head and big eyes who, as a mayor, looks after a village full of anthropomorphic animals. As a player, you can chat with villagers, exchange gifts, plant trees and flowers, collect bugs, fossils and fish, and design and style your home. The gameplay is one which lends itself well to practicing cuteness, and that's what this chapter is about. And no, this chapter won't try to make the argument that it was the first cute game, nor the best cute game, but rather simply that *Animal Crossing* is cuter than Mario in a tanooki suit and we should talk about it.

Of course, we could justify *Animal Crossing*'s place in this list of key video games because of its popularity, legacy or financial success, but that would be missing the core of its contribution to this book and to games as a field—cuteness. In 2001, the top three Metacritic titles as listed on their website in 2021 (Metacritic, 2021) were *Tony Hawk's Pro Skater 3* (Neversoft, 2001), *Grand Theft Auto III* (DMA Design, 2001), and *Halo: Combat Evolved* (Bungie, 2001), and while these are legendary games to be sure, they aren't cute. In a market which was dominated by extreme sports, extreme crime, and extreme violence, there's *Animal Crossing*, the antithesis of extreme anything.

So why should we, as game developers, scholars, and fans, care about *Animal Crossing* and its cuteness? This chapter makes the argument that *Animal Crossing* provides a unique gameplay experience and aesthetic which, on a deeper level, represents resistance to a dominant culture that mocks, derides, and dismisses cute things. This game affords us an opportunity to pick apart why our cultures and societies scoff at all things adorable. To do this, I use Judith Butler's (1999) idea of gender hierarchies to break down and discuss how cuteness became synonymous with not being taken seriously and how this is rooted in hegemonic masculinity. Using this paradigm, we can see how and why *Animal Crossing*'s gameplay and aesthetic stand out from other titles released in 2001 and continues to stand out, and why it matters for the development of game genres.

What is Cute and How is *Animal Crossing* Cute?

Before we can move on to discussing the larger implications cuteness has to games as an entertainment medium, we first need to define what we mean by cuteness. Starting with a biological definition, Konrad Lorenz (1943) described the baby/child schema (*Kindchenschema*) theory which states that visual features of juvenile animals and humans trigger an emotional and physical response in observers. In his description of the visual features of juvenile animals and humans, Lorenz perfectly describes *Animal Crossing*'s mayor and villagers: heads too big for their bodies, enormous eyes, chubby cheeks, and tiny arms and legs. Scholars of cuteness, and I am happy to say they exist, say that humans respond to cute features by either reading the baby-like mien as weakness, and subsequently feel the urge to protect the creature or reading the countenance as whimsical and want to play with it (Lieber-Milo, 2021). In the case of *Animal Crossing*, both reactions seem appropriate as players of the franchise feel an emotional responsibility toward their villagers (Kalinowski, 2021; Bohunicky, 2021) and an invitation for social play among them (Comerford, 2021).

Not only is *Animal Crossing* cute in its baby/child schema representation of characters in the game, it is also cute in its gameplay. The most literal example of this is when an animal villager catches the flu. The villager will ask the player-character to fetch them medicine which, given the above discussion of how baby-like cuteness inspires caregiving, causes the player to care for the physical wellbeing of the villager like a parent would for a child. Abstracting from this, all fetch-quests villagers ask the player to complete can be seen as caregiving tasks taken on simply because the player feels an obligation to the safety and wellbeing of a lump of (very cute) polygons. That is to say, there is no direct reward for completing fetch-quests (no armor unlocks, no level progression, no new area on the map), just the satisfaction that you helped an adorable virtual animal in need and perhaps they like you a little more. Whether or not a villager likes the player can be important to gameplay, because if they don't, there is a potential that they could move away and thus deprive the player of their cuteness.

On a deeper level, the structure of the play experience in *Animal Crossing* invites whimsical playfulness. Instead of having a strictly linear progression of in-game activities, quests, and missions, the game uses a real-time clock to advance the game according to the time of day, month, or season. Any pressure to complete tasks players may feel is not due to competition with other players or game NPCs, but due to time-sensitive activities, like fishing tournaments, or collecting unique holiday items during their respective seasons. The latter time-pressure example was actually a source of a family-wide argument in November 2002 as I refused to attend our family Thanksgiving dinner. I preferred instead to complete all the turkey-day-themed tasks in *Animal Crossing*. For concerned readers, a compromise was struck, and I successfully negotiated bringing the GameCube to grandma's house, so don't worry.

Competing against time in this game does not necessarily take the form of a time-trial, but rather the form of having windows of opportunity. The game's open and flowy structure affords the player the opportunity to do what they like in-game and, instead of punishing them if they run out of time like in racing games, the window on those opportunities merely closes with an invitation to try again the following year. This structure is whimsical and reinforces the cute aesthetic through that whimsy. Players complete activities not according to when the game instructs them, but according to their whim.

Further to this idea of whimsical cuteness, if a player attempts to cheat the game by resetting their GameCube's internal clock, the only punishment is getting yelled at by a mole named Mr Resetti. Now I don't want to minimize how unpleasant Mr Resetti is, because his scolding does make cheating players feel awful for cheating, but in terms of game punishments, it is still pretty cute.

Finally, *Animal Crossing* is cute because it is a game which rewards the cutefication of the game's environment. The game begins with the central task of increasing the size of the player's house, customizing it, and paying off the subsequent mortgage. While the real-life process of buying a house, remodeling, and paying off debt is the antithesis of cute, the game somehow manages to make it so. Instead of working a tedious nine-to-five job, you catch butterflies, go fishing, and tend brightly colored fruit trees to earn money. In addition to being fictional, the debt in *Animal Crossing* is also fairly easily paid off. In keeping with the game's open structure, the player is afforded a lot of freedom in how they choose to customize and decorate their house, and they can pay off the mortgage whenever they want or not at all. Despite this flexibility, the player is incentivized to decorate their home in prescribed ways to get a better score from the Happy Room Academy. The Happy Room Academy judges the composition of the player's house and awards more points for styles which are harmonious in color scheme and theme, or, put another way, homes which are cute.

The game has stores in which the player can purchase items to assist in customizing their home, such as music or furniture, and items which can be used to customize the avatar. *Animal Crossing* rewards players who make their mayor character cute, too. At the Able Sisters' clothing shop, players can purchase new clothing or create their own custom designs, allowing them to creatively experiment with ways of making the game even cuter.

Why Does This Matter for Society and Games?

Now that we've established just how cute *Animal Crossing* is, let's talk about why it matters. The game has a troubled place in larger popular conversations about the role of games in society. On the one hand, it is often discussed as the title to "get your girlfriend into games," a phrase problematic for the underlying assumptions that all gamers are heterosexual men, and that *Animal Crossing* will appeal to all women because of an essential biological mandate. On the other hand, it is often pointed to in media effects debates to illustrate that games aren't always a violent bloodfest (Mulkerin, 2016). Keeping both of these aspects in mind, I argue that *Animal Crossing*'s cuteness matters not because of its ability to argue for the cultural legitimacy of games in circles outside of self-identified gamers, but because it has a profound impact, whether we acknowledge it or not, on both society and games. As a cute game which is unique in its aesthetic and gameplay from other titles popular at the time, it illustrates not only that a game *not* about extreme sports or violence is commercially viable, but that games which appeal to sensibilities gendered as traditionally feminine have a place in gaming. The rest of this chapter will break down and describe the lasting impacts *Animal Crossing* has had on society and games.

First, let's discuss the lasting impact of *Animal Crossing*'s cuteness on society. Its cuteness challenges the way hegemonic culture frames gaming as a uniquely masculine pursuit because the game world rewards behaviors traditionally framed as feminine, like caregiving, interior design, and fashion design. Although it is out of the scope of this chapter to trace the origin of cuteness being tied to femininity, we can briefly discuss where it fits within the gender hierarchy. At the core of the issue, Judith Butler writes that "...reason and mind are associated with masculinity and agency, while the body and nature are considered to be the mute facticity of the feminine, awaiting signification from an opposing masculine subject" (1999, p. 48). When applied to society's perception of gaming, we can say that games with foundations in cerebral pursuits of strategy, even if that strategy is managing health bars and ammunition, are elevated as valuable pursuits and learning opportunities. When games, on the other hand, focus on creativity or design, they are too focused on the aesthetics of the body and are thus classed as feminine and unworthy of being taken seriously, according to popular culture. Butler points out that it isn't just that women have been associated with bodies, flesh, and pleasure, as there is nothing wrong with any of those things, but that women have been placed there by, and in their opposition to, masculinity. So even if we look at *Animal Crossing* as a cerebrally challenging game where you must catalog complex relationships with villagers and multitask to keep them happy, it will still be contextualized against more traditionally masculine gaming pursuits and found to be wanting. It isn't enough that the game is found pleasing by traditionally feminine measures, it will always be judged by what it can offer hegemonic masculinities.

This pattern of a hierarchy of valuation, with masculine-coded gaming behaviors highly valued and feminine games always receiving less than their fair share, reverberates throughout gaming culture at large. Not only do women often reject the title of gamer despite making up half of the gaming population (Shaw, 2011; ESA, 2021), boundaries are created and enforced to define masculine forms of gaming as authentic and all others as imposters attempting to corrupt gaming culture (Eklund, 2016). And in circles adjacent to gaming, the same arguments are levied against women video-game streamers—that women only stream games for pleasure and fun, and not for serious, rational, or competitive reasons (Dargonaki, 2018). Again, saying that people are interested in different types of gaming isn't the issue. The issue is that one is heralded as "true" gaming, while the other (feminine) is looked upon as an inauthentic dalliance.

On the one hand, *Animal Crossing* illustrates that there is a market for cute—and not just graphically cute—games, and on the other hand, it illustrates that there is a firm resistance in the player base to the dominant hegemonic ideals behind traditional modes of gameplay. *Animal Crossing* represents a significant objection to the valorization of video gaming as a masculine activity, but not because it counters it head on or vies for cultural legitimacy. *Animal Crossing* is too cute to care.

Ashley Guajardo

References

Bohunicky, K. M. (2021). Dear Punchy: Representing and feeling writing in *Animal Crossing*. *Loading*, 13(22), 39–58. doi.org/10.7202/1075262ar

Butler, J. (1999). *Gender trouble: Feminism and the subversion of identity*. New York: Routledge.

Comerford, C. (2021). Coconuts, custom-play & COVID-19: Social isolation, serious leisure and personas in *Animal Crossing: New horizons*. *Persona Studies*, 6(2), 101–117. doi.org/10.21153/psj2020vol6no2art970

Dargonaki, S. (2018). Performing gender on Twitch.tv: Gendered playbour through Butlerian theory. *International Journal of Media & Cultural Politics*. 14(1). Retrieved 4 October, 2021, from https://search.ebscohost.com/login.aspx?direct=true&db=ufh&AN=128856763&site=ehost-live

Eklund, L. (2016). Who are the casual gamers? Gender tropes and tokenism in game culture. In M. Wilson, & T. Leaver (Eds), *Social, casual and mobile games: The changing gaming landscape* (pp. 15–29). New York, NY: Bloomsbury.
ESA. (2021). *2021 Essential Facts About the Video Game Industry*. Entertainment Software Association. Retrieved 4 October, 2021, from https://www.theesa.com/resource/2021-essential-facts-about-the-video-game-industry/
Kalinowski, A. M. (2021). "My Pockets Are Full": The emotional and mechanical function of goodbyes in *Animal Crossing*. *Loading*, 13(22), 59–71. Retrieved 4, October 2021, from https://journals.sfu.ca/loading/index.php/loading/article/view/299
Lieber-Milo, S. (2021). Pink purchasing: Interrogating the soft power of Japan's kawaii consumption. *Journal of Consumer Culture*. doi.org/10.1177/14695405211013849
Lorenz, K (1943) Die ngeborenen Formen möglicher Erfahrung. *Zeitschrift für Tierpsychologie* 5, 233–409.
Metacritic. (2021). *Game Releases by User Score 2001 All Platforms. Metacritic.com*, Retrieved 4 October, 2021, from https://www.metacritic.com/browse/games/score/metascore/year/all/all?year_selected=2001
Mulkerin, T. (2016). The 12 Best Games That Aren't About Killing Stuff. *Business Insider*. Retrieved 4 October, 2021, from https://www.businessinsider.com/the-12-best-non-violent-relaxing-games-2016-6
Shaw, A. (2011), Do you identify as a gamer? Gender, race, sexuality and gamer identity, *New Media and Society*, 14 (1), 28–44. Retrieved 4 October, 2021, from https://journals.sagepub.com/doi/full/10.1177/1461444811410394

Further Reading

Brown, A. M., & Berg Marklund, B. (2015). Animal crossing: New leaf and the diversity of horror in video games. In DiGRA 2015, May 14th-17th, Lüneburg, Germany. Digital Games Research Association (DiGRA). Retrieved 4 October, 2021, from http://www.digra.org/wp-content/uploads/digital-library/160_BrownMarklund_Animal-Crossing.pdf
Scully-Blaker, R. and Flynn-Jones, E. (eds). (2020). Animal Crossing Special Issue. *Loading: The Journal of the Canadian Game Studies Association*. 13(22), 1–134. Retrieved 4 October, 2021, from https://journals.sfu.ca/loading/index.php/loading/issue/view/25

DOI: 10.4324/9781003199205-4

ASSASSIN'S CREED ORIGINS (2017)

Assassin's Creed (hereafter *AC*) is a series of twelve main video games in which, since 2007, players have taken the role of a hero (and now a heroine), some with supernatural powers (such as "eagle vision," which reveals things beyond normal sight), but all with similar exceptional and spectacular physical abilities. They receive quests from historical personae and conduct them through the action of a phantasmagorical device (the Animus). To complete those quests, they freely explore an open virtual world in third-person view using different types of jumps and moves to climb up buildings, infiltrate exotic and often urban settings, and interact in real-time with other characters, including antagonists they must avoid or kill as stealthily as possible, to avoid being killed or to continue their exploration. In the most recent games, they engage in group battles with armies, raiders, or naval ships. The series is set largely in the past, as made clear by Ubisoft's tagline for the series 'History is our playground': Greece (fifth century BC); Egypt (first century BC); Norway and England (ninth century); Middle East (twelfth century); northern Italy (fifteenth century); the Antilles (eighteenth century); the northeastern coast of the current US (eighteenth century); Paris (eighteenth century); and London (nineteenth century). *Assassin's Creed Origins* (herein *ACO*) represents a significant evolution of the series' core premise of mixing fantasy and historical realism and is a key video game because of its engagement with history through its Discovery Tour feature.

Assassin's Creed and the Origins of the Tour

In *ACO*, players explore the genetic memory of Ptolemaic (ancient Greek kingdom based in Egypt) police officer Bayek who, together with his spouse Aya in 49 BC, decides to avenge their son's death by executing his abductors. They succeed thanks to help received from pharaoh Cleopatra, who directs them to members of the Order of the Ancients (precursors to the Knights Templar), masked men who removed her from the throne and replaced her with her younger brother Ptolemy XIII to control the kingdom. Cleopatra obtains Caesar's help to be restored to the throne, and they make a deal with the Order of the Ancients, betraying Bayek and Aya before returning to Rome. Aya decides to leave for Rome and inflicts the first injury on Caesar during his assassination. Before her departure, she and Bayek had laid the foundations for the brotherhood of "the hidden ones" (future Assassins), whose creed is to work in the shadows to protect the people's freedom against tyrants.

As can be seen from the narrative of *ACO*, the series draws on the intertextual library of secular legends and myths to create a fiction that combines the genres of the fantasy adventure and historical documentary. The product marketing in this cross-media universe is based in part on the historical expertise used to make the games more realistic. The profession of the consultants recruited for this purpose lends credibility: most are trained in and earn their living from history, often as university history professors. Thematic issues of popular history magazines, popular reviews, and recent in-game educational modes pioneered in *ACO* also cultivate this impression. These educational modes are called Discovery Tours (hereafter DTs). DTs are downloadable extensions of recent *AC* games allowing users to visit the games' universe. They occupy a growing place in classrooms, because they are presented in a mode that lets visitors freely roam the games' sites to learn more about their history and daily life or embark on guided tours curated by experts, without worrying about combat or quests.

Upon entering the DT Origins (aka DT Ancient Egypt), players choose their avatar. If they choose a guided tour, they have the choice of five (Egypt, Pyramids, Alexandria, Daily Life, and Romans). They must follow a path marked by a luminescent trail. The tour is a guided interaction, the texts of which can also be read. These texts have been written by, among others, archeologists, historians, and linguists. They are accompanied by photographs of artifacts, monuments, or archeological sites and interactive maps that help to understand the physical geography and organization of the territory. Each of these tours has five to twenty stations (eighty-five in total) about architecture, the arts, the natural environment, philosophy, politics, science and technology, and the daily lives of ordinary people, such as religious beliefs and practices, education, leisure, customs, modes of transportation, and the work of farmers and artisans. For example, there are stations about the Library of Alexandria, the Hippodrome of Alexandria, the Greek pharaohs, the construction of the Pyramids, the fauna of ancient Egypt, the Nile, slavery, the flora of ancient Egypt, the embalming of mummies, Egyptian fashion, the making of beer and bread, the seasons and agriculture, domestic animals, Roman military equipment, crucifixions, and Roman aqueducts.

If the players choose to take a self-guided tour, they select a location on the map of Egypt to visit and then navigate the open environment on their own. They can walk, swim, ride an animal (including an eagle), ride a boat, and even teleport to a site of interest on the map and observe the animals, buildings, non-player characters (NPCs), and natural landscapes. They can also take the place of an NPC who is surrounded by a white circle, to see what gestures the person made and have the meaning of these gestures explained to them.

Assassin's Creed and History

Whereas those who engage in scholarly, educational, or official history discourses claim (and can believe in, often rightly) the verifiability of their statements, the general public who partake in lay history (a wide range of practices dealing with the past in a variety of settings) often renounce this ideal, even acknowledging from the outset that it is a fictional creation or entertainment (Éthier & Lefrançois, 2021). While lay history can base itself on scholarly work for its credibility and revenue, research regularly uncovers inaccuracies in form and substance in films; for instance, whether or not by design (a trait shared by scholarly history), women are portrayed in cartoonish ways. Plus, it often showcases elements of the past that generate support for causes (but not always those of the current elite) and, even when it is not edifying, conveys a range of values.

One current mode of consumption of historical references has achieved cultural prominence: historical video games (HVGs), such as *Age of Empires* (Ensemble Studios, 1997) or *Crusader Kings* (Paradox Entertainment AB, 2004). Like other lay history, HVGs inflect real references or place them in a fantasized historical frame, or even alter what we know as "history"; HVGs illustrate visions of the past circulating within society and are not ideologically neutral (Chapman, 2016; Kee, 2014). They engage the participant in thinking, deciding, and "acting" in a historical context. Their immersive and interactive nature distinguishes them from other lay history insomuch as they mediate a rapport to historical references, notably as they let the players' actions impact their "destiny". Indeed, Gilbert's (2019) study confirmed that high-school students believe that the immersive experience of the video game contrasts with school because of the feeling that they have been playing the games in the *AC* series, given the immediate access to history it offers, and because of the empathy they say they feel toward the people of the past.

Ubisoft's reputation of being historically accurate raises the question of relationships between games and the different types of history, as well as efforts to conform to scholarly history that gives the brand its credibility. The traces of the past visible through virtual historical tourism can create a personal connection to history, as when players explore the city of Alexandria in *ACO* and realize that the capital city of Egypt was a major center of Greek culture, but they can barely question it or think of it independently, since the narrative creation is not apparent to them and is more artistic than historical. In fact, while the game designers' interest in history serves the story's continuity, it is like the practice of many re-enactors who conduct in-depth but selective research on material history to create an immersive reconstruction experience. As such, several editorial choices reinforce the cliché images that players have of the sites represented (e.g., a *Ben Hur*-like hippodrome, instead of a Greek one), and human behavior and relationships (seen as changeless), or serve the needs of the narrative. DT *Origins* unveils those choices, with a "behind-the-scenes" marker that explains what and why creative liberties were taken.

Like many video games, *ACO* offers an experience of control in an orderly, simulated environment. Players may have a vicarious experience by observing not only the great figures of the elite, but also of the governed (exploited workers, oppressed peoples, etc.) who "make history" (to use Ubisoft's slogan). This might also prompt them to think about subjects that have an impact on history. For instance, in DT *Origins*, they can interact with bakers, farmers, sailors, and sculptors.

Several video games prominently showcase re-enactments of past events, like *Age of Empires* or *Sid Meier's Civilization* (MicroProse, 1991). Despite some "superficial" faults (errors, violence, anachronisms, etc.), the classroom use of HVG intensifies the circulation of factual knowledge resulting from historiographical work and increases pupils' motivation. Nonetheless, even well-done HVGs regrettably short-circuit the imparting of the approach that lies at the heart of historical thinking: its critical, heuristic, and interpretative process which is subject to evidence-based debates, as is any scientific process. Might playing video games make it possible to develop a critical approach to historical sources, and to utilize it to analyze "popular" history or current political discourse?

A Discovery Tour of Classrooms

Students consume a wealth of information about the past outside of school in a variety of formats, mostly fictional (Wineburg, 2018). In 2020, with COVID-19 closing schools, some teachers turned to video games for help. For example, Péloquin, a high-school teacher who organizes academic trips, explained in *The Washington Post* (Favis, 2020) that having an open world without conflict where students discover additional content is a useful part of *Assassin's Creed: Odyssey* (2018), although a school trip experience, be it virtual, is not automatically a source of learning, especially while the use of traces from the past to allow students to problematize and reconstruct history is seldom at the center of teaching practices. Péloquin adds that the exploration of sites needs to be intellectually nurtured to help students figure out what they do when they collect and analyze (virtual facsimile) traces of the past, if they are to understand how historians work, to learn to inquire, to obtain information from recollections and make sense of them.

Taking advantage of *ACO* to teach history, one study we have conducted is really revealing. We have used DT *Origins* with students aged twelve to thirteen in Montreal area French schools that were asked to investigate different sociohistorical phenomena. The students were given three independent assignments: to investigate the Greek aspect of Syria in the first century BC; to investigate how the Egyptologist Champollion achieved the first modern translation of ancient Egyptian hieroglyphic writing; and to investigate sedentarization. The goal was to identify, locate in time and space, observe, describe, and explain phenomena. Questions also asked students to specify the actors involved.

DT *Origins* is an excellent tool for such a task. From the guided tour or their free navigation of the environment, students can look at, and concentrate on, elements catching their attention. Yet, they should also be looking for answers. In both cases, to find these, they have access to animated video capsules, maps, images, and texts. Finally, they have the opportunity to take the place of a baker, a mummy embalmer, or another NPC to understand their life.

In writing their answers, students had to clarify and document the evidence found in DT Origins on which they were based. They were also asked to evaluate and validate this evidence. To find clues in their free exploration, they could, for example, go to high ground (e.g., climb to the top of a pyramid) to observe three features of the space in a region, or take a boat ride to find three advantages of living near the Nile. To document what they discovered, they could build a portfolio of images to support their argument by taking a snapshot of the evidence from the Photo mode (by clicking with the virtual camera and exporting the image to an external hard drive; this is another great tool found in DT *Origins* to record history).

From this study, we found that students learned about culture (including artifacts, notably tools), daily life (including that of women), social relations, as well as the geographical context. They also felt they had learned as much history as usual, yet on different topics and in a different way; less fluid and structured, but more enjoyable and less constrained. However, according to the teachers, students did not perform differently in their class, compared to similar tests or groups from previous years. They appeared more motivated and focused than before the experiment and were even heard talking more regularly about the topic outside of the classroom, although very few said that they delved more than usual into history outside of school. Teachers noted that the stimulation of students was at first intense but decreased somewhat after three sessions of a one-hour history class. Students appreciated seeing the monuments and being able to decide for themselves what to visit.

A New Historical Literacy

If it weren't for DT *Origins*, students wouldn't have made these visits on their own and they wouldn't have sought out what they learned on their own. While not a decisive answer to any issue around the use of HVGs in a classroom context, the DT mode of *ACO* represents a leap forward in this direction. In fact, educational use of DT *Origins* specifically shows that it is a key game within the HVG genre, because it offers a violence-free environment, freedom of choice of sequences, a great historical wealth, and a diversity of possible explorations.

Marc-André Éthier and David Lefrançois

References

Chapman, A. (2016). *Digital games as history*. New York: Routledge.
Éthier, M.-A., & Lefrançois, D. (2021). *Histoire profane*. Québec: PUL
Favis, E. (2020, April 15). With coronavirus closing schools, here's how video games are helping teachers. *The Washington Post*. Retrieved November 28, 2021, from https://www.washingtonpost.com/video-games/2020/04/15/teachers-video-games-coronavirus-education-remote-learning/
Gilbert, L. (2019). 'Assassin's Creed reminds us that history is human experience': Students' senses of empathy while playing a narrative video game. *Theory & Research in Social Education*, 47(3), 1–30. Retrieved 2021-11-28, from https://doi.org/10.1080/00933104.2018.1560713
Kee, K. (Eds) (2014). *Pastplay: Teaching and learning history with technology*. Ann Arbor: University of Michigan Press.
Wineburg, S. (2018). *Why learn history (when it's already on your phone)?* Chicago: University of Chicago Press.

Further Reading

Éthier, M.-A., & Lefrançois, D. (2020). *Assassin's Creed vu par les historiens*. Montréal: Del Busso.
Joly-Lavoie, A. (2019). *Assassin's Creed*: implications pour l'enseignement de l'histoire. In Éthier, M.-A., & Lefrançois, D. (Eds). *Agentivité et citoyenneté dans l'enseignement de l'histoire* (pp. 203–217). Montréal: M Éditeur.
McCall, J. (2011). *Gaming the past*. New York: Routledge.

DOI: 10.4324/9781003199205-5

BEJEWELED (2001)

Bejeweled is a game so ubiquitous that it is easily overlooked within the broader scope of video-game history and culture. It has neither the grand narratives of many games we think of when considering the medium, nor does it have the contemporary popularity of games like *Candy Crush Saga* (King, 2012), which *Bejeweled* surely influenced. As a historical object, *Bejeweled* also lacks the stark brutishness one might associate with a game like *Tetris* (Alexey Pajitnov, 1984). But *Bejeweled* is a gem in the rough (so to speak) that, while lacking the stylistic excess of contemporary casual games, has been overall deeply influential in the genre of match-3 casual games and the medium of video games more explicitly. It was an early game to court the casual and feminized player, and it helped to reformat how popular culture might think about video games, writ large.

The History and Gameplay of *Bejeweled*

Bejeweled was first released in 2001 by developer PopCap Games as a game played in web browsers via Flash. An earlier version of the game was titled *Diamond Mine* (named after a country song), but when Microsoft offered them a partnership, the name was changed to *Bejeweled* (Edwards, 2013). It was not the first match-3 game—this honorific belongs to a 1994 MS-DOS game called *Shariki*, developed by Russian Eugene Alemzhin (The N3TWORK, 2018). But, even further back, one could link its origins to the famous 1980s puzzle game *Tetris*; to this point, scholar Jesper Juul (2009, p. 84) argues that all matching tile games can ultimately be linked back to *Tetris*. Regardless, more than any other matching tile or match-3 game, *Bejeweled* became a household name in a space where copycats and reskinned mechanics are plentiful. While it (perhaps) did not define the genre, it has changed with it and changed it, with subsequent releases and titles including *Bejeweled Twist* (Popcap, 2008), *Bejeweled Blitz* (Popcap, 2008), *Bejeweled Stars* (Popcap, 2016), and *Bejeweled Champions* (Popcap, 2020). In 2011, PopCap Games was acquired by mega game corporation Electronic Arts (Rao, 2011), which now owns the game series.

Gameplay in a match-3 game—and more specifically in *Bejeweled*—is relatively simple. The mechanics involve lining up three or more of a kind (matching shapes or colors) by exchanging two items. When the three or more items are in line, they disappear, moving the other shapes on the board and creating a modified version where the player (once again) must match a new set of three things. In the case of the original game, shapes and colors were designed as gems: green squares, turquoise diamonds, purple triangles, white circles, and yellow squares (turned on an angle). In *Bejeweled*, as well as other match-3 games, the primary mechanics of play involve swapping—if you swap a green square for a purple triangle you will have three items in a row, allowing those three items to disappear and reshuffle the board each time. At different levels, the specifics of constraints might vary through different board shapes and light changes to the mechanics. In future games of the series, mechanics became even more varied with some games focusing more on time challenges (get as many matches as you can in the shortest period of time), while in others the primary constraint might be the number of moves you get to collect a certain kind of color or shape (collect a certain number of yellow gems in twenty moves), and others were pushing players more toward a zen-like repetition of gameplay.

In addition to game sequels that lightly change the mechanics, the past two decades have expanded the number of platforms a simple game like *Bejeweled* can be played on. While it started as a browser game, versions of the game are now available on practically any platform from mobile phones (iOS and Android) to consoles (all or most have had versions made for it), to arcade versions and a litany of antiquated technologies (even a version for the Palm Pilot). The simplicity of the game and ease of making new versions have helped to create its ubiquity and accessibility.

Video Games and Expanding Markets

Part of the beauty of *Bejeweled* lies within its flexibility—there are any number of ways to make these seemingly simple puzzles vary between one another, yet remain identifiably part of the series. This combination of recognizability and incremental difficulty is what has made the match-3 subgenre a mainstay of casual games for such a long time. The frequent cloning of the games that are similar but different, as well as the ability to find these types of games on almost any platform, has made it an easy entry point for novice players who had not previously thought of themselves as "gamers" per se. Juul explains that "playing a matching tile game does not signal special knowledge of video games" (Juul, 2009, p. 85) within the broader culture of the medium. In other words, *Bejeweled* (and the games that it influenced afterwards) erected a space within video games that continues to deliberately appeal to non-gamers.

As previously noted, the game is neither particularly unique, nor was it "the first." *Bejeweled*'s popularity is—at least in part—a consequence of its timing onto the market. Being released in 2001 put it in the world in a cultural moment where more people had access to a variety of game-ready technologies (personal computers, consoles, and eventually smartphones), making it a game that was both easy to learn *and* readily accessible. Its popularity has influenced the thousands of clones that have been produced—many which have never achieved popularity and others (such as *Candy Crush Saga*) that have exceeded it in popularity. This is all to say: *Bejeweled*'s importance is due less to being innovative than to how it innovated in the right way at the right moment—just as the technology and culture around video games were dramatically changing.

The Emergence of Casual Games

This cultural moment in the video-game industry is often referred to as the emergence of the "casual" game. When referring to video games, "casual" is a label that implies that they are cheap or free, can be played for longer or shorter periods of time, and have low entry points in terms of difficulty levels (Casual Games Association, 2007). Many early casual games were computer- or browser-based games (such as *Bejeweled*), but later Nintendo capitalized on the emerging market with their release of the Wii and the DS Lite, both in 2006. Casual games sit as the alternative to what is often referred to as "hardcore"—games that have more temporal and monetary investment and were long treated as the bread-and-butter of the video-game industry, although a shift has occurred in the last few decades (Juul, 2009, pp. 8–10).

More specifically, there has long been a chasm of gender difference aligned with these terms— hardcore and casual—wherein hardcore is typically associated with masculine gamers and casual is typically associated with feminine gamers (Chess, 2017; Vanderhoef, 2013). This trend was only beginning in 2001 with the emergence of *Bejeweled* onto the market, but the so-called casual games from that time period—whether match-3 (like *Bejeweled*), time management like *Diner Dash* (Playfirst, 2003), or hidden object like *Mystery Case Files: Ravenhearst* (Big Fish Games, 2006)—all helped to contribute to a growing zeitgeist, wherein games no longer needed to be big, expensive, and difficult in order to be successful. Up until the early 2000s, the majority of video games were designed and intended for male audiences, and while there are many instances where women and girls did make a space for themselves within video-game culture, those moments were not necessarily taken as the opening of a new market. Casual games helped to create a new play aesthetic within the video-game industry. There was a shift of intention, and with this a broadening of audiences that went beyond the typical "gamer" (regardless of gender identity). The terms "casual" and "hardcore" are not without much-warranted critique; they force the games we play into binary categories that are both misleading and fortify a toxicity within a culture that was already full of poor behavior (Consalvo, 2011). However, they are also industry terms that have stuck and become difficult to side-step when discussing a game such as *Bejeweled*.

The market shift of the early 2000s was not without pushback. 2008 saw the beginning of the "filthy casual" meme which had the intention of deriding those who played casual games, suggesting that casual game players are not as impressive nor as important to the industry as hardcore players (Chess & Paul, 2019). Industry debates continue to discuss topics whether specific games are "real games" (Consalvo & Paul, 2019), and casual puzzle games become part of that larger conversation and gate-keeping. All of this is to say, casual games sit in a precarious but valuable place within the broader industry.

Why *Bejeweled*?

So, to return to the question "Why *Bejeweled*?" and to what has been said, some of the answer has to do with timing, some of the answer has to do with changes to the industry, and some of it has to do with the ease and beauty with which the game construction presented itself to players. As with all casual games, the ability to be played for shorter and longer periods of time makes it easier for people with busy schedules to find snippets of time in their everyday lives. Its low price points (often free to play with micro-purchasing options for boosters) makes it a low-cost alternative to expensive console games. It carries a well-known name brand that allows novice players to dabble and try new things, not forcing commitment of financial or time investment. Like any other well-known casual activity, this makes it a particularly powerful product within the broader market.

Pattern-matching games, and match-3 games in particular, create a sense of order within a disordered world. Just as constructing a jigsaw puzzle helps make the hobbyist feel a sense of control over chaos, so too does a match-3 game where the right solution not only removes stray items from the screen but rewards the player with bursts of color and movement. In this way, *Bejeweled* can be understood similar to the hidden-object game mechanic (where players find objects in a messy room that subsequently disappear (Chess, 2017). *Bejeweled*'s function, which is similar to that, might ultimately be understood as a "cleaning" mechanic. The inherent organization involved in the match-3 game makes it satisfying in that a short period of play time can create a strong sense of satisfaction for the player.

Casual games function in a unique way, compared to hardcore games (if we are going to use these still somewhat troubling terms).

Because of casual games' ability to create this sense of satisfaction with such low financial and time cost, they can be squeezed into the everyday life of the player with ease. One can argue that games like *Bejeweled* are played in the in-between times—the time spent not doing more "productive" things in one's life. From this perspective, casual games such as this one both provide a sense of relief from the grind of everyday life via play, but also a work-like ethic of constantly producing, being in motion, and feeling productive. A game like *Bejeweled* creates a sheen of false productivity, but also can replicate the anxieties inherent in our everyday lives.

And yet, the title of the game, *Bejeweled*, creates a sense of gendered expectations built into all of these things, and as a reflection on its emergence as an early popular casual game. The stereotypes of consumptive femininity seem to wink at the audience behind the pixelated jewels, promising the nascent audience of 2001 a different kind of experience in digital play. "*Bejeweled*" suggests that when played properly, the player is able to shimmy themselves into the existing industry and brightly shine through, lighting a new path forward for not only the games that existed twenty years ago, but the ones that could be. They can, it would seem, "be jeweled" or adorned by the spectacle of what was then a new experience. Two decades later, *Bejeweled* remains important because it was part of the revolution that changed the industry forever.

Shira Chess

References

Casual Games Association. (2007). *Casual Games Market Report 2007*. Retrieved October 27, 2021, from http://issuu.com/casualconnect/docs/casualgamesmarketreport-2007/6?e=2336319/1145366

Chess, S. (2017). *Ready Player Two: Women gamers and designed identity*. Minneapolis, MN: University of Minnesota Press.

Chess, S., & Paul, C. A. (2019). The end of casual; Long live casual. *Games and Culture, 14*(2), 107–118.

Consalvo, M. (2011). Confronting toxic gamer culture: A challenge for feminist game studies scholars. *Ada: A Journal of Gender and New Media Technology, 1*(1). Retrieved October 27, 2021, from http://adanewmedia.org/2012/11/issue1-consalvo/. DOI: 10.7264/N33X84KH

Consalvo, M., & Paul, C. A. (2019). *Real games: What's legitimate and what'snNot in contemporary video games*. Cambridge, MA: MIT Press.

Edwards, J. (2013, September 11). The History of Bejeweled. *Business Insider*. Retrieved October 27, 2021, from https://www.businessinsider.com/the-history-of-bejewled-2013-9

Juul, J. (2009). *A casual revolution: Reinventing video games and their players*. Cambridge, MA: MIT Press.

Rao, L. (2011, July 12). EA Buys PopCap Games For As Much As $1.3B. *TechCrunch*. Retrieved October 27, 2021, from https://social.techcrunch.com/2011/07/12/confirmed-ea-buys-popcap-games-for-750-million-plus-earn-out/

The N3TWORK. (2018, April 23). A Brief History of Match-Three Games. *Medium*. Retrieved October 27, 2021, from https://medium.com/@john_23522/a-brief-history-of-match-three-games-31233dcdfcc5

Vanderhoef, J. (2013, June 1). Casual threats: The feminization of casual video games. *Ada: A Journal of Gender, New Media, and Technology*. Retrieved October 27, 2021, from http://adanewmedia.org/2013/06/issue2-vanderhoef/. DOI: 10.7264/N3V40S4D

DOI: 10.4324/9781003199205-6

BRAID (2008)

Indie Darling

On a sunless day in the winter of 2012, I (Adam) found myself in a car, snowed in on a mountain pass trying to reach the Sundance Film Festival in Park City, Utah. A blizzard had been raging all day and I was unable to make any progress until the highway was cleared. I was joined in the wait for the snowplows by two film directors, and though our conversation was wide ranging in the hours spent together in the cozy SUV, much of it revolved around the film they had brought to the festival, *Indie Game: The Movie* (Pajot & Swirsky, 2012). One of the main topics we discussed was the recent rise of solo developers who could create games and find great success outside of the traditional game studio system. *Indie Game: The Movie* celebrates some of these video-game visionaries as auteur-like artists[1] while it chronicles the travails of hopeful independent game developers. Rather astutely, Lisanne Pajot and James Swirsky also invited on the journey one of the most quintessential independent game developers of all, Jonathan Blow.

Blow's game *BRAID* (Number None, 2008) hit the Xbox Live Arcade[2] in August of 2008 with a slew of other independently made games, and the gaming world hasn't been the same since. *BRAID* initially looks like a standard puzzle-platforming experience. However, integrated into the genre's familiar jumping and climbing is a brain-bending and sometimes brutally difficult time manipulation mechanic. Each painterly level contains puzzles that test players' critical and lateral thinking abilities, all in service to an obscured narrative woven throughout the game's progression. Over the course of the game, players navigate their way through six worlds, each with their own variant of the time mechanic and their own haunting musical score.

Interspersed between these worlds are narrative clues hinting toward the game's overarching story, which is never fully revealed, even at the end.

Disguised Complication

From the puzzles to the metaphorically relevant time mechanic, Blow deliberately layers complexities throughout the game. For example, the "How to Play" menu describes three easy tasks: 'Press A to jump,' 'Bounce on monsters' heads to get higher,' and 'Collect puzzle pieces.'[3] From there, players are transported to a world of peace and serenity: the moving brushstroke scenery and melodic violin music seem much more at home in a romanticized garden party than in a video game, and the initial few obstacles are easily overcome. Things change dramatically when players inevitably miss a jump or touch a monster: the music stops abruptly, the motion of the background halts, and a simple prompt to press a new button is shown on the screen. When players press this button, the music plays in reverse, the colorful backgrounds lose their saturation, and the player-character (Tim) moves backward along his original path. It seems that the "How to Play" menu left out one incredibly important detail: players can reverse time.

This time reversal is not just reserved for a simple button press to undo mistakes; instead, each of the game's worlds centers around an additional time-altering mechanic. In one world, the passage of time is directly correlated to Tim's forward and backward movement, and in another, players create a shadow version of Tim that performs a set of already completed and reversed actions. In the game's more difficult levels, players must combine multiple time-altering abilities together to solve puzzles. This theme, that of pulling back the curtain to reveal a more complex world, is the common thread in *BRAID* and as each new mechanic is introduced, players quickly understand the tacit promise that more complexity will follow.

The narrative proves to be no less intricate. The game's story starts at a familiar and fairly tropey place: 'Tim is off on a search to rescue a Princess.' The books found at the beginning of each world tell an emerging tale of a hero on a quest to rescue a princess. However, this story quickly breaks from the trope by admitting that the reason the Princess 'has been snatched by a horrible and evil monster' is 'because Tim made a mistake.' As the game progresses, players witness firsthand the lengths that Tim will go to twist his version of the story in a bid for sympathy from the audience, and to convince himself that his manufactured memories are objective truth. For example, the first level players can enter is called "World 2," not "World 1" as would be expected. It appears that Tim is showing players "World 2" first in an attempt to gloss over his "mistake." This untrustworthy narration continues throughout, and ultimately culminates in the final level. In the end, players learn that while Tim may be the protagonist of the game, he is very much the villain of the story: it is revealed that he stalked a girl outside her bedroom window while she was sleeping, and then twisted his own perception of reality to turn the literal knight in shining armor who rescued her into a monster who stole her away from him.

A Singular Vision

Despite all the game's complexities, and probably because of them, *BRAID* was a commercial success: one perhaps Blow was not prepared for. Several years later, when Blow appeared in *Indie Game: The Movie*, he was shown as an older but wiser developer, a sage who realized his own authorial vision with *BRAID* but was changed by the process. In the documentary, he nods toward the similarities between film (and film auteurs) and video games (and indie game developers):

> So, the way that I'm approaching design in this case really is kind of experiential. Right, I'm thinking about "when the player comes on the screen, what's going to be happening, right?" You know, not quite in the same way that you think of it in a movie, but sort of.
>
> (Pajot & Swirsky, 2012)

Blow's desire to express his own singular vision through his game— and having the tools and programming ability to create it on his own—was not a new thing in the world of game development. In the earliest days, teams were typically very small. *Adventure* (Atari, 1979), the game that popularized the concept of an "Easter egg" and was featured prominently in the video-game nostalgia novel *Ready Player One* (Cline, 2011), was programed and designed by a single Atari employee named Warren Robinett. Even the original *Super Mario Bros.* (Nintendo, 1985), one of the most successful and well-known video games in the world, was developed by a small group of people.[4] Within these small teams, a game's creative vision, story, and themes could often be traced to a single person. However, as the game industry grew past a handful of studios, controlling every detail in a game became more difficult for solo developers as the technology, costs, and player demands for "higher quality" increased.[5] When Blow began development on BRAID, he made a conscious choice to make the game on his own and to distance himself from the common studio model:

> Back when Braid came out, there certainly had been independent games that people were paying attention to before that. But that year, 2008, saw a number of indie games that... [had] enough meat here to this game that you might care about this as much as you care about a AAA retail game.
>
> (Gamespot, 2012)

This is a critical point. Virtually everything that makes BRAID the game it is—including both its triumphs and its shortcomings—is there because Blow, and Blow alone, meticulously determined it should be there. As he said in *Indie Game: The Movie*:

> Things that are personal have flaws. They have vulnerabilities. If you don't see a vulnerability in somebody, you're probably not relating with them on a very personal level. So, it's the same with a game design. Making [BRAID] was about, "let me take my deepest flaws and vulnerabilities, and put them in the game, and let's see what happens."
>
> (Pajot & Swirsky, 2012)

Time and Mystery

Since BRAID's release, a number of questions about the game have been discussed in the gaming community. For example, is the narrative reflecting some part of Blow's personal history? Is it possible that an in-game achievement earned for standing motionless for two straight hours is a cynical commentary on extrinsic motivation? Is Tim responsible for the game's books and level progression, or are they a product of a separate, darker Tim that is trying to lock the truth away from both players and himself? And possibly the most talked about question: why are there so many references to the atomic bomb throughout the game? Players want to understand why the Princess explodes if Tim manages to catch her in the final level, why there is a quote from Manhattan Project physicist Kenneth Bainbridge[6] in the epilogue, and what significance there is to the game's initial release date falling on the anniversary of the bombing of Hiroshima.

These issues can only be explored if players discover them, since they have been deliberately obscured by their creator. And yet, after the game was released, Blow went out of his way in many interviews to discuss "the meaning" of the game. In an interview with Chris Dahlen of the AV Club, he alluded to both the "obvious" meanings, as well as the other details that no one seemed to be seeing:

> I did leave the game very open to interpretation. [But] I feel that a lot of people are a little bit too quick to take concrete bits of evidence that they find and that they recognize, and to use those to create a definitive explanation of everything and to bend all other facts to fit that explanation.
>
> (Dahlen, 2008)

Still, even for those of us who have played the game multiple times over the years, we are left with questions that may never be answered. With the upcoming anniversary edition of the game slated to be released (at the time of this writing) that will contain, in Blow's words, "the craziest, most in-depth commentary ever put in a video game"[7] (Blow, 2020), there will no doubt be further revelations.

Perhaps that was Blow's intention all along, and the simplest aspect of the game—the title itself—is the first of the many simplicities that turn out to be anything but: strands that are connected and woven together, easy to get lost in, and impossible to examine without looking at the entire braid.

Corrinne Lewis and Adam Hunter

Notes

1. To quote the *Encyclopedia Britannica*, "Auteur theory, [is the] theory of filmmaking in which the director is viewed as the major creative force in a motion picture... [and] is more to be considered the 'author' of the movie than is the writer of the screenplay."
2. Xbox Live Arcade was announced in May 2004 as Microsoft's foray into digital game distribution for the original Xbox. It focused on arcade-style games and demos which were small enough to download easily. In November 2005, it was relaunched for the Xbox 360, which was where *BRAID* launched in August 2008 as part of the XBLA Summer of Arcade.
3. These stripped-down instructions echo the very simple instructions from the first game mega-hit, *PONG* (Atari, 1972): "Deposit Quarter. Ball will serve automatically. Avoid missing ball for high score."
4. In an interview on Nintendo.com, Shigeru Miyamoto, Takeshi Tezuka, and Koji Kondo—three of the main developers of many of the early Super Mario Bros games—note that the original *Super Mario Bros.* was developed by a team of only "about seven or eight people" (Sao, 2016).

5. In a 2004 article entitled "Death of The Bedroom Coder," Rhianna Pratchett (now a very well-known game writer in her own right) interviewed Archer McLean, studio head for Awesome Developments and creator of the hit game *Dropzone* (Sparkypants Studios LLC, 2017), for *The Guardian* about this issue at the time: "It's extremely difficult to get into games these days if you want to be a one-man-band, unless you want to do mobile games ... Now there's a huge infrastructure of publishers controlling developers, lots of financial strings being pulled, the marketing machines, the magazines and the charts, and that's usually much more complex than the whole development cycle." (Pratchett, 2004).
6. Kenneth Bainbridge was one of the chief physicists who worked on the Manhattan Project. Upon seeing the atomic bomb's first "foul and awesome display" at the Trinity Site, he famously remarked to his fellow scientists, "Now we are all sons of bitches."
7. The Anniversary Edition of *BRAID* was announced on August 6, 2020 (fitting that Blow chose the same date as the date when the original game was released). They were "aiming" for a release in the first quarter of 2021, but as of this writing (October 2021) it has yet to be released.

References

Britannica, T. (2017, December 27). Editors of Encyclopedia. *Encyclopedia Britannica*. Retrieved October 14, 2021, from https://www.britannica.com/art/auteur-theory

Bainbridge, K. (1975, May). 'All in our time'—A foul and awesome display. *Bulletin of the Atomic Scientists. Educational Foundation for Nuclear Science, Inc.* 46.

Blow, J. (2020, August 6). Announcing Braid, Anniversary Edition. Retrieved October 14, 2021, from http://braid-game.com/

Cline, E. (2011). *Ready Player One*. New York, NY: Crown Publishers.

Dahlen, C. (2008, August 27). Game Designer Jonathan Blow: What We All Missed About Braid. *AV Club*. Retrieved October 14, 2021, from https://www.avclub.com/game-designer-jonathan-blow-what-we-all-missed-about-b-1798214678

GameSpot. (2012, March 8). Jonathan Blow: How Mainstream Devs Are Getting It Wrong [Video]. *YouTube*. Retrieved October 14, 2021, from https://www.youtube.com/watch?v=I1Fg76c4Zfg

Pratchett, R. (2004, January 24). Death of the Bedroom Coder. *The Guardian*, Retrieved October 14, 2021, from https://www.theguardian.com/technology/2004/jan/24/games.gameswatch

Sao, A. (2016). NES Classic Edition, Developer Interview: Super Mario Bros. & Super Mario Bros. 3. *Nintendo*. Retrieved October 14, 2021, from https://www.nintendo.com/nes-classic/super-mario-bros-and-super-mario-bros-3-developer-interview/

Further Reading

Juul, J. (2019) *Handmade pixels: Independent video games and the quest for authenticity*. Cambridge, MA: MIT Press.

Zagal, J. P. & Mateas, M. (2007). Temporal Frames: A Unifying Framework for the Analysis of Game Temporality. In Situated Play, Proceedings of DiGRA 2007 Conference. 516–523, Retrieved October 14, 2021, from http://www.digra.org/digital-library/publications/temporal-frames-a-unifying-framework-for-the-analysis-of-game-temporality/

DOI: 10.4324/9781003199205-7

CALL OF DUTY: MODERN WARFARE 2 (2009)

Call of Duty: Modern Warfare 2 (Infinity Ward, 2009), the sixth iteration of the *Call of Duty* franchise and a direct sequel to a reinvention of the series, hews closely to its predecessors in terms of its aesthetic design and gameplay. As a war game, it signals a profound change in the representation of military conflict, turning the domestic spaces where the game is played into the battlefield where war unfolds. As it represents the symbolic leveling of American suburbia, the game also upends ideas sacrosanct to its predecessors, specifically that American-led military conflict is just and that its enemies are clearly defined, and that the United States and its allies are safe due to their spatial distance from conflict and the temporal distance of history.

Invoking the invasions of Iraq and Afghanistan, representing an aerial assault on the United States that clearly recalls September 11, 2001, and making playable a terrorist attack on an airport, *Modern Warfare 2*'s topicality foregrounds a willingness to depict violence that is brutal even by the genre's standards, discursively contextualizing it as realistic, or at least knowable, through references to television and cinema. Simultaneously, the narrative's characters bluntly rationalize engaging in such violence as a way to seize power and subvert the historical record. With a performative display of self-censorship, allowing players to skip a level that the game itself deems potentially too graphic even for fans of militarized shooters, *Modern Warfare 2* situates itself as unique within the *Modern Warfare* series, *Call of Duty* as a franchise, and the genre as a whole. Few games that represent such spectacular levels of violence have such an uneasy relationship with their performance, and few military shooters prior to *Modern Warfare 2* depict contemporary military conflict as wholly uncontainable and fundamentally egoistic.

Standard Formation: Aesthetic and Narrative Design

Modern Warfare 2 does little to innovate the military shooter subgenre or the *Call of Duty* franchise, instead utilizing established game mechanics and streamlining design elements from previous titles that benefit from player familiarity. As is standard in first-person shooters, the player is represented onscreen by the weapon they carry, which is the locus of interactivity. The goal is to dominate space through violent means, and interaction focuses primarily on pointing and shooting available weapons at oncoming enemies, tactically or frenetically, and avoiding damage from an increasingly overwhelming onslaught.

The layout of the visual field—the heads-up display, or HUD—and the information it contains communicate immediate objectives, pertinent information such as remaining ammunition and health, and nearby locations of interest. Although populating the visual field with information either narrational or actionable was not new to first-person shooters, *Modern Warfare 2*'s aesthetics emphasize militarism, with objectives and information displayed in a typeface that replicates official government memoranda, and glowing neon symbols in the mini-map evoking night vision colors that have been associated with televised warfare since the Persian Gulf War. Additionally, the weapons to which the player has access are all faithful replicas of real military hardware, painstakingly reproduced with an attention to detail that includes incorporating the sound the weapons make when discharging, continuing *Call of Duty*'s valorization of weaponry's technical minutiae—this, the player is told, is how war looks and feels.[1]

Much as *Modern Warfare 2* replicates its predecessors in aesthetics, interface design, and gameplay, the game utilizes a narrational template present from the first iterations of the franchise, intertwining the stories of a multinational group of soldiers fighting from different vantage points against a common foe. In *Call of Duty 2* (Infinity Ward, 2005), for example, the player must defend Moscow as a Soviet private, stage an attack on German troops in North Africa as a British sergeant, and participate in D-Day as an American corporal, always pressing forward into German-occupied territory. The stories of these soldiers are told both through the play of individual levels and through intra-level cut-scenes that simultaneously work to provide expository grounding for the ensuing action of gameplay and communicate the trajectory of the war itself. In *Call of Duty: World at War* (Treyarch, 2008), Kiefer Sutherland's voiceover contextualizes statistics and World War II film footage, celebrating the determination of the war effort and situating the forthcoming battle in a larger unfolding history, retold with an eye toward factual detail. These cut-scenes provide an air of verisimilitude to the ensuing action and embody, through their juxtaposition with gameplay, the multiple modes of historical representation possible.[2] *Modern Warfare 2* continues this tradition of representing war as multifaceted and vast, yet it notably eschews the historical accuracy its predecessors embellish in favor of speculative fantasy, portraying the goal of military conflict as the erasure of history itself.

Surprise Attacks: Boundless Warfare and Offensive Topicality

The complexity of *Modern Warfare 2*'s narrative reinforces the grandiose scope of the war represented, uniting spatially disparate locations—places that are the subject of nightly newscasts, the settings of popular films, and the target market for the game itself—through a complicated plot, which entwines the nuclear fears of an unending Cold War with the War on Terror's vicious unpredictability. The game's narrative concerns Lieutenant General Shepherd, commander of both the army rangers and Task Force 141, a clandestine international military outfit, as he hunts for Vladimir Zakarov, a Russian Ultranationalist and international terrorist. One of Shepherd's ploys, to place a ranger, Private Joseph Allen, near Zakarov during a brutal assault on a Moscow airport, backfires, leaving Allen dead and Russia declaring war on the United States. Russia invades the US, seen from the perspective of Private James Ramirez, while members of the 141, including former SAS officers "Roach" Sanderson, "Soap" Mactavish, and Captain John Price, realize that Shepherd is himself responsible for the attack, in an insane bid to become an international hero, and confront him at his secret base in Afghanistan. Playing alternatively as Allen, Roach, Ramirez, and Soap, and briefly as an unfortunate astronaut who witnesses an EMP blast firsthand, over the course of eighteen missions the player must fight through cities in Afghanistan, favelas in Brazil, and townhouses in Virginia, as well as fortified oil rigs and dilapidated castles on the Bering Sea, and briefly float above the chaos in outer space.

Notably, the linear missions in earlier *Call of Duty* titles echo the spatiotemporal progression of the individual soldiers pushing forward against the Axis powers, contextualizing war as both complicated and vast but also interconnected and causal. In *Modern Warfare* 2, the spatial disparity between the represented locales exists in tension with the linearity of the individual levels. The globetrotting narrative presents great variety in terms of place, but negates interconnectivity, literally positioning military conflict as an unbounded and randomized collapse of barriers between different locations vivid in the popular imaginary. The game's cut-scenes reinforce this immediacy, displaying the perspective of a spy satellite's eagle eye that can instantly focus in detail anywhere around the globe, notifying the player of where the next mission will begin, and continually zooming in on and revealing the component parts of the tanks, submarines, aircraft, and missiles that will be the focus of the mission, providing a visual deconstruction of the machinery that constitutes the industry of war itself. The characters Shepherd and Price narrate these moments, predicting the future instead of recounting the past, issuing ominous platitudes about how history is written—or erased—through unwavering determination and superior force.[3] Bringing *Call of Duty* into the present moment by emphasizing and accentuating its tropes, *Modern Warfare 2* succeeds in destabilizing its predecessors' achievements: here, the accurate depiction of weaponry becomes fetishization, a multifaceted perspective on war is undone through spatial incoherence, and the representation of historical events transforms into a celebration of history's negation.

The narrative's sprawling complexity and blustering grandiosity are outdone perhaps only by the gameplay's intensity. In the opening Afghanistan mission, the player, strapped into the gunner position atop a tank and therefore wholly exposed—a perspective frequently visualized in newscasts of the invasion of Iraq in 2003—crawls through a claustrophobic city seemingly devoid of life, until a firefight begins, and bullets and rockets rain down from above as the tank speeds recklessly through alleyways in an attempted escape. In the level "Wolverines!"—an overt reference to John Milius's 1984 film *Red Dawn*, in which a ragtag militia must fight back against a Russian and Cuban invasion of the US—the player as Private Ramirez witnesses the destruction of Northeastern Virginia by Russian troops firsthand, as F/A-18s screech across the sky, homes burn, and smoke fills the air. Defending a main street populated with fast-food restaurants, banks, and gas stations from both land and aerial assault, the player, as Ramirez, must race between storefronts and rooftops, dodging and returning gunfire as multiple waves of enemy troops advance. In "No Russian," a mission so notable for its brutal violence that the game features a "Disturbing Content Notice" at the beginning of the campaign and provides an option to skip the mission in its entirety, the player accompanies the terrorist Zakarov in an attack on Russian citizens in a Moscow airport. Whether or not they choose to participate in the killing spree, simply walking through the level produces grizzly images of numerous civilians being bloodily executed.

Although players can expect gameplay in the World War II-era *Call of Duty* games to be assaultive, as it recreates historical conflict that resulted in an astounding loss of life, *Modern Warfare 2*, freed from a historical record that its own characters proclaim must be expunged, instead trades on a general topicality which allows for an exhaustive embellishment of violence. The intertextual referentiality to celebratory newscasts and Hollywood cinema provides a foundation upon which notably recent and deeply traumatic events can become grist for playable entertainment. However, though the game attempts to acknowledge its own brutality, its performative act of self-censorship positions the other overwhelming violence in the game as neither disturbing nor offensive, a rhetorical revision that negates the trauma of engaging in war and the inherent brutality of ending lives with military firepower. In proposing that only some of its content is disturbing, *Modern Warfare 2* deviates from both the other games in the franchise and military shooters more generally, which situate violence as an unfortunate necessity with deleterious effects upon both its recipients and its perpetrators.

Depicting contemporary military conflict as diffuse in its reach, overwhelming in its violence, and totalitarian in its impetus, *Modern Warfare 2* destabilizes the jingoistic truisms associated with historical war and historical wargaming, instead providing a withering critique of modern warfare itself. While previous games required the player experience endless hardship as they sacrifice themselves as part of the greatest generation, here they must defend the burger joints and banking centers that define American consumer capitalism at the whim of a murderous narcissist. The call of *Modern Warfare 2* is not one of collective action and a defense of freedom, but instead of erasing knowledge so as to rewrite history itself, through violence that is at points excessively brutal and rarely heroic. Neither total critique nor passionate celebration of US-led military might, and in awe of modern firepower yet uncomfortable with its excesses, *Modern Warfare 2* continually occupies an uncomfortable middle ground.

Impact: Genre Influence

Modern Warfare 2's immense popularity, selling over 14 million copies, makes the game a profoundly visible example of the military shooter's changing relationship to warfare's representation. Though the *Call of Duty*, *Battlefield*, and *Medal of Honor* franchises all began by representing World War II-era combat, they turned to contemporary militarized conflict in the mid-2000s. *Modern Warfare 2* only accelerated this trend, with the game's influence felt over its own direct sequels and later entries in the franchise, notably *Call of Duty: Black Ops II* (Treyarch, 2012), which focuses on both historical clandestine military operations and a futuristic Cold War. Competing franchises concocted fictional warfare across the Middle East, China, Africa, and, notably, America itself, with a strand of increasingly fantastical FPS titles, notably *Homefront* (Kaos Studios, 2011) and *Wolfenstein II: The New Colossus* (MachineGames, 2017), depicting the United States as an occupied battlefield. None, however, would be as audacious in their brash topicality or their uncomfortable brutality

Given its profitability, acclaim, and influence, it can easily be forgotten that *Modern Warfare 2* does not simply endorse the conflict it represents and the violence it imagines. It stands in difficult relation to them, critiquing contemporary war as waged at the whim of those in power and with a far-reaching impact on the innocent, arguing that, in global conflict, collateral damage cannot be contained. Its gameplay is at once exciting and thrilling, but also overwhelming and viciously brutal. Nonetheless, it deems only some of its content disturbing and offensive, implying that armed military conflict in general should not be considered to be either. Indeed, no matter the in-game obstacle, violence is always the only solution. While helping thrust an entire subgenre into the present and bringing war home in a way that rippled beyond military games, *Call of Duty: Modern Warfare 2* interrogates both the impetus for and the breadth of contemporary warfare, proposing that the erasure of history, from both war and its representation as consumable, commodifiable entertainment, results in spectacular and violent excess.

Harrison Gish

Notes

1. Josh Smicker discusses historical *Call of Duty* games as "*re-enactment* games," which attempt to "recreate and reproduce, as accurately as possible, specific wars, battles, armies and equipment," and pay "fastidious attention to artifactual and organizational detail" (2010, p. 112).
2. In their writing on the project of New Historicism, Catherine Gallagher and Stephen Greenblatt propose understanding the historical object as existing within "a tangle of crossing lines" (2000, p. 54), a multitude of possible contextualization. Historical *Call of Duty* games enact such a project, representing World War II as existing at a nexus of different forms of historical representation, most notable in the disparity between cut-scenes and gameplay.
3. Matthew Thomas Payne notes that "the *Modern Warfare* games [tap] into a different register of political anxieties than does fighting yesteryears Nazis in World War II shooters" (2016, p. 75). While the representation of warfare in historical shooters provokes questions of accuracy, but is morally unassailable, the *Modern Warfare* games, having comparatively little history to interrogate, instead explore contemporary questions of morality.

References

Gallagher, C. & Greenblatt, S. (2000). *Practicing new historicism*. Chicago: The University of Chicago Press.
Payne, M.T. (2016). *Playing war: Military video games after 9/11*. New York: New York University Press.
Smicker, J. (2010). Future combat, combatting futures: Temporalities of war video games and the performance of proleptic histories. In N.B. Huntemann & M.T. Payne (Eds), *Joystick soldiers: The politics of play in military video games* (pp. 106–121). New York: Routledge.

Further Reading

Ouellette, M.A. & Thompson, J.C. (2017). *The Post-9/11 video game: A critical examination*. Jefferson: McFarland & Company, Inc., Publishers.
Stahl, R. (2010). *Militainment, Inc.: War, media, and popular culture*. New York: Routledge.

DOI: 10.4324/9781003199205-8

DANCE DANCE REVOLUTION (1998)

Most people's experiences with *Dance Dance Revolution* (Konami, 1998; *DDR*) fall into one of two categories: their experiences as players, likely introduced to the game by friends or family (in Höysniemi's 2006 study more than half of all participants started playing in this way) or their experiences as spectators, watching those players particularly skilled at the game perform in front of arcade audiences. The two categories, of course, overlap, with Höysniemi finding that many players actually tried the game *because* of the performances they had seen (2006, p. 11). The game's simple mechanics, yet with broad affordances, allowed for a wide range of experiences, from relatively intimate sessions with friends or strangers to the incomparable footwork of the e-sports professionals, some exemplified in iconic scenes in popular films. It's a game that offers its players and spectators multitudinous, multitiered, multisensory experiences, and it all begins with the arcade machine itself: its attention-grabbing arcade cabinet and all-important dance stage.

Take the Stage

The raised metal dance stage itself consists of two dance pads, each with four pink and blue arrows as iconic as the action buttons on a PlayStation controller, and two associated safety bars, so important to professional players, as balance for furiously fast footwork or as balletic interface for spectacular freestyling. The dance stage is the first thing you see when approaching the game in an arcade, but also the first thing you forget when you play, lost in embodied performance. It is as well the first thing dedicated players try to recreate in the home, often going beyond the branded soft pads available as part of home editions of the game and buying specialized third-party hard pads or even making their own. Nearly twenty-five years after its release, *DDR*'s dance stage remains the most iconic controller you primarily operate with your feet and is not only important in terms of nostalgia or hardware fetishism, but in terms of its role and influence.

Distinct physical interfaces have been part of rhythm games since their inception—before video games—with Ralph Baer's handheld electronic game *SIMON* (Milton Bradley, 1977) and the continuity in terms of game mechanics is such that Knoblauch even describes the "four-button pad" of *DDR* as "essentially a SIMON-like platform" (2016, p. 36). There are, of course, important rhythm games which do not require special hardware, like the wildly influential *Pa-Rappa the Rapper* (NanaOn-Sha, 1996), another contender to the title of the first rhythm game, the idiosyncratic *Vib-Ribbon* (NanaOn-Sha, 1999), or more contemporary games like *Thumper* (Drool, 2016). Nevertheless, some of the biggest titles associated with the genre are well known for their hardware, including the mimetic cabinet of *Beatmania* (Konami, 1997) in Japanese arcades (which would provide the name for Konami's *Bemani* music game division of which *DDR* is part) and later *Guitar Hero* (Harmonix, 2005) throughout Western homes. Juul focuses on the effect of the *DDR* dance stage on gamespace, arguing that the game "shifted the focus from 3-D space to the physical movement of the players on the game's dance pads." He noted that "the game does feature a display, but most of the game's spectacle is in player space, the real-world area in which players move about" (2010, pp. 17–18). It is this movement on its stage, and this particularly embodied experience, both quite novel at the time, that not only contribute to *DDR*'s wide appeal and influence on subsequent casual and rhythm games but also constitute a very specific gameplay experience.

Play and Perform

Demers discusses the transformation of the player into a cyborg "whose physical actions are amplified by a computer" (2006, p. 405). While she doesn't here explicitly recall Haraway's conceptualization of the cyborg (Haraway, 2016) with its utopian transgression of social, cultural and physical boundaries, this is particularly apt when discussing *DDR*. Demers draws an implicit connection between the game's wide range of avatars (unusual for the time, and to a certain degree even today) and its player base, whereby "the majority of *DDR* participants were teenage girls, while the players of most other arcade games are almost exclusively adolescent boys" (2006, p. 407). At the same time, this was not a domain where boys did not enter as "DDR prowess almost always seemed to make boys more popular among friends and potential romantic partners" (2006, p. 405). This play space that crosses gender boundaries—sadly quite rare in gaming history—has also been used in popular films to illustrate both friendship and romance bordering the nerdy and the cool in both *Scott Pilgrim vs. the World* (Edgar Wright, 2010) and more recently *The Kissing Booth 2* (Vinve Marcello, 2020). While both illustrate male–female friendships as well as heterosexual romance (in the case of *Scott Pilgrim* the first evolving into the latter), the plot of *Kissing Booth 2* also centers around a *DDR* competition, building on the central friends' love for the game in the first film of the franchise, and later exploring more of the culture surrounding the game, whereby its affordances (as those of many subsequent dance games) allow for a variety of gameplay experiences and types of spectatorship.

Performance, in both senses of the term, plays an important role here, and one that prefigures both the rise of international competitive e-sports scenes, and the rise of performance-focused rhythm games like *Guitar Hero* and *Rock Band* (Harmonix, 2007). There is a degree to which all video games feature an element of performance that is systemically evaluated, of course. Nitsche describes this type of performance as "the effectiveness in successfully mastering a game or game situation" (Nitsche, 2014, p. 388) and Karhulahti notes that this process is not only compulsory in the case of video games, but also performed by the game itself (2015). In *DDR*, this is evaluated through what Miller describes as "encouraging exhortations and playfully insulting feedback on players' dancing in both screen-text and voiceover forms" (2017, p. 8). When a human audience is involved in *DDR*, however (which is more often than not), a different kind of performance is involved, one that is more of an "expressive and artistic practice" (Nitsche, 2014, p. 388). This is the meaning of the term that Austin uses when describing his first experience of watching someone play *DDR* and notes that he and his friends had "never before […] seen anyone *perform* a game […] and certainly not with that level of virtuosity" (2016, p. 15, emphasis in original). He contrasts this with previous experiences in the arcade whereby his friends "were embarrassed to even be seen" there while "these guys had come to put on a show with their acrobatic and energetic dance moves, hoping to draw an audience from the crowd of field trippers and mall walkers who happened to pass by" (2016, p. 15). Importantly, he is not only describing a performance with an audience, but a performance *for* an audience. These types of performances can be technical or artistic (or a combination of the two), competitive or collaborative, with relatively small audiences in local arcades like the one Austin describes, or on the stage of larger competitions. *The Kissing Booth 2* paints one such stage, with freestyle collaborative duets emphasized by stage costumes, appropriate lighting, and audience cheers. In the real world, Konami's competitive Arcade Championship features a different kind of spectacle of largely young men in branded T-shirts demonstrating their technical proficiency, arguably to more knowledgeable audiences than those of the popular film. Ultimately, *DDR* offers space for all these different players and audiences. But despite its breadth, it is also a fertile ground for a more dedicated following, one for whom the game's music plays a role beyond the game's mechanics.

Miller notes the game's "reliance on popular music as a driver of affective experience" is one of its qualities often described as revolutionary (2017, p. 8) and on its release, *DDR* was certainly at the forefront using larger amounts of popular music in games. Demers also links the game's imagery to club culture, and the game's lights and large speakers create a multisensory experience for both its players and its audience. Moreover, she argues that the game's marketing as 'hip' (Demers, 2006, p. 409) and the sale of its soundtracks as "separate, purchasable collections of underground techno, house, and drum'n'bass," (2006, p. 401) emphasize the matter of musical taste and frame the experience of dedicated players as one that is both musical and distinct from the mainstream. Beyond this framing, Demers also describes the musical selection as limited in terms of the "relatively homogeneous rhythmic profile" required by its mechanics (2006, p. 412). For Auerbach, it is this very "insistent, metronomic beat" of the type of music featured in the game "that suggest the game's relevance to rhythm drilling" and broader potential in terms of musical instruction, including sight-reading (2010, p. 2). Discussions of the game's potential benefits to musical pedagogy and musicality are, however, massively outweighed by discussions of the game's physical benefits as a form of exercise.

Effect and Influence

So far, I have discussed *DDR* primarily as a rhythm game, but one of its longest lasting influences has been on what is often referred to as *exergaming* (or simply *exercise games* for those not fond of the portmanteau). Its potential benefits to fitness were widely discussed in the media, and it was even integrated into some schools and gyms explicitly as a form of exercise. Moreover, this was also an important motivation for continued play, outweighed only by its entertainment factor in Höysniemi's 2006 study of 556 players. Even Wikipedia classifies *DDR* and its successors as both music *and* exercise games. The athleticism of *DDR* play also placed the game at the forefront of the debate surrounding video games as sports, bypassing common counterarguments, and being declared as an official sport in Norway in 2003 (Höysniemi, 2006, p. 22). Competitions in the sport can be either technical, focusing on the speed and accuracy of players' footwork, or freestyle, where some accuracy is still necessary, but the criteria focus on the showmanship and creativity of the dancers. While these two distinct forms have parallels in the real world, like ice skating in the form of speed skating and figure skating, outside of dancing games the two types of competition (and forms of the sport) are not commonly found in e-sports. The range of competitive play is only telling of the range of possibilities afforded by the game and is why *DDR* has been not only an incredibly popular game, but one with a large influence.

DDR's direct legacy lies in its direct sequels, spinoffs, and clones. Home releases of *DDR* for PlayStation quickly followed the arcade release and were accompanied by soft-pad peripherals (often maligned by dedicated arcade players). It has also had a number of arcade successors, with the most recent at the time of writing—*Dance Dance Revolution A20* (Benami and Konami)—released in 2019. Following *DDR*'s initial release, a number of other dance games also appeared on the scene, some so closely resembling the game that they incurred lawsuits from Konami. Major later dance series, particularly those for home consoles, moved away from dance mats, most notably *Just Dance* (Ubisoft Milan and Ubisoft Paris, 2009) for the Nintendo Wii, which did not have a dedicated peripheral, but used the Wii Remote to measure accuracy (current iterations of *Just Dance* still do not require extra peripherals), and *Dance Central* (Harmonix, 2010) for the Xbox 360, which used the Kinect motion controller (the most recent version of *Dance Central* expanded to VR in 2019). While dance games remain at the margins of so-called gamer culture, the influence of *DDR* beyond these explicit examples illustrates the potential of these games to both subvert and expand what video games are, or rather what they are commonly understood to be.

Juul places the game at the forefront of mimetic interfaces that would define an important trend in casual games of the 2000s, particularly in the form of games for the Wii and *Wii Sports* (2006), contemporary games in the genre including *Ring Fit Adventure* (Nintendo, 2019) for Nintendo Switch. At the same time, its use of soft pads in the home paves the way for other rhythm games like *Guitar Hero* to require specific hardware independent from the main controller (Miller, 2017, p. 9). Finally, its competitive scene is arguably one of the earliest in the history of video games that is both international and fragmented, with local and transnational variants still relatively widespread.

To this day, *Dance Dance Revolution* continues to subvert many of the clichés about video games that continue to be perpetuated: that they encourage a lack of physical activity, that they are violent, that their graphical fidelity or other graphical qualities are paramount, that they are either solitary or aggressively competitive. At the same time, *DDR*'s innovations can often be overestimated, and it's important to note that foot-operated pads and controllers had existed since the 1970s, that there are a number of important rhythm games that predate it, that games had featured popular music as soon as it was technically possible, and that despite its wide appeal, both Demers's study and contemporary competitions are heavily male dominated. Nevertheless, it is difficult not to consider *DDR*'s disruptions and influence with some element of utopianism. Ultimately, there are few video games that offer such a diversity of social play that can be competitive and collaborative, local and international, and that can offer such means for artistic expression and performance.

Andra Ivănescu

References

Auerbach, B. (2010). Pedagogical applications of the video game *Dance Dance Revolution* to aural skills instruction. *Music Theory Online*, 16(1). Retrieved November 6, 2021, from https://mtosmt.org/issues/mto.10.16.1/mto.10.16.1.auerbach.html

Austin, M. (2016). Introduction—Taking note of video games. In M. Austin (Eds), *Music video games: Performance, politics, and play* (pp. 1–22). New York and London: Bloomsbury Academic.

Demers, J. (2006). Dancing machines: "Dance Dance Revolution", cybernetic dance, and musical taste. *Popular Music*, 25(3), 401–414.

Haraway, D. J. (2016). *Manifestly Haraway*. Minneapolis: University of Minnesota Press.

Höysniemi, J. (2006). International survey on the *Dance Dance Revolution* game. *Computers in Entertainment*, 4(2), 8.

Juul, J. (2010). *A casual revolution: Reinventing video games and their players.* Cambridge, MA: MIT Press.

Karhulahti, V.-M. (2015). Defining the videogame. *Game Studies*, 15(2). Retrieved November 6, 2021, from http://gamestudies.org/1502/articles/karhulahti

Miller, K. (2017). *Playable bodies: Dance games and intimate media*. Oxford: Oxford University Press.

Nitsche, M. (2014). Performance. In Wolf, M. and Perron, B. (Eds) *The Routledge companion to video game studies* (pp. 388–395). New York and London: Routledge.

Further Reading

Behrenshausen, B. G. (2007). Toward a (kin)aesthetic of video gaming: The case of *Dance Dance Revolution*. *Games and Culture*, 2(4), 335–354. doi.org/10.1177/1555412007310810

Kocurek, C. A. (2015). *Coin-operated Americans: Rebooting boyhood at the video game arcade*. Minneapolis: University of Minnesota Press.

Summers, T. (2016). *Understanding video game music*. Cambridge, MA: Cambridge University Press.

DOI: 10.4324/9781003199205-9

DIABLO (1996)

Diablo (Blizzard North, 1996) became a hit PC game in 1997[1] with an initial print of 500,000 copies to match its phenomenal 450,000 pre-orders (Next Generation Online, 1996). Hype around the game was building from mid-1996 thanks to enthused advance press coverage and a pre-release demo circulated over the Internet and in gaming magazines. *Diablo* dominated computer game sales charts for months, passing two million copies and becoming a flagship franchise for Blizzard Entertainment. It soon received an expansion, *Diablo: Hellfire* (Synergistic Software, 1997), and a successor which dwarfed its popularity: *Diablo II* (Blizzard North, 2000). These, along with other releases (the *Diablo II: Lord of Destruction* expansion [Blizzard North, 2001], *Diablo III* [Blizzard Entertainment, 2012], and other titles in development as of 2021), iterated on the first game's innovations and took the series into the 35 million copies territory. *Diablo* inspired a slew of similar games (labeled "Diablo clones" by critics) and was impactful for concretizing the action-RPG genre, for its approach to complexity and use of random generation, and for its online multiplayer integration.

Aesthetics: A Dark Gothic Fantasy

Diablo can be described as a gothic roguelike action role-playing game. While its gameplay and design are the all-important centerpiece to the discussion about its influence, it is worth covering its audiovisual aspects first. When inserting the CD-ROM into a computer's drive, the AutoPlay function automatically showed a menacing portrait of the giant titular demon with his deep, evil laugh over the ominous music before displaying the options for installing and playing the game. The mood and atmosphere were reinforced in the game's introductory cut-scene, full of slow, shadowy drawn-out images presenting an abandoned town, a crow pecking out the eye of a corpse, hanged bodies dangling in the wind, and a warrior exploring warily. The game's manual also set the tone, with gothic lettering on parchment, citations about Hell and demons from Dante's *Inferno* (1320), Nietzsche and the Egyptian Book of the Dead among others, and a sprawling 5,000-word epic on the war between Heaven and Hell that serves as backstory to the player's immediate quest of hunting down the Lord of Terror across sixteen dungeon floors.

Diablo represented a significant shift from the usual orcs-and-elves medieval fantasy imagery, drawing not only on the gothic, but on the occult and satanic as well. As players venture into the labyrinth, they meet pagan shrines, goat demons, inverted burning crosses, and pentagrams. Environments and characters were modeled and exported as fully rendered sprites, providing a dreary realistic look and fluid animation—with violence and gore everywhere. Composer and sound designer Matt Uelmen's work is still saluted to this day as a key factor in setting the game's foreboding ambience with the soundtrack's low, deep drums meeting industrial elements, distorted noises, screeches and wails in the dungeons, and the hauntingly tragic twelve-string guitar theme in the town of Tristram.

Genre: A Roguelike RPG for the Masses

"The sanctity of this place has been fouled!", your character exclaims as they enter the desecrated church's underground labyrinth. Playing *Diablo* is easy: it's a point-and-click game. Click somewhere on the stone pavement to move there; click on that door to open it. When something moves in the darkened corner of the screen beyond your tenuous ring of light, click on the creature to attack and bring it swift, gory death (most enemies die in one to three hits). If it drops something, click on it to pick it up, before another enemy arrives. Each of these horrors is weak alone, but the danger of being swarmed is ever present. Right-click to cast spells or drink the potions in your belt, a vital skill when you need urgent healing since everything unfolds in real-time. Killing enemies nets you experience points; in a matter of minutes, you gain a level and invest points into your core attributes

(Strength, Magic, Dexterity and Vitality), which upgrades your combat efficiency as reported on your "character sheet" in Damage, To Hit, Mana, Life, and Armor Class (perhaps the strongest *Dungeons & Dragons* convention in there). As you collect weapons, armor pieces, gold, and potions, your limited inventory space fills up, prompting return trips to buy and sell stuff in town. Even as you progress, the core gameplay remains surprisingly stable: click to attack and retreat, avoid getting swarmed, use your resources well, and buy or find better gear as you explore (and eventually, buy a replacement mouse after all that clicking).

This apparent simplicity is the reason for *Diablo*'s success, especially compared to dungeon-crawler computer role-playing games like the *Wizardry* (Sir-Tech, 1981–2001), *Might & Magic* (New World Computing, 1984–2003), and Gold Box series from Strategic Simulations Inc. (1988–1992). These revolve around fantasy hack-and-slash inspired by Tolkien and *Dungeons & Dragons* (Gary Gygax & Dave Arneson, 1974) and they are quite complicated: players must manage parties of four to six characters (which they create by a lengthy process of carefully balancing various intersections of racial bonuses, class requirements, and character attributes), remember lots of rules, statistics, and action possibilities in a complex interface, draw maps, and take notes. Some RPGs had started to move away from traditional turn-based gameplay by incorporating real-time elements, as in *Dungeon Master* (FTL Games, 1987) and series like *Eye of the Beholder* (Westwood Associates/Strategic Simulations Inc, 1991–1993). Compared to them, *Diablo* plays more like the *Gauntlet* (Atari, 1985) action arcade game, or Blizzard's real-time strategy game, *Warcraft: Orcs & Humans* (Blizzard, 1994).

Real-time or turn-based RPGs remained difficult to approach—aside from *Lands of Lore: The Throne of Chaos* (Westwood Studios, 1993), with which *Diablo* shares an orientation toward simplicity. As game designer David Brevik recounts in a retrospective interview (Ars Technica, 2020), this starts with the alleviated character creation process: "We wanted to be everything that RPGs weren't, and one of those things was, we want to just press a few buttons and get right into the game." Barton and Stacks concur that the series attracted "millions of gamers who had never played any of the classic CRPGs, much less a tabletop AD&D game" (2019, p. 366). Brevik also acknowledges *Angband* (Alex Cutler & Andy Astrand, 1990) as a major influence for the development of *Diablo*. *Angband* was a popular game in the niche genre of the roguelike, austere text-and-ASCII-characters-based programs popularized by *Rogue* (Michael Toy & Glenn Wichman,

1980) and *Moria* (Robert Alan Koeneke & Jimmey Wayne Todd Jr., 1983) among others, and circulated on mainframe computer systems in United States university and research environments through the ARPANET. Roguelikes had a single character to manage, but more complex rules leading to limitless combinations of possibilities, with an even steeper difficulty curve.

Diablo does lift a lot from *Angband*: you must venture ever deeper into dungeon levels with increasingly powerful enemies and treasures, with limited light, to ultimately defeat Morgoth (the final boss), starting in a town with shops providing supplies. More specifically, *Diablo* took two key mechanics from the roguelike genre: *permadeath* (if your singular character dies, you must start over with a new one) and *procedural generation* (each game, a new dungeon, enemies and treasures are randomly generated), but reworked them for greater accessibility to a wide audience. You can save and reload in single-player games (which makes death not permanent), but you cannot have multiple saves, so you must still commit to your progress, just as in roguelikes. More uniquely, the game is designed to not be won on your initial attempt, as the strength of enemies and overall difficulty scale up quickly, and a first run will be full of poor choices. Instead of dying and restarting from scratch (as in typical roguelikes), you can at any time start a new game and transfer your character with all experience and possessions to take on a new randomly generated dungeon. *Diablo* actively encourages this, as there are more enemy types, quests, and unique mini-bosses than you can encounter in a single playthrough, which means starting a new game allows you to discover new content. It also means you can never get stuck in an unwinnable scenario. These design decisions substantially alleviate the difficulty, to the point where dedicated roguelike fans consider Blizzard's game to not qualify, calling it a "roguelite".

Design: A Clockwork Slot Machine Draped in Simplicity

Diablo exemplifies what Noah Wardrip-Fruin (2009, pp. 169–229) calls the *Tale-Spin* effect (after James Meehan's 1976 story generator program), which describes works that appear, on the surface, significantly less complex than they are internally. There's a lot of complexity under the clicking hood of Blizzard's game, as even the seemingly transparent statistics in To Hit % and Armor Class are cogs in a clockwork incorporating more hidden data (Faria, 2001). Comparing *Diablo* to other RPGs that display lists of statistics and virtual dice rolls and concluding that it's too simple misses the mark: the game eschews its computer RPG and roguelike cohorts' ambition of achieving Wardrip-Fruin's (2009, pp. 299–352) *SimCity* effect (that is, systems that effectively communicate on the surface their underlying computational complexity).

Diablo's complexity manifests in its flexible three-class system that offers distinct gameplay experiences. Warriors hate chasing archers around, rogues hate open areas where they are exposed, and sorcerers hate switching spells because of enemies' resistances to fire, lightning, or magic. On the surface, warriors can cast spells and sorcerers can use a sword and shield, for instance, if they invest in their Magic or Strength attributes, but the game upholds soft general orientations through its hidden clockwork: a sorcerer take 0.6 seconds to swing a sword and 0.3 to block an attack, instead of 0.45 and 0.1 respectively for a warrior (Faria 2001, pp. 9–11). These tiny decimals make the difference between withstanding or succumbing to the swarm; *Diablo*'s fast pace is not a gimmick, but the structural spindles around which the clockwork operates.

The other site of considerable complexity in the game's design is the loot system, which Brevik describes as a slot machine (Ars Technica, 2020). Opening a chest or killing an enemy grants a spin at the loot subsystem, which has very few unique, hand-built items (with their name displayed in gold). Base items (in white) can be bought or found in the early game, but the vast majority of loot will be magic (blue) items, which are randomly generated by applying a prefix and/or a suffix to a base item. These 176 modifiers are distributed across twenty-six groups with varying levels of quality as you progress. An iron or mithril weapon gets a bonus to hit between six and ten percent, or forty-one and sixty percent respectively. With seven equipment slots (weapon, shield, helmet, armor, amulet, and two rings), the possibilities are gigantic and there's always something to improve. Combined with the flexible classes, the loot subsystem creates meaningfully different experiences: a lucky sorcerer finding an Obsidian (forty percent resistance to all elements) Plate Mail of Sorcery (+20 magic) could consider slowly raising their Strength to eventually wear it. *Diablo*'s color-coded loot subsystem would be reused by Blizzard in *Diablo II* and *World of Warcraft* (2004), and eventually most games incorporating such tiered items logic.

Battle.net: Hell Is Other People

Diablo's box exclaims "Compete FREE over the Internet", advertising Blizzard's battle.net service, which let players chat in group channels, and create or join multiplayer games of up to four players.

Providing this without a subscription fee was an unusual move in 1996/1997, and battle.net was very successful (Walter, 1997). Multiplayer *Diablo* was subject to different rules: no saving or reloading, and you must restart a game every time you play (but all dungeon zones are unlocked from the start). Dying to monsters has dire consequences: your hard-earned equipment and half your gold fall on the ground. Unless a comrade resurrects you, you must restart in town, hopefully with some leftover gear or the help of friends—assuming they didn't also die—to go back and reclaim your equipment. If everyone quits the (non-persistent) game, your items disappear forever.

While the game allows cooperation, "friendly fire" means players can accidentally hurt teammates. They can also toggle a switch from "player friendly" to "player attack" and directly target and backstab others, making them player killers (PKs). The game rewards this with a trophy collectible: their victim's ear. "PKing" was a major source of contention among players, as expressed in the Usenet newsgroup alt. games.diablo. As dying from a player had benign consequences (you only lose gold), some "griefer" PKs schemed to cause maximum distress, for example by luring players into packs of monsters so they die from them and lose their gear.

This was exacerbated by the much larger problem *Diablo* became infamous for: the rampant cheating that prevailed over battle.net. To reduce lag and costs, the game data was not handled on a Blizzard server, but locally on a player's computer—and hence easily tampered with. As Kücklich (2008, p. 66) writes, the "developers unprepared for the invasion of cheaters that followed its release" resulted in *Diablo* being "the showcase example of the damage cheaters can do to an online role-playing game". Cheaters could "dupe" (duplicate) items, use "trainer" programs to boost their characters to obscene levels or fabricate impossible items. Griefers installed Townkill or Autokill to instantly kill other players, even in town. Soon cheating programs were presented as a necessity for guarding against malicious cheaters and enjoying the game.

Through both its single-player and multiplayer modes, *Diablo* proved influential with its point-and-click interface, distinctive dark gothic art direction, procedural generation mechanics for environments, enemies, and items, and its loot system. Parts of the game's legacy on players is yet to be documented. *Diablo* may have been the most successful attempt at turning players into gears for its clockwork to run smoothly, a precursor to contemporary games of the attention and microtransactions economy. The intersection of its aesthetics, mechanics, and early online culture may also prompt ethical reflection, as foreshadowed by the game's manual, which cites Nietzsche on the "Multi player instructions" page: "He who fights with monsters might take care lest he thereby become a monster". What kind of player is produced by a gothic slot machine of loot draped under violence and gore, in a world where virtue has no place?

Dominic Arsenault

Note

1. Retailer shipments started at the end of December 1996 for an early January launch, but some retailers started selling on 31 December, which Blizzard retrospectively decreed to be *Diablo*'s anniversary. See https://diablo.fandom.com/wiki/Diablo_(Game) for relevant discussion using interviews, period websites, and press releases.

References

Ars Technica. (2020). *War Stories: Diablo's Loot Lottery was Almost a Turn-based Affair*. Retrieved November 15, 2021, from https://arstechnica.com/gaming/2020/08/war-stories-how-diablo-was-almost-a-turn-based-strategy-game/

Barton, M. & Stacks, S. (2019). *Diablo and the rise of action RPGs. Dungeons & desktops. The history of computer role-playing games* (pp. 357–382). Boca Raton, FL: A K Peters / CRC Press.

Faria, P. (2001). *Jarulf's Guide to Diablo and Hellfire*. Retrieved November 15, 2021, from http://www.lurkerlounge.com/diablo/jarulf/jarulf162.pdf

Kücklich, J. (2008). Forbidden pleasures: Cheating in computer games. In Melanie Swalwell & Jason Wilson (Eds), *The pleasures of computer gaming: Essays on cultural history, theory and aesthetics* (pp. 52–71). Jefferson, NC: McFarland.

Next Generation Online staff. (December 1996; archived June 6, 1997). *Diablo Demand Skyrockets*. Retrieved November 15, 2021, from https://web.archive.org/web/19970606035803/http://www.next-generation.com/news/121796d.chtml

Walter, B. (1997). Battle.net Defines its Success: Interview with Paul Sams. Game Developer (formerly Gamasutra), November 28. Retrieved November 15, 2021, from https://www.gamedeveloper.com/business/battle-net-defines-its-success-interview-with-paul-sams

Wardrip-Fruin, N. (2009). *Expressive processing: Digital fictions, computer games, and software studies*. Cambridge, MA: MIT Press.

Further Reading

Craddock, D. L. (2013). *Stay awhile and listen: How two Blizzards unleashed Diablo and forged a video-game empire*. Canton, OH: Digital Monument Press.

Harris, J. (2020). *Exploring roguelike games*. Boca Raton, FL: CRC Press.
Usenet newsgroup archive for alt.games.diablo: (n.d.). Retrieved November 15, 2021, from https://groups.google.com/g/alt.games.diablo/
DOI: 10.4324/9781003199205-10

DONKEY KONG (1981)

As the creation myth goes, in the beginning Shigeru Miyamoto wanted to name his first-ever game, a challenging four-level visual and aural extravaganza with unprecedented attention to character and story for an arcade game, "Stubborn Gorilla." As frequently happens with creation myths, there are various tellings of the story. In many, the Japanese–English dictionary Miyamoto consulted offered up "Donkey" and "Kong" as synonyms, and thus began the legend of one of video games' most iconic characters when the coin-operated arcade game with that cryptic title, *Donkey Kong* (Nintendo, 1981) was released.[1] Nintendo initially planned to make its way into US arcades with a top-down shooter, following in the genre of earlier successes like *Space Invaders* (Taito, 1978) and *Galaxian* (Namco, 1979), called *Radar Scope*; while *Radar Scope* was successful in Japan, the early test markets in the US were decidedly underwhelming. Nintendo gambled on an unknown designer (Miyamoto) and a literally game-changing plan to re-purpose the underperforming *Radar Scope* machines into something previously unseen in the video-game world.

Donkey Kong established not only Nintendo, but also its creator (Miyamoto), as major forces within the video-game industry. The game introduced several important innovations in game design: it was the first highly successful example of the platform genre, where characters moved an avatar through a computer-animated space while avoiding obstacles, as opposed to firing at descending invaders (like in *Space Invaders*) or navigating through a maze (as in *Pac-Man* [Namco, 1980]). The shift in the game's basic action for the player was distinctive, as it introduced the potent activity of "rescuing" together with what had previously been limited to verbs like "shooting" and "chasing" (in *Space Invaders* and *Pac-Man*, respectively).[2] The player's avatar—initially a carpenter called "Jumpman"—had no extraordinary abilities, just the capacity to run, jump, and occasionally grab a hammer. Jumpman would get a career and name change, becoming the plumber Mario in later games. Yet *Donkey Kong* also stands apart from its fellow quarter-gulping games for offering up more narrative information than was revealed in other arcade video games and for the relative complexity of its musical accompaniment.

Narrative and Character in *Donkey Kong*

The efforts at storytelling within *Donkey Kong* were unprecedented within arcade video games up to its time. In his analysis of *Centipede* (Atari, 1981), Richard Rouse III has astutely observed that most early arcade games avoided a story, but instead focused just on establishing a setting (2005, p. 465); neither the game nor its paratextual elements (like cabinet illustrations) explained why there were insects dropping down from the top of the screen, nor why the player should try to shoot those insects, and similarly mysterious settings could be described in *Space Invaders*, *Pac-Man*, *Frogger* (Konami, 1981), and many others. *Donkey Kong* uses introductory and inter-level animated sequences (early examples of what would later be called "cinematics" or "cutscenes," following the inter-level animated shows in *Pac-Man*, which did not explain anything about the story and only highlighted the playfulness of the characters) to reveal a story where a giant ape (in Miyamoto's imagination, the ape had been owned by Jumpman) has abducted a woman (Jumpman's girlfriend), climbed up a ladder, and then jumps with such force that it causes the girders to bend. Jumpman must then run, jump, and climb up the girders to try and rescue the woman. That the woman in the game would eventually be known as "Pauline" is explained (by Jeff Ryan 2011, pp. 29–30) as an homage to the wife of the warehouse manager, Polly, who was assisting in the conversion of unsold *Radar Scope* machines in *Donkey Kong* cabinets.

Intentionally or not, the name Pauline creates a connection to the early twentieth-century film series, *The Perils of Pauline*. Ben Singer has written about *The Perils of Pauline* as the lone surviving vestige of a genre he labels the "serial-queen melodrama"; these films stressed "female independence and mastery" (2001, p. 224) and pointed to the youthful film industry's interest in cultivating a female audience.[3] Indeed, there are important parallels between the early film industry and early video-game industry's efforts to create more products with female protagonists, as occurred in 1982 with *Ms. Pac-Man* (General Computer Corporation, 1982), a game that, like *Donkey Kong*, also borrows the visual and musical vocabularies of early cinema. The Pauline of the early film serials was a bold adventurer, making the hapless Pauline of *Donkey Kong*, whose sole purpose in the game is to cry "Help!", a politically reactionary reconfiguring of what had earlier been a far more active and heroic female character. If we can conceive of *Donkey Kong* as a nostalgic and even perhaps postmodern reworking of early cinema conventions, it is also relevant to note that the narrative device of the cliffhanger, such a central feature of early serial cinema, finds a modern parallel in the way that games like *Donkey Kong* lead the player through a level, only to discover that the damsel is still in distress and will need saving in the next level.

Donkey Kong's postmodern pastiche extends beyond allusions to early cinema and into a landmark early example of Hollywood's adventure and fantasy films: RKO Pictures' *King Kong* (Merian C. Cooper & Ernest B. Schoedsack, 1933). One of the most iconic moments from this influential film has Kong, a giant ape, kidnapping a blonde, white woman and scaling the heights of the recently completed Empire State Building. *Donkey Kong* also features a giant ape stealing away with a white woman to the top of a high building as well as seeming to share the family name from RKO's earlier film. When *Donkey Kong* began generating massive revenue for Nintendo, Universal Studios lodged an infringement suit against them (*Universal City Studios Inc. v. Nintendo Co., Ltd.*), citing similarities in the likeness and name of the title characters.[4] Histories of the Nintendo company and *Donkey Kong* often relay, with no dearth of glee, the poetic irony of Nintendo's lawyer pointing to a 1975 suit of Universal's against RKO where Universal had successfully argued that King Kong was in the public domain, hence negating their own claims of ownership. RKO's original 1933 film was remade in 1976 by John Guillermin, and perhaps some of the Japanese company Nintendo's fascination with the US figure of King Kong may make sense within the context of a moment when Stuart Hall said that postmodernism "is about how the world dreams itself to be 'American'" (Grossberg, 1986, p. 46).

Donkey Kong's Music

Beyond its fairly oblique reference to *The Perils of Pauline* and its use of early cinema conventions like the chase, the damsel in distress, and the cliffhanger, *Donkey Kong*'s accompanying music also points back to the traditions of early cinema in several ways. For instance, the introductory animation that begins every game of *Donkey Kong* is accompanied by a melodramatic cue, in parallel fifths, whose penultimate note trills in a manner approximating the way a pianist accompanying an early film might apply tremolo to a suspenseful scene. That melodic phrase is in fact part of the famous opening from the *Dragnet* television series that Jon Burlingame describes as "the decisive and melodramatic four-note phrase [that] became a kind of American musical code for 'you're in trouble now'" (1996, p. 15). Although the *Dragnet* phrase does not appear to be a direct quotation from the early twentieth-century photoplay books, its diminished harmonic structure and exaggerated character nonetheless tie it to that musical world. Other games from the early 1980s utilized this same melody: *Wizard of Wor* (Midway, 1980) opens each level with the first four notes of the phrase, withholding the final chord until a successful completion of a level, while *Pitfall* (Activision's game for the Atari 2600, 1982) accompanies each death of Pitfall Harry with the same tune.

Donkey Kong was exceptional for the harmonic coherence that ran through the game. Each level of *Donkey Kong* begins with an identical cue that playfully establishes a B-flat major triad as the home tonality. The first level has a constant syncopated bass line that spells out a B-flat triad, while each time Mario successfully jumps over one of the barrels thrown at him by the ape, it is accompanied by a rapid five-note melody that momentarily introduces an E-flat chord, the subdominant harmony, into the mix. That melody's rapidly rising and falling contour matches Mario's physical movements as he rapidly jumps up and down over a barrel. Should Mario grab a hammer, the time in which he wields it will be accompanied by a B-flat major fanfare. Each of Mario's deaths unleashes a torrent of chromatically related sixths and fifths before delivering a return to the relative stability of diatonicism and the familiarity of B-flat major. If the player has remaining lives, the death music is then followed by the level introductory music, returning to the key of B-flat major.

Completing each level brings a musical reward, although each respite from the ape's assaults lingers but for a moment. Successfully completing the first level elicits a short, happy moment in the music before the cabinet emits three ominous low F-sharps, which accompany the ape again stealing Mario's girlfriend and causing the heart above them to break, only then to be followed again by the introductory level music. Three of *Donkey Kong*'s four levels have continuous musical accompaniments; the bass lines of the Rivet level and the Conveyor Belt level also support the B-flat tonality. (The fourth level, the Elevator level, has no musical accompaniment, only the constant sound effect of the bouncing springs.) Defeating the Rivet level on the first stage, which causes the ape to fall, allowing Mario and Pauline a brief moment together, triggers a ragtime-inflected cue that ends with a B-flat seventh chord; defeating the Rivet level on the second stage also carries with it a brief whiff of ragtime syncopations and blue notes. With the start of the next level, B-flat major returns as the primary tonality. The entire game thus uses a single key area to unify the various levels and actions, using the brief disruption of the chromatic death music as contrast to the rest of the music that occurs as frame and within each level (i.e., the level introductory music, the ostinato bass line, plus any jumping and hammering that the player may elect to do) and to add momentum back into the home key. *Donkey Kong* was not the first game to use music, nor even the first game to have interesting and distinctive music. By the time *Donkey Kong* arrived on the scene, there had already been various musical accompaniments that used repeating basslines of increasing speed (e.g., *Space Invaders* and *Asteroids* [Atari, 1979]) or that opened a game with a memorable fanfare (e.g., *Pac-Man* and *Galaga* [Namco, 1981]).[5] What sets it apart from the games that came before it is the tonal coherence that binds together various cutscenes, levels, and game actions.

Donkey Kong Beyond the Arcade

Donkey Kong became the first game to earn an extra life beyond its pixels and into the world of breakfast cereal when, in 1982, Ralston Purina released their "crunchy barrels of fun," as the cereal box described its contents. (General Mills would follow a year later with *Pac-Man* cereal.) The 1982 Game and Watch version of *Donkey Kong* contained the first use of a cross-directional pad as a controller, a feature that would become a standard controller configuration with the Nintendo Entertainment System/Famicom (Donovan, 2010, p. 158). The rapper Ice Cube signaled the game's continuing and widespread familiarity on the 1992 album *The Predator* with "Now I Gotta Wet'Cha," in which he declared that "it's on like Donkey Kong." The game's increasing difficulty and limit of only 256 levels (a common feature in eight-bit games from that era) made it a contested area for record high scores, and the 2007 documentary *The King of Kong: Fistful of Quarters* (directed by Seth Gordon) presents the tribulations of an underdog gamer seeking the accomplishment of a record high score.[6] Still, among *Donkey Kong*'s many innovations, the introduction of what would become one of Nintendo's most familiar characters, Mario, is perhaps its greatest historical achievement.

Neil Lerner

Notes

1. Extended histories of Nintendo and its rise in the video-game industry include Sheff (1999), Kent (2001), Donovan (2010), and Ryan (2011).
2. Ryan (2011) notes the addition of "rescuing" to "shooting" and "escaping" (p. 35).

3. See Chapter 8, "Power and Peril in the Serial-Queen Melodrama"; this quotation is from page 224.
4. See Sheff (1999, pp. 118–127), Kent (2001, pp. 172–179), and Ryan (2011, pp. 39–44).
5. For more on the history of musical style in the early years of arcade games, see Lerner 2014a.
6. Kocurek discusses *The King of Kong* and observes how the film's focus serves to "bolster the notion that gaming is achievement oriented and that kind of achievement is satisfying and desirable for both children and adults" (2015, p. 181).

References

Burlingame, J. (1996). *TV's biggest hits: The story of television themes from "Dragnet" to "Friends."* New York: Schirmer Books.
Donovan, T. (2010). *Replay: The history of video games.* East Sussex: Yellow Ant.
Grossberg, L. (1986). On postmodernism and articulation: An interview with Stuart Hall. *Journal of Communication Inquiry, 10.* 45–60.
Kent, S.L. (2001). *The ultimate history of video games.* New York: Three Rivers Press.
Kocurek, C.A. (2015). *Coin-operated Americans: Rebooting boyhood at the video game arcade.* Minneapolis: University of Minneapolis Press.
Lerner, N. (2014a). The origin of musical style in video games, 1977–1983. In D. Neumeyer (Eds), *The Oxford handbook of film music studies* (pp. 319–347). New York: Oxford University Press.
Rouse, III, R. (2005). Game analysis: Centipede. In K. Salen and E. Zimmerman (Eds), *The game design reader* (pp. 460–473). Cambridge, MA: MIT Press.
Ryan, J. (2011). *Super Mario: How Nintendo conquered America.* New York: Portfolio/Penguin.
Sheff, D. (1999). *Game over: How Nintendo conquered the world.* Wilton, CT: Gamepress.
Singer, B. (2001). *Melodrama and modernity: Early sensational cinema and its contexts.* New York: Columbia University Press.

Further Reading

Herman, L. (2001). *Phoenix: The rise and fall of videogames,* third ed. Springfield, NJ: Rolenta Press.
Lerner, N. (2014b). Mario's dynamic leaps: Musical innovations (and the Specter of Early Cinema) in *Donkey Kong* and *Super Mario Bros*. In K.J. Donnelly, W. Gibbons, and N. Lerner (Eds), *Music in video games: Studying play* (pp. 1–29). New York: Routledge.

DOI: 10.4324/9781003199205-11

DOOM (1993)

In 1992, id Software completed and published *Wolfenstein 3D*, a groundbreaking first-person shooter (FPS) game that is today often referred to as the "grandfather" of its genre. The American company's next major project would be *DOOM*, an even more ambitious FPS. The success of *Wolfenstein 3D* meant that *DOOM* had a lot to live up to, but the developers—five young men[1]—were unfazed by expectations. In January of 1993, they issued a press release heralding the release of the game later that year. With characteristic bravado, they claimed that *DOOM* would represent a "technical revolution in PC programming" that would make *Wolfenstein 3D* look "primitive" by comparison. *DOOM*, moreover, would be "the first game to really exploit the power of LANs and modems to their full potential." Finally, the developers promised to make *DOOM* an "open game" in allowing players "to easily write and share" their own modifications to the software (id Software, 1993a). Impressively, they delivered on all these counts.

Presentation and Gameplay

To the modern eye, *DOOM* looks like a generic first-person shooter, but it only seems generic because of its deep and enduring influences on the genre (Pinchbeck, 2013). The player navigates the game world from a first-person perspective, with the currently equipped weapon projecting into that world as though the player were actually holding it. The player is represented by an animated portrait of a tough-looking man—the nameless Doom Marine. This portrait appears in the center of the status bar, at the bottom of the screen, which informs the player of their current health and weapon loadout.

DOOM's backstory, which takes inspiration from 1980s action-horror films like *Aliens* (James Cameron, 1986) and *Evil Dead II* (Sam Raimi, 1987), is tongue-in-cheek and not very important.[2] The player is a space marine stationed on Mars as security for the Union Aerospace Corporation (UAC). The military uses the UAC's facilities to experiment with inter-dimensional space travel. This dangerous experimentation eventually results in the opening of a portal to Hell, which evil demons use to attack humanity. At the start of the game, the player-character finds himself at an overrun military compound and must fight his way out.

There is a little more detail in the game's manual (1993b), but all the player needs to know is that they are supposed to clear the levels by killing the demons, which range from possessed humans through humanoid imps to hulking cybernetic monstrosities. The manual's description of a common enemy, the generic "Demon," should help convey the somehow both terrifying and silly nature of these enemies: "Sorta like a shaved gorilla, except with horns, a big head, lots of teeth, and harder to kill. Don't get too close or they'll rip your fraggin' head off" (1993b). The ultimate boss of the game is the Spider Mastermind—an arachnoid terror consisting of an enormous brain-with-a-face resting on a four-legged metallic exoskeleton with an incorporated chaingun on the front. A typical level in *DOOM* features scores of demons, but the player has access to enough firepower to even the odds: chainsaw, pistol, shotgun, chaingun, rocket launcher, plasma rifle, and the BFG ("Big Fucking Gun") 9000, an especially powerful plasma rifle. These weapons are scattered around the sprawling levels, whose abstract designs blend gothic science fiction with organic surrealism in the spirit of H. R. Giger.

Of course, the shooting-based gameplay is *DOOM*'s main attraction. It is unrelentingly fast and pulse-poundingly frantic. The player-character can move at superhuman speed while shooting continuously. While weapons can run out of ammunition, they never need reloading and can be switched in the blink of an eye. The enemies, though deadly, are slower than the player and have at most a couple of different types of attack at their disposal. Some of these attacks are projectiles that can be avoided. For example, the Imp hurls fireballs in a straight line toward the player, which the player should dodge by moving sideways ("strafing") out of the way. Other monsters rush down the player to connect a biting attack. They can be dealt with by running backward while shooting. The real havoc begins when multiple monsters of different kinds attack the player simultaneously. Whenever that happens, the player should focus on blasting the most dangerous foes while dashing around to avoid incoming attacks. Skilled players can make this deadly dance look almost graceful. Aside from engaging in combat, the player will spend time navigating the levels, many of which frustrate progress with hidden keycards.

Impact

To get a sense of *DOOM*'s impact, consider that for years after its release the term "*DOOM* clone" was used to designate any entry in the FPS genre (see Therrien, 2015; the use of "first-person shooter" would only overtake "*DOOM* clone" in the late 1990s). Much of this influence was doubtless due to *DOOM*'s distribution model, which offered the first of the original game's three chapters as free shareware.

While the full version of *DOOM* sold over one million copies, the shareware version achieved a much larger install base—likely over 10 million (for estimates, see Pinchbeck, 2013, p. 4).

What, exactly, did *DOOM* bring to subsequent generations of FPS games? Certainly, a conviction that satisfying gunplay and violent spectacle were enough to carry a game, and perhaps even a genre. Story would eventually come into focus with games like *Half-Life* (Valve, 1998), which had a slower pace and more deliberate shooting than *DOOM*. Today, these two games are often considered the respective forbears of two distinct styles of FPS gameplay. *DOOM*'s focus on speed and dynamic gunplay defines "movement-based" shooters like *Titanfall II* (Respawn Entertainment, 2016) and *Unreal Tournament* (Digital Extremes & Epic Games, 1999), as well as the 2016 reboot of *DOOM*, whereas *Half-Life* inspired slower shooters like *Call of Duty: Black Ops* (Infinity Ward, 2007). In addition, *DOOM* provided the FPS genre with much of its semantic repository: cheesy movie tropes, generic "alien" enemies, tough-guy protagonists, and weapon archetypes (such as the iconic rocket launcher).

In being arguably the most recognizable and controversial first-person shooter ever made, *DOOM* also deeply influenced modern gaming culture. I will touch on three areas: multiplayer, the PC gaming modding scene, and the cultural discourse surrounding violent video games.

I will never forget the day, in the summer of 1996, when I entered my first local *DOOM* multiplayer tournament—or, rather, the day I entered the hall in which the tournament took place. I had never seen anything like it. Dozens of bulky beige desktop PCs were lined up on long wooden desks. About thirty participants, most of them teenaged males, were playing, chatting, laughing, and generally having a good time. My best friend and I, both nine years old at the time, arrived at the scene with what we thought was well-earned confidence. After all, we had practiced on *DOOM*'s challenging single-player campaign for months. But competitive multiplayer was a different beast; we could not believe the speed and accuracy of our would-be opponents. After watching the action for just a few minutes, we understood that all that was there for us was abject humiliation and slinked home.

For me and for many other players in the mid-1990s, *DOOM*'s multiplayer was something new and special. Just the idea of a friendly shootout in a virtual 3D environment was exciting. To be sure, *DOOM* was not the first game to offer networked FPS multiplayer. That honor goes to 1973's *Maze War*. But *DOOM* popularized it and put it online.

DOOM offered two multiplayer modes, each available for two to four players. Cooperative gameplay allowed players to take on the game's monster-infested levels together. The second mode had players shoot at each other instead, earning a "frag" with each successful kill. Designer and programmer John Romero coined the term "deathmatch" for this mode (Takahashi, 2013), a label that still shows up in modern FPS games.

About *DOOM*'s multiplayer, the developers' original press release had made the bold prediction that it would become "the number one cause of decreased productivity in businesses around the world." They may actually have been right about that. In 1994, *Computer Gaming World* reported that Intel had banned *DOOM* from the work environment. This happened "after several Intel subnets were rendered inoperable during lunch hour, as employees raced to get in a game of multiplayer *DOOM* DeathMatch" (p. 14). Other businesses and universities would go on to ban the game because it stole employees' time and hogged computer networks (Kushner, 2004, p. 160).

Also buttressed by the developing online infrastructure was *DOOM*'s influence on the PC modding scene. As promised by the developers, the game made its data—notably, level designs, sprites, and sound effects—accessible and modifiable to players in so-called WAD files (short for "Where's All the Data?"). Players could then mix and match these elements as they pleased, creating new levels or even completely new games based on *DOOM*'s software engine. The Internet allowed for the widespread sharing of these creations, which were also distributed commercially on CD collections.

Violence

Finally, and inevitably, violence. In the United States, serious controversy over violent video games began with the release of the Big Three in the early 1990s: *Night Trap* (Sega, 1992), *Mortal Kombat* (Midway Games, 1992), and *DOOM*. These games were all violent, graphically advanced, and highly popular. They had what it took to make parents worry about their children's amusements, and thereby to force the issue. *Night Trap* and *Mortal Kombat* became main targets of the 1993 congressional hearings on violent video games.[3] According to Senator Joseph Lieberman's opening remarks, these games contained "the most horrible depictions of graphic violence" and "teach a child to enjoy inflicting torture" (C-SPAN, 1993). He was unaware that *DOOM*, a game whose violence topped that even of *Mortal Kombat*, would be released to the public just one day later, on December 10 of 1993.

In the years following its release, *DOOM* became the centerpiece of debates surrounding violent video games and the wisdom or folly of their censorship. A main reason for *DOOM*'s infamy was the game's many technical achievements, which brought a sense of grounded realism to the violent depictions. These achievements included fully texture-mapped levels, high-framerate combat, dynamic lighting, gorily fluid death animations, and impactful sound design (such as the wet crunch of an Imp being splattered by an exploding barrel). Another factor was the game's literal perspective on its violent depictions. For so many players and parents, *DOOM* was the first they had ever seen of the *first-person* shooter genre. This mode of presentation can seem disturbing to onlookers in its suggestion that the player is present in the game world, aiming and shooting at seemingly real agents. That view is taken to an extreme by the media psychologist Dave Grossman, who has repeatedly used the term "murder simulator" to refer to first-person shooters and to *DOOM* in particular.

DOOM again caused controversy in the summer of 1999 when it was linked to the Columbine High School massacre. Armed with guns and strapped with homemade explosives, Eric Harris and Dylan Klebold murdered twelve fellow students and one teacher before shooting themselves in the head. Investigations into the backgrounds of the shooters revealed that they were both fans of *DOOM* and other violent media, with Harris having remarked on a tape shot in the basement of his house that the massacre was "going to be like fucking *DOOM*." In his journal, he wrote that he would force himself "to believe that everyone is just a monster from *DOOM*" so as not to be "sidetracked by my feelings of sympathy, mercy, or any of that" (October 23, 1998). Harris had also made and shared homebrewed levels for *DOOM*, which stirred a now debunked rumor that one of his levels staged the planned massacre as a sort of dry run.

It is no coincidence that research into the effects of playing violent video games really took off in the wake of the Columbine massacre. One of the most cited academic papers on the matter, a 2001 article published in the journal *Psychological Science*, opens by recounting the shootings and linking them to *DOOM* in particular (Anderson & Bushman, 2001, p. 353). Today, however, the evidence suggests that violent games like *DOOM* do not promote real-world violence, with recent findings even suggesting that mass shooters are *less* likely to be avid players of violent video games than their peers (Markey & Ferguson, 2018).

Technically innovative, brutally competitive, and violently controversial, *DOOM* remains emblematic of the modern first-person shooter. And by setting the terms of this hugely popular genre, it is certainly one of the most important video games of the 1990s.

Jens Kjeldgaard-Christiansen

Notes

1. Through most of *DOOM*'s development, the team consisted of Adrian Carmack, John Carmack, Kevin Cloud, Tom Hall, and John Romero. Creative differences caused Tom Hall to leave the team in July of 1993. Sandy Petersen and Dave Taylor joined the team later that year (Kushner, 2004).
2. The story world that was originally planned for *DOOM*, as laid out in early development by Tom Hall in a document entitled the "Doom Bible," was quite elaborate. The rest of the team eventually decided to drop most of Hall's Bible, with John Carmack famously remarking that "story in a game is like a story in a porn movie. It's expected to be there, but it's not that important" (Kushner, 2004, p. 128).
3. These hearings resulted in the establishment of the Entertainment Software Rating Board (ESRB), an organization that assigns age and content ratings to video games released in the US.

References

Anderson, C.A., & Bushman, B.J. (2001). Effects of violent video games on aggressive behavior, aggressive cognition, aggressive affect, physiological arousal, and prosocial behavior: A meta-analytic review of the scientific literature. *Psychological Science, 12*(5): 353–359.

C-SPAN. (1993). *Video game violence*. Retrieved August 27, 2021, from https://www.c-span.org/video/?52848-1/video-game-violence

Computer Gaming World. (1994, March). Intel bans *DOOM*! *Computer Gaming World*, 116. Russell Sipe.

Harris, E. (1998). *Eric Harris's journal*. Retrieved April 6, 2021, from http://acolumbinesite.com/eric/writing/journal/journal.php

id Software. (1993a). *DOOM press release*. Retrieved March 28, 2021, from https://tcrf.net/Prerelease:Doom_(PC,_1993)

id Software. (1993b). *The DOOM manual*. Retrieved March 28, 2021, from https://www.starehry.eu/download/action3d/docs/Doom-Manual.pdf

Kushner, D. (2004). *Masters of Doom: How two guys created an empire and transformed pop culture*. New York, NY: Random House.

Markey, P.M., & Ferguson, C.J. (2018). *Moral combat: Why the war on violent video games is wrong*. Dallas, TX: Benbella Books.

Pinchbeck, D. (2013). *DOOM: SCARYDARKFAST*. Ann Arbor, MI: University of Michigan Press.

Takahashi, D. (2013). After 20 years, Doom co-creator John Romero looks back on the impact of a seminal (and satanic) game (interview). *Venturebeat*.

Retrieved August 26, 2021, from https://venturebeat.com/2013/12/11/after-20-years-doom-co-creator-john-romero-looks-back-on-the-impact-of-a-seminal-game-interview/2/

Therrien, C. (2015). Inspecting video game historiography through critical lens: Etymology of the first-person shooter genre. *Game Studies*, *15*(2). Retrieved April 1, 2021, from http://www.gamestudies.org/1502/articles/therrien

Further Reading

Kjeldgaard-Christiansen, J. (2020). "Unbreakable, incorruptible, unyielding": *Doom* as an agency simulator. In J. Carroll, M. Clasen, & E. Jonsson (Eds), *Evolutionary perspectives on imaginative culture* (pp. 235–253). New York: Springer.

Voorhees, G.A., Call, J., & Whitlock, K. (2012). *Guns, grenades, and grunts: First-person shooter games*. New York, NY: Bloomsbury Publishing.

DOI: 10.4324/9781003199205-12

DRAGON'S LAIR (1983)

Dragon's Lair (Advanced Microcomputer Systems, 1983), first displayed to the public at the 1983 Amusement Operator Expo in Chicago, arrived at an auspicious period in video-game history, commonly referred to as the North American video-game crash. This epoch-forming, industry-wide event resulted in the massive financial contraction of the business and the quick exit of several formerly dominant companies. *Dragon's Lair* entered the market in this competitive context armed with a definitive technological difference, using laserdiscs to display its hand-drawn graphics and operate its specific form of interactivity, and organizational innovation, positioning a deeper connection between enterprising old and new media producers, an assemblage which briefly found promotion as a fix to the crash as both makers and pundits sought redemptive hope in laserdisc technology.

By most measures, both financial and critical, *Dragon's Lair* was an immediate success. The game presented users with thirty-seven and a half minutes of sword-and-sorcery-themed animation, featuring a brave knight, a kidnapped princess, and an evil dragon, punctuated by occasional quick decision points with single solutions. Although out of step with contemporary standards of gameplay, the game drew attention from the spectacle of its visual decision and its core promise to "play" a fully drawn cartoon. Upon its June 1983 release, reports bragged of long lines and intense interest at flagging local arcades. One such piece claimed that the game was twice as profitable as a typical arcade machine, returning investment in only four weeks, and that the game's very presence had increased arcade foot traffic by twenty-five to fifty percent (Bierbaum, 1984). Cabinet sales, too, were robust; by January 1984, it had sold approximately 8,500 units at $4000 apiece, twice the price of traditional arcade cabinets (Harmetz, 1984). However, the sales were lower than the optimistic projections, seemingly hindered by the limited production capacity for laserdisc players, the game's necessary component. Nevertheless, in response to the immediate buzz and returns around the game, its makers announced a new and ambitious business plan of producing five similar "movie games" a year and selling the new games to existing cabinets owners (Harmetz, 1983; Brownstein, 1984).

Technology and Design

Dragon's Lair is a platform whose internal components determined the look, design, and experience of the game itself. The cabinet included a Pioneer LD-V1000 or a PR-7820 laserdisc player, to store and reproduce the game's audio and visual elements in a stable, un-manipulable format as well as a single eight-position joystick and action button. This form of data storage and retrieval allowed for "full pictorial animation" (Dyer, 1984) at a time when competing publishers still mostly relied upon an abstracted iconography to represent players, objects, and game worlds. Technical documents drafted by the game's designer Rick Dyer describe the game's use of the laserdisc's unique ability to store and retrieve information in order to sustain a sense of interactivity. Dyer discusses *Dragon's Lair*'s Russian doll structure of nested temporalities—from represented narrative time, down to frame screen time, down to clock time of the microprocessor—and how each is reconciled in the operation of the game through its use of what Dyer calls rooms, nodes, and windows. In the game, users enter rooms where they encounter visual representations of nodes in which a correct action must be taken to overcome some visually represented obstacle (swinging vines, rolling boulders, etc.). At these nodes, users are confronted with timing windows, a limited portion of time, or literally spiralized bands on the laserdisc encoded with single film frames, in which they must engage the correct input action. While many of the game's nodes necessitate that a user respond as swiftly as possible to an accompanying visual cue, constituting what is commonly now called a "quick-time event," many other obstacles demand that users act swiftly, but also within the exact appropriate window. The result is a game that combines waiting-acting in that order of prominence. Dyer referred to his game's construction of interactivity, contrasting it with contemporary games' "multiplicity of choices...[and their] virtually unlimited number of permutations and combinations of action" (1984, p. 1). Instead, *Dragon's Lair* presents "incidents being portrayed [that] include physical and other constraints which severely limit the options available to the protagonist... [who] does not have many options" (1984, p. 8). Dyer's design deviated significantly from contemporary arcade games and used the laserdisc to take advantage of the depiction of space, the non-linearity of game order, and the manipulation of cues derived from cinematic storytelling.

Spaces and Control

Dragon's Lair presents a user with a visually rich world supplemented with an inverse paucity in terms of control. *Dragon's Lair* is represented from a shifting, deep, third-person perspective, unlike the flat-plane perspective of then contemporary arcade games. In the game, the seemingly stable background and environment suddenly act upon the user, who is subjected to everything from avalanching ceilings to collapsing floors to shrinking platforms, etc. The game's rooms also host many inanimate objects that spring to life to provide more environmental dangers. Playing the game entails quickly and decisively reacting to environments and their objects rather than acting upon them. In other words, the game combines the visual design of an adventure game with the pace of an action game.

For both economic and technical reasons, many early arcade games present an unalterable order of events both within levels and between levels, or some other temporal marker. A single play of *Dragon's Lair*, unique among its contemporaries, is built around a series of rooms which contain one or more selection nodes but which in themselves have no set order. The makers of the game took advantage of the non-linear access of the laserdisc drive in which the point of address could be quickly shifted without complicating in-game calculations. Like all video games, this one is also based on a set of finite visual parameters, but by using the non-linearity of the laserdisc to randomize room order in regular play and between tries, the game presents users with an experience of a procedurally generated game space, albeit built with a relatively modest number of variables. In order to give shape and logic to this non-linear construction, the game's makers deployed specific visual elements of character and setting.

Using familiar fantasy imagery, *Dragon's Lair* invokes the specific subgenre of sword-and-sorcery and, more broadly, the mode of fantastic and fairy-tale storytelling. Critical work on these narrative traditions focuses on the modularity of their represented events, their use of repetition, and their own peculiar temporality, usually denoted with "once upon a time," all elements echoed in *Dragon's Lair*'s own use of quasi-non-linearity.

Because of its lack of continuous control, *Dragon's Lair* requires a user to occupy the positions of both a spectator and a player at the same time, or literally become an "active" viewer. Tellingly, many of the game's cabinets famously were equipped with two monitors: one below for the actual user and one above for people to gather and watch the game being played. The scopic combination of represented depth and fixed angle was the unique resource and limitation of *Dragon's Lair*'s laserdisc storage and provided the game's specific technique of combining cues and actions, testing a user's tacit sense of film conventions such as angle, composition, and screen direction. Perhaps the best example of this technique can be observed in the game's boulder room. This room depicts the player avatar, Dirk, running from an enormous billiard ball in a parabola-shaped gully while avoiding a set of perpendicular boulders running along the gully's curve. Echoing the iconic shot from *Raiders of the Lost Ark* (Steven Spielberg, 1981), the room and its shots depict the principal ball coming down along the z-axis, from the presumed background, or frame top, toward the user who must depress the joystick down in time to avoid both the main boulder, as well as the cross-traffic of boulders moving from frame left to frame right, to escape through frame bottom. The room repeats this node four times, cycling the animation, while only changing the color of the horizontally crossing ball. After establishing this vector moving down and away through four successive nodes and shots, the game suddenly places the virtual camera behind Dirk, as a user must jump across another pit to escape the room for good and allow the chasing boulder to crash down. Or a user must press up on the joystick after visual cues and repetitive actions had conditioned her that "up" would spell certain doom. Constrained, fixed framed shots accompanied with spatial continuity in these shots established a pattern of image and action which was confounded in the room's ultimate solution. In other words, interaction in *Dragon's Lair* necessitates a different form of visual activity, soliciting a user to keep track of spatial cues and read them critically.

Production and Industrial Context

These unique design decisions were informed by the technical structure of the game's hardware as well as the unique combination of producers, drawn from adjacent media industries, who collaborated on

Dragon's Lair's construction. The producers of *Dragon's Lair* assembled their work through a disorganized division of labor atypical of video games at a time when production was characterized by in-house producers wholly designing arcade cabinets. Working at toy-maker Mattel during the boom in electronic games, Dyer devised a sword-and-sorcery game that utilized an automatic paper scroll, similar to cash register tape, to cycle between narrative encounters (Robley and Kunkel, 1984). Upon leaving the toy-maker in 1979, Dyer and his new independent venture Advanced Microcomputer Systems (later renamed RDI Systems) pitched their invention to fledgling animation studio Don Bluth Productions as a prototype for a new laserdisc game. Bluth and company organized between fifty and seventy of their staff on a four to six month production schedule to create twenty-two minutes of cel-animated game footage (Brownstein, 1984). Meanwhile, El Cajon-based Cinematronics, a company already struggling with bankruptcy (Skelly 2012), handled the production and distribution of the games' physical cabinets to video game arcades. A contemporary *Variety* article described the production of *Dragon's Lair*: "RDI employs a 25-person staff that scripts arcade games. Company artists draw out storyboards from which Bluth's artists perform the animation. RDI engineers complete the programming and engineering of the games before Cinematronics takes over [physical] production and distribution" (Bierbaum, 1984). *Dragon's Lair* was also an expensive game to produce, costing approximately $3 million ($1.2 million from Bluth, $1.2 million from RDI, and $600,000 from Cinematronics), or between two and four times as much as other contemporary games (Harmetz, 1983; Winslow, 1984). The expensive gambit was informed both by the volatility of each company's native industries as well as the utopian hope placed in laserdisc as a transformative medium.

Dyer turned to laserdiscs to leave the toy industry, which was then undergoing waves of boom and bust related to the growth of new media. In less than a decade, the toy industry saw the rise of electronic devices such as Mattel's *Electronic Football* (1977) and Milton Bradley's *Simon* (1978), their replacement with emerging console gaming, and home gaming's collapse with the video-game crash. A "baby boomlet" in the US population, as baby boomers increasingly entered into childrearing, prompted weary toy companies to return to reenergized legacy brands and products. For example, Mattel, Dyer's former employer, had been a pioneer in electronic games and console gaming, but after the collapse of its Intellivision home console, the company had divested of "everything but its traditional operations" (Hollie, 1984).

Bluth's core industry, too, was plagued with turmoil. On September 13, 1979, animation director Don Bluth offered his resignation to Disney Animation, quickly prompting the exit of approximately one-fifth of that firm's total creative personnel (Goldrich, 1979). And while the exact motivations behind this exodus are a matter of debate, Bluth used the exit as an opportunity to espouse his belief in so-called full animation, separating himself from his contemporaries focused on so-called limited animation (Summers, 1980; "Branching Out..." 1982). Unfortunately, larger changes in the animation business left Bluth Productions' house style increasingly difficult to sell to the major studios, who preferred inexpensive, overseas animation labor. As a result, the company considered other avenues for the type of animation work that they produced. Bluth found that other venue in video games, which the animator himself called "participatory movies" and which he cast as a vehicle to finance feature animation, a "training ground for animators" to learn the meticulous art of full animation, and an opportunity to train younger audiences to appreciate it (Beckerman, 1983; Arnold, 1983).

Despite *Dragon's Lair*'s initial success, the "laser craze" around laserdisc games quickly subsided as many critics attacked the flood of subsequent games as empty iterations of previous titles or otherwise lacking (Crook, 1982). Following this second-wave reaction, today's pundits often frame *Dragon's Lair* as a historical curiosity or negative example of design, and this failure is frequently attributed to the game's lack of so-called "interactivity." *Dragon's Lair* arrived as a product and example of this heady period where discursive speculation around the laserdisc's ability to grant so-called interactivity, and precisely what interactive experiences were, was widespread across technical documents and prototypes. In this spirit, the design and production of *Dragon's Lair* is more productively understood as one experiment among other interactive TV devices consumed with examining the possibility of deeper engagement with media imagery, and as one production among others using the new medium of digital media discs to manage risk and create opportunity.

Michael J. Clarke

References

Arnold, G. (1983, July 17). Snow White reawakened. *Washington Post*. Retrieved November 4, 2021, from https://www.washingtonpost.com/archive/lifestyle/style/1983/07/17/snow-white-awakened/e7055651-c591-4573-9244-0a6b84766736/

Beckerman, H. (1983, July 15). Animation spot. *Back Stage*. 26.
Bierbaum, R. (1984, Feb. 8). Laser game plan sees 'revolution' heading for home. *Variety*. 3, 178.
Branching out with classical style. (1982, July 31). *Screen International*. 13.
Brownstein, M. (1984, April). The Computer Games interview: Don Bluth. *Computer Games*. 24–27.
Crook, D. (1982, January 11). Video game makers offering new twists. *Los Angeles Times*. G1.
Dyer, R. (1984). *Full pictorial animation video game*. World Intellectual Property Organization. WO 84 / 03792.
Goldrich, R. (1979, November 16). Animation newcomer. *Back Stage*. 29, 34–35.
Harmetz, A. (1983, August 2). Hollywood playing harder at the video games. *The New York Times*. C11.
Harmetz, A. (1984, January 20). Video arcades' new hope. *The New York Times*. D1.
Hollie, P. (1984, June 27). The risky business of toys. *The New York Times*. D1.
Robley, L. and B. Kunkel. (1984, January). Games on disc. *Electronic Games*. 41–46.
Skelly, T. (2012). Rise and fall of Cinematronics. In M.J.P. Wolf (Eds), *Before the crash: Early video game history* (pp. 139–167). Detroit: Wayne State.
Summers, J. (1980, March 17). Disney alum prescribes cure for animation's ills? *Boxoffice*. 2.
Winslow, K. (1984, April 14). Fast forward. *Billboard*. 36–37.

Further Reading

Clarke, M. (Forthcoming). *Dragon's Lair and the fantasy of interactivity*. Lanham, MD: Lexington Books.

DOI: 10.4324/9781003199205-13

THE ELDER SCROLLS II: DAGGERFALL (1996)

Dungeons and Daggers

Released in 1996, *Daggerfall* is the second game in the *Elder Scrolls* role-playing game (RPG) series. By pushing the boundaries of the series and extending playable space, the designers of the first game, *Arena*, would set new expectations for play, as grounded in the roots of the seemingly directionless *Dungeons & Dragons* (*D&D*) model of tabletop play. *Arena* laid the foundation for the sandbox genre the *Elder Scrolls* series ultimately defined, but Bethesda looked for every opportunity to build something to stand out in a crowded RPG market. That year also saw the release of Blizzard's dungeon crawler *Diablo*, with its greater emphasis on combat, and *Nemesis: The Wizardry*

Adventure (Sir-Tech, 1996), which offered a hybrid adventure-RPG spin-off on one of the most extensive D&D-esque RPG series of the time. Ultimately, *Daggerfall* set new expectations for RPGs thanks to two innovations: an emphasis on procedurally generated content to allow vast dungeons and exploration, creating an expansive, sandbox world; and a skill-based model centered on progression, rewarding players for investing in certain paths. *Daggerfall* also introduced a new skills paradigm, which designer Todd Howard notes would move the game away from some of its *D&D* elements toward a more distinctive system of character generation:

> We were never sure if it was big to just be big, since it was randomly generated. We could dial up or dial down the size very easily. But it became the sum of its parts. You could do so much. It's also the *Elder Scrolls* game that introduced the skill system, and the whole "you improve by doing" paradigm, which I think defines the series in many ways. You really felt like the character you played was up to you, and not the game.
>
> (Miller, 2010)

Unlike *Arena*'s intensely similar dungeons, these not only offered a superior level of variations, but also revealed a fundamental design problem of *Elder Scrolls*: how can even the designers speak to content that they can never fully experience themselves? The vastness risked repetition, thanks to a reliance upon formulaic structures, but proved invaluable in extending the player's experience of a world as sandbox play. The *Daggerfall* experiment crafted a foundation that the sequels (and competitors) would extend, pushing further as graphical enhancements allowed this realism to move toward a higher sense of graphical fidelity, and thus paving the way for near-endless exploration that became a hallmark feature of subsequent *Elder Scrolls* iterations.

These changes were recognized immediately by computer game players. In *Computer Gaming World*'s December 1996 issue, reviewer Scorpia asked and answered two questions about *The Elder Scrolls II: Daggerfall*: "Is it better than the game's prequel, *Arena*? Is it as buggy as *Arena*? The answer to both questions is yes" (1996, p. 281). Players and critics alike concluded that the sequel was better than *Arena*, even with glitches. Bethesda had much to improve and spent nearly three years developing *Daggerfall* as the company began work immediately after *Arena*'s March 1994 release. To run the game, Bethesda incorporated a new game engine that replaced *Arena*'s 2D illusions. According to an interview with game director Todd Howard (in Miller, 2010), the design team opted to develop and utilize a 3D game engine called XnGine. This took the series in a different direction than *Arena*'s reliance upon the raycast engine, which utilized 2D world-building that only appears to be 3D. Consumers initially disliked the "mouse-look interface" seen in games like the first-person shooter *Terminator: Future Shock* (Bethesda, 1995), but it eventually became quite popular in computer games (Miller, 2010).

Sandbox games have rightly been criticized for offering players opportunities for endless action with very little meaning or impact, as Tanenbaum and Tanenbaum argue in their discussion of player agency:

> There may be limitless permutations of these activities with enough variation and emergent moments to support hours of unique play. However, there is a comparatively small range of meanings to which that player is committing. She may either commit crimes or obey the law; she may follow the structured quests or she may ignore them, in which case the world remains static.
>
> (Tanenbaum & Tanenbaum, 2009)

Tanenbaum and Tanenbaum situate the *Elder Scrolls* series alongside *Grand Theft Auto* (Rockstar, 1997–2017) in this discussion of the weaknesses of sandbox games. Yet, the "growth by doing" model of *Daggerfall* offered an early model for how sandbox role-playing games could craft meaning through a combination of exploration and player action. While sandbox games such as *Minecraft* (Markus Persson, 2010) rely on the player creating their own direction in what might otherwise be seen as a "goal-less game," sandbox RPGs combine the best aspects of sandbox games—"creating space for player agency, as they allow players to be creative in setting their own goals" (Waern, 2012)—with the structures of a role-playing game to incentivize forward progress in the world. James Paul Gee described this engagement as "co-creative," suggesting that it is this aspect of play that makes games enticing to educators who might look to the *Elder Scrolls* model for inspiration (Gee, 2003, p. 2).

Daggerfall as Sequel

In retrospect, it is perhaps surprising that a game centered on a generic relic like the "Staff of Chaos" would generate any momentum for a sequel. Many of the designers were aware of the struggles of crafting meanings at a scale the size of *Arena*, and several tried to push for more specificity and complexity as the series moved forward. For instance,

Ted Peterson tried to subvert the generic feel of the original in his work on *Daggerfall:*

> The reviews for *Arena* were pretty good, but as a writer, it definitely pained me that the lackluster, cliched [sic] plot and game world was called out. I made it my mission to create the most complicated story I could wrap my head around, subverting expectations wherever possible. I wanted to give the player tons of choices, from character creation to which side of the conflict you wanted to champion…Yes, it all hinged on a MacGuffin, a hoary old literary device you can find in everything from the *Maltese Falcon* to *Pulp Fiction*, but with the competing groups not being so black and white, the player was given some real meaningful choices about how to play the story.
>
> (Peterson, 2019)

A massive sequel to a game like *Arena* would require some connections to its predecessor, and Peterson's personal challenge resulted in one of the most complex *Elder Scrolls* narratives. In the year 3E 405, Uriel Septim VII commands the protagonist to travel to the Daggerfall region of High Rock in the northwest corner of the world to investigate the suspicious death of his loyal subject, King Lysandus, whose spirit walks the streets of his kingdom at night with vengeance on his ghostly mind. That said, Emperor Septim has another job for his trusted warrior: to discover the whereabouts of a private letter he sent to King Lysandus' widow, Queen Mynisera. The contents of the letter can significantly impact the six possible endings in *Daggerfall* as the player can decide what to do with a totem that controls a giant golem called the Numidium. More importantly, the various factions in the politically unstable region of Daggerfall that were painstakingly created by Peterson play a major role in crafting the lore that would take *Elder Scrolls* through the next several decades.

The lore was not the only tradition Bethesda improved in the *Elder Scrolls* series as *Daggerfall*'s primary contribution was its enhanced skill system with a "you improve by doing" leveling up paradigm (Miller, 2010). *Daggerfall* retains some elements from *Arena*, including a class system and an attributes system using both familiar role-playing stats (such as strength and intelligence) and more unusual character-focused traits (including personality and luck). In the sequel, however, three boxes on the character creation screen determine how the protagonist will level up: "Primary Skills" (three), "Major Skills" (three), and "Minor Skills" (six). Once these skills are properly tiered, the next step is to select advantages or disadvantages that will influence the difficulty level for skill advancement. Players then determine the "Reputations" of the character among various social classes in the game. Finally, a questionnaire determines the backstory of the created character.[1] When all of these mechanisms are finalized, a character levels up by using their preferred skills during the game. The more a skill is used, the more it increases, determining how or when a customized character reaches a new level. This novel leveling system meant that each playthrough could produce an entirely different experience than previous ones.

Daggerfall was so ambitious that Bethesda's designers surprised even themselves. Former Bethesda designer Ted Peterson expressed that with canonical information after *Daggerfall* and leading into *Morrowind*, "It's almost mind-boggling to imagine what they're going through right now. I'm happy to watch from the side lines" (Italia, 2001). Kurt Kulhmann was hired toward the end of *Daggerfall*'s development. He notes, "I still remember my amazement at being able to put together a dungeon or quest, fire up the executable, and see what I'd just done right there on my computer screen in an actual game. I'm still occasionally floored by that magic, even after all these years" (in Miller, 2010). Design director Bruce Nesmith said, "this game looks amazing. Little did I know what the future held" (in Miller, 2010). Nesmith's words foreshadow *Daggerfall*'s role in setting internal expectations for subsequent iterations in the *Elder Scrolls* series.

Daggerfall in Review

Reviewers unaffiliated with the project seemed similarly impressed. *Gamespot*'s Trent Ward stated, "From start to finish, *Daggerfall* shows itself to be an epic product that surpasses the time-crunching power of even the legendary RPGs of old" (1996). Ward emphasized the vastness of the game world, noting that: "To play *Daggerfall* successfully requires one of two mindsets: to remain ever-vigilant, taking notes and going exactly when and where you're told; or to relax and let life take you where it will." This combination of play styles would continue to serve Bethesda's interests with their future titles. *Game Revolution*'s Jonathan Leack gave *Daggerfall* a perfect score and wrote, "If you're tired of shotguns and chainsaws and need to play a game that takes brains, strategy, character development, role-playing, magic, and much more, BUY DAGGERFALL NOW!!!!! You are guaranteed hours of excitement in a constantly changing world" (1996). Reviewer Scorpia concluded, "*Daggerfall* is the closest thing to real role-playing I've seen outside of the *Ultimas*, and that's saying a lot. It will definitely keep you busy and happily occupied for quite some time to come" (1996, p. 293). Unlike *Arena*, *Daggerfall* emphasized wandering between locations over fast travel. This feature expanded the sense of the world, eclipsing the size of its predecessor. Echoing fantasy tropes in its structure, the world map is about the scale of Great Britain, offering 15,000 towns to visit and 750,000+ NPCs to interact with (*The Elder Scrolls Wiki*, n.d.). The scale is such that when an adventurous YouTuber sought to venture across the full map, the effort took sixty-two real-time hours (Plunkett, 2016).

Yet, like *Arena*, the world's sense of scale dwindled during long playthroughs because the reliance upon randomness would lead to continual encounters with the familiar. Designers reflected on the lessons learned after the game's initial success, recognizing the challenges that vastness presented to meaningful world-building. As Todd Howard noted when looking back on the project: "*Daggerfall* in my memory is mostly flavored by how large it was. It was something we really struggled with during the project" (in Miller, 2010). Howard later admitted to *Computer Gaming World* in February 2001 before *Morrowind*'s release:

> We didn't really like the result of *Daggerfall*....There were about 20 to 30 hours of good gameplay, but then it began to just be the same thing over and over again. We went into *Morrowind* thinking that less is definitely more.
>
> (Green, 2001, p. 53)

Nevertheless, despite the gimmick of the game world, *Daggerfall* inspired Bethesda's modding scene as well as the spin-off games *The Elder Scrolls Legend: Battlespire* in 1997 and *The Elder Scrolls Adventures: Redguard* in 1998. Unfortunately, both games were buggier than their predecessor and not well received (Gallagher, Jong, & Sinervo, 2017, p. 37). Like *Arena*, *Daggerfall* began to show its age soon after its technology became outdated. It would be up to *Morrowind* to carry the *Elder Scrolls* torch into the next computer age, while inspiring innovation across the genre building on *Daggerfall*'s foundations.

Anastasia Salter and Mark Kretzschmar

Note

1. For a thorough description of this process, see the Let's Play "#02: Character Creation In-Depth — [Daggerfall]" https://www.youtube.com/watch?v=ADoM94ZrIgM.

References

Gallagher, R., Jong, C., & Sinervo, K. A. (2017). Who wrote the *Elder Scrolls*?: Modders, developers, and the mythology of Bethesda Softworks. *Loading...*, 10(16). Retrieved October 1, 2021, from http://journals.sfu.ca/loading/index.php/loading/article/view/169

Gee, J. P. (2003). What video games have to teach us about learning and literacy. *Computers in Entertainment*, 1(1), 1–4. doi.org/10.1145/950566.950595

Green, J. (2001, February). *Morrowind*: Bethesda readies its new *Elder Scrolls* RPG—finally. *Computer Gaming World*, 199, 52–54.

Italia, M. (2001, April 9). *General: Ted Peterson Interview I. The Unofficial Elder Scrolls Pages*. Retrieved October 4, 2021, from https://en.uesp.net/wiki/General:Ted_Peterson_Interview_I

Leack, J. (1996, November 5). *The Elder Scrolls II: Daggerfall Review. Game Revolution*. Retrieved October 4, 2021, from https://www.gamerevolution.com/review/33031-daggerfall-review

Miller, M. (2010, December 26). *Decrypting The Elder Scrolls. Game Informer*. Retrieved October 4, 2021, from https://www.gameinformer.com/b/features/archive/2010/12/26/decrypting-the-elder-scrolls.aspx

Peterson, T. (2019, April 19). *The Elder Scrolls at 25: How I Created Bethesda's Legendary RPG Series. Escapist Magazine*. Retrieved October 1, 2021, from https://www.escapistmagazine.com/the-elder-scrolls-at-25-how-i-created-bethesdas-legendary-rpg-series/

Plunkett, L. (2016, November 13). Old *Elder Scrolls* Game Takes over 60 Hours to Walk Across. *Kotaku*. Retrieved October 1, 2021, from https://kotaku.com/old-elder-scrolls-game-takes-over-60-hours-to-walk-acro-1788931074

Scorpia. (1996, December). Here at last, *Daggerfall* is a real, epic RPG of a lifetime. *Computer Gaming World*, 149, 281–293.

Tanenbaum, K., & Tanenbaum, J. (2009). Commitment to Meaning: A Reframing of Agency in Games. *eScholarship*. Retrieved October 4, 2021, from https://escholarship.org/uc/item/6f49r74n

The Elder Scrolls II: Daggerfall. (n.d.). *The Elder Scrolls Wiki*. Retrieved October 1, 2021, from https://elderscrolls.fandom.com/wiki/The_Elder_Scrolls_II:_Daggerfall

Waern, A. (2012). *Framing games. Proceedings of Nordic DiGRA. Nordic Digital Games Research Association*. Retrieved October 1, 2021, from http://www.digra.org/wp-content/uploads/digital-library/12168.20295.pdf

Ward, T. (1996, September 26). *Daggerfall Review. Gamespot*. Retrieved October 1, 2021, from https://www.gamespot.com/reviews/daggerfall-review/1900-2538495/

Further Reading

Piero, M., & Ouellette, M. (Eds). (2021). *Being dragonborn: Critical essays on The Elder Scrolls V: Skyrim*. Jefferson, MC: McFarland Press.

Voorhees, G. A., Call, J., & Whitlock, K. (Eds.). (2012). *Dungeons, dragons, and digital denizens: The digital role-playing game*. New York: Bloomsbury Publishing USA.

DOI: 10.4324/9781003199205-14

ELITE (1984)

Few games have had a greater impact than David Bell and Ian Braben's *Elite* (1984). Despite being launched on one of the less popular home computer platforms at the time, the educational BBC Micro Model B (and its smaller sibling, the Acorn Electron), it is easily the most influential game made for the home computer market from the early 1980s. At that time, the popular game genres were either text adventures, sometimes with simple still graphics, or 2D action games like *Donkey Kong* (Nintendo R&D1, 1981). *Elite* sold phenomenally well, despite its, for the time, high price tag of £15 or US $20 (around £50 or US $65 in 2020). It was later ported to a dozen other platforms, and was followed by eight sequels, the latest from 2021. The original box also broke new ground by including a print novella, *The Dark Wheel*, by the successful fantasy and science fiction author Robert Holdstock, thus making it the earliest example of a tie-in novelization.

In the novella, we follow Alex Ryder, a young space trader who survived the deadly attack on his father's merchant ship, and who eventually avenges his father through extraordinary natural-born skills as a space "combateer." *The Dark Wheel* is a competently written David/Goliath tale that portrays the game's world and gameplay in useful detail, providing an effective motivation and background, setting the atmosphere for the player. Novelizations of popular games and game series later became quite normal, but here, possibly for the first time, we observe two unusual aspects: a tie-in with the game box, and a launch text.

Gameplay Innovations

Elite features a classic rags-to-riches scenario, where the player starts out as the rookie pilot of a lightly armed space trader-fighter, the Cobra MK III. There is no Alex Ryder, instead, the player can assume the default name "Jameson" or replace it with any other name. Through successful trades, mining asteroids, or by looting other ships, the player earns enough money to enhance their ship with better equipment and stronger weaponry. Unlike somewhat similar-looking 3D space-action games, such as *Star Raiders* (Atari, 1979) or *Rescue on Fractalus* (Lucasfilm Games, 1984), *Elite* is set in a complex, large, open-world universe of eight galaxies with 256 planets each. The player can choose whether to be good or evil, pirate or law enforcer, miner, fighter, or trader. Or, more likely, most of the above. Bad behavior will be noted by the space authorities and attaining the status of "fugitive" will make travel in policed space, typically near the space stations, very difficult.

Elite also had far superior graphics to any other contemporary game on similarly priced platforms, with its vector graphics showing objects with increasingly more detail upon approach, compared to the typically crude, pixelated sprites at the time. The interface controls were especially complex, using virtually the entire keyboard for trade, navigation, or fighting. The world of the game is unusually detailed as well, with dozens of different ship models, space objects, and weapons, enabling numerous variations of strategy. An impressive innovation was the 3D radar display under the viewscreen, which allowed the player to determine enemy positions at any angle around the ship, instead of constantly and frantically swirling the ship or flipping between front, back, and side views during dogfights. This second perspective on the battlefield seats the experienced player in the ship and makes them the center of the action, rather than someone who is always trying to find where the action is, confused by the six directions of 3D navigation.

The Cruelest Game of the 80s?

For the novice, the game is punishingly hard. If the last decade has seen a rising popularity of abusively difficult games, fueled by the publication of *Dark Souls* (FromSoftware, 2011), a quick glance at the reception of *Elite* tells us that this is nothing new (Gazzard, 2013). I spent countless late hours in my bedroom trying to achieve "Elite" status, but gave up after many months of nightly space-action at "Deadly," the next highest level. The progress was simply too painfully slow.

Elite is cruelly difficult from the start. The first real challenge, for the initial generation of players who were not at all used to the freely rotational perspective of outer space, was to dock, manually, at the nearest Coriolis space station. There is a Coriolis station near every planet and, to progress and trade, one must first dock there. The station spins, so the player must align the spin of the ship with the spin of the station, while slowly approaching the docking opening at a straight 90° angle. Too fast or slow, and you crash. This is the first very frustrating test and, ironically, when players finally have mastered the art of docking, they typically also will have made enough money to buy a Docking Computer, thereby automating the process forever after. This must be one of the most no-brainer investments in all of game history and is certainly not an "interesting choice" in Sid Meier's sense of the phrase.

The creation of *Elite* also incarnates the classic inventor story, so common in computer history, of the two friends who start out in a garage, or a bedroom—or in this case, a dormitory in Jesus College,

Cambridge (Edge, 2003, p. 61)—and end up creating or revolutionizing a whole new market or product. Braben and Bell met at Cambridge University in 1983, and quickly found they had compatible interests in game design. By Fall of 1984, they had produced a working prototype of the game. This was first rejected by publishers, notably Thorn/EMI, as too complex and containing dubious content, such as the trading of narcotics. The fact that the in-game ethics also forbids this and will get the player a "fugitive" status seemed not to matter. Bell and Braben then pitched the game to Bell's previous publisher, Acornsoft, where the impressive programming and world-building was appreciated, probably because Acornsoft also developed its own games and software. Then, Acornsoft's business relationship with the BBC provided the cross-medial sensibility that led to the lavish paratextual marketing and wrapping. Here was indeed something special, and prepublication expectations were high.

What *Elite* did, in a miraculously small space of 32K memory, where one-third was used for the screen, was to create a deep, open, playable "world." *Elite* was a world, not a game. The game was up to the player.

What's so Special About *Elite*?

Elite's status as revolutionary and groundbreaking may not be obvious, especially in the hindsight of nearly forty years. Today, we have a much better overview of the history of the early home computer and arcade games than the game's contemporaries had. In the late 70s and early 80s, there were no Internet databases, search engines, or shared historical game resources, and there was no common, vernacular canon of great video games. Game platforms were expensive, and few young people (the main market) at the time could afford more than one platform, and so were locked in by their choice. And different game platforms dominated the different continents of Asia, Europe, and North America. Differences in voltage and TV-signal standards made imports impractical across continents. The most popular home computer in the USA in the early days of home computer gaming, the Apple II series, was mostly sold domestically, and in Europe, British machines dominated the market, although the Commodore 64 became a great transatlantic success, unlike the Apple II. Some of the print magazines and TV programs at the time would cover more than one platform, but game canons would develop around a specific platform, unless the games were ported to other machines, a much more difficult and expensive feat in an era that lacked today's cross-platform development tools. Thus, as Gazzard (2013) has pointed out in her excellent article on *Elite's* reception, awareness of important games and the development of a canon were local and platform dependent. In those days, a game could easily be considered groundbreaking and original by those who had access to it and other games from the same techno-culture, even if, unknown to them, other cultural platforms might have earlier games with the same features.

What, if anything, made *Elite* special? Other and earlier games had space travel and the trading motif, and others had first-person 3D space combat or a persistent and large, complex world, where the game state could be saved and reloaded later. But no earlier game had all of these. *Elite's* first-person exploration of a large universe and the freedom to decide one's moral orientation, and the nature of one's ambition, where to go and what to do there, were a powerful mix of game elements that had not been experienced together in earlier games. *Elite* demonstrated a state-of-the-art game-world representation, and a continuously progressive gameplay that could develop at the player's pace over days and months. And while the initial game platform, the BBC Model B, was quite expensive for a home computer (around €2000 or US$2250 in today's currency, with the Acorn Electron at half that), other platforms the game was later ported to were not.

Is It Possible Not to Canonize *Elite*?

Discussing what makes games great or important inevitably entails a glorifying rhetoric of firstness or uniqueness, which may lead to exaggerated or even false claims of grandeur and originality on the part of the discussed work, to justify its inclusion in a canon. Canons, whether vernacular or academic, are unavoidable and should always be treated with deep suspicion. But false or exaggerated claims about *Elite* reflect on the claimer, not on the game itself. The more notable the work, the more mythologized it will be. The one prior game that most resembles *Elite* is Doug Neubauer's *Star Raiders* (1979). Braben is often cited (e.g., Helion 2015) saying that he and Bell had not heard of that game, but it does have some very similar traits, like 3D first-person space battles, navigating by galactic charts and hyperdrive, and docking at space stations for repairs and refueling. However, *Star Raiders* lacks the progressive elements, trading, and the ability to get better equipment for your ship, and both games deserve to be recognized for their influential, innovative design and technology. Important milestones both, in the tradition that started with Russell et al.'s *Spacewar!* (1962).

Elite's legacy continues unabated today, both in the eponymous series still directed by Braben (after a famous falling out, Bell left the franchise before the publication of *Frontiers: Elite 2*) and through countless clones, derivatives, and innovative revisions, from *Wing Commander* (ORIGIN Systems, 1990), via EgoSoft's *X* series (1999–), to *No Man's Sky* (Hello Games, 2016) and *EVE Online* (CCP Games, 2003). Can *Elite*'s relative importance in this tradition somehow be assessed, or is that question merely naïve and incommensurate with a modern, historiographical approach? In the unavoidably glorifying spirit of canonization, I will attempt the contemptible, but with full subjectiveness and personal bias engaged: playing *Elite* in the year it was first published was a revelation only matched by two other peak game experiences—my first ever encounter with a video game, Taito's *Speed Race*, as an eight-year-old, in 1974, and the first time I played *DOOM* (id Software), in 1993. For different reasons, each of these experiences changed me, and while such anecdotal evidence is, of course, no evidence at all, or of anything, in the case of *Elite*, it was clear to me in 1984 that being perceptually and mentally seated in a virtual world, where one's actions had a lasting effect and there was a whole possibility space of strategic choices to explore, was more than a novelty, it was a new mode of play. Perhaps a game's importance can be measured simply by comparing its combination of achievements to those of the games that came before, and to those that come after. There is a steep rise to *Elite* from the earlier 3D and open-world games, and a much gentler inclination from *Elite* to its later incarnations and mutations. This relative difference between before and after, this standing out rather than "being first," is what characterizes *Elite*. Admittedly, this is a poor and probably useless method for measuring the importance of most games. But *Elite* is not most games.

Espen Aarseth

References

Edge (2003). Elite. *Edge presents: Retro. "The making of…" special*, 60–63.

Gazzard, A. (2013). The Platform and the Player: Exploring the (Hi)stories of *Elite*. *Game Studies, 13*(2). Retrieved November 27, 2021, from http://gamestudies.org/1302/articles/agazzard

Helion, M. (2015, February 13). The Elites: David Braben Talks *Elite: Dangerous* and Space Sims. *The Escapist*. Retrieved November 27, 2021, from https://www.escapistmagazine.com/the-elites-david-braben-talks-elite-dangerous-and-space-sims/

Further Reading

Bell, I. (2021). The Elite Home Page. Retrieved November 29, 2021, from http://www.iancgbell.clara.net/elite/

Braben, D. (2011). GDC Postmortems: Elite. Retrieved November 29, 2021, from https://www.gdcvault.com/play/1014628/Classic-Game-Postmortem

DOI: 10.4324/9781003199205-15

EVE ONLINE (2003)

EVE Online (EVE) is a space-themed massively multiplayer online game (MMOG) developed by CCP Games. Set in a speculative future where humanity has perfected long-range space travel, players pilot spaceships, mine for raw materials, manufacture items, and engage in combat throughout the single-shard universe of New Eden. A single-shard server means that players all connect to the same gameworld, the only exceptions being players located in China, who have a separate server to accommodate the country's firewall (Page, 2018). Subscriptions peaked at about 500,000 and, while these numbers have decreased in recent years, *EVE* has been lauded for its fiercely loyal fandom, many of whom have played since its initial release in 2003. While it never achieved tens of millions of subscribers like MMOG juggernaut *World of Warcraft* (Blizzard Entertainment, 2004), *EVE* is a "key game" because it breaks from conventions typically found elsewhere in the MMOG genre. However, this chapter also serves as a warning: an overemphasis on *EVE*'s uniqueness is used as a form of gatekeeping, creating a barrier to participation in this gameworld.

A Brief Introduction to *EVE Online*

Since its original launch, some elements of *EVE* have evolved dramatically, while others have hardly changed at all. Yet, *EVE* today is not the same game that was released almost two decades ago. As a MMOG, it follows the typical pattern of regular updates to add new features, patch bugs, and it continues to unfurl a loose narrative that serves as an optional backdrop to *EVE*'s gameplay. Players require an active Internet connection and a fairly good computer to run the game software. In its early days, *EVE*'s software was installed via a CD-ROM, but now the game client is downloaded from the developer's website. While a credit card was previously required for a subscription, the developer began offering a free-to-play option in 2016. These are all fairly consistent with the evolving MMOG genre; nothing about these features makes *EVE* particularly unique.

Where *EVE* begins to break from other MMOGs is with humanoid avatars (or, in *EVE's* case, the relative lack thereof). It is notable that there is a robust full-body avatar creation tool that allows customization of a highly realistic human avatar—one that is far more customizable and realistic than allowed by the avatar creation tools found in comparable games (McArthur, 2019)—but it is only really visible in a player's personal, private quarters. Only a small passport-style photo of this avatar is shown to others; a player's primary in-game representation is their ship. Unlike other MMOGs, where avatars remain cosmetically consistent (perhaps changing their armor or their avatar's hairstyle), ships in *EVE* are frequently discarded as a player acquires upgraded equipment, or they can be destroyed in combat against non-player characters (NPCs) or other players.

When we talk about other ways that EVE is unique, the game's economy (and CCP's hiring of an economist to oversee it) is often flagged as being a departure from MMOG genre conventions. In-game goods and currency are generated almost exclusively via player actions—players must mine the raw materials that are essential to all other components of the game. Those who collect raw materials or manufacture items can sell them to NPCs in space stations, or list them for sale for other players to purchase in the marketplace. Buyers can purchase goods directly, or post contracts where they indicate what materials they would like to purchase and set the price they are willing to pay.

In addition to the resource acquisition and manufacturing elements of gameplay, there is also a robust player versus player (PVP) system in place. To summarize briefly, there are some areas of New Eden (high-sec) that are under the protection of NPC police (known as CONCORD) who will target players that attempt to attack a fellow player. However, much of the gameworld is classified as null-sec, where no NPCs will come to save you, even if you are ambushed. The stakes of *EVE* are particularly high, as the gameworld employs a "permadeath" mechanic—if a player's ship is destroyed in combat, everything they were carrying is lost. If their escape pod is destroyed, they must start over again with a clone. These high stakes have led to *EVE*'s reputation for being less than welcoming to newcomers (Paul, 2016) and only recently has CCP overhauled the new player tutorial to make it friendlier to novice players. It remains to be seen if these changes will provide inroads for new demographics to join an otherwise difficult to access inner player community. Those who do make it through the "learning cliff" of *EVE* tend to do so because they quickly found a support network, such as joining a temporary group (fleets) or becoming a member of a corporation (*EVE*'s term for guild). Corporations can band together into larger Alliances, which in turn allows groups of players to claim and defend their dominion over wide swaths of New Eden.

Finally, real money trading is typically considered by most MMOG developers to be a black or gray market practice. *EVE* offers its players a roundabout way to exchange in-game currency (Interstellar Kredits, shortened to ISK) to real-world dollars. While ISK cannot be purchased directly, it *can* be converted to a Pilot License Extension (PLEX), a form of in-game currency that can be bought and sold for US dollars. This in turn creates an "exchange rate," allowing for the astronomically high costs of *EVE*'s PVP wars to be calculated, which tends to be a focal point when non-players discuss *EVE*. For example, the mainstream press reported on the "bloodbath" of B-R5RB because the destruction cost 11 trillion ISK, which converts to roughly $300,000 USD (Taylor et al., 2015). These exceptionally large battles (and their associated costs) is something that *EVE* has become particularly well-known for, and indeed is one of the primary reasons the game receives press coverage (Bergstrom, 2019a).

CCP's approach to avatars and their game's economy makes *EVE* slightly different from other MMOGs. I now turn my attention to EVE's most unique feature: being a sandbox-style game. This structure has allowed for interesting emergent play practices. However, I urge caution if this is presented as the *only* reason *EVE* is a key game. It is my argument both here and throughout my writing about this game that an overemphasis on what makes *EVE* special can act as a form of gatekeeping.

The Unregulated Sandbox

In the context of MMOGs, sandbox-style games are generally understood to offer a degree of player agency not found in other genres; sandbox games allow players to determine their activities in a relatively open gameworld. The term sandbox is typically used in opposition to "theme park" style games where the player experience is on rails, encountering content in a sequence pre-determined by the developer. Content in other games might take the form of quests or dungeons, which reward experience points used to "level up" an avatar to a level cap, which then allows players to engage in "end game" encounters. In *EVE*, there is nothing that is considered typical of a MMOG end game (e.g., high-level dungeons);, instead, long-term *EVE* players spend their time creatively pushing the game's affordances to their limits.

Since its release, CCP has remained hands-off from *EVE*'s gameworld, only intervening in extreme situations. Scams, cheating, griefing, or other forms of dark play (Carter, 2015) may result in a player being banned in other games, but not in *EVE*. It is a space for deviant leisure, a place for players to push the boundaries of "acceptable" behavior that would result in punishment or outright bans in other, more regulated gaming environments (Bergstrom, 2020; Taylor et al., 2015). Deviant leisure is defined as "behavior that violates criminal and non-criminal moral norms" (Williams, 2009, p. 208) and the experiences relayed to me by *EVE* players frequently meet that definition (Bergstrom, 2020).

In other games, such as *World of Warcraft*, players can opt to play on a server that best fits their preferred style of gameplay (Billieux et al., 2013). Players who wish to opt-in to a gameplay experience where PVP is prevalent will create their avatar on a designated PVP server. Players who wish to be left in peace while they adventure may opt for a non-PVP or perhaps even a role-play server. Players who purposefully engage in PVP in areas not specifically designated for PVP are understood to have violated the norms of *World of Warcraft* and will be punished—PVP is something that must be consented to. This is not the case for *EVE*. Instead, the idea of "non-consensual PVP" is an emergent sandbox behavior that has come to be accepted by a vocal segment of *EVE*'s player community. Players who would otherwise decline to participate in PVP (e.g., people who prefer to play *EVE* as a resource acquisition or manufacturing game), are eventually goaded into PVP by players who view combat as the "correct" way to play *EVE*. One such example of disciplining non-conforming players was an annual event known as Hulkageddon, where bounties were put on the heads of *EVE*'s miners and their ships were destroyed for sport (Bergstrom, 2019b). None of this was against the game's terms of service, nor did CCP step in to stop these attacks that effectively prevented some members of the *EVE* community from playing according to their preferences. This disruption was so severe that some of my informants reported just not logging into the game during Hulkageddon. This antagonism inspired some players to refit their ships with weapons and fight back in their own event known as Griefergeddon. While Griefergeddon was short-lived and never had the same level of participation as Hulkageddon, the result was what the original antagonists wanted: miners picked up their weapons and engaged in combat, conforming to this more vocal group's view of the "correct" way to play *EVE*. To be clear: while *EVE* may be marketed as a sandbox, the reality is that not all players are completely free to play the way they *want* to play.

The Danger of a Single Story

EVE is not a game that easily lends itself to dabbling. Most MMOGs have a robust new player onboarding system where the user is given the skills they need to succeed in the gameworld. *EVE*, at least prior to the new tutorial revamp, throws players right into the deep end with no life raft (Paul, 2016). The difficulty and time required to obtain an "insider" view of *EVE* has led to its reputation of being a hostile and unwelcoming gameworld. Indeed, much of what is written about by journalists (both by the games enthusiast press and in more mainstream outlets), as well as early academic writing about the game, emphasized the destructive battles or the ethical/norms violations that are present in this gameworld (Bergstrom, 2019a). These scandalous stories circulate more readily as they make for interesting reporting that is easily understood by non-players. A second generation of *EVE*-scholarship, drawing on participant observation and in-depth interviews with current and former players, reveals the hidden-in-plain-sight alternative ways of playing *EVE*, such as robust role-play communities or the pacifists who avoid combat entirely (Carter et al., 2016).

Despite a growing understanding of the diversity of play that occurs in and around *EVE*'s gameworld, the game continues to be framed as an edge-case that departs from expected MMOG norms and conventions. Throughout my decade of research about this game, I have argued such reporting is problematic as it is frequently the *only* public-facing narrative about *EVE*. Helping to reinforce the belief that the game is special or unique acts as a form of gatekeeping, creating a public-facing narrative that *EVE* is not a game "for" the average player interested in MMOGs. My research on *EVE*'s former and non-players has found they opt out because these public conversations work to reinforce a false idea that it is too difficult, too cutthroat, or too time-consuming for all but the most dedicated players. There is a danger in perpetuating a single story about *EVE*—or any of the games in this book. Players who would enjoy *EVE*'s many non-PVP communities (e.g., role-play, resource gathering, etc.) will never find it if the only narrative we share about *EVE* is that it is an unforgiving PVP sandbox MMOG.

Kelly Bergstrom

References

Bergstrom, K. (2019a). *EVE Online* is not for everyone: Exceptionalism in online gaming cultures. *Human Technology, 15*(3), 304–325.

Bergstrom, K. (2019b). *EVE Online*. In M. T. Payne & N. Huntemann (Eds), *How to play video games* (pp. 301–308). New York: NYU Press.

Bergstrom, K. (2020). Destruction as deviant leisure in *EVE Online*. *Journal of Virtual Worlds Research, 13*(1), 1–10.

Carter, M., Bergstrom, K., & Woodford, D. (Eds). (2016). *Internet spaceships are serious business: An EVE Online reader*. Minneapolis: University of Minnesota Press.

Billieux, J., Van der Linden, M., Achab, S., Khazaal, Y., Paraskevopoulos, L., Zullino, D., & Thorens, G. (2013). Why do you play World of Warcraft? An in-depth exploration of self-reported motivations to play online and in-game behaviours in the virtual world of Azeroth. *Computers in Human Behavior, 29*(1), 103–109.

Carter, M. (2015). Massively multiplayer dark play: Treacherous play in *EVE Online*. In T. E. Mortensen, J. Linderoth, & A. M. L. Brown (Eds), *The dark side of game play: Controversial issues in playful environments* (pp. 191–209). New York: Routledge.

McArthur, V. (2019). Making ourselves visible: Mobilizing micro-autoethnography in the study of self-representation and interface affordances. *Loading: The Journal of the Canadian Game Studies Association, 12*(19), 27–42.

Page, R. (2018). To win at life: Tradition and Chinese modernities in *EVE Online*. *Journal of Virtual Worlds Research, 10*(3), 1–10.

Paul, C. A. (2016). *EVE Online* is hard and it matters. In M. Carter, K. Bergstrom, & D. Woodford, *Internet spaceships are serious business: An EVE Online reader* (pp. 17–30). University of Minnesota Press.

Taylor, N., Bergstrom, K., Jenson, J., & de Castell, S. (2015). Alienated Playbour: Relations of Production in *EVE Online*. *Games and Culture, 10*(4), 365–388.

Williams, D. (2009). Deviant leisure: Rethinking "The Good, the Bad, and the Ugly." *Leisure Sciences, 31*(2), 207–213.

Further Reading

Groen, A. (2016). *Empires of EVE: A history of the great wars of EVE Online*. Chicago: Lightburn Industries.

DOI: 10.4324/9781003199205-16

FARMVILLE (2009)

FarmVille (Zynga) was first launched on Facebook in June 2009. That same year saw the release of games like *Flower* (Thatgamecompany), *BRAID* (Number None), *Wii Sports* (Nintendo), *Uncharted 2: Among Thieves* (Naughty Dog), *League of Legends* (Riot Games), and *Call of Duty: Modern Warfare 2* (Infinity Ward). While the other titles can be found named among the top games of the year, *FarmVille*'s reputation is arguably less flattering. Instead of considering the game on a par with Triple-A titles, *FarmVille* is perhaps better compared to other casual games, such as *Angry Birds* (Rovio Entertainment) and *Plants vs. Zombies* (PopCap Games), that were also released in 2009. However, beyond being a casual game among others, *FarmVille* gained strong criticism for its business model and "dark" design patterns (Tanz, 2011; Karlsen, 2019). It was even named one of "The 50 Worst Inventions"—together with the insecticide DDT and asbestos—by *Time* magazine (Fletcher, 2010). The "poisonous" invention in *FarmVille* was the expectation of repetitive, daily maintenance on the farms players had first created.

Over the years, *FarmVille* evolved with its players—the emerging group of casual gamers—with Facebook as its notorious platform, and with the genre of social network casual games that it came to shape. Many of us only learned the microskill of turning off Facebook notifications because of *FarmVille*, and games researchers, together with the industry, were forced to adjust the definitions of in-game purchases, in-game advertising, and incremental games because of it.

FarmVille was closed at the end of December 2020. Notwithstanding its continuing popularity, the enabling technology, Adobe's Flash player, faced technological obsolescence and *FarmVille* was entombed with it. This means that *FarmVille* remained active on Facebook for eleven years (including two years of beta, as will be explained further). There's *FarmVille 2* (Zynga, 2014), of course, and *FarmVille 3* (Zynga, 2021), launched on November 4, 2021 (Business Wire, 2021). But this chapter focuses primarily on the first, original game and explains why and how it has earned its place in the history of games, and on the legacy of *FarmVille* in the video game industry, culture, academia, and design. Regardless of the raging criticism the game received, *FarmVille*, as operated by the developer Zynga, shaped the game industry and culture alike.

Social Gaming on Social Networks

FarmVille would not exist without Facebook as a base platform. Its methods of user acquisition and user retention, as well as features of actual gameplay, were all tightly built on Facebook's existing social functions. Notoriously, players would contribute to the introduction of new players by leveraging their friendships on Facebook, and seek to support their game progress by invitations posted on Facebook timelines. This resulted in a flood of unwanted notifications on people's Facebook accounts and became a meme that has already outlived the game itself.

As the player endlessly improves their farm estate with money earned from selling produce from crops and livestock, they accept farmer friendships to complete individual tasks on each other's farms, which also results in continuous comparisons of progress and achievements between co-players. The breadth of one's social network on Facebook would then potentially influence the player's progress in the game. Mary Flanagan and Helen Nissenbaum suggest that while the game "relies on community, trust, and friendship" it also "involves the exploitation of these values, and this exploitation often negates the positive values" (2014, p. 28). A prompt to rescue dying crops on an offline friend's farm, for example, encourages empathy, but the effortless incorporation of friends' time, effort, and goodwill into one's own farm assumes a built-in value according to which "friends are cultivated as easily as the corn" (2014, p. 29).

As one of the first major games on Facebook, *FarmVille* was among the platform's longest-lasting and top-grossing games. In the developer Zynga's portfolio, it was followed by numerous games designed for the platform and the companies had a long-lasting partnership. Tellingly, Zynga entered the public stock market in December 2011, followed by Facebook only six months later. The mutually beneficial relationship brought Facebook thirty percent of Zynga's sales on the platform, while ninety percent of Zynga's revenue came in through Facebook (MacMillan, 2012). Both *FarmVille*, and its successor *CityVille*, had surpassed 80 million players at the time, making them important contributors to Facebook's revenue in 2011, as twelve percent of it came from Zynga (Raice, 2012). It is therefore fair to acknowledge that the early success of the two companies was reliant on each other and that *FarmVille* had a role in making Facebook the giant it is today.

New Models of Monetization, Game Analytics

Two aspects that made *FarmVille* immensely successful as well as profitable—a free-to-play (F2P) business model and the use of game analytics in development and marketing—were meaningfully connected in the game. Like many games today, *FarmVille* allowed a smooth, free start for a player yet asked for personal information and rights to use game data in return. *FarmVille* was one of the key games in the beginning of the F2P business model and, according to Matthew A Chew, "the game that marked the opening up of the trend toward f2p in the USA" (Chew, 2016, p. 230). Microtransactions allowed players small benefits in the game and offered the possibility of purchasing items that seemed otherwise unreachable.

Since it was a social network game, *FarmVille*'s developers were able to learn about players' behavior through the user data provided by Facebook. The game remained in an unfinished development state—beta—for nearly two years, allowing constant and often sudden changes to various aspects, regardless of players' ability to make real money purchases in the game. While this may have been for the benefit of the players, player data was collected for various purposes, often not transparent to the players themselves. Michele Willson and Tama Leaver (2015) criticize how *FarmVille*'s data mining brought Zynga significant revenue in the form of in-game microtransactions, though users rarely understood what they had signed up for. *FarmVille*'s connectedness with Facebook secured the developers a wide understanding of the use patterns and preferences of players, together with information from their personal Facebook profiles.

Such business intelligence—game analytics—has grown into a major domain of video game development in the past decade, but *FarmVille* was, again, among the first ones to adopt related practices. According to Magy Seif Al-Nasr and Alessandro Canossa, "Zynga has been on the forefront of using and establishing game analytics techniques both as a method to enhance the user experience and the design of games and as a business model to increase profit and make more successful games" (2013, p. 73).

Constant Care and Attention

But who were the players of such a carefully calculated game and why does the theme of the game matter? If anything, the above-mentioned negative meme of *FarmVille* requests being received from acquaintances and distant relatives reveals something about the era in video gaming that prevailed during the game's early years. Jesper Juul (2010) discusses and rightly contests the stereotypical player type who, at the time, was considered "casual". Casual games and casual players were often attacked by self-identified "gamers," whose knowledge in the areas of game history, game types, and game cultural conventions greatly surpassed that of the assumed casual player. The identity of a casual player was considered feminine and farm simulations were commonly seen as a women's genre (Kowert, Breuer, & Quandt, 2017).

If *FarmVille* has its place in the history of games that have been particularly popular among female players, it is not least because the game brought together the themes of caring and domesticity (Wirman, 2011), the ease of access for non-players, and the non-criticality of play time and length that attract more female players into games

(Kowert, Breuer, & Quandt 2017). We can therefore identify a sexist undertone in the hatred toward *FarmVille*—one that goes beyond the game's design and exploitative F2P monetization; one that was fueled by a need to gatekeep games from people who were not seen as players in the traditional sense. Here, then, *FarmVille* has a place in the power struggles that led to the "Gamergate controversy" (e.g. Chess & Shaw, 2015) and questioned what counts as a game and who counts as a player.

Eco-Criticism of Farming Simulations

In *FarmVille*, as in most farm simulation games, the daily grind of completing tasks is made to match the simulation of an increasingly factory-like farm with animals and plants. In such a game, livestock and crops are reduced to sources of income and, eventually, contribute toward in-game profit, game progress, and bettering of the player's status among co-players. *FarmVille* can be seen as a simulation of capitalism that exploits natural resources for the sake of accumulating more profit (Cole & Stewart, 2017). It commodifies nature and contributes to "cultural legitimation of nonhuman animal exploitation through establishing emotional connections with idealized representations of nonhuman animals at the same time as they inhibit the development of awareness and empathy about the exploitation of real nonhuman animals" (Flanagan & Nissenbaum, 2014, p. 402). Among other aspects, animal suffering and simulations of animals' actual life cycles are excluded from the game.

Alenda Chang has scrutinized how farming games, and *FarmVille* in particular, combine the pastoral ideal of idyllic rural life with high technology and industrial capitalism within and outside of the game. Paying attention to animal and human labor and to the specific context of North American agricultural tradition, she suggests that "just as farm games overlook the politically unpalatable realities of exploited and historically excluded agricultural workers, they also turn a blind eye to nonhuman labor and the equally unpalatable ecological realities of industrial waste, entropy, and resource limitation" (2012, p. 8). The intrinsic values of farming simulations are rarely questioned by players, possibly because they are based on common tropes familiar from other forms of entertainment and popular culture, and possibly because they are easily accepted as established genre conventions. *FarmVille* is neither the first nor the last farming simulation but, because of its popularity, it encouraged more similar games to the market and contributed to the longevity and stability of farming simulation games and their associated ideology.

What is Left of *FarmVille*?

FarmVille came out during a transitional moment in game development and game cultures when traditional platforms were facing a loss of players and casual (social) play gained a victory. At the same time, traditional game monetization models were challenged by F2P and microtransactions. From a player's point of view, a very different set of games and norms in game cultures were present in 2009 than at the time of *FarmVille*'s closure in 2020. *FarmVille* had a part in these changes. It was among the first games to show us, through the unique albeit annoying linkages to Facebook walls, that players are everywhere and anyone can be a player. It had a unique role in normalizing play and playerhood and in making casual play a thing to take seriously.

Hanna Wirman

References

Business Wire. (2021, 6 October). Zynga Opens Pre-Registration for FarmVille 3 Ahead of November 4, 2021 Launch. *Business Wire*. Retrieved October 25, 2021, from https://www.businesswire.com/news/home/20211006005037/en/Zynga-Opens-Pre-Registration-for-FarmVille-3-Ahead-of-November-4-2021-Launch

Chang, A. (2012). Back to the virtual farm: Gleaning the agriculture-management game. *Interdisciplinary Studies in Literature and Environment*, 19(2), 237–252.

Chess, S., & Shaw, A. (2015). A conspiracy of fishes, or, how we learned to stop worrying about #GamerGate and embrace hegemonic masculinity. *Journal of Broadcasting & Electronic Media*, 59(1), 208–220.

Chew, M.M. (2016). Contested reception of the free-to-play business model in the North American video game market. In A. Fung (Eds), *Global game industries and cultural policy* (pp. 227–252). Cham, Switzerland: Palgrave Macmillan.

Cole, M., & Stewart, K. (2017). 'A new life in the countryside awaits': interactive lessons in the rural utopia in 'farming' simulation games. *Discourse: Studies in the Cultural Politics of Education*, 38(3), 402–415.

Flanagan, M., & Nissenbaum, H. (2014). *Values at play in digital games*. Cambridge, MA: MIT Press.

Fletcher, D. (2010). The 50 Worst Inventions. *TIME*. Retrieved August 23, 2021, from http://content.time.com/time/specials/packages/article/0,28804,1991915_1991909_1991768,00.html

Juul, J. (2010). *A casual revolution: reinventing video games and their players*. Cambridge, MA: MIT Press.

MacMillan, D. (2012, 22 April). Zynga and Facebook. It's Complicated. *Bloomberg*. Retrieved August 23, 2021, from https://www.bloomberg.com/news/articles/2010-04-22/zynga-and-facebook-dot-its-complicated

Karlsen, F. (2019). Exploited or engaged? Dark game design patterns in *Clicker Heroes*, *FarmVille 2*, and *World of Warcraft*. In K. Jørgensen & F. Karlsen (Eds), *Transgression in games and play*, 219–234. Cambridge, MA: MIT Press.

Kowert, R., Breuer, J., & Quandt, T. (2017). Women are from FarmVille, men are from ViceCity. The cycle of exclusion and sexism in video game content and culture. In R. Kowert & T. Quandt (Eds), *New perspectives on the social aspects of digital gaming. Multiplayer 2* (pp. 136–150). New York and Oxon: Routledge.

Raice, S. (2012, February 2). Facebook and Zynga: Sharing Riches isn't Always Easy. *The Wall Street Journal*. Retrieved August 23, 2021, from https://www.wsj.com/articles/SB10001424052970204662204577199403545189294

Seif El-Nasr, M. and Canossa, A. (2013). Chapter 5: Interview with Jim Baer and Daniel McCaffrey from Zynga. In M. Seif El-Nasr et al. (Eds), *Game analytics: maximizing the value of player data*, 73–82. London: SpringerVerlag.

Tanz, J. (2011, 20 December). The Curse of Cow Clicker: How a Cheeky Satire Became a Videogame Hit. *WIRED*. 2011. Retrieved August 23, 2021, from https://www.wired.com/2011/12/ff-cowclicker/

Willson, M. and Leaver, T. (2015). Zynga's FarmVille, social games, and the ethics of big data mining. *Communication Research and Practice*, 1(2), 147–158.

Wirman, H. (2011). Playing The Sims 2: Constructing and negotiating woman computer game player identities through the practice of skinning. PhD dissertation.

Further Reading

Kuittinen, J., Kultima, A., Niemelä, J. and Paavilainen, J. (2007). Casual games discussion. In *Proceedings of the 2007 conference on Future Play (Future Play '07)*. Association for Computing Machinery, New York, NY, 105–112. doi.org/10.1145/1328202.1328221

Vanderhoef, J. (2013, June). Casual threats: The feminization of casual video games. *Ada: A Journal of Gender, New Media, and Technology*, (2). Retrieved October 25, 2021, from https://adanewmedia.org/2013/06/issue2-vanderhoef/

DOI: 10.4324/9781003199205-17

FIFA 14 (2013)

It comes as no surprise that a sport as widely televised, watched, and played in the world as soccer played a meaningful role in the development and further popularization of video gaming. While David J Leonard's claim that "(t)he sports gaming industry is the crown jewel of the video games world" (2005, 110) remains contestable, digital sports games certainly mark a cornerstone within the video games industry, gaming practice and fandom, and—more recently—within the growing field of so-called e-sports. Along with the more obvious examples of "Games of Empire" (Dyer-Witheford & de Peuter, 2009), soccer video games have become a staple of global media cultures and the global capitalism these media are entangled with. Within these media cultures, sports video games in general, and soccer video games specifically, have a long history. As soon as programmers could program code to simulate a complex set of rules and some graphic elements to move across a playing field representing a soccer pitch, digital soccer games became available for almost any of the early video game consoles and computers.

Soccer Video Games before *FIFA 14*

In 1993, one year before the FIFA World Cup in the United States, Electronic Arts published *FIFA International Soccer*, the first game in the *FIFA* series. In 1994, Japanese publisher Konami released a soccer game, *International Superstar Soccer*, for the Super Nintendo Entertainment System that would provide the foundation for the *International Superstar Soccer* (*ISS*) franchise, which itself was revamped as *Pro Evolution Soccer* in Europe and *Winning Eleven* in North America, starting with the sixth console generation. For more than twenty-five years, Konami and EA have battled for the respect and attention of digital soccer fans across the globe with FIFA shattering its competition in terms of sales and overall popularity. By May 2021, the latest installment at the time, *FIFA 21* (2020) had sold more than 25 million copies worldwide, according to EA's earnings report (Minotti, 2021).

As holds true for a number of digital sports games, the *FIFA* series features a decisive effort to recreate the televised live event of the respective sport across its off-line and online modes, on at least three levels: first, on the level of graphics and visuals, starting with the televisual logics of the camera as the organizing principle of the games' aesthetics, to the motion-capture of key players (and the atmosphere of a live event filmed in a stadium); second, on the level of licenses, not only including original team and player names, pre-ranked by the producers in accordance with their collective and individual levels of skill, but also featuring the voices and commentary of broadcasting personnel of the TV stations televising the real-life leagues and competitions featured in the games; third, on the level of the assumed realism of the gameplay and the overall physical reality of the video game version of the soccer game at hand. Naturally, as TV productions of live sporting events have evolved, especially in relation to camera angles, commentary, and the use of second screens, so has the aesthetics of soccer video games changed with regard to game modes, camera angles, commentary, and more. For example, recent installments of the *FIFA* series have premiered, among other features: an inclusion of female soccer teams; a narrative (or story) mode entitled *The Journey*, which allows players to customize an avatar/hero called Alex Hunter and simulate his career in the English Premier League; and a new game engine called Frostbite 3. However, it was arguably the game that first featured the previous game engine, Ignite, that stands out as the most balanced soccer game of the series: *FIFA 14*.

Seasonal Seriality and *FIFA 14*

Released in November 2013, *FIFA 14* not only featured the Ignite engine, it was also the first game of the franchise to be released for the eighth console generation, most prominent among them being the PlayStation 4 and the Xbox One consoles. This double transition from older to new systems and new game engines always provides a simultaneous challenge and opportunity for game developers of serial games. The seasonal seriality of many sports game franchises poses an additional challenge to their development, as they need to align themselves—for marketing and sales purposes—with the seasonal logics of the sports they bring to the digital devices. In any given year, serial franchise games thus face considerable pressure to be released during a specific time of the year (in the late summer/early fall for soccer and American football games).

Shane Denson and Andreas Sudmann have carefully analyzed the multiple ways processes of serialization inform and make video games that go beyond the obvious kind of franchise serialization outlined above in my history of the digital soccer game. Even though to them, "[t]he history of digital games is above all a history of popular series: it is the story of countless sequels, prequels, remakes, hacks, mods, copies, updates, and franchises," the individual games themselves have been serial at least since they "had begun introducing the mechanism of save points, thus ordering gameplay itself as an episodically segmented but continuing serial activity" (2017, p. 262). Consequently, to Denson and Sudmann, gaming as practice becomes decisively serial, adding to the narrative logic of games in their deployment of levels and the serialized logic of gaming industry production in installments or series.

Digital sports games produce a specific, seasonal form of seriality. This also holds true for the *FIFA* series and *FIFA 14* is no exception. Structurally, the season informs digital soccer games in three interrelated, yet slightly distinct ways: first, in that the release of digital soccer games happens annually in the fall season; second, which—of course—corresponds with the seasonal logics of the real-life sports in the Northern hemisphere; and third, the intradiegetic season marks a crucial and distinctive formal feature of the "narrative" of digital sports gaming, resembling the save point or the level as ordering principles of the gaming experience, while maintaining its own distinct quality. *FIFA 14*'s two most prominent modes, the career mode and FIFA Ultimate Team (FUT), are premised on seasons as a structuring principle. While this was not new at the time, nor was it unique to *FIFA*, the introduction of ten divisions to FUT increased the significance of the season for players taking part in the mode.[1]

The annual release of the installments of the games adheres to the seasonal logics of the real-life sports. This is why, after all, the installments typically feature the year of the season they are released in correspondence with as part of their title. *FIFA 14* was released in 2013 but for the 2014 season. For players then, the seasonal logics are equally relevant, with fall and winter featuring the release of the new games. Additionally, with trading and transfer windows closing in late summer in most professional soccer leagues (at least in Europe), the games almost have to follow a similar rhythm of release. As a consequence, the discussions and speculations among users about upcoming installments of the respective franchise naturally intensify in the weeks before the release, which puts these discussions in sync with the flow of news pertaining to the real-life pre-season period, which is marked by transfer rumors and the general murmurs regarding strengths and weaknesses of teams in the upcoming season (cf. Buehler, 2018, pp. 4–5). Not surprisingly then, a new season of a digital sports game, coinciding with an altogether new generation of gaming consoles and the implementation of new gaming engines, always adds to the anticipation and expectations among fans of digital gaming franchises; and *FIFA 14* lived up to the hype. While the game only mildly adjusted its major modes, it fully utilized the next-gen moment that coincided with the anticipation of the 2014 FIFA World Cup to happen in Brazil in the summer. The larger technological transitions, more often than not, provide ample opportunity for what has been deemed "failing forward" for many digital sports game franchises. Here, *FIFA 14* arguably marks a laudable exception to the rule. Indeed, it delivered in terms of gameplay and graphics, and utilized the then-new affordances of the consoles of the eighth generation and the new engine. The graphics were critically enhanced and the grass on the pitch and the training ground, for example, looked refined and much more detailed than in previous installments. What really stood out to players, however, was the way the game played in this new enhanced graphical setting. The gameplay in *FIFA 14* was improved in two ways: on the level of the collective/general and of the individual/skill.

Playing *FIFA 14*

Two general features were heavily marketed by EA, the shooting system and what the marketing team referred to as the "protect the ball" feature. While the shooting system is regularly overhauled from one installment to the next, the "protect the ball" feature was intended to provide players with a better sense of controlling the speed of the overall game (i.e., the way in which the on-screen midfield players could speed-up or slow-down the buildup of their attacks). The individual level featured the improvement of special skill moves, not only in terms of how and when to perform them, but also with regard to their respective usefulness. While the allure of serial development might be to steadily increase the efficiency of individual skill moves, *FIFA 14* actually decreased the frequency and efficiency of the so-called scoop turn. In *FIFA 13*, the scoop turn provided the most powerful skill to dribble past players, especially when performed at full speed. *FIFA 14*—much in line with how the move is performed in real-life soccer—disabled the scoop turn in full sprint, which accomplished two things: the scoop would now be more measurably deployed and at slower dribble speed which, consequently, increased the sense of realism of the move itself and the overall gaming experience.[2]

As mentioned, the game received mostly positive reviews from critics and fans alike, and the general consensus was that the game marked a crucial step toward a more realistic simulation of a professional soccer experience, while not giving up on its playability.[3] *FIFA 14* included an impressive number of licenses for original team and player names, as it also continued previous installments' aspiration to capture the excitement of soccer as broadcast on TV. As holds true for the fierce competition regarding the rights to broadcast certain sports competitions nationally and globally, the number of licenses in digital sports games depends mostly on the economic prowess and business strategy of the producers of digital games; here, *FIFA 14* and EA once again outperformed Konami, with more than "30 leagues, 600 teams, and 16,000 players".[4]

As a central element for gamers to experience the realism of a digital sports game, the licensing of leagues, teams, and players marks a cornerstone for digital sports games and has certainly contributed immensely to the success of the *FIFA* franchise. Konami's *PES* franchise, for example, has never featured a version of the German Bundesliga nor a fully licensed English Premier League, two of the major professional leagues in soccer, and two important marketplaces for digital soccer gaming (in Europe). While the question of licenses remains crucial for gamers playing digital sports games, gameplay and the overall physical reality of the games remains a more contested issue in discussions online (and equally significant to the perceived realism of the games); as a consequence, EA and their competitors have placed great emphasis on the tangible physical realness of the recent installments of their digital sports games.

In addition to new graphics and (some) new licenses, *FIFA 14* struck a careful balance with regard to innovation and continuity in terms of its gameplay, even though it was built with a new engine. This, arguably, made the game such a critical success; the transition to a new system and engine increased the visual realism, while the gameplay still resembled that of earlier installments and thus allowed players to adapt easily to new graphical and atmospheric environments. Of course, even *FIFA 14* could not satisfy each and every digital soccer aficionado, especially because the franchise's games typically invite gamers to master dribbling in general and special moves in particular. While these serve as crucial elements in the history of video games, they arguably take away from the game's aspiration to simulate the real-life sporting event, which has become extremely passing-based and immensely tactical in the past twenty years (or so). Still, with *FIFA 22* on the horizon at the time of writing, *FIFA 14* provides EA Sports with a great example of a successful transition to next-gen technology and it thus deservedly holds a place in the hall of fame of great digital sports games.

Martin Lüthe

Notes

1. https://fifauteam.com/year-by-year-history-fifa-ultimate-team/
2. https://www.youtube.com/watch?v=D_SeaCrdjL8
3. On metacritic.com the PlayStation 4 version of the game has scored considerably higher with critics (87) than with players (6.3). Not to dismiss the latter, but reviews by users are decisively more heterogeneous and players tend to respond to very specific concerns more dramatically than critics. (https://www.metacritic.com/game/playstation-4/fifa-14).
4. https://www.ea.com/de-de/games/fifa/fifa-14.

References

Buehler, B. (2018). White-Collar play: Reassessing managerial sports games. *Velvet Light Trap*, 81, 4–17.
Denson, S., & Sudmann, A. (2017). Digital seriality: On the aesthetics and practice of digital games. In F. Kelleter (Eds), *Media of serial narrative*. (pp. 261–283). Columbus: Ohio State UP.
Dyer-Witheford, N. & de Peuter, G. (2009). *Games of empire: Global capitalism and video games*. Minneapolis: University of Minnesota Press.
Leonard, D. J. (2005). To the white extreme: Conquering athletic space, white manhood, and racing virtual reality. In: N. Garrelt (Eds), *Digital gameplay. Essays on the nexus of game and gamer*. (pp. 110–128). Jefferson, NC: McFarland.
Metacritic. FIFA 14. *Metacritic.com*. Retrieved September 20, 2021 from https://www.metacritic.com/game/playstation-4/fifa-14
Minotti, Mike (May 11, 2021). FIFA 21 has Attracted over 25 Million Players, Ultimate Team up 16%. *VentureBeat*. Retrieved September 20, 2021, from https://venturebeat.com/2021/05/11/fifa-21-has-attracted-over-25-million-players-ultimate-team-up-16

Further Reading

Baerg, A. (2013). It's in the game: The history of sports video games, in D. Coombs & B. Batchelor (Eds), *American history through American sports: From colonial lacrosse to extreme sports*. (pp. 75–90). Vol. 2, New York: Praeger.
Baerg, A. (2017). It's Game Time: Speed, Acceleration, and the Digital Sports Game. *Temporalités*, 25. Retrieved September 20, 2021, from https://journals.openedition.org/temporalites/3655
Pursell, C. (2015) *From playgrounds to PlayStation: The interaction of technology and play*. Baltimore: Johns Hopkins UP.

DOI: 10.4324/9781003199205-18

FINAL FANTASY VII (1997)

Since its release by Square Soft in 1997, *Final Fantasy VII*'s powerful narrative has resonated deeply with players. The technological advancements of the PlayStation afforded the game's developers unprecedented artistic freedom, and the resulting game featured immersive 3D graphics and an extensive storyline. The sweeping cinematic cut-scenes that illustrated the game's most significant narrative moments were accompanied by rich symphonic music. Finally, the psychologically detailed character backstories enhanced a player's ability to identify with the characters, heightening the emotional impact of the game's narrative. This chapter examines the relationship between these elements more closely, exploring how the increased technical capabilities of the new console contributed to the emotional intensity of some of the game's most poignant narrative moments.

The Franchise

Final Fantasy (*FF*) stands out as one of the longest-running and best-known video game franchises in history. The majority of main titles in the franchise fall into the role-playing game (RPG) genre, with the exception of two massive multiplayer online RPGs (*FFXI* [2002] and *FFXIV* [2010]); additional spin-off games encompass a variety of genres, from fighting games to third-person shooter and tactical RPGs. Originally released for the Nintendo Famicom in Japan in 1987, *FF*'s success led to its North American release for the Nintendo Entertainment System (NES) in 1990. Releases for several subsequent games in the franchise remained limited to Japanese markets, with the exception of *FFIV* (1991) and *FFVI* (1994). In order to keep naming conventions consistent, Nintendo altered the titles for the North American releases of these games to *FFII* (1988) and *FFIII* (1990), respectively.[1] When Square Soft released *FFVII* in 1997, the title remained the same for both international and Japanese audiences, and all subsequent games in the franchise followed suit.

Unlike other video game franchises, in which all games tend to share a core universe, each main title game in the *FF* franchise offers a unique gameworld and experience. Early games featured fantasy plots that generally involved four or more playable characters who work together to save the world from imminent destruction. Due to the technical limitations of early home gaming systems, games produced for the NES and Super Nintendo Entertainment System (SNES) relied on pixelated 2D graphics and 8- or 16-bit audio. Later games in the franchise (*FFVII* and beyond), featured plots with more complex philosophical and narrative implications, as well as substantially improved graphics and sound capabilities. Main title games in the series through *FFX* (2001) share a turn-based RPG format, in which players experience random enemy encounters while exploring a dungeon or world map. During these encounters, members of the player's party and enemy combatants select actions (attacking, using magic or items, etc.) during their respective turns to complete the battle. Like their narrative worlds, the action options and rules for determining the sequence of turns varies depending on the game.

When considering the franchise as a whole, games produced between the mid-1990s and the early 2000s transformed the narrative, artistic, and musical expectations for games bearing the *FF* title. Among the games produced during this critical period, *FFVII* remains the most influential, not only within the franchise, but also for the broader RPG genre. Of all the *FF* titles, *FFVII* possesses the most extensive game universe; more spin-off games and films have been created in association with this game than any other main title in the series. With over 13 million copies sold, it is also the highest-selling game in the franchise (Adler, 2020) and the first Japanese RPG to break through to North American markets (Kent, 2001, p. 542). In addition, the game's success set the tone for future games in the genre more broadly, helping to establish narrative, cinematic, and gameplay expectations for other RPGs designed for the new console.

PlayStation Changes the Game

As the first main title to be released for the Sony PlayStation, *FFVII* benefited greatly from the expanded hardware capabilities of the new console. According to creator Hironobu Sakaguchi, the increased artistic freedom allowed by the PlayStation directly influenced Square Soft's decision to leave Nintendo and produce games for Sony instead (Kent, 2001, p. 542; Donovan, 2010, p. 279). The PlayStation's 32-bit processing power and increased storage of the CD format made 3D graphics using pre-rendered backgrounds and polygonal characters possible for the first time in a *FF* title (TG Staff, 2017). Unlike earlier games produced for the NES and SNES, in which the limitations of the hardware influenced decisions on narrative content, the PlayStation achieved Sakaguchi's artistic and narrative vision in full (Kent, 2001, p. 541). The result was an RPG with a larger world and more complex narrative presentation than any that came before.

While gameplay in *FFVII* remained consistent with prior games in the franchise, the technological leap to the PlayStation resulted in notable shifts in the game's visual and narrative presentation. Its cinematic cut-scenes acted as critical anchors for the narrative, illustrating key moments of the story in rich visual detail. Due to the 3D graphics, each CGI cut-scene acted like a short movie, drawing players deeper into the story and more closely connecting the narrative experience with gameplay elements. Other changes included the presence of blood and the use of explicit language (TG Staff, 2017); although minor, these additions signaled a shift to a more mature target audience and helped reinforce other narrative content, such as the science-fiction setting, which re-envisioned the series in a more modern light.

Alongside these striking visual and narrative features, the ability to produce CD-quality sound significantly increased the narrative impact of the music, which directly informs players' emotional responses to game events. In composing the music for *FFVII*, Nobuo Uematsu chose to rely on MIDI, which allowed for more dynamic music with fewer repetitive loops and quicker transitions between tracks (Collins, 2008, p. 69). With the PlayStation, Uematsu had twenty-four channels of 16-bit sound at his disposal, far more than the eight channels available on the SNES (Collins, 2008, p. 69). As a result, the soundtrack for *FFVII* featured more complex musical textures and more realistic instrument sounds than those heard in previous titles. A full symphonic score accompanied the game's striking cinematics, and tracks like "One-Winged Angel," the music associated with the final boss battle, quickly became fan favorites.

Narrative Experience in *FFVII*

Unlike its predecessors in the franchise, which relied on fantasy-based narratives, *FFVII* drew heavily on science-fiction themes. The game focuses on the conflict between the Shinra Electric Company, which is extracting life energy from the planet to power a post-industrial society, and Avalanche, a small group of eco-terrorists attempting to preserve the planet's life force, known as the Lifestream. As the conflict progresses, Sephiroth, a former elite soldier for Shinra, becomes the game's primary antagonist. Having been the subject of experimentation at the hands of Shinra scientists, Sephiroth becomes determined to merge with the Lifestream, effectively destroying all life on the planet while making himself into a god-like being. In response to Sephiroth's ambitions, Avalanche takes on a new mission, working to stop him while continuing to oppose Shinra.

As the story progresses, players encounter several characters that become central to the game's narrative and eventually become playable. Avalanche hires the primary protagonist, a mercenary named Cloud Strife, to help with a bombing mission at the outset of the game. A series of events introduce players to other members of Avalanche, including Tifa Lockheart, a childhood friend of Cloud, and Barret Wallace, the leader of Avalanche. Cloud also meets Aeris Gainsborough, a flower seller and the last descendant of an ancient race known as the Cetra. Over time, players encounter additional characters who become members of the player's party, including a talking animal with red fur, a retired pilot, and a robotic cat controlled by a member of Shinra. Players also have the option to recruit a shuriken-wielding ninja or an immortal marksman.

The rich narrative context provided for each character imbues them with clear goals and motivations for action, making them much more relatable than standard non-playable characters (NPCs).

Philosopher Christopher Wood (2009) addresses the significant impact this narrative context has on player experience:

> From an innocent and seemingly simple flower girl living in the slums of a harsh and desolate super-city, to a short-tempered and headstrong man with undying aspirations to become an astronaut, there is nothing tremendously unbelievable about the game's main characters that might prevent us from relating to them on a deep and sympathetic level....All of the game's playable characters are accompanied by a rich backstory that...helps to drive their actions and aspirations just that much closer to home and into the hearts of the game's players.
>
> (p. 168)

As Wood notes, it is the everydayness of the characters that makes the narrative of the game so compelling.

While several moments in the narrative illustrate this effect, two of the most striking occur during extended cut-scene sequences involving a loss of life. The first happens during the destruction of the Sector 7 slums in the city of Midgar, and the second occurs when Sephiroth murders a playable character, Aeris. In these moments, the game's technological advancements in 3D imagery and detailed cinematics work together with the symphonic music and relatable characters to create a deeply emotional experience for players. In both instances, the music sets the emotional tone for the scene, while players' knowledge of the characters' backstories heightens their emotional responses to the events on the screen.

The destruction of the Sector 7 slums begins with a brief in-game cut-scene that has players click through dialogue, followed by a short cinematic cut-scene depicting an explosion and the collapse of a large metal plate that smashes into the slums below. The screen goes black, then gradually reveals the player's party lying in the rubble of a nearby playground for another dialogue-based cut-scene. During the initial in-game cut-scene, players are told by the NPC about to detonate a bomb that they don't have much time to escape, and the music played during this sequence invokes a sense of urgency, including the underlying sound of a ticking clock. As the game transitions into the cinematic cut-scene, this music fades out. Players see the plate collapse onto the homes below and hear the sounds of crashing metal and of people crying out, but no music. After a brief view from the Shinra president's office as he watches the destruction while listening to classical music, the screen fades to black and the game's main theme begins to play. In the final dialogue-based scene of the sequence, players must grapple with a sense of tragedy, horror, and loss, as playable character Barret repeatedly cries out for his young daughter, who he believes died in the collapse. Since players have been introduced to Barret's child during prior gameplay, the loss becomes more personal. Meanwhile, the music reinforces the strong emotional impact of the scene, using the main theme's distinctive melody to create a sense of yearning and loss.

For many players, the most memorable cut-scene of the game occurs when Sephiroth murders Aeris Gainsborough as she kneels in prayer. Donovan (2010) describes it as "one of the most iconic moments in game history" (p. 279). The loss shocked players and moved them deeply, as evidenced by the number of Internet rumors about ways to revive the character (TG Staff, 2017). Players who invested in leveling up Aeris before this scene faced not only the emotionally charged narrative loss of the character, but also the loss of time spent in developing her skills (Chandler, 2009, p. 14). The perceived innocence of the character, developed consistently over prior narrative interactions with Cloud and others, made her unexpected death even more shocking.

Similar to the scene depicting the destruction of the Sector 7 slums, the music that underlies Aeris' death sequence forces players to dwell on the depth of the tragedy. During her death, careful synchronization of the character's musical theme with detailed cinematic visuals holds players' attention on the scene. Notably, the music continues into the ensuing boss battle, emphasizing the loss of the character over the excitement of conflict. Prolonging her theme into the battle forces players to dwell on the events of the cut-scene and narratively suggests the depth of loss felt by other characters within the story. Following the boss battle, the music continues as a poignant dialogue-based cut-scene shows characters saying final goodbyes and laying Aeris to rest.

Conclusion

As scenes like the destruction of the Sector 7 slums and the death of Aeris demonstrate, the detailed characters, rich visual graphics, and carefully designed music heightened the emotional intensity of these moments and deeply moved players. *FFVII*'s legacy, seen in countless re-releases, remakes, and spin-off games and films, owes much to the game's initial ability to resonate with players. It resonated because the narrative was compelling, the characters were relatable, and the visual and musical aspects of the game made players feel deeply about their struggle. Combined with the technological advancements of the PlayStation, these features made *FFVII* a key video game of its generation and a landmark game for the RPG genre.

Jessica Kizzire

Note

1. Games with limited releases have since been re-released to international audiences under their original titles; all references in this chapter rely on the original Japanese titles.

References

Adler, M. (2020). *Why Final Fantasy is the Biggest RPG Series of All Time*. Retrieved June 10, 2020, from https://www.ign.com/articles/why-final-fantasy-is-the-biggest-rpg-series-of-all-time

Chandler, B. (2009). The spikey-haired mercenary vs. The French narrative theorist: *Final Fantasy VII* and the writerly text. In Blahuta, J.P. and Beaulieu, M.S. (Eds), *Final Fantasy and Philosophy: The Ultimate Walkthrough* (pp. 5–19). New Jersey: John Wiley & Sons, Inc.

Collins, K. (2008). *Game sound: An introduction to the history, theory, and practice of video game music and sound design*. Cambridge, MA: The MIT Press.

Donovan, T. (2010). *Replay: The history of video games*. East Sussex: Yellow Ant.

Kent, S.L. (2001). *The ultimate history of video games*. New York: Three Rivers Press.

TG Staff, TheGamer. (2017). *15 Awesome Things You Didn't Know About Final Fantasy VII*. Retrieved June 10, 2020, from https://www.thegamer.com/15-awesome-things-you-didnt-know-about-final-fantasy-vii-2/

Wood, C.R. (2009). Human, all too human: Cloud's existential quest for authenticity. In Blahuta, J.P. and Beaulieu, M.S. (Eds), *Final fantasy and philosophy: The ultimate walkthrough* (pp. 167–184). New Jersey: John Wiley & Sons, Inc.

Further Reading

Anatone, R. (Eds). (2022). *The music of Nobuo Uematsu in the Final Fantasy series*. Bristol: Intellect Publishing Group.

DOI: 10.4324/9781003199205-19

FORTNITE BATTLE ROYALE (2017)

The highly successful release of *Fortnite Battle Royale* (hereafter *Fortnite*) could suggest meticulous planning leading to its release on September 26, 2017 as an alternative game mode to *Fortnite: Save the World* (hereafter *Fortnite: StW*), launched on July 25, 2017. However, the advent of this multiplayer game created by Epic Games, a company famously known for its game engine Unreal, can be perceived as a particularly serendipitous event. After a long and challenging development phase (*Fortnite* was unveiled back in 2011), Epic Games tried to boost their product by capitalizing on the success of the Battle Royale genre, particularly in fashion following the success of *PlayerUnknown's Battlegrounds* (PUBG Studio, March 2017; hereafter *PUBG*). Epic Games had provided technical support to PUBG Studio during the development and launch of their game in early access, the latter running on Epic Games's Unreal Engine 4. *PUBG* was finally released on December 12, 2017. Meanwhile, Epic Games developed *Fortnite*'s Battle Royale mode in two months.[1] The proximity between these companies, and *Fortnite*'s success overtaking *PUBG*'s, incidentally led to a lawsuit for copyright infringement (later abandoned)—the first of many in the history of *Fortnite*.

Fortnite: A User's Manual

In the original game, *Fortnite: StW*, players use building mechanics reminiscent of *Minecraft* to create forts in order to withstand repeated assaults by waves of computer-controlled opponents (based on the Tower Defense game format). The unexpected merger of this gameplay with the codes and conventions of Battle Royale led to the core structure of *Fortnite*, which quickly overshadowed its parent title.

The name is derived from the Japanese dystopian film *Battle Royale* (Kinji Fukasaku, 2000) in which a group of students trapped on an island are forced to kill each other in order to be the last survivor of a satirical TV show. Battle Royale games were initially developed within the modding communities of warfare simulations (see the *ARMA* series, Bohemia Interactive, 2006–). A game of *Fortnite* starts with a hundred players, confined in a flying school bus, being parachuted onto a fictional island. Each player (or team) chooses a landing spot, finds material and equips themselves to fight their opponents. A "storm" progressively engulfs the island and tightens the game space to force the players to converge toward the same location. This extrinsic constraint sets a time limit to the game experience (around 15–25 minutes) until only a single person (or team) remains.

Fortnite specifically taps into the intensity of the DeathMatch multiplayer mode introduced by *DOOM* (id Software, 1993), while replacing the cramped corridors of first-person shooters (FPSs) with the vast expanses of open-world games. To some extent, *Fortnite*, in which the character is seen from a third-person point of view, offers an alternative to the "tunnel vision" that Rune Klevjer argued was a necessity in FPS games, in that "enemies can potentially attack from any direction (this is why there will always be corridors in the fps no matter how capable the technology: the tension of having free space in all directions must be carefully regulated)" (Klevjer, 2006, p. 2). It is precisely this permanent threat of being attacked "from any direction" that the game fosters, all the more so as the players' initial positions can lead to immediate confrontations. In the case of *Fortnite*, the regulation of this tension is achieved through the agency offered by the building mechanics. By erecting temporary barricades, ramps, or roofs out of various materials collected on the island, players can protect themselves from attack, while creating a secure space to spot opponents and plan their response. Such a high-intensity multiplayer experience is also reinforced by the direct elimination of players when they reach zero hit points and are automatically switched to the point of view of their victorious foe, enjoying a brief respite before being sent to the next match (a fate shared by all but one players/teams in every match!).

Fortnite distinguishes itself from its Battle Royale predecessors by moving away from visual and physical realism, in favor of a cartoonish and colorful fictional universe. Despite the presence of pistols and rifles, age ratings suggest that *Fortnite* is suited in most countries for children aged twelve or thirteen. The aesthetic choices favored by Epic Games have thus allowed the company to reach a larger audience than previous multiplayer shooters.

Playing on a Transmedia Island

Following the example of contemporary media franchises and TV series, *Fortnite* has built its success by harnessing the serial dynamics of recent cultural productions (Denson & Jahn-Sudmann 2013). The game world is a testament to the sophisticated use of "transfictionality" logics at work in many cultural productions today (Saint-Gelais, 2001). The game is structured in "seasons", leading to a renewal of characters and items in-game as well as a partial reconfiguration of the island. Usually lasting from two to three months, each game "season" gives access to new characters (skins) that draw on established cultural tropes (aliens, secret service agents, superheroes, etc.), franchises (e.g., Marvel, 2018; John Wick, 2019; Star Wars, 2019; NBA, 2021) and personalities (e.g., Marshmello, 2019; Travis Scott, 2020; Neymar, 2021), as well as emotes, dances, and various cosmetic objects (gliders, pickaxes, etc.). None of these assets provide advantages in game in regard to the winning conditions, other than the potential psychological impact of the avatar's look on other players.

The in-game store has been available through the game's main menu since the launch of *Fortnite*. The selection of objects for sale refreshes every twenty-four hours to further incentivize purchases. Backpacks, weapon skins, musical tracks, and loading screens have been added months and years later, with the same time-constrained purchasing technique.

On December 13, 2017, Epic Games launched "Season 2", retrospectively naming the first period of the game "Season 1". Season 2 saw the creation of a paid option, called "Battle Pass", providing weekly quests that allow players to obtain in-game assets that are otherwise impossible to buy. This system, as well as the in-game store, generates significantly higher revenues than previous shops in free-to-play games, often focused on attracting "whales"—a minority of players who spend large amounts of money to acquire virtual assets or in-game advantages (Tassi, 2018). Since *Fortnite*'s launch, this in-game store has generated significant revenue, with sales figures of up to $300 million per month.

Despite using assets created for *Fortnite: StW*, *Fortnite* rapidly took its own narrative path, developing stories in-game through cut-scenes and environmental storytelling (Carson 2000). This parodical—and somewhat paradoxical—universe facilitates the integration of various media and cultural contents, such as the secondary mechanics of dances and tags (further discussed below).[2] It also allows an almost perpetual renewal of the game, through the regular addition of new avatars, equipment, or dance moves, without undermining the coherence of the game world. To the contrary, the constant addition and mixing of cultural icons has led to the participative creation of cross-franchise narratives by the players, often shared and discussed on social media. This notably happened in April 2020 when Xbox's mascot Master Chief, from the *Halo* franchise, became available in the game store at the same time as Sony's mascot Kratos, from the *God of War* franchise. In-game screenshots of both characters fighting side by side were massively shared on social media, eventually fueling the game's marketing campaign, and more specifically its cross-play feature that allows users on most platforms (including the PS4 and Xbox One) to play together.

Since 2018, to stimulate purchases on the in-game store and to integrate high-value media content into the game, Epic Games has been multiplying partnerships with various franchises and personalities. Meanwhile, they have been accused of pillaging famous moves from pop culture without any compensation to their authors, in particular dances from African-American musicians or actors (e.g., 2 Milly,

Alfonso Ribeiro), provoking a significant media backlash. Although such practices are widely perceived as unethical, online platforms such as *Fortnite* deliberately exploit the limitations of the current legal framework, allowing for the reappropriation of such cultural assets without infringing on copyright law (Ravetto-Biagioli 2021).

Cross-Play: *Fortnite* on Every Platform

From a technical standpoint, *Fortnite* is made with Epic's Unreal Engine. The game originally ran on Unreal Engine 3, and later moved to Unreal Engine 4 to display the technical capabilities of the company's latest engine. *Fortnite* demonstrates the in-game chat feature (text and vocal) available through the engine, running independently of any platform's vocal communication system. Available at launch for Windows, MacOS, PlayStation 4, and Xbox One, Epic Games released versions for Nintendo Switch, iOS, and Android in 2018, showing that one given game could be developed, played, and regularly updated on numerous competing platforms. Epic Games's strategy has further involved the promotion of cross-playability between different versions of the game.

Beside the technical challenges involved, the studio also had to convince Sony, notably known to be reluctant to allow this feature on the PlayStation 4. In August 2019, Sony accepted cross-play as a result of a financial agreement with Epic Games (Warren, 2021). The deployment of the game on numerous platforms, as well as the economic weight acquired by Epic Games in the wake of the game's success, has led to structural changes within the "duopoly" model that Apple and Google maintain in the digital applications market. In August 2020, Epic attempted to circumvent the fees charged by these two companies by changing the way the game's virtual currency (V-bucks) was purchased on iOS and Android versions. This led Apple and Google to remove the game from their online store. Epic Games immediately lodged complaints against Apple and Google and launched a public campaign rallying companies like Spotify and Match Group (*Tinder*) within the "Coalition for App Fairness".[3]

Of Battle Passes and Pickaxes: *Fortnite*'s Business Model

The business model of *Fortnite* is based on practices in the online gaming and mobile application market that have been in place for a decade. In 2012, Epic Games allowed Chinese company Tencent to acquire forty percent of the company's shares in a move toward the development of products based on the "game as a service" model. That is to say, games regularly updated with new content, in which players are invited to spend money in the long run, either on a subscription (E.g., *World of Warcraft*, Blizzard Entertainment, 2004), or on virtual in-game assets (e.g., *Candy Crush Saga*, King, 2012). Five years on, the success of *Fortnite* validated that strategy, providing Epic Games with large revenues and allowing the company to diversify its investments.

The commercial success of *Fortnite* attracted substantial media coverage as early as 2018, partly reconducting the discourses of "moral panic" already at work in the reception of video games and "new media" in general (Bowman, 2016). One could easily stumble upon articles arguing: that the game was sending legions of young teenagers to detox (Bloomberg, 2018); that it was the source of many divorces (Darby, 2018); that *Fortnite* is as addictive as cigarettes (Fournier, 2019); or that Prince Harry considered the game harmful and wanted it banned in the United Kingdom (Lanier, 2019)!

The media coverage of the game was all the more important as the latter went far beyond the sole practice of online shooters. Indeed, *Fortnite*'s dances were quickly mimicked by soccer stars, or reinterpreted by YouTubers. The game's competitive mechanics and scoreboards led to heated discussions in schoolyards. And the game also generated a lot of para-ludic activity, through Twitch channels, content creation by YouTubers, and the emergence of a professional scene heavily bankrolled by Epic.

Generating and fostering a myriad activities related to the game itself, such as watching videos online, establishing Twitch channels, or participating in forums, are certainly not specific to *Fortnite*. Nor is its financial model, which is partly based on predatory logics aimed at harnessing the purchasing urges of its (partly young) audience. That being said, *Fortnite* has managed to combine a variety of trends from contemporary game and business models in a single game, making it a platform for sharing and socializing capable of "capturing" a wide variety of practices—and data. This is demonstrated by the celebrity concerts organized within the game, such as Ariana Grande's in 2021, or by the Playground mode, launched in 2018, which allows groups of friends to meet on an island, to interact or play freely without the competitive constraints of standard matches.

Epic Games has endured its share of controversy with *Fortnite*, from the traditional moral panics to issues related to cultural appropriation and platform capitalism. As a "game as a service", *Fortnite* will keep going through regular updates and experimenting with business models that are deemed the most profitable. In the coming years, studying this game, or rival games such as *PUBG*, *Destiny 2* (Bungie, 2017), and *Apex Legends* (Respawn, 2019), will offer insights on the evolution of multiplayer shooter games and their business models.

Selim Krichane and Yannick Rochat

Notes

1. Note that a PvP mode for *Fortnite* had been envisioned years prior to its release.
2. Players can make their avatar initiate a dance sequence, or graffiti on the in-game environment at any time. These mechanics are often used to interact with other players.
3. It is well worth keeping in mind that this "crusade" against the digital distribution giants took place as the studio was branching out into online distribution through the creation of the Epic Games Store, largely funded by the success of *Fortnite*.

References

Bloomberg (2018, November 28). *Fortnite Battle Royale addiction is forcing kids into video-game rehab*. Retrieved September 1, 2021, from https://www.scmp.com/tech/apps-social/article/2175334/fortnite-battle-royale-addiction-forcing-kids-video-game-rehab

Bowman, N. D. (2016). The rise (and refinement) of moral panic. In Rachel Kowert and Thorsten Quandt (Eds), *The Video Game Debate* (pp. 22–38). New York: Routledge.

Carson, D. (2000, March 01). *Environmental Storytelling: Creating Immersive 3D Worlds Using Lessons Learned from the Theme Park Industry*. Retrieved October 24, 2021, from https://www.gamedeveloper.com/design/environmental-storytelling-creating-immersive-3d-worlds-using-lessons-learned-from-the-theme-park-industry

Darby, L. (2018). *Fortnite Is Now Responsible for At Least 200 Divorces*. Retrieved September 1, 2021, from https://www.gq.com/story/fortnite-ending-lots-of-marriages

Denson, S., & Jahn-Sudmann, A. (2013). Digital seriality: On the serial aesthetics and practice of digital games. *Eludamos. Journal for Computer Game Culture*, 7(1), 1–32.

Fournier M.-E. (2019). *Demande d'Action Collective: Fortnite, Comme la Cigarette?* Retrieved September 1, 2021, from https://www.lapresse.ca/actualites/justice-et-faits-divers/2019-10-04/demande-d-action-collective-fortnite-comme-la-cigarette

Klevjer, R. (2006). La via della pistola. L'estetica dei first person shooter in single player. In M. Bittanti & S. Morris (Eds), *Doom. Giocare in prima persona*. Milano: Costa & Nolan. English translation: https://folk.uib.no/smkrk/docs/wayofthegun.pdf

Lanier, L. (2019). *Prince Harry Wants 'Fortnite' Banned*. Retrieved September 1, 2021, from https://variety.com/2019/gaming/news/prince-harry-fortnite-ban-1203180583/

Ravetto-Biagioli, K. (2021). Whose dance is it anyway?: Property, copyright and the commons. *Theory, Culture & Society*, 38(1), 101–126.

Saint-Gelais, R. (2001). *Fictions transfuges. La transfictionnalité et ses enjeux*, Paris: Éditions du Seuil.

Tassi, P. (2018). *Study Says 69% Of 'Fortnite' Players Spend Money On The Game, $85 Spent On Average*. Retrieved September 1, 2021, from https://www.forbes.com/sites/insertcoin/2018/06/26/study-says-69-of-fortnite-players-spend-money-on-the-game-85-spent-on-average/

Warren, T. (2021, May 3). *Sony Really Hated PS4 Crossplay, Confidential Documents Reveal. Epic Games was Trying to Force Sony to Budge*. Retrieved September 1, 2021, from https://www.theverge.com/2021/5/3/22417560/sony-ps4-cross-play-confidential-documents-epic-games-agreements

Further Reading

Hurel, P.-Y., Krichane, S., Rochat, Y. (Eds) (to be published, 2023), *Fortnite: Battle Royale—Au prisme des game studies*. Liège: Presses Universitaires de Liège.

Jarrett, J. (2021). Fortnite. In Mark J. P. Wolf (Eds), *Encyclopedia of video games: Theculture, technology, and art of gaming*, 2nd Edition (pp. 354–355). Santa Barbara, California: ABC-CLIO, LLC.

DOI: 10.4324/9781003199205-20

GRAND THEFT AUTO III (2001)

Released in 2001, Rockstar's *Grand Theft Auto III* (*GTA III*) would change the landscape of video games in significant ways. Immensely popular, with more than 14 million copies sold, *GTA III* has also found critical acclaim. It frequently appears on lists highlighting the greatest games of all time. For example, Evan Narcisse sees a paradigm shift resulting from the release of *GTA III*. "Video game level designs were like hotel floor layouts before *Grand Theft Auto III*: opulent rooms that you enjoyed immensely while in them but connected by dreary hallways of necessity," writes Narcisse as part of *Time's 100 Greatest Games of All Time* (2012).

> What Rockstar Games' open-world revolution gave players, then, was an estate, one where you became a demigod of chaos without consequence. *Grand Theft Auto III* turned PlayStation 2s everywhere into roiling vistas of possibility where the id could run free and even the drudgery of getting around was a thrill.
>
> (2012)

Despite its innovation, at its core *GTA III* is a conventional game about revenge, betrayal, and the American Dream. Set in Liberty City (inspired by, if not based on, New York City), the game's main character, Claude (he is not named until he appears in *GTA: San Andreas*), is initially betrayed by his girlfriend Catalina, resulting in his arrest. On his way to jail, Claude escapes, setting off a series of missions that sees his rise through the ranks of the Mafia and other criminal syndicates as he seeks revenge against Catalina and all those who have betrayed him. Offering a series of missions alongside of its built-in freedom to simply explore, *GTA III* tells the story of a crime-ridden community—"the worst place in America"—being overrun by corruption, violence, and despair, and your effort to bring order and stability into that community by any means necessary.

A Virtual Sandbox

Describing it as a "masterpiece of interactive design,", as creating "a highly traversable space" (Murray 2005, p. 91) where players are offered a world of "unscripted, performed, free-play" within a "highly-articulated-place," (p. 92) Soraya Murray argues that while *GTA III* prompted debates about racial and gender representation and, at times hyperbolic, discussions over violence, its spatial and temporal organization embodies the most transformative and powerful intervention in game design. "GTA, through a simulated 'realistic' sense of space and time, conveys an expansive sense of 'place.'... a player's ability to act within a gaming environment is made palpable through the successful combination of image, tactility, and sound," writes Murray. "It represents a compelling human-computer encounter between informational space and lived space" (Murray 2005, pp. 91–92). While the game's narrative and remixing of longstanding tropes of Hollywood were compelling, its construction of a world defined both by detailed 3D renderings of space and place, each of which sparked clear connections to understood geographic signifiers, and by the freedom to move, explore, and otherwise make choices at the push of the button, was truly revolutionary. Whether stealing an ambulance, walking the streets of Liberty City, or starting up a side mission, *GTA III* changed the gaming world by providing ample choices and freedom alongside of its structured narrative and clear objectives. Structured and unstructured, nonlinear yet propelled by the completion of missions, offering a clear rendering of space and the freedom to either go on a murderous rampage or simply drive around the city to see the sights, *GTA* reimagined interactive play. Scholars and gamers alike have celebrated the game for its design, for its aesthetics, and for creating a world defined by freedom and movement (Frasca, 2003).

Ushering in an era of games focused on organized crime, on "urban life," or what S. Craig Watkins (1999) describes as "the ghetto-centric imagination," *Grand Theft Auto* would provide a template for future game designers that built upon the popularity of hip-hop and the longstanding cinematic crime genre. It would also spark endless debates, discussions, scholarly inquiries, and reflections about the impact of the game, on its message and ideology, on whether it was harmful or dangerous. In many ways, the game's importance stems from it becoming a vehicle for broader debates about video games and popular culture, about violence, sexism, racism, and the gaming industry. While some critics and scholars would lament the game's embrace of societal sexism, others celebrated the game's innovation as a satirical commentary of society's ills.

Social Commentary or the Glorification of Violence?

With its embrace of narratives centering on murder, destruction, and graphic psychopathic behavior, *GTA III* would elicit widespread debate about the harm of the game, especially on youth. Manifesting in everything from parental advisory notices to an outright ban in Australia, from politicians and other critics denouncing the game as a corrosive threat to basic human decency, to scholars examining the impact of playing games and views about violence, *GTA III* would generate ample discussion. Pushing back against the abundant criticism, was the argument that the game was, in fact, a satirical taken on societal violence rather than an effort to glorify it. For them, *GTA III* exposed the ideologies and narratives that normalized violence. In "Play-Fighting: Understanding violence in Grand Theft Auto III," Tanner Higgin argues "GTA provides a space for the player to act out and stage a performance of this type of violence in situations which reflect, distort, and exaggerate those of real life yet are contained within the safety of the virtual sphere" (2006, p. 77). For the game's defenders, *GTA III* reflected hegemonic militaristic tendencies, exposing the history of violence that is central to American history

Embracing similar arguments, others have dismissed criticisms which see the game as too violent or as a teacher of violence, concluding that the game is a satire of violence. According to Keith Stuart,

> Rockstar North has built an extraordinary universe that functions not only as an exciting, diverse setting but also as a pulverizing,

nihilistic satire on western society Reality TV, celebrity magazines, social media, plastic surgery, pop psychology books—all get savaged via the often hilarious commercials on the game's many radio and TV stations.

(2013)

Such defenses, however, have been less commonplace with respect to gender and race, given the game's dehumanization of people of color and white women, and given its centering of a physically powerful and intellectually dominating white masculinity.

A White Man's World

Danielle Paquette (2019), in "What happens to boys who kill women in video games," identifies the many ways that *GTA III* deploys "blatant sexism" right alongside its embrace of a world of violence and brutality. Evident by the fact that women are often dressed in bikinis or close to nothing at all, which does little to contain their ample breasts and skinny waists, *GTA III* embodies a world where women serve men. In the game, women exist to serve, help, and pleasure men; for the game's player, they exist as bodies to dominate, control, and exert power over. "They are, quite literally, disposable. A player can pay a sex worker for 'everything,' promptly run her over with his car and then reclaim his money," notes Paquette. Yet, as with so much of *GTA III*, its importance rests not just on the world that its designers imagined and the dialectics between the virtual and real, between the hyperreal and those mundane ideologies that shape society, but also on the ways the game could be understood as embodying the sexism, racism, homophobia, and xenophobia that has plagued gaming since its inception.

Grand Theft Auto III has been at the center of debates about race, representation, and white supremacy within gaming. While the releases of *Vice City* (2002) and *San Andreas* (2004) prompted widespread discussion within both gaming circles and academic spaces about GTA's racialized world and what it reveals about the video game industry, the racial landscape of *GTA III* offers a clear example of the ways in which games have consistently dehumanized and stereotyped communities of color. In fact, the game deploys racial stereotypes entrenched within the dominant imagination: the Italian mobster, the Black criminal "thug," the East Indian cab driver, the Chinese crime boss, and the Latino drug dealer. Yet, the game's depiction of the Italian crime family is distinct from those other characters. The game's instructions describe the Leone family as a "charming, smart, traditionally well-dressed, strong Sicilian family." Exhibiting strong family values, discipline, and etiquette (a moral compass) that privileges loyalty, rules, and a proper way of doing things, this crime family is exceptional in the game. Their enemies, which the player-controlled character must disarm, defeat, and destroy, are pathological, violent, and without redemption. Compare this sort of humanizing representation with that of the Triads, the game's Chinese gang. The game's instructions describe the Triads as "obsessively territorial maniacs," which is evidenced by the fact that members are ready to shoot or attack anyone who enters their neighborhood. Often patrolling their neighborhoods with baseball bats and brandished guns, the Triads are not only violent threats to the social order, but also cultural disruptions. They are not alone. The game offers, similarly racially, Othered signifiers in the form of crime communities. Reflective of entrenched ideologies within gaming and the broader cultural landscape, the few African-American characters are part of the South Side Hoods. Its incorporation of longstanding stereotypes about African Americans (as poor, as wearing hip-hop clothes; associated with games) highlights how the game goes further with its inscription of Blackness. As with the Diablos, who drive low-riders and speak with accents commonplace for Mexican bodies within mediated culture, the Yardies (dreads), the Columbia Cartel, and the Yazuka (Japanese crime family), *GTA III* replicates longstanding images, signifiers, and narratives of communities of color (Leonard, 2003). Seen as foreign, violent, and Othered, they exist as a foil to a vision of whiteness, which, despite the presence of criminal activity, is humanized, empowered with voice, and given a level of depth unseen in the other characters.

Defenders of the game have challenged such criticisms, arguing that, as a satire parody, *GTA III* challenges entrenched racial stereotypes. In other words, *GTA III* creates a world of extreme racial stereotypes, offering an opportunity for players to see, witness, and even experience the absurdity of prejudice and racial generalizations. Such arguments are difficult to digest given the lack of purpose and clear intervention against hegemonic understandings that emanate from white supremacist ideologies. *GTA III* is, at best, conventional in its representation of communities of color as dangerous villains devoid of humanity; likewise, whiteness, even of those engaged in crime is, yet again, a source of beauty, order, and humanity.

A Paradigm Shift

Twenty years after its release, *GTA III* remains one of the most important games in history. With the release of several other installments in the series—*Grand Theft Auto: Vice City; Grand Theft Auto: San Andreas; Grand Theft Auto IV* (2008); *Grand Theft Auto V* (2013)—and numerous expansion packs, across multiple platforms, *GTA III* was the start of a gaming empire for Rockstar. Equally important, it would shape the types of games going forward, from its use of Hollywood actors to its embrace of a sandbox framework, from its embrace of narrative-based missions to its allowance of free movement, from its creation of complex and detailed virtual cities that resembled places throughout America to its engagement with dominant ideologies, tropes, and representation, *GTA III* would serve as a compass of sorts over the following two decades. With its focus on offering an expansive gaming landscape and the freedom to explore, alongside the tried and tested bankable gaming tropes and commonplace characteristics of both gaming and the larger culture (excessive violence; hyper-sexualization of women; white heroism; dehumanization of people of color), it found both commercial and critical successes. Yet, its legacy sits with the problematic representations that it would normalize; it rests with its dehumanization of bodies and communities of color, with its reduction of women to objects of desire and white male domination and power (Lewis 2013); it exists with the movements, particularly from gamers and scholars of color, who demanded a virtual (and lived) world where their lives, voices, and presence mattered. To understand the history of gaming requires understanding *GTA III* not only for its innovation and its contribution to a paradigm shift, but also through the discussions that resulted from the violence it both represented and embodied on multiple levels.

David J. Leonard

References

Frasca, G. (2003, December). Sim Sin City: Some thoughts about *Grand Theft Auto 3*. Game Studies 3(2). Retrieved November 7, 2021, from http://www.gamestudies.org/0302/frasca/

Higgin, T. (2006). Play-Fighting: Understanding violence in *Grand Theft Auto III*. In Nathan Garretls, ed. *The meaning and culture of Grand theft auto: Critical essays* (pp. 70–87). Jefferson City, NC: McFarland & Company.

Leonard, D. (2003, November). "Live in your world, play in ours": Race, video games, and consuming the Other. *Studies in Media & Information Literacy Education*, 3(4), 1–9.

Lewis, H. (2013 September, 21). "Yes, it's Misogynistic and Violent, but I Still Admire *Grand Theft Auto*". *The Guardian*. Retrieved November 7, 2021, from https://www.theguardian.com/technology/2013/sep/21/grand-theft-auto-5-women-misogynistic-violent

Murray, S. (2005). High art/low life: The art of playing *Grand Theft Auto*. *PAJ: A Journal of Performance and Art*, 27 (2), 91–98.

Narcisse, E. (2012, November 15). All-TIME 100 Video Games. *Techland*. Retrieved November 7, 2021, from https://techland.time.com/2012/11/15/all-time-100-video-games/slide/grand-theft-auto-3-2001/

Paquette, D. (2019, April 29). What Happens to Boys who Kill Women in Video Games? *Washington Post*. Retrieved November 7, 2021 from, https://www.washingtonpost.com/news/wonk/wp/2016/04/15/what-happens-to-boys-who-kill-women-in-video-games/

Stuart, K. (2013, September 16). *GTA 5 Review: A Dazzling but Monstrous Parody of Modern Life*. *The Guardian*. Retrieved November 7, 2021, from https://www.theguardian.com/technology/2013/sep/16/gta-5-review-grand-theft-auto-v

Watkins, S. C. (1999). *Representing: Hip hop culture and the production of black cinema*. Chicago: University of Chicago Press.

Further Reading

Gray, K. *Intersectional tech: Black users in digital gaming*. Baton Rouge: LSU Press.

Kushner, D. 2012. *Jacked: The outlaw story of Grand Theft Auto*. Nashville: Turner Publishing.

Malkowski, J. and Russworm, T.M., eds. 2017. *Gaming representation: Race, gender, and sexuality in video games*. Bloomington: University of Indiana Press.

Murray, S. 2021. *On video games: The visual politics of race, gender and space*. New York: Bloomsbury Academic.

DOI: 10.4324/9781003199205-21

GUITAR HERO (2005)

Introducing Rhythm Games

Whether used as a tool to communicate with the player or implemented to create atmosphere and ambience, almost all video games have some musical element to them. Then there are games that put the music front and center as a primary gameplay mechanic. Within the music and rhythm genre, gameplay is most often tied to keeping the beat of the music, often through a unique controller in a range of play contexts. From dance games such as *Dance Dance Revolution* (Konami, 1998) and *Just Dance* (Nintendo/Ubisoft, 2009), to games that aim to put the player in the role of a musician, such as *Guitar Freak* (Konami, 1998) and *Rock Band* (Harmonix Music Systems, 2007) among many others, the use of popular music has grounded the genre firmly within the broader video game landscape. The genre has steadily expanded beyond simple mimicry, as seen through games that use rhythm as an auditory cue for core gameplay, such as *Beat Saber* (Beat Games, 2018), where the player must dodge oncoming obstacles to the beat of the music, or *Audica* (Harmonix Music Systems, 2019), where the player must shoot targets on the ever-increasing beat. Though the music and rhythm genre has had a steady, yet often low-key level of success over the years, arguably it is the *Guitar Hero* franchise (2005-2015) that has seen the most mainstream success and longevity within the genre.

In what would become the first game in the franchise, *Guitar Hero* was developed by Harmonix, published by RedOctane, and released on the PlayStation 2 in 2005 in North America, and 2006 in Europe (April) and Australia (June). Though there have been other games that aimed to teach players how to play the guitar, such as *Rocksmith* (Ubisoft, 2011) and *Bandfuse: Rock Legends* (Realta Entertainment Group, 2014), the aim of *Guitar Hero* was not to teach the player how to play an actual guitar, but to mimic the overarching movements of playing a guitar. The game gave the player just enough referential information, so they "felt" like they were playing but without the dexterity and mental challenges of learning real musical chords, allowing players to immerse themselves in the guitar player fantasy in their own homes.

Playing Guitar (Hero)

The 2005 release of the game was packaged with a black and white, three-quarter scale model of the Gibson SG guitar with an adjustable strap. Replacing the PlayStation's standard handheld controller and its traditional input buttons—the classic green triangle, red circle, blue cross, and pink square—the gameplay input on the stringless plastic guitar controller consisted of five colored buttons (green, red, yellow, blue, and orange), each spanning the width of their own fret on the neck of the guitar. The guitar came equipped with a whammy bar, which was used for collecting power ups and changing the pitch of the notes—most often used to collect more points—and a white strum bar, which the player moved up and down while pushing down the appropriate colored buttons to simulate "strumming". It also included two navigation buttons where tone and volume knobs would otherwise be, to enable the player to access the main and option menus. The plastic guitar was lighter and smaller than the Gibson SG it was modeled after, affording the player to interact with the game through the imagined skills and movements of playing guitar, but it was in no way an actual simulation.

Before starting the game, players could select a character from eight preset options. This character would perform on stage during gameplay, though they had no bearing on the actual gameplay or the game's progression. In career mode, players were able to customize elements of their character and purchase different guitars. Interestingly, while the player selects the character, the gameplay perspective faces the stage so the player can see the band—including the character they selected—which implies that the character selected is not actually the player but is a fellow bandmate. Further, while the player could purchase different in-game guitars, the visual representation in the game did not translate to any change in the actual plastic guitar the player used to play the game, nor did it change any of its functionality.

On the bottom center of the screen sits the image of a large, fretted guitar neck where the notes scroll by at varying paces, depending on the difficulty level. Basic gameplay consisted of matching the notes on their guitar to the scrolling notes on the screen by pressing down on the correlated colored buttons on the neck of the guitar. If the player missed a note, they would lose points. To successfully complete a song, the player must match a certain number of notes to achieve a rating of at least three stars (out of five). As songs are completed successfully, more tour locations and set lists become accessible.

Even in a crowded room, gameplay could often become mesmerizing, as the player focused on the scrolling musical notes speeding across the screen while simultaneously trying to hone their dexterity to match the notes on the guitar. After several hours of gameplay, it was not uncommon to log off and still see the scrolling notes before one's closed eyes. This residual post-play visual effect increased as the difficulty levels were amped up and the player was required to concentrate and react to the increasing pace of gameplay.

Difficulty levels focused on both the speed of the scrolling notes and the complexity of the button combinations. For example, when playing on Easy, the player only uses the red and green buttons, whereas on Hard the player uses all five buttons, challenging the player's dexterity and concentration abilities. With the option to play either career mode or Quick Play and three difficulty levels, the player can power their way through sets of six songs to unlock more content, or select any unlocked song, pick a difficulty level, and jump right in.

This core gameplay of scrolling notes on the screen followed over into other Harmonix games, including *Rock Band* (2007), a cooperative game where you could play up to four people on guitar, bass, drums, and vocals (each with its own unique plastic peripheral). While other games within the franchise expanded the gameplay by introducing multiplayer elements (battle and cooperative) and a new guitar with a different button schema, with each release, the core gameplay remains the same regardless of platform and controller. At the heart of the *Guitar Hero* experience, there is always the plastic guitar.

Plastic Guitars

It could be argued that a large part of *Guitar Hero*'s success lay in the plastic guitar controller. While there were other games with specific supplementary peripherals—*Duck Hunt*'s plastic gun being one of the most iconic (Nintendo, 1984)—the plastic guitar changed the way the player interfaced with the game (Parisi, 2011) and shifted the gameplay from seated play to standing performance. While the player could sit down if they wanted to, there was something to be said about standing up, settling into a guitar-playing stance, and giving in to the embodied, performative nature of being on stage (Jenson & De Castell, 2008). Not quite feeling like the real thing, the plastic guitar nonetheless contributed to the guitar hero fantasy.

Though the original guitar controller was wired to the PlayStation 2, limiting the player's movement to a few feet from the television, the controller still shaped the ways the player engaged with the game. Bound by the materiality of the guitar, the player's stance, arms, and hands were forced to assume the embodied experiences of holding and playing guitar, even if they were not truly creating notes or strumming on strings. For experienced video game players, the novelty of the guitar controller as an immersive gameplay element could, at times, be countered with frustration as the control schema was different to players' mental mapping of typical handheld video game controllers, many of which have similar button layouts and mapping. So, while the guitar controller contributed to the simulation of an authentic guitar-playing experience, the disconnect between playing a real guitar (no strings!) and the new interfaced control schema a player may otherwise not be used to, had the potential to break the immersive "guitar hero" fantasy.

With each new release within the franchise, the player could acquire different iconic guitars; Gibson guitars in different colors, including wireless options that allowed for more freedom of movement for the player. Luckily for owners of the first *Guitar Hero*, all subsequently released guitars were compatible with the original 2005 game and the original controller was compatible with future releases. This influx of plastic guitar controllers led some to complain that they were more of a problem than an asset (Stein, 2017), though the plastic invasion of controllers (and other rock instruments from other titles), was only an issue if players upgraded or wanted a different style of guitar—there was no technical need to upgrade.

Social Gameplay: Music Brings People Together

Although the first *Guitar Hero* is a single-player game, the performative nature of the gameplay meant that people often played the game in a range of social settings. From small groups gathering in domestic environments to more public venues such as birthday parties, team-building events, and bars, players and spectators alike would cheer each other on, laugh, and even help each other complete a song to unlock more options (or so they don't have to hear yet another failed attempt!). *Guitar Hero* became such a popular social event beyond the living room that some bars even hosted *Guitar Hero* nights (similar to karaoke), where players got up on stage and performed a song from the game's unlocked playlist. The better the player was, the more they could perform without looking at the screen with the notes scrolling behind them and focus on entertaining the crowd while (ideally) hitting every note perfectly. While there may have been prizes for the best performance, it is clear that one of the main draws for entrants was the opportunity to live out their dream of being a "guitar hero" even more with the opportunity to be on a real stage in front of a real audience cheering (or booing) them on.

Further to the appeal of the performance of the player as spectacle, it could be argued that the soundtrack and set lists were another strong element that contributed to the game's (and the franchise's) success. The main setlist ranged from Motörhead's *Ace of Spades* and David Bowie's *Ziggy Stardust* to the Ramones' *I Want to be Sedated* and the Red Hot Chili Peppers' *Higher Ground*, anyone familiar with popular rock and roll from the late 1960s onwards would recognize at least some (if not all) of the songs in the game. While the 2005 release of the game had all cover versions rather than original recordings, they were performed as close to the originals as possible. Players could also purchase seventeen bonus songs with their in-game earnings from career mode. These songs were more obscure and performed by the original artists. It was a novel way of introducing players to new music, especially given the fact that players often had to play many times over to successfully complete a song and get a high score.

Whether the player was interested in playing out their rock star dreams or simply wanted to unlock as many songs as possible, the music selection—ranging from classic rock hits to lesser-known alternative songs—the game had something for everyone. Future releases within the franchise would focus on specific bands or eras, and even included motion capture of the artists to lend an air of authenticity to in-game performances (Boudreau & Poremba, 2019). But arguably, it was the increasing use of popular mainstream music that kept players coming back for more, challenging themselves and their friends to unlock more songs.

Guitar Hero players and spectators alike want to be able to play and sing along to something they already know, to be able to play their favorite song, or travel down a nostalgic road of musical favorites. Undoubtedly, the use of mainstream popular music contributed to the game's success as a performative and social gaming experience that helped kickstart the growing trend in social rhythm games such as *Rock Band* and *Just Dance* to use music the target audience would be familiar with.

Setting the Stage for the Franchise and the Future of Music and Rhythm Video Games

While many other games in the music and rhythm genre have been released since 2005 that are memorable and fun to play, *Guitar Hero* has helped put popular music at the forefront of game design, using it as a core gameplay mechanic instead of being relegated to an atmospheric tool or narrative device. Through embodied gameplay, unique peripheral controllers, and familiar, if not nostalgic, musical favorites, the game clearly set the stage for players to live out their rock star fantasies in the comfort of their living rooms.

Kelly Boudreau

References

Boudreau, K., & Poremba, C. (2019). Rock stars & plastic guitars: Designing and playing with captured experiences in music videogames. In *Abstract Proceedings DiGra'19: Game, Play and the Emerging Ludo Mix. August 6–10*. Kyoto, Japan. Retrieved August 16, 2021, from http://www.digra.org/wp-content/uploads/digital-library/DiGRA_2019_paper_186.pdf

Jenson, J., & De Castell, S. (2008, October). From simulation to imitation: new controllers, new forms of play. In *Proceedings of the 2nd European Conference on Games-Based Learning*, Barcelona, Spain (pp. 213–218). Retrieved August 16, 2021, from http://www.digra.org/wp-content/uploads/digital-library/09287.28053.pdf

Parisi, D. (2011). Game interfaces as bodily techniques. In *Gaming and simulations: Concepts, methodologies, tools and applications* (pp. 1033–1047). IGI Global.

Stein, S. (2017, December 17). *I am Buried in Plastic Instruments: Why Guitar Hero III and Rock Band are Ruining the Videogame Industr. Esquire Online*. Retrieved September 05, 2021, from https://www.esquire.com/news-politics/a4066/rock-band-121307/

Further Reading

Brown, N. (2015, June). Tough gig. *Edge*. 61–67.
Dozal M.A. (2016). Consumerism hero: The "selling out" of *Guitar Hero* and *Rock Band*. In Austin, M. (Eds). *Music video games: Performance, politics, and play*. New York: Bloomsbury Publishing USA.
Wixon, D. (2007). *Guitar Hero*: the inspirational story of an "overnight" success. *Interactions*, 14(3), 16–17.

DOI: 10.4324/9781003199205-22

HALF-LIFE (1998)

Players, journalists and scholars have praised *Half-Life* (Valve, 1998) for many reasons, including its artificial intelligence (enemies work together to coordinate their attack, and guards follow and protect the playable character), its art direction (the eerie atmosphere and gritty realism of the Black Mesa research facility), as well as its contribution to the modding landscape (by turning some mods into retail games such as *Counter-Strike* [Le and Cliffe, 1999; Valve, 2000]). Its narrative was also widely acclaimed, but the common view has never been that *Half-Life* presents a remarkable story.

In this first-person shooter, we play as scientist Gordon Freeman, who has to save himself from a disastrous scientific experiment which has created a portal between an alien world and his workplace, the Black Mesa laboratories. Bloodthirsty aliens are now teleporting everywhere in the research complex and the military has come to clean up the place, killing both aliens and scientists on sight. Freeman must safely go through various sectors of Black Mesa to locate an exit, retaliating against human and nonhuman enemies thanks to a significant arsenal, ranging from common military weapons to experimental firepower, not to mention his famous crowbar, useful to bash "headcrabs" and make one's way through boxes, gates, and windows. Meeting surviving colleagues along the way, Freeman finally finds a way to stop the vicious aliens from traveling to Earth. This is not a ground-breaking story nor is it that different from what first-person shooter aficionados were accustomed to at the time. It reminds one of *DOOM* (id Software, 1993), with its space marine having to take care of murderous monsters which, following a technological failure, started showing up on human facilities set on Mars' moons. In both cases, it comes down to saving mankind after science went too far.

What is impressive with *Half-Life* is rather *how* it presented its story in an era where action games were still struggling to effectively implement narratives. Cut-scenes, levels, textual windows, and extra-diegetic elements were largely left out of the game. *Half-Life* rather resorted to devices that contributed to constituting a cohesive space, continuous time, and actional uniformity, thus generating ludonarrative harmony, in which gameplay and narrative are united instead of clashing with each other or simply being disconnected.[1] Three devices are especially relevant to the game's ludonarrative harmony: environmental storytelling; mimetic narration; and aesthetics of continuity. In its attempt to weave parts into a whole, *Half-Life* evolved the first-person shooter genre.

On Genre Evolution

To understand how *Half-Life* is a major step in the evolution of first-person shooters, it is important to make a couple of remarks on the development of genres. As a biological metaphor to describe genres, the term "evolution" has been historically contested in fields such as film and literary studies. Despite this reluctance, Arsenault has pointed out that we should not get rid of it and make the mistake of claiming that genres do not evolve in some ways and that games are devoid of "any generational gap between them" (2009, p. 150). Key first-person shooters such as *DOOM*, *Half-Life*, and *Halo: Combat Evolved* (Bungie Studios, 2001) are not experiments made in isolation from each other, without any family ties. They share a "lineage" that can be traced in the production problems they all faced and the solutions they came up with. If we argue that, for its time, *Half-Life* exemplifies a form of evolution of first-person shooters, as we do here, we have to identify what solutions it provided to a historically situated problem typical of its genre, and how successful it was in doing so. A fundamental difficulty first-person shooters of the 1990s had to deal with was how to incorporate a story without diminishing familiar and pleasurable aspects of the genre experience, such as fast-paced action and uninterrupted interactivity. One might be skeptical that first-person shooters were truly concerned with narratives in the 1990s, but the fact that many action games from this era used to establish their fictional context in a game manual indicates the contrary. Some first-person shooters also included narrative fragments we could gather by exploring their world. This is true for *Marathon* (Bungie, 1994) and *Unreal* (Epic Games, 1998), in which we find terminals and logs warning about the threat of a cruel alien species. However, these solutions kept the game's narrative separated from gameplay. They asked players to stop engaging with the 3D environment to read static paragraphs. Instead of going that route, *Half-Life* adopted a different approach.

When Narrativity and Interactivity Collide: Environmental Storytelling

Half-Life's ludonarrative harmony is well served by its environmental storytelling. As an alternative to the usual opening cut-scene, the game begins with a fairly long sequence in which we are free to move and look around as Freeman takes a tram ride in Black Mesa's underground facilities to go to work. A robotic voice greets us with safety measures and factual information about Black Mesa while the tram traverses various sectors. Heavy hydraulic doors close behind the vehicle as it slowly sinks into the depth of the facilities, isolating us from the rest of the world. If we are attentive to what is outside the tram, we might get a glance of radioactive pools, gigantic pistons producing lightning bolts, and machines welding steel and transporting crates. This early sequence gives us a certain responsibility in discovering Black Mesa and learning that it is a highly dangerous place where top-secret projects are conducted. It is not an ordinary narrative exposition since the game encourages us to seek out environmental details, immediately fostering an attitude typical of gameplay.

After the tram docks at the anomalous materials laboratories, we can run (not walk) around the entrance hall, the dining, locker, and computer rooms as well as through numerous corridors while characters speak to Freeman, reminding him that he's late to the test chamber and has to get his hazard suit. This is how the first objective is transmitted. We may ignore the security guards and scientists we stumble upon, but if we are confused, it is probably because we disregarded what they had to say. We are not reminded of our goals in any other way. No textual message urges us to get back on track. Nothing interrupts us from our exploration (beside walls and locked doors). The first few moments of the game hence undermine the dichotomy between spectatorship and interactivity, narrativity and gameplay. Instead of merely receiving information about Black Mesa and what our objectives are, we have to "work" to obtain some of them by examining places, moving around, meeting characters, and listening to them. Even before handling weapons and fighting enemies, we are presented with a certain degree of ergodicity, thanks to the environmental storytelling.[2]

Mimetic Narration

Another device for ludonarrative harmony in *Half-Life* is mimetic narration, a mode of narrativity according to which traces of narrative discourses (such as the enunciation "once upon a time") disappear, making the narratorial figure not easily discernible (Ryan, 2006, p. 13). In his close reading of the game, Atkins claims: "it is the distance that *Half-Life* has traveled along this axis [between the diegetic pole and the mimetic pole], the extent to which mimesis is approached, that has resulted in the plaudits of its critics and the readerly satisfaction of its audience" (2003, p. 74). We have already stated that game objectives are communicated by characters, never by a voice external to the fictional world. Another mimetic particularity in *Half-Life* is that the heads-up display is not extra-diegetic. Information about ammunition, health, armor, and battery status appears once Freeman puts on his hazard suit, meaning that they are displayed by the uniform. Even though it is now a convention among games in which we play as a cyborg (e.g., *Deux Ex: Human Revolution* [Eidos, 2011]), this kind of information is traditionally provided by an abstract entity, one could say a narratorial figure, who is not part of the fictional world, thus creating a clear divide between what is exclusively for our attention and what is for our playable character's attention and ours.

Moreover, health, armor, and ammunition are scattered in a way that makes more narrative sense than first-person shooters of the time had accustomed us to. These resources often seem like they have been placed by an "invisible hand," that they exist solely because we are playing the game. They lie on the ground in the middle of rooms, as if they were waiting for us to pick them up. In *Half-Life*, ammunition is stored in crates and storage rooms when not gathered from dead soldiers. First aid stations and hazard suit chargers are placed on the walls of the facilities, making us believe they are available to all Black Mesa staff. The location of most, if not all, of these strategic resources are narratively justifiable. They do not convey the impression of being there exclusively for gameplay purposes, as in *DOOM*, *Duke Nukem 3D* (3D Realms, 1996), and *Blood* (Monolith, 1997). Hence, the placement of resources reinforces the coherency of Freeman's world while still assisting our in-game progression, reuniting narrative with gameplay.

Aesthetics of Continuity

Half-Life's ludonarrative harmony is also reflected in its aesthetics of continuity. This concept was introduced by Manovich, who observes that:

> Many computer games also obey the aesthetics of continuity in that, in cinematic terms, they are single-takes. They have no cuts. From beginning to end, they present a single continuous trajectory through a 3D space. This is particularly true for first-person shooters such as *Quake* [id Software, 1996]. The lack of montage in these games fits in with a first-person point of view they employ. These games simulate the continuity of a human experience....
>
> (2002, p. 135)

Half-Life goes further than *Quake* in incorporating an aesthetics of continuity since it gives up the notion of levels. In popular first-person shooters from the 1990s, gameplay is halted at the end of each level as a screen tells us how long it took to complete the previous segment, how many secrets we have found, and how many enemies we have killed. Instead of relying on levels, *Half-Life*'s narrative is marked by chapters. On arrival at a new place, a title fades in gently in the center of the screen, without disrupting our navigation, to foreshadow where we're arriving at or what is coming up. These titles are some of the very few signs of non-mimetic narration, but they are important in directing us in the narrative as the game goes on. On the contrary, end-level screens inform us about our performance and have not much use from a narrative point of view. Levels are, in essence, disparate fragments, independent of each other: we can add or remove levels from a game without affecting its coherence or continuity. Chapters in *Half-Life* are points of reference in a sequence of interconnected places. We cannot "teleport" from one chapter to another since they are designed to be experienced in a pre-established order.

Additionally, levels imply something akin to montage: a gameplay sequence is cut to a stats screen and back to gameplay. *Half-Life* is known for its "lack of montage".[3] This is why Nitsche compares it to a play set on a virtual stage rather than to a film (2008, p. 105). One problem with filmic strategies is that they produce actional discontinuities through predetermined camera movements and transitions to cut-scenes. What was under our control, the playable character and the point of view, has suddenly been taken away from us. In these moments, we are put back into a spectator posture and inclined to separate what is part of the narrative from what is part of the gameplay. These discontinuities are accentuated by "cut-scene signifiers", such as a change in aspect ratio, the disappearance of the heads-up display, and a sudden cut to a new camera angle, which prepare us to stop playing (Howell, 2002, pp. 118–119). With this forewarning, the narratorial figure reveals itself (in a way not that different from saying "once upon a time") and then takes over the action. However, in addition to chapters, *Half-Life* depends mostly on event triggers to structure Freeman and our journey. Headcrabs falling through collapsing ceilings, shoot-outs between humans and aliens, scientists barricading themselves in safe rooms and asking for help are some of the situations which coincide with our exploration of Black Mesa. Even though our spatial position sets them off, they maintain the illusion of occurring despite our coming. Hence the narratorial figure fades away, hiding behind gameplay to support it, without provoking any actional discontinuity.

Conclusion

The legacy of *Half-Life* is multifaceted, but there's no doubt that its narrative dimension represents one of its most important contributions to the first-person shooter genre. The game tells a story without suspending interactivity, contrasting narrated time with narrative time, or jumping from place to place. When we play *Half-Life*, we take part in its story. Our experience does not alternate between narrative and gameplay, as stopping movement to read journal entries or putting the controller down to watch cut-scenes involves. These two dimensions are united, creating a single cohesive whole. This is how the game achieves ludonarrative harmony.

Maxime Deslongchamps-Gagnon

Notes

1. Many scholars have studied ludonarrative "consonance", "resonance," or "harmony" in games, following Clint Hocking's (2009) critique of ludonarrative dissonance in *BioShock* (2K Games, 2007). We won't be able to discuss the usage of these terms here.
2. Ergodicity being defined as the: "nontrivial effort...required to allow the reader to traverse the text" (Aarseth, 1997, p. 1).
3. Of course, the start of a new chapter generally comes with a loading time, which freezes the screen, but this is due to unavoidable technological constraints.

References

Aarseth, E. (1997). *Cybertext: Perspectives on ergodic literature*. Baltimore: The John Hopkins University Press.
Arsenault, D. (2009). Video game genre, evolution and innovation. *Eludamos. Journal for Computer Game Culture*, 3(2), 149–176.
Atkins, B. (2003). *More than a game: The computer game as fictional form*. Manchester: Manchester University Press.
Howell. S. (2002). Watching a game, playing a movie: When media collide. In G. King and T. Krzywinska (Eds), *Screenplay: Cinema/videogames/interfaces* (pp. 110–121), London: Wallflower Press.
Nitsche, M. (2008). *Video game spaces: Image, play, and structure in 3D worlds*. Cambridge: MIT Press.
Manovich, L. (2002). *The language of new media* (electronic Eds). Cambridge: MIT Press.
Ryan, M-L. (2006). *Avatars of story*. Minneapolis: University of Minnesota Press.

Further Reading

Carless, S. (2003, August 8). Marc Laidlaw On Story And Narrative. *Gamasutra*. Retrieved August 16, 2021, from https://www.gamasutra.com/view/feature/131227/marc_laidlaw_on_story_and_narrative.php
Hocking, C. (2009). Ludonarrative Dissonance in Bioshock: The Problem Of What the Game Is About. In D. Davidson (Eds), *Well Played 1.0: Video Games, Value and Meaning* (pp. 268–274), Pittsburgh: ETC Press.
Mactavish, A. (2002), Technological Pleasure: The Performance and Narrative of Technology in Half-Life and other High-Tech Computer Games. In G. King and T. Krzywinska (Eds.), *Screenplay: cinema/videogames/interfaces* (pp. 33–49), London: Wallflower Press.
Valve. (2004). *Half-Life 2: Raising the Bar*. Roseville: Prima Games.

DOI: 10.4324/9781003199205-23

JOURNEY (2012)

As I write this, almost ten years after its release in PlayStation 3's digital store, *Journey* (thatgamecompany, 2012) is a pivotal game that redefined the limits for the design of commercially successful video games. It is also a game whose lessons have been absorbed piecemeal into the mainstream. When it arrived, *Journey* stood out for its calm, its scale, its nearly absent difficulty, and its wordless multiplayer interaction.

Playing *Journey*

As you start *Journey*, your masked and near-faceless character moves across a pastel-color desert landscape, whose central guiding post is a distant mountain with a seeming beacon shining toward the sky. The frame of reference for the world is seemingly Tibetan, with textile pieces in the wind, like Tibetan prayer flags in high altitude locations, but it is also an ambiguous reference that does not signal any one culture or location.

At first, the game world looks like an open world where you can go anywhere, but you *want* to go toward the mountain. Movement is slow and deliberate in the beginning. You can interact with only a few things, some cloth blowing in the wind, some creatures, some switches. You mainly move along. As you play, you often meet other players, though one at a time. It's a silent and low-key interaction, where you can help each other by opening doors, pressing buttons; your only means of expression is a general ping, which can mean both "here!", "thanks!", or "watch out!" Players often cite the experience of a shared journey through a strange land with a stranger as touching. It's not communication the way you'd expect, but bonding, perhaps.

What you do with other players can best be described as gestures. You can give energy to the other player such that they can fly more, only that extra energy is surprisingly not needed for progress in the game. You can point to an exit or entrance to guide the other player, yet players rarely get lost in this game. You can toggle a switch needed for progress, but switches are easily found and activated, and there are no puzzles that require coordination between players. The lesson here is that even though the help players give each other is of minor importance in relation to completing the game, it still feels like friendly and generous gestures that bind strangers together.

The World Leading to *Journey*

Let us look at the cultural moment in which *Journey* first appeared. In the history of video games, and especially since the 1990s, it has been a recurring argument that video games should expand their range of subject matter, sometimes to mirror stories (Crawford, 1992), sometimes to provide new role models (Costikyan et al., 2005). Some developers have specifically singled out the challenge and rule-bound nature of video games as detrimental to the range of experiences they could provide (Juul, 2018). In their 2010 manifesto, US-Belgian duo Tale of Tales argue that video games are "stuck" in violence and unnecessary challenge, and have stopped evolving, and propose a new kind of game, or *notgame*:

> A time in which we can play with autonomous characters (without having to trick their dialog trees).
> A time in which we can climb the colossus

(without being forced to strike it with our little sword).
A time in which we can play.
Without rules or goals or winning or losing.
A time in which we can make love, notgames.

(Harvey & Samyn, 2010)

Indeed, the games of Tale of Tales, like *The Graveyard* (2008) and *Bientôt l'été* (2012), eschew the conventional goal structure and the try-fail-repeat cycle of video games.

2012 was also the year *Dear Esther* (The Chinese Room) was released commercially, often referred to (sometimes disparagingly) as a *walking simulator*—a game that does not simulate any of the traditional crafting, shooting, building, trading, or other mechanics that we expect from video games, but only the act of walking through a landscape. In *Dear Esther*'s case, the walking is accompanied by a metaphor-heavy narration of a relationship and a car crash.

This gives some historical context for an interview with *Journey* game director Jenova Chen at the time of the game's release, showing how he taps into this rhetoric, rejecting the violence and challenge of traditional video games, focusing instead on new emotions for video games: wonder and awe. As Chen stated,

> I started to realize there is an emotion missing in the modern society, and of course missing in the online console games. It is the feeling of not knowing, a sense of wonder, a sense of awe, at the fact that you don't understand, at the fact that you are so small and you are not empowered. And so our focus for *Journey* was to make the player feel small and to feel wonder, so when they run into each other in an online environment, rather than thinking about how am I supposed to use my gun on the other player, we wanted them to feel a connection to another player.
>
> (in Ohannessian, 2012)

It is also worth noting that Chen describes the game's design as starting not with a genre, but with an emotion. This is an influential method of development, popularized around 2004, according to which game development should be guided by the intended experience or emotion of players (Hunicke et al., 2004; Fullerton et al. 2004).

Journey and the thatgamecompany Oeuvre

Journey was the third release by thatgamecompany. Their first game, *flOw*, was a 2006 master's thesis project and its later 2007 PlayStation

3 release was a surprise success, at the time the most downloaded game on the PlayStation Network store. In *flOw*, you control a small underwater creature that grows from eating other creatures, and progress in the game leads to meeting ever larger and more dangerous enemies. Ostensibly, *flOw* was about being in a state of *flOw* (Csikszentmihalyi, 1990), though the actual experience was often a meditative one. *Flower* (2009) was a more linear game of restoring a landscape ravaged by industrial decay, in order to nurture the titular flowers. These three games are readable as an *oeuvre*, a body of work from the same (collective) author. The later *Sky* (2019) continues the wordless interaction of *Journey*.

Journey as an Independent Game

Journey has an odd position in the ecology of video games. On the one hand, it is easily placed in a history of independent and experimental games, as a game that rejects many conventions of big-budget commercial games and focuses on new experiences and peaceful interaction. Many of the team members are also active in the independent game community, and some come out of a university game design program (University of Southern California). On the other hand—and I will discuss why this is sometimes perceived as a contradiction—it is a game made with a considerable budget and with close ties to Sony's Santa Monica division. The game was developed in a three-game deal with Sony (Rutkoff, 2006), and was exclusive to Sony PlayStation platforms from 2012 to 2019, when it was launched on Windows and iOS.

But rather than asking if *Journey is* an independent game, it can be productive to think about how it functions *as* an independent game. Building on the work of cinema scholar Geoff King (2005), I have proposed that we distinguish between three kinds of independence (Juul, 2019, p. 12). A game can be:

1. *financially independent* in terms of how it was funded, and under what circumstances it was made, typically meaning that the game is not beholden to large publishers or investors
2. *aesthetically independent* by looking, sounding, or feeling different to mainstream games
3. *culturally independent* by making larger cultural or political arguments.

Read this way, the status of *Journey* becomes a little clearer as it is aesthetically independent in that it promotes a new emotion and mood, and in its visual aesthetics. Going back to the Jenova Chen quote, the alleged lack of awe is discussed not just for video games, but for society at large. *Journey* is thus promoted as culturally independent, as making a larger cultural point, and perhaps even solving a spiritual malaise in our culture. Finally, the close ties to Sony and its apparently substantial budget makes it comparatively less financially independent than other experimental games. In combination, this constitutes the unique status of *Journey* in the ecology of video games.

The Traditionality of an Innovative Game

I have pointed to the radicality of *Journey*. But we can also see in it a range of traditional video game elements. For example, many sections of the game involve gliding through sand, which is distinctly similar to snowboarding games like *SSX* (EA Canada, 2003): gaining speed from going downhill, drawing a trail in the surface, navigating obstacles. In short, *Journey* shares this kinesthetic pleasure (Swalwell, 2008) with *SSX* and many other sports games. This is quite different from the promotion of the game, which emphasized its difference from video game tradition.

I said that *Journey* is a game where challenge or difficulty is not meant to hinder the player's progress, yet the game often imparts a sense of danger. Towards the end, you ascend a windswept and snowy mountain, and walk on a high ledge ruffled by strong winds. You fall down easily, but the character always manages to survive, and it is only a short walk back to where you fell from. What may be less obvious is that this type of design is extremely resource-intensive and requires extensive playtesting and tweaking of levels. It would be cheaper to make a more punishing game.

Structure

Journey is very linear. We are presented with many open vistas, only to find that there is just one way we can go, which usually coincides with the way we want to go. The promotion and media coverage of this game also means that we are perhaps too primed to think of it in a particular way, as a liberatory reaction to the confines of rules and goal structures, which is strange given how much its overall structure in practice follows a strict single-player adventure game template. As you play the game, you can feel like a quite powerless entity, capable of minimal change in the world, journeying from point A to B, going through a series of locations with changing color schemes. The game communicates structure explicitly, with cloaked figures appearing in cut-scenes, showing us a simplified version of our journey so far and prefiguring what we must do next. What you notice or do, it seems, makes little difference in the game, but it makes perfect sense in the fiction: you are small and can only do small things next to ancient and divine powers.

The Afterlife of Journey

At the very end, our character collapses in the snow, is met by the silent entities, is seemingly lifted to a colorful afterlife, and then walks into the light in the middle of the mountain. Fade to white. Mountains are of course used in many religious traditions as places where divine powers live or appear, and the game is easily read as a religious allegory or journey.

Journey presents ideas of calm and quiet interaction, it is a *slow game*, in opposition to video game tradition, but also—contrary to promotion and press coverage—includes ample amounts of traditional video game enjoyment, especially in its high production values and well-executed periods of satisfying kinesthetic movement.

| Smaller games have followed *Journey*, such as *Abzû* (Giant Squid Studios, 2016), but like other wildly successful games such as *The Sims* (Maxis Software, 2000), it is striking how few attempts there are to make big-budget commercial games with this template. The main influence of *Journey* on larger titles is in the silent, constructive, and nonverbal communication and interaction with other players. At a time where many online games have had to deal with toxicity between players, *Journey* has shown how to create supportive and peaceful multiplayer experiences. The imprint of *Journey*, then, is that of popularizing experimental game ideas, coming up with new design ideas, and subtly feeding these ideas into the mainstream.

Jesper Juul

References

Costikyan, G., Spector, W., Laurel, B., Rocca, J. D., Hecker, C., & Zimmerman, E. (2005, March 11). *Burning down the house—Game developers rant*. Game developers conference, San Francisco. Retrieved November 1, 2021, from http://crystaltips.typepad.com/wonderland/2005/03/burn_the_house_.html

Crawford, C. (1992). *The dragon speech*. Computer game developers conference. Retrieved November 1, 2021, from http://www.youtube.com/watch?v=_04PLBdhqZ4

Csikszentmihalyi, M. (1990). *Flow: The psychology of optimal experience.* New York, NY: Harper & Row.
Fullerton, T., Swain, C., & Hoffman, S. (2004). *Game design workshop: designing, prototyping, & playtesting games.* San Francisco, CA: CMP Books.
Harvey, A., & Samyn, M. (2010). *Over Games.* Retrieved November 1, 2021, from http://tale-of-tales.com/tales/OverGames.html
Hunicke, R., LeBlanc, M., & Zubek, R. (2004). MDA: A formal approach to game design and game research. *Proceedings of the Challenges in Games AI Workshop, nineteenth national conference of artificial intelligence.* Retrieved November 1, 2021, from https://users.cs.northwestern.edu/~hunicke/MDA.pdf
Juul, J. (2018, August 14). The aesthetics of the aesthetics of the aesthetics of video games: Philosophy of Games Conference. *Proceedings of the 12th international conference on the philosophy of computer games.* Retrieved November 1, 2021, from https://www.jesperjuul.net/text/aesthetics3/
Juul, J. (2019). *Handmade pixels: Independent video games and the quest for authenticity.* Cambridge, MA: The MIT Press.
King, G. (2005). *American independent cinema.* Bloomington, IN: Indiana University Press.
Ohannessian, K. (2012, March 12). Game Designer Jenova Chen on the Art Behind His "Journey." *Fast Company.* Retrieved November 1, 2021, from https://www.fastcompany.com/1680062/game-designer-jenova-chen-on-the-art-behind-his-journey
Rutkoff, A. (2006, November 28). How a Grad-School Thesis Theory Evolved Into a PlayStation 3 Game. *WSJ.Com.* Retrieved November 1, 2021, from https://web.archive.org/web/20070319210051/http://online.wsj.com/public/article/SB116460570723333343-_wOSu3g2II5Vtw_TIMRN2noG0TQ_20061227.html
Swalwell, M. (2008). Movement and kinaesthetic responsiveness: A neglected pleasure. In M. Swalwell & J. Wilson (Eds), *The pleasures of computer gaming: Essays on cultural history, theory and aesthetics* (pp. 72–93). Jefferson, NC: McFarland.

Further Reading

Carbo-Mascarell, R. (2016). Walking simulators: The digitisation of an aesthetic practice. *Proceedings of the first joint FDG/DiGRA conference.*
Leino, O. (2013). Playability and its absence—A post-ludological critique. *Proceedings of the 2013 DiGRA international conference: DeFragging Game Studies.*
Soderman, B. (2021). *Against flow: Video games and the flowing subject.* Cambridge, MA: The MIT Press.

DOI: 10.4324/9781003199205-24

KING'S QUEST (1984)

In the wake of the North American Video Game Industry Crash of 1983, Sierra On-Line published what is arguably designer Roberta Williams's most influential title: *King's Quest* (later retitled *King's Quest I: Quest for the Crown*). This game introduced arcade-style real-time EGA (enhanced graphics adapter) color graphics to the established adventure game genre, combining the text-based interface exemplified in games such as *Zork* (Infocom, 1977) with a graphical avatar that could move in a complex environment with direct control by the player, similar to arcade games of the time. In addition to becoming a defining game of the adventure game genre (Ju & Wagner, 1997), *King's Quest* established Sierra On-Line as a major player in the video game industry and Roberta Williams as one of the most influential designers of the twentieth century.

The Game: Story, Play, and Technology

In *King's Quest*, the player guides Sir Graham through the kingdom of Daventry to complete a quest given to him by King Edward, who promises the crown in exchange for retrieving three magical objects: a chest that is always filled with gold; a shield that protects the bearer from harm; and a magical mirror that shows the future. The mirror is the only one of the three treasures that features in later *King's Quest* games as a major plot device.

Unlike many games of the same time, *King's Quest* offers sufficient plot information in the game itself to understand the premise without the addition of a manual. However, as was common practice in the early 1980s, the different manuals for *King's Quest* reiterate the premise and expand somewhat on it. The initial IBM PCjr edition's manual (1983) depicts "Grahame" in comical cartoon drawings that had little similarity to any later depictions. The plot summary in the IBM manual is perfunctory, focusing on King Edward's commission for Graham with minimal elaboration. But when the game was published for other home computer systems, the manual text included with those editions develops more of a backstory, which blames the decline of the kingdom on the deceptions of an evil witch in disguise who causes King Edward to lose the three treasures in the first place. These manuals also abandoned the cartoonish illustrations in favor of a more serious, medievalized fantasy aesthetic that became associated with the series (for a digitized collection of manuals, see Sierra Manuals, 2006).

Graphically, *King's Quest* took advantage of the IBM PCjr's enhanced display with a full sixteen colors; the game was developed as part of a deal with IBM to encourage sales of the new home computer by showing off its capabilities (Mills, 2020, pp. 33–34). To facilitate production of the game, Sierra On-Line developed what would now be understood as a game engine: AGI, or the Adventure Game Interpreter. With some subsequent iterations and improvements, AGI was used to produce much of Sierra On-Line's early catalog, including *Space Quest (1986)*, *The Black Cauldron (1986)*, *Police Quest (1987)*, and others before it was replaced by SCI, the Sierra Creative Interpreter, which was used for later titles. As Ken Williams, Roberta Williams's husband and founder of Sierra On-Line, explains: games made in AGI "gave the impression of 3D by working with twelve 2-dimensional layers" that created a "priority map" that controlled how graphical elements overlapped and how the "sprites," movable objects and characters, interacted with the static backgrounds (2020, p. 163).

Similar to earlier text-based adventure games, *King's Quest* is primarily played through the use of a parser, which interprets typed commands, although AGI's parser is robust and complex compared to earlier parsers. However, in addition to the usual typed commands, the player could also use the escape key to access menu options, including save and restore and turning the sound on and off in a style that is now familiar to users in almost any operating system. Thus, although not as noticeable as the graphical innovations, *King's Quest* also helped establish a convention used not only in games but also nearly any other kind of application: drop-down menus.

Gameplay in *King's Quest* is primarily advanced through object-based puzzles, interrupted by occasional action sequences that also use real-time, arcade-like controls. Although the game famously exhibits what is sometimes called "moon logic," a fairly common feature of the adventure game genre in which puzzle solutions defy common sense, most of the pleasure and logic of the puzzles offered in the game rely on recognition of and (sometimes loose) associations between fairy tales, myths, and fantasy fiction conventions. There are multiple ways to solve most puzzles in the game. Generally, the points system rewards non-violent solutions and discourages using treasure instead of situation-specific solutions. Solving the puzzles is largely non-linear; there are three objects necessary to win the game, which can be obtained in any order, and the player may work toward these three objects simultaneously.

Of particular interest in *King's Quest* is one of the most infamous action sequences in the adventure game genre: the beanstalk. In a mashup of the tales of "Rumpelstiltskin" and "Jack and the Beanstalk," the player is invited to guess the name of an old gnome. If the player guesses the thematically obvious choice, Rumpelstiltskin (or Rumplestiltskin [sic]), the game responds "That is very close but not quite right!" As per the fairy tale, the player may guess three times. If the player does not guess the name, the old gnome disappears and leaves behind a key that opens an easier but less valuable path. If the player ultimately guesses correctly, answering "ifnkovhgroghprm" derived from a backward alphabet cipher (or, in some later editions, the somewhat easier "nikstlitselpmur"), the gnome gives Graham magic beans that must be planted to create a beanstalk. The beanstalk is a complicated sequence that must be climbed precisely over three screens. This climbing is made particularly challenging because the priority map does not exactly match the visual map on the beanstalk screens, resulting in certain areas that appear safe to climb but are not, and other areas that appear unsafe but are actually safe. The combination of the backward name-guessing puzzle and the subsequent frustrating arcade sequence have made this specific puzzle notorious as one of the most challenging sequences in adventure gaming.

The Creator: Roberta Williams

Little research on and criticism of *King's Quest* itself exists in comparison to the range of material published on its creator Roberta Williams, who has become a somewhat legendary figure in the history of computer games. One important part of Williams's role in the development of *King's Quest* is that she was primarily a designer and storyteller rather than a programmer; although this is typical of game design teams today, in 1984 most game designers were also coding their games, and the role of designer or writer was generally not separate from other roles.

King's Quest was notably not Roberta Williams's first game, nor even her first commercial success. Previously, she had designed and written several graphical adventure games known as the Hi-Res Adventures, published under the company name On-Line Systems: *Mystery House* (1980), *The Wizard and the Princess* (1980), *Mission: Asteroid* (1981), and *Time Zone* 1982). These represented an innovation in adventure games: the adding of static CGA color images to what had previously been a text-based genre. The key innovation with *King's Quest* relative to these titles lies specifically in the implementation of animated, layered, real-time graphics in sixteen-color EGA.

Roberta Williams herself has gained a near-legendary status and is often offered as a counterpoint to claims that the video game industry has always been dominated by men. Laine Nooney (2013) noted that the mere fact that Williams is a woman has significantly shaped the narrative around her designer status. Interviews and press releases from the 1990s about Williams and her games at the height of her fame often referred to her as a "queen" in the industry, in part referring to *King's Quest*'s role in establishing her reputation (as, for instance, in Landis [1993] or Levy [1997]). More recently, as interest in the history of video games becomes more mainstream, Williams's role as designer has been presented as part of the origin story of video games in popular narratives such as Netflix's 2020 *High Score* documentary series. Although the nature of Roberta Williams's legacy is multifaceted, she undeniably occupies a central role in video game history, especially regarding personal computers and the adventure game genre.

Criticism and Legacy

Because Roberta Williams may seem an ideal counterpoint to male-dominance in early video game history, one of the more significant fields of inquiry regarding *King's Quest* is feminist criticism. Williams is often credited with creating the first playable female character in computer games with Rosella in the later *King's Quest* games, although that claim depends heavily on technical definitions and may be disputed (Graner Ray, 2004). However, in critical work on *King's Quest*, Cox (2018) finds that Williams's early work, especially as exemplified in *King's Quest*, lacks any overtly feminist qualities, relying heavily on androcentric narrative conventions that were already present in video game fantasy settings. Indeed, *King's Quest* features exactly three female characters, representing less than one-fifth of the on-screen characters: a good fairy, a woodcutter's wife, and an evil witch. Furthermore, not one of these characters plays an essential role in the game's narrative or play.

Recently, there has been a revival of interest in Sierra On-Line's history, including two crowdfunded books narrating the company's history, including significant sections discussing the flagship role of the *King's Quest* series, as each of the eight games represented an incremental innovation for the company or the genre. The first is Shawn Mills's (2020) extensively researched history *The Sierra Adventure*; the second is Ken Williams's memoir of the company, *Not All Fairy Tales Have Happy Endings*, in which he argues that "Roberta is the true founder of Sierra and was always Sierra's bestselling author," alongside a narrative that locates *King's Quest* as bringing the company back from the brink of ruin and establishing its reputation as a maker of graphic adventures (2020, p. 171).

These books express the most common way in which *King's Quest* is discussed in the overall history of video games and, especially, in adventure games—as an important technical turning point and the establishment of Sierra On-Line's and Roberta Williams's dominance in the adventure game genre—but little critical attention has been paid to the game itself as an object for analysis. Thus, there remains a significant gap in video game research in the close analysis and game-specific research on earlier influential games, such as *King's Quest*. Such research may be supported by readily available tools, such as open-source and public domain versions of the AGI engines, ample documentation of Sierra On-Line's history, and existing research from various fields that intersect with *King's Quest* and Roberta Williams's other work. As can be seen in Nooney's (2020) response to her own previous work (Nooney, 2013), developing a corpus of research on early influential games such as *King's Quest* helps promote a better understanding of video game history, culture, and practices.

Ultimately, *King's Quest*'s legacy is best understood in three parts: as an innovation that made video games on home computers financially and technologically accessible; as a shift in genre conventions for text-based adventure games toward a visual and more complex interaction; and by establishing Sierra Online and Roberta Williams as dominant players in the adventure game genre and history of video games.

Angela R. Cox

References

Cox, A. R. (2018). Women by women: A gender analysis of Sierra titles by women designers. In K. L. Gray, G. Voorhees, & E. Vossen, *Feminism in play* (pp. 21–36). Cham: Palgrave Macmillan.

Graner Ray, S. (2004). *Gender inclusive game design*. Hingham: Charles River Media.

Ju, E., & Wagner, C. (1997). Personal computer adventure games: Their structure, principles, and applicability for training. *The Data Base for Advances in Information Systems, 28*(2), 78–92.

Landis, D. (1993, May 27). A Genre Built on 'Mystery House'. *USA Today*, p. 3D. Retrieved January 29, 2011, from *LexisNexis*

Levy, S. (1997, March 31). Sierra's Queen Is Still on Top of Her Game. *Newsweek*, p. 80. Retrieved January 29, 2011, from *LexisNexis*

Mills, S. (2020). *The Sierra adventure*. Shawn Mills.

Nooney, L. (2013, December). A pedestal, a table, a love letter: Archaeologies of gender in videogame history. *Game Studies, 13*(1), n.p. Retrieved July 6, 2021, from http://gamestudies.org/1302/articles/nooney

Nooney, L. (2020). The uncredited: Work, women, and the making of the U.S. computer game industry. *Feminist Media Histories*, 6(1), 119–146.
Sierra Manuals (2006). *The Sierra Help Pages*. Retrieved July 26, 2020, from: http://sierrahelp.com/Documents/Manuals.html
Williams, K. (2020). *Not all fairy tales have happy endings*. Ken Williams.

Further Reading

Cassell, J., & Jenkins, H. (1998). Chess for girls? Feminism and computer games. In J. Cassell, & H. Jenkins, *From Barbie to Mortal Kombat* (pp. 2–45). Cambridge, MA: MIT Press.
Cox, A. (2014). *Gwydion to Alexander: Colonialism in King's Quest III*. Retrieved July 28, 2021 from https://www.playthepast.org/?p=4920
Juul, J. (2019). *Handmade pixels*. Cambridge, MA: MIT Press.
Nooney, L. (2017). Let's begin again: Sierra on-line and the origins of the graphical adventure game. *American Journal of Play*, 10(1), 71–98.
Salter, A. (2019). 3. King's quest: Narrative. In M. Payne & N. Huntemann (Eds), *How to play video games* (pp. 29–35). New York: New York University Press.
Salter, A. (2009). "Once more a kingly quest": Fan games and the classic adventure genre. *Transformative Works and Cultures*, 2. https://doi.org/10.3983/twc.2009.033
Sierra On-Line. (1997). *King's quest collection series manual*. Oakhurst: Sierra On-Line.
Spear, P. (1993). *The King's Quest companion* (3rd Eds). Berkeley: McGraw Hill.
The Sierra Chest. (2021). Retrieved (October 28, 2021), from http://www.sierrachest.com/

DOI: 10.4324/9781003199205-25

THE LEGEND OF ZELDA (1986)

In an interview for the release of *The Legend of Zelda: Sound & Drama* music album (1994), Shigeru Miyamoto, game designer and director of Nintendo, described his game with a simple premise: "An everyday boy gets drawn into a series of incredible events and grows to become a hero" (Shmuplations, 1994). Such a common, even clichéd, "hero's journey" tale description is a rather humble one given the massive critical and commercial success of Nintendo's 1986 game *The Legend of Zelda*. The title would eventually sell more than 6.5 million copies and grow into a series of eighteen games and a global multimedia franchise.[1] In 2016, the Strong Museum of Play inducted *The Legend of Zelda* into their World Video Game Hall of Fame, citing its then-novel combination of story, exploration, puzzles, and mechanics that would serve as inspiration for many games to come. At the time of writing, more *Zelda* games are in development as the series is firmly established as a Nintendo flagship title. (In this chapter, italicized *Zelda* and *The Legend of Zelda* are interchangeable terms.)

The Adventure Begins

The Legend of Zelda begins with a prologue detailed in the game's instruction manual. Princess Zelda has hidden eight pieces of the mythical Triforce of Wisdom throughout the land of Hyrule, hoping to keep it away from the game's chief antagonist, Ganon. Ganon seeks world domination by obtaining all of the pieces of the Triforce, which would bestow upon him unparalleled abilities. Having already stolen the Triforce of Power, Ganon imprisons Princess Zelda; her nursemaid Impa is sent to find someone courageous enough to destroy Ganon. Impa finds that person in a boy named Link, and the story begins. The player, as Link, must explore the land of Hyrule to acquire the pieces of the Triforce of Wisdom in order to find and defeat Ganon. Through a landscape of mountains, caves, deserts, and other (mostly) natural topography, players battle enemies, meet friendly characters, discover treasure, and solve puzzles. Their major available actions thus include moving about the two-dimensional map in a top-down perspective, occasionally moving objects, and attacking enemies with various acquired weapons.[2]

The three central characters, Link, Zelda, and Ganon, persist throughout the franchise, their roles changing very little from their original incarnations in the 1986 title—even Impa is a frequently recurring side character who always comes to Zelda's aid. In interviews, Miyamoto and his team credit varied sources as loose inspiration for these characters: Link's youthful, elfin androgyny an homage to Peter Pan (Audureau, 2012); Zelda from Zelda Fitzgerald, F. Scott Fitzgerald's wife ("The History of Zelda," 2008, p. 29); and Ganon's piglike appearance to Chohakkai, a literally pig-headed character from a sixteenth-century Chinese novel *Xī Yóu Jì* (Iwata, n.d.). Other aspects of the game would also continue throughout the series (for instance, the Triforce has become part of the essential iconography of the game).[3] Along with characters and objects, the origins of many narrative features, gameplay elements, art, and music in later games can be traced back to *The Legend of Zelda*.

On the whole, Miyamoto cites adventure-based films that were popular at the time—specifically the *Indiana Jones* franchise—as the inspiration for developing *The Legend of Zelda* (Sao, n.d.). Something about the treasure-hunting epic adventure was yet to be captured on game consoles, where the player could become the adventurer. But *Zelda* was not the first action-adventure video game to hit global markets. Predecessors include Atari's *Adventure* (1979), *Superman* (1979), and yes, even a video game version of *Raiders of the Lost Ark* (1982).⁴ At their core, these games were similar to *The Legend of Zelda*: control a character to explore a world and defeat evil. However, Nintendo's relative success with *Zelda* points to a kind of magic synergy of factors that propelled the game to popularity and admiration worldwide, some of which could be attributed to game design, some to Nintendo's technology, and some to marketing decisions. A powerful Triforce indeed.

Technology and Marketing

Nintendo shipped *The Legend of Zelda* as a flagship title for their Family Computer Disk System (FDS), a peripheral upgrade for the original Family Computer (more commonly known as the Famicom and later redesigned as the Nintendo Entertainment System or NES in Western markets). The Famicom was already a popularly selling system in Japan. But the introduction of the Disk System, which utilized relatively inexpensive floppy disks compared to cartridges, created more buzz around the console.

The FDS offered increased sound channels, storage capacity, and the ability to rewrite disks with new game data. As an FDS launch title, *The Legend of Zelda* was the very first console game to allow the player to save their game progress, an innovation that greatly expanded gameplay horizons. Designers could introduce greater levels of difficulty and complexity in games now that players had a "safety net" in case of failure. On this measure alone, *The Legend of Zelda* felt like a big and expansive game. If players could pick up where they left off, they could spend more time invested in the world and their progress through it. This technological feature thus enabled a feeling of "epic adventure" in a way that prior games could not.⁵ It also set it apart from its immediate Nintendo predecessor, *Super Mario Bros.* (1985), which was modeled more closely on its arcade origins: a *Mario* game offered relatively accessible, discrete level-based challenges that allowed for racking up points and achieving high scores. *The Legend of Zelda*, on the other hand, drew more inspiration from the *feeling* of an epic adventure rather than from a set of fun interactive mechanics.

Miyamoto credited his experiences as a child exploring nature around his home in Kyoto, Japan, as his inspiration, pointing to a particular sense of wonder and discovery that he wanted to capture (NPR Staff, 2015). Miyamoto aimed to bring that explorative affect to *Zelda*, stating that he "wanted to create a game where the player could experience the feeling of exploration as he [sic] travels about the world, becoming familiar with the history of the land and the natural world [they inhabit]" (Shmuplations, 1994). Of course, a totally unbounded game could engender frustration and confusion in players, so balancing traditional elements of goal-oriented gameplay and player guidance was a key factor in the design process. In *Zelda*'s early stages, game testers complained about its high level of difficulty. Miyamoto responded by taking Link's sword away, having the player start off with no weapon at all, which forces them to begin the game in exploration mode: where is the weapon I need to defeat these monsters? ("The Legend of Zelda," 2016). (It's with the old man in a cave—featuring the now iconic line in the English translation: "IT'S DANGEROUS TO GO ALONE! TAKE THIS.")

The decision to have players search for Link's sword at the very beginning meant that Link was likely to die at least once before the player realized what to do, presumably leading to even greater frustration than the playtesters had initially noted. But Miyamoto banked on something else: that players might go beyond the game itself to try to figure things out. He expressed the hope that players would seek out each other to form a community around playing *Zelda* and discovering its secrets. He'd seen it in communities that had developed around role-playing games and was thus inspired to try to proactively foster these conversations through the complexities in Nintendo's new, expansive game (Sao, n.d.).[6]

Another strategy for developing the world of *Zelda* was to make significant use of the instruction manual that came with the game, as well as including a map. This essentially expanded the world of the game beyond the screen, a deliberate goal of the team who sought to "reinforce the feeling of the game's epic setting" (Sao, n.d.). After the title screen, an opening crawl displaying numerous and diverse items and icons in the game scrolls until Link appears, holding up a sign that says "PLEASE LOOK UP THE MANUAL FOR DETAILS." The manual was full of extra material such as story lore, character information, and helpful hints for solving puzzles. The difficulty of the game, alongside this title screen directive, encouraged players not only to read the manual but also to buy a hard copy of the game rather than acquiring it at an FDS disk-rewriting kiosk. Placing greater value on material aspects—rather than just the virtual elements—helped plant the seed of the game's lasting legacy. As one nostalgic gamer put it, "This was a ridiculously premium product, a Faberge [sic] egg in a black sleeve, and—as a kid holding both the gold box and the gold cartridge—you felt like you'd just unearthed a treasure" (Ozzy, 2021).[7]

The Sound of Adventure

The Legend of Zelda is a game premised around the feeling of adventure, a feeling generated not simply by its story and gameplay, but significantly by its aesthetics—which was difficult to develop with the audio and visual capabilities of gaming consoles in the 1980s. Nonetheless, *Zelda* made its mark, and its music is a large part of its enduring appeal. Composed by Koji Kondo, who also wrote the music for *Super Mario Bros.* around the same time, the soundtrack for *The Legend of Zelda* featured music that would be significantly reused and adapted in later games; much like the central characters and locations being established in the 1986 title, so was its sound. When asked about composing for the *Zelda* series, Kondo remarked that his inspiration was rather pastoral: "open, grasslands…the feeling of running or rushing through open spaces…[W]ith *Zelda*, I don't go for conventional chord structures, but instead focus more on the atmosphere" (Shmuplations, 2001).

Kondo's deliberately atmospheric music similarly set the game's stage as much as Miyamoto's decision to hide the sword at the beginning—creating the conditions for that *feeling* of an epic adventure, regardless of console limitations. That the music carries strong connotations of that epic *Zelda* adventure feeling is particularly evident in the scope and longevity of Kondo's original themes, which are not only featured in later games but also in symphonic concerts dedicated to the series. *The Legend of Zelda: Symphony of the Goddesses*, a concert series that debuted in 2012, featured orchestras performing arrangements of Zelda music to sold-out concert halls. This, perhaps, is that *Zelda* essence writ large, that "epic feeling" through music that is able to hold court in halls normally reserved for classical music. And, inasmuch as the Triforce is visually emblematic of *The Legend of Zelda* series, Kondo's original soundtrack contains something of its affective essence. In Iwata Satoru's interview with the developers of *The Legend of Zelda: Spirit Tracks*, he remarked that Kondo's puzzle-solving musical cue defined the entire series, which the developers easily agreed with (*NES Classic Edition Developer Interview*, n.d.).

While there was clearly a precedent for a fantastical adventure game before *The Legend of Zelda*, what set the game apart was a kind of felicitous combination of a solid adventure story, interesting and appropriately challenging puzzles, relatively intuitive gameplay controls, and a world design that captured the imagination with colorful and musical environments—not to mention Nintendo's smart marketing strategies. But Miyamoto's emphasis on that feeling of adventure seems to be what sticks in the minds of reminiscing players writing retrospectives: "There's really no other experience like *The Legend of Zelda* was in 1986," wrote journalist Evan Griffin (2015). To many, *The Legend of Zelda* has reached its own "legendary" status, inviting us to reflect not only on games as objects of interaction design, but also as experiences of wonder.

Julianne Grasso

Notes

1. This number does not include remakes, unreleased games in development, spinoffs, or unlicensed titles, which would bring the number closer to thirty or more.
2. While players can also press a button to interact with characters, Link himself does not speak; this remains largely consistent throughout the franchise. Thirty-five years after the first game was released, producer Eiji Aonuma has stated that this is now solidly part of Link's character (Richards, 2016).
3. Early conceptions of the Triforce were designed as computer chips (Audureau, 2012).
4. It is worth noting, however, that Atari is a company that originated in the United States and so their games were not nearly as popular in Japan, where Nintendo would reign as champion of console video gaming throughout the eighties and nineties.
5. While the FDS never made its way westward, Nintendo still made room in a golden-colored cartridge for a small internal battery that would allow for saving game progress. That gold casing—plus a year between release dates to hype up the game—helped solidify the game's commercial success in its various markets (Ozzy, 2021).
6. Part of the game's large sense of scope could also be attributed to the "Second Quest" option, in which players repeated the adventure at a greater difficulty.
7. Licensed publications such as the *Hyrule Historia* volume continue the booklet's legacy around collectable material objects that supplement video games.

References

Audureau, W. (2012, November 1). Miyamoto, la Wii U et le secret de la Triforce. *Gamekult*. Retrieved November 26, 2021, from https://www.gamekult.com/actualite/miyamoto-la-wii-u-et-le-secret-de-la-triforce-105550.html

Griffin, E. (2015, February 26). The Legend of Zelda: NES Retrospective. *The Young Folks* Retrieved November 26, 2021, from https://www.theyoungfolks.com/video-games/51491/legend-of-zelda-nintendo-nes-anniversary-nes-1986-link-evan-griffin/

Iwata, S. (n.d.). Volume 2: The History of Handheld: The Legend of Zelda Games. *Iwata Asks*. Retrieved November 26, 2021, from https://iwataasks.nintendo.com/interviews/#/ds/zelda/1/0

NPR Staff. (2015). Q&A: Shigeru Miyamoto on the Origins of Nintendo's Famous Characters. *NPR*. Retrieved November 26, 2021, from https://www.npr.org/sections/alltechconsidered/2015/06/19/415568892/q-a-shigeru-miyamoto-on-the-origins-of-nintendos-famous-characters

Ozzy, D. (2021, February 21). Looking Back to 1986 and the One that Started it All: The Legend of Zelda. *The Xbox Hub*. Retrieved November 26, 2021, from https://www.thexboxhub.com/looking-back-to-1986-and-the-one-that-started-it-all-the-legend-of-zelda/

Richards, B. (2016, January 29). Aonuma Unsure about Having Link Speak in Zelda Games. *Nintendo Everything*. Retrieved November 26, 2021, from http://nintendoeverything.com/aonuma-unsure-about-having-link-speak-in-zelda-games/

Sao, A. (n.d.). *NES Classic Edition Developer Interview: Interview with Shigeru Miyamoto, Takeshi Tezuka, and Koji Kondo*. Retrieved November 26, 2021, from https://www.nintendo.com/nes-classic/the-legend-of-zelda-developer-interview/

Shmuplations (tr.). (1994). Legend of Zelda Developer Interview. Liner Notes to "The Legend of Zelda: Sound and Drama" Audio CD. Retrieved November 26th, 2021, from http://shmuplations.com/zelda/

Shmuplations (tr.). (2001). Koji Kondo—2001 Composer Interview. *Game Maestro, 3*. Retrieved November 26, 2021, from http://shmuplations.com/kojikondo/

"The History of Zelda." (2008). *Retro Gamer*, 51, 26–37.

"The Legend of Zelda." (2016). Retrieved November 26, 2021, from https://www.museumofplay.org/games/the-legend-of-zelda

Further Reading

Cirilla, A.G. & Rone, V.E. (Eds). (2020). *Mythopoeic narrative in The Legend of Zelda*. New York: Routledge.

Richardson, M., Miyamoto, S., & Thorpe, P. (Eds). (2013). *The Legend of Zelda Hyrule Historia*. Milwaukie, OR: Dark Horse Books.

Tanner, A., Kotobuki, H., & Plechl, H. (Eds.). (2017). *The Legend of Zelda: Art & artifacts*. Milwaukie, OR: Dark Horse Books.

White, K. C. & Tanaka, S. (Eds.). (2018). *The Legend of Zelda encyclopedia*. Milwaukie, OR: Dark Horse Books.

DOI: 10.4324/9781003199205-26

MINECRAFT (2009)

It is hard to overstate the significance of *Minecraft* (2009). As I write this, it is the best-selling video game, ever; by September 2021 it had sold over 238 million copies, and the free Chinese version had been downloaded over 400 million times. It is also one of the most well-known games, with 90 percent of the US online population aware of *Minecraft*. It is historically and culturally significant for its distinctive aesthetic, accessible gameplay, indie development process, modifiability, and massive popular adoption as a platform for artistic, educational, and virtual world goals.

Minecraft is a sandbox game that can be played on mobile, computer, console, or in VR. Represented by a blocky avatar, a player breaks and places cubes of different materials in a procedurally generated, three-dimensional environment that spawns non-player character creatures, some of which are hostile. Players can choose different modes of gameplay, including Creative mode (in which they have unlimited resources, can fly, and cannot die) or Survival mode (in which they avoid dying by gathering or mining and crafting materials into shelter and other resources, and maintaining levels of health and hunger). Swedish programmer Markus "Notch" Persson created it in the Java programming language and initially released it on the independent game developer online forum TIGSource (2009), and then as a public alpha in 2009. Mojang, the independent game development company Persson founded, released *Minecraft* in beta in 2010, and the full version in 2011. In 2014, Mojang (now Mojang Studios) was acquired by Microsoft Game Studios (now Xbox Game Studios). As of this writing in 2021, the game continues to grow as a cultural phenomenon.

Minecraft is often described as a computer game version of LEGO because of its looks and unstructured play. It is characterized by a high degree of player agency; players choose whether resources are infinite or mined, whether objectives are set for them, whether they play alone or with others, and whether they modify the look and/or the mechanics of the game they purchased.

Distinctive Aesthetics

Minecraft's distinctive aesthetic is based on pixelated graphics, cubic blocks, melodic ambient and piano music, first-person perspective with abstracted avatars, and procedurally generated content. These, and other elements, contribute to the distinctive blend of look, sound, movement, and game feel that comprise its aesthetics. *Minecraft*'s juxtaposition of blockiness with beauty, of unyielding horizontal and vertical constraint with the unlimited possibilities of transformation, sets it apart. It is stimulating, but the details in the game don't overwhelm the player's imagination. Everything is abstracted, dialing down the demanding details of everyday life. A *Minecraft* world is a place of possibility, of fun, and, for many, of nostalgia.

The *Minecraft* aesthetic is expressed in every aspect of the game. It is found in the visual style: the square, pixelated look of *Minecraft* blocks; the tones of monochromatic colors; and the iconic recognizability of non-block items like flowers, rails, and carrots, reminiscent of needlepoint and beadwork. It is communicated in movement: flowing lava; the way avatars move; how beings in the world respond to proximity. It is perhaps most profoundly experienced in Persson's choices of music, sound design, and additional content, all of which originated in the indie game community. The achingly beautiful ambient melodic music of composers C418 (Daniel Rosenfeld) and, more recently, Lena Raine, and the sounds of Creepers, Villagers, and other entities in the world, are not what players heard in other games in 2009. When Persson decided to give *Minecraft* the win condition that appears after the Ender Dragon has been defeated, he chose the brilliant and unusual writer Julian Gough to create an eight-minute scrolling text to conclude the game that "makes clear the ancient ties between creativity and survival, and the wonder of collaboration, cooperation, and community, both in its world and in the reality on the other side of the screen" (Parkin, 2013).

First-person perspective was a key factor that Persson added to *Infiniminer* (2009), the open-source block and construction game that inspired the first iterations of what he made into *Minecraft*. Equally significant was the engagingly abstracted avatar who, like the world, is devoid of curves and comprised of pixels. Similar to a pointillist painting made with a crayon, an avatar's face peers back at you when you toggle the third-person camera mode, or see another player. As Scott McCloud insightfully comments about comics, you have no choice but to fill in the gaps: "icons demand our participation to make them work. There is no life here except that which you give to it" (McCloud, 1993, p. 59).

Accessible, Scalable Gameplay

Minecraft is characterized by accessible and versatile gameplay, with multiple game modes, cross-platform play across devices, and limitless replayability. The core gameplay of punching trees, of placing and destroying blocks, are all easy to do. Players can choose how much risk they want when they choose between the play modes: Creative or Spectator for low risk, and Survival, Adventure, or Hardcore as variations with scarce resources and the possibility of losing one's items and of game death. Four difficulty settings (Peaceful, Easy, Normal, Hard) allow players to further modulate their risk.

There are multiple ways to play *Minecraft* by oneself or with others. Multiplayer is varied, with subscriptions to Mojang-hosted private

Minecraft Realms servers, LANs (local access networks) in a single location, one of the handful of featured servers on Bedrock, or one of the thousands from the Java edition. Additionally, *Minecraft* has unlimited replayability. Each unique, procedurally generated world is a navigable space with places ready to be explored and discovered, and it can be further fashioned by players. The world is created anew.

As players grow in age, interests, and skills, *Minecraft* grows with them. What might engage a young player may cease to fascinate a tween or teen, but they can shift to harder Survival modes, challenge themselves with Redstone, explore, make animations, participate in a lore server that has a narrative, or endeavor to build more extensively. Wherever you are, on whatever device, you can play *Minecraft* and connect with friends. With the "Better Together" update (2017), Mojang established one of the most extensive systems for unifying cross-platform play so players can use their account across devices and platforms. As of September 2021, *Minecraft Bedrock* (coded in C++) can be played on Xbox One, mobile on iOS and Android, VR, Nintendo Switch, PS4/5, and Windows 10 devices. The original Java edition allows cross-platform play across Mac, Windows, and Linux computers.

Moreover, *Minecraft* has benefited from Microsoft's commitment to accessibility in gaming. For example, a group of 2019 Microsoft Garage interns, sponsored by the Minecraft Education team, used inclusive design to build features that improve accessibility for the autism community, while also enhancing accessibility for everyone. Both the recent dungeon crawler stand-alone game *Minecraft Dungeons* (Mojang Studios, 2020) and *Minecraft* ranked in the top fifteen games with accessibility features, out of 740 games reviewed (Family Video Game Database, n.d.).

Indie Development and an Indie Ethos

Minecraft's visual aesthetic and versatile gameplay reflect its origins as an indie game, with an emphasis on creative use of minimal assets. It's about making more than what is originally there out of simple blocks, colors, and mechanics like mining, crafting, building, and modding. Persson developed *Minecraft* like the independent game developer he was, both in process and in spirit. For him, being indie meant being more interested in fun, both for the developer and the player, than in popularity or financial success. *Minecraft*'s successful development process pioneered an early access model based on player feedback that was revolutionary for indie developers in the video game industry.

From 2009 to 2011, Persson and then Mojang (Swedish for gadget) incorporated input from the community of players who were, in the earliest stages, alpha testers and predominantly indie game developers. Before Persson established Mojang in 2010, he posted daily builds on the indie developer forum TIGSource, and wrote about it on his blog, *The Word of Notch*. Mojang continued to embrace the player community of *Minecraft* as co-creators with: an extended development phase; an End User License Agreement (EULA) that encourages players to create content for and with the game, including mods (modifications) of the original game that players could share with each other that enabled *Minecraft* to become a platform; and by leaving gaps that the community could and did fill, such as instructions for gameplay. Greg Lastowka (2011) considers not having an instruction manual "an ingenious design decision" because when players look for help, they must turn to the online community of wikis, videos, blogs, and forums about *Minecraft*, but outside of Mojang. Reliance on user-generated content in lieu of official documentation is an aspect of *Minecraft* that is changing. In October 2021, Microsoft terminated the ten-year old agreement with Fandom (previously Curse) to use *Minecraft* branding and call the wiki "official." The wiki is still in good standing, but only minecraft.net, now with official documentation, can use *Minecraft* logos.

Although a game owned by Microsoft cannot be considered indie, Mojang has retained its characteristic focus on indie game development, despite growing to over 600 employees since 2014, when Mojang was acquired for $2.5 billion by Xbox Game Studios, formerly Microsoft Studios. Current Mojang Chief Creative Officer Jens "Jeb" Bergensten became Lead Creative Designer when Persson stepped down in December 2011, and he has been a steady presence since Persson left the company in 2014. Bergensten's approach to the multiple forms of *Minecraft* is based on a recognition that "we need to grow slowly in all directions" (Peckham 2016). Bergensten recognizes that *Minecraft* has always been based on multiplicity, on options, and on choice.

Mods

Modding (modifying) a video game predates *Minecraft*, but *Minecraft* brought modding into the mainstream. Mods are user-created modifications of the *Minecraft* game engine that provide additional content which alters the audiovisual, kinetic, and interactive aspects of *Minecraft* (in contrast to content built with the game engine). Undoubtedly,

Minecraft would not have been as successful without mods and the community which made, reviewed, disseminated, and hosted them. Persson and the other Mojang founders tried to balance fostering community creative participation in mods and derivative works with protecting the company's intellectual property. Instead of legalese, the Mojang EULA uses regular language to encourage content creation, as long as users don't distribute Mojang's content without their permission. The player has ownership of tools, plugins, and content they create in the game, but it must be noncommercial and not officially connected to the game.

Other mods were developed to serve the needs of specific segments of the community. Autcraft was established in 2013 by and for people with autism and their families (Huang, 2019), and MinecraftEDU was started in 2011 by teachers who licensed *Minecraft* from Mojang. In 2016, Mojang acquired MinecraftEDU and released *Minecraft: Education Edition*. In 2021, over 35 million students and teachers in 115 countries use the licensed *Education Edition* (Xbox Game Studios, 2021). If learning works best when education meets students where they are at their skill level, building on existing knowledge, providing models of possible results, challenging them enough to interest them without overwhelming them, then it is no wonder teachers have sought out *Minecraft*. A *New York Times Magazine* cover story entitled "The Minecraft Generation" speculated on the transformative effect that "an almost perfect game for our current educational moment" could have (Thompson, 2016). Further, *Minecraft* is the platform of choice for a range of expressive projects. For example, in Australia's first Indigenous Digital Skills training program, students at Governor Stirling Senior High School in Perth used Minecraft to construct animated worlds from local elders' stories, bringing to life a retelling of a story about the *weitj* (emu) (Warriner, 2020). During 2020–2021, students across the world used Realms to host collaborative builds of their college campuses for social gatherings, including graduation activities canceled because of COVID-19 (Kohli, 2020). *Minecraft* succeeds as a teaching and learning environment because it is a transitional object-to-think-with (Landay, 2016).

Lasting Influence

The *Minecraft* multiverse is a breakthrough virtual world, in which a generation of children and adolescents form their expectations of computer-mediated experiences as content creators, active participants, and modders, within community-created narrative structures and in an infinitely expandable universe. As youth grow accustomed to participatory imaginary worlds where they can communicate with friends, customize avatars, create, play, share information, have fan experiences, follow characters and stories, compete in games, and strengthen media and computer skills to show off to and compete with their peers, they bring the elements of virtual world participation into everyday life (Landay, 2017). As they expand their use of Discord and other communication channels to augment games and social media, as a generation's social experiences flow between digital and physical spaces with the growth of augmented and mixed realities, the possibilities afforded in *Minecraft* will be foundational. In an article in *Forbes* magazine, Jordan Shapiro (2014) concludes, "*Minecraft*'s success tells us that the future generation of grown-ups understand that there is only iteration. We constantly reframe. We perpetually redefine. We try on new categories and always see that there is room for improvement. Everything is dynamic and flexible. Nothing is fixed; neither in time, nor space." *Minecraft* shapes the horizon: discoverable, transformable, and mine.

Lori Landay

References

FamilyVideo Game Database. (n.d.). *Accessibility Dashboard*. Retrieved September 18, 2021, from https://www.taminggaming.com/accessibility-data

Huang, M. (2019, October 29). Minecraft Now more Autism Friendly with Accessibility Features built by Garage Interns. *Microsoft*. Retrieved September 18, 2021, from https://www.microsoft.com/en-us/garage/blog/2019/10/minecraft-now-more-autism-friendly-with-accessibility-features-built-by-garage-interns/

Kohli, D. (2020, March 26). College Students Re-create Campuses and Plan Virtual Graduation, on 'Minecraft', *The Boston Globe*. Retrieved October 20, 2021, from https://www.bostonglobe.com/2020/03/26/arts/college-students-re-create-campuses-plan-virtual-graduation-minecraft/

Landay, L. (2016). Minecraft: Transitional objects and transformational experiences in an imaginary world. In Wolf, M. J. (Eds), *Revisiting imaginary worlds* (pp. 157–178). New York: Routledge.

Landay, L. (2017). Persson's Minecraft. In Wolf, M. J. P. (Eds), *The Routledge companion to imaginary worlds* (pp. 410–424). New York: Routledge.

Lastowka, G. (2011). Minecraft as Web 2.0: Amateur Creativity & Digital Games. *SSRN Electronic Journal*. doi.org/10.2139/SSRN.1939241

McCloud, S. (1993). *Understanding comics: The invisible art*. Northampton, MA: Kitchen Sink Press.

Parkin, S. (2013). Review: Minecraft's Magic Made it a Gaming Phenomenon. MIT Technology Review. Retrieved November 5, 2016, from https://www.technologyreview.com/s/516051/the-secret-to-a-video-game-phenomenon/

Peckham, M. (2016, 16 November). Exclusive: 'Minecraft' Luminary Jens Bergensten Talks About the Game's Future. *Time*. Retrieved November 16, 2016, from https://time.com/4568843/minecraft-exploration-update-jens-bergensten-interview/

Thompson, C. (2016, 14 April). The Minecraft Generation, *New York Times Magazine*. Retrieved 19 September 2021, from https://www.nytimes.com/2016/04/17/magazine/the-minecraft-generation.html

Shapiro, J. (2014, June 24). Generation Blockhead: How Minecraft Mods the Grown-Ups of Tomorrow. *Forbes*. Retrieved September 19, 2021, from http://www.forbes.com/sites/jordanshapiro/2014/07/22/generation-blockhead-how-minecraft-mods-the-grown-ups-of-tomorrow/

Xbox Game Studios. (2021, April). Minecraft Franchise Fact Sheet. *Xbox. com*. Retrieved September 19, 2021, from https://news.xbox.com/en-us/wp-content/uploads/sites/2/2021/04/Minecraft-Franchise-Fact-Sheet_April-2021.pdf

Warriner, J. (2020, November 7). Minecraft and Augmented Reality Helping Indigenous Elders Keep Stories Alive for the Next Generation. *ABC News*. Retrieved September 19, 2021, from https://amp.abc.net.au/article/12858252

Further Reading

Duncan, S. (2011). Minecraft, beyond construction and survival. *Well Played*, *1*(1), 9–30. Retrieved October 30, 2016, from http://press.etc.cmu.edu/wellplayed

Stuart, K. (2014). How Daniel Rosenfeld wrote Minecraft's Music. *The Guardian*. Retrieved October 29, 2016, from https://www.theguardian.com/technology/2014/nov/07/how-daniel-rosenfeld-wrote-minecraft-music

DOI: 10.4324/9781003199205-27

MORTAL KOMBAT (1992)

Upon its premiere in October 1992, Midway's *Mortal Kombat* became a strong competitor in the coin-op market for fighting games—an American upstart rivaling its primary source of generic inspiration, Capcom's *Street Fighter II: The World Warrior* (1991). Given East Asia's popular (albeit reductive) association with martial artistry, the highest-quality fighting games have often been credited to Japanese studios like Capcom—although *Street Fighter II*'s largely bloodless combat opened the door for North American rivals like Midway to use explicit gore as an eye-catching gimmick (Harper, 2014; Goto-Jones, 2016). The respective battle between these games, along with the many imitators they spawned, helped transform fighting games from a relatively minor phenomenon into one of the most popular genres in 1990s gaming, bringing fresh blood to North American arcades and an emerging generation of 16-bit home consoles. Building on earlier genre conventions (e.g., in-round health meters, multi-round matches, two-player competitive play), *Street Fighter II* had added new dimensions of gameplay strategy (e.g., a full roster of playable characters, each with their own visual design, special moves, simple combos, and distinct sets of strengths and weaknesses) and thereby created a template that most other fighting games would follow. The distinctive features that *Mortal Kombat* innovated, however, proved as controversial as they were profitable, especially once parents and media watchdog groups became increasingly alarmed about video game violence entering the domestic sphere.

The Origins of *Mortal Kombat*

By 1988, three Chicago-based amusement firms—Midway, Bally, and Williams Industries—had merged into a single corporation, with Midway as the brand name of their successful arcade division. Programmer Ed Boon and artist John Tobias originally pitched *Mortal Kombat* as a fighting game that would digitize martial-arts star Jean-Claude Van Damme via pixilation—a stop-motion technique in which photographic stills of live actors are edited together to create the illusion of movement—as a licensed tie-in with the film *Universal Soldier* (1992). Although the *Universal Soldier* deal ultimately fell through, Boon and Tobias (plus background artist John Vogel and composer/sound designer Dan Forden) decided to carry on without Van Damme's involvement, instead filming local martial artists for rendering as photorealistic character sprites who would battle within hand-drawn background arenas. Boasting greater realism than hand-drawn sprites, Midway had already used pixilated actors for the characters in its platform-shooter game *NARC* (1988) and would successfully combine this more "cinematic" aesthetic with cross-promotional development deals for the rail-shooter *Terminator 2: Judgment Day* (1991) and the basketball game *NBA Jam* (1993), especially after *Mortal Kombat*'s success helped prove pixilation's overall viability as a marker of product differentiation (Ali, 2019). Indeed, unlike *Street Fighter II*'s colorful, anime-inspired sprites, which make Capcom's game a cartoonish tournament of fights between various national-cultural stereotypes from around the world, *Mortal Kombat*'s photorealism proved one of its most immediately striking features—especially when combined with the gouts of animated blood that spill from the combatants during each match.

Without a direct movie tie-in for *Mortal Kombat*'s original story, Tobias drew narrative inspiration from films about mysterious and deadly martial-arts tournaments, such as Bruce Lee's *Enter the Dragon* (Robert Clouse, 1973) and the Van Damme vehicle *Bloodsport* (Newt Arnold, 1988), plus elements of supernatural magic drawn from more fantastical films like *Zu: Warriors from the Magic Mountain* (Hark, Tsui, 1983) and *Big Trouble in Little China* (John Carpenter, 1986). Whereas early fighting games often depicted martial arts as simply a form of competitive sport, loose narrative justification about "good" heroes versus "evil" bosses had become a generic convention by the late 1980s—former comic-book artist Tobias used his cinematic inspirations to flesh out *Mortal Kombat* with far more backstory than seen in any previous fighting game. Told via the game's attract mode and a mail-order comic book, *Mortal Kombat* is a shadowy martial-arts tournament that was once held by the legendary Shaolin Temple, but which has since been commandeered by an evil sorcerer, Shang Tsung, with the help of a monstrous, four-armed demigod named Goro. Each of the seven playable characters also has specific motivations for participating in the tournament, but they must ultimately fight their way up to the two boss characters to prevent Shang Tsung from gaining immortality by continuing to harvest fallen combatants' souls. While some of these characters—such as Liu Kang and Johnny Cage as Bruce Lee and Jean-Claude Van Damme analogues—originated as allusions to Tobias's filmic influences, their individual narratives would become increasingly complex as sequel games developed a dense cosmology of alternate dimensions, rival deities, overlapping timelines, and plenty of other lore.

Already dripping in orientalist texture, *Mortal Kombat*'s diegesis gained an even darker and more mysterious ambience through Midway's deliberate inclusion of various "Easter eggs" (e.g., an unlockable fight against the hidden character Reptile) whose existence arcade gamers largely spread via word of mouth, leading to further rumors and speculation about what other hidden features might be encoded in the game. Indeed, *Mortal Kombat*'s creative team would increasingly seed Easter eggs and running jokes into the series, whether as nonexistent features teased in the games' audit menu (accessible only to arcade operators) or by incorporating the ideas developed by fans' overactive imaginations into new features present in later games (Church, 2022).

Mortal Kombat's most notorious hidden feature, however, was the ability for a match's winning player to perform a "fatality" upon their defeated opponent, as a bloody *coup de grâce*. Among the most emblematic fatalities were Sub-Zero's extraction of his opponent's head and spinal column, and Kano's extraction of his opponent's still-beating heart—both of which were highlighted during the high-profile concern over video game violence that would erupt in fall 1993. Although Midway did not publicize how to perform these so-called finishing moves, their existence circulated as an open secret, becoming a major part of the game's draw. While successfully executing fatality moves is not a prerequisite for winning *Mortal Kombat*, the novelty value of the game's gore meant that winning players were socially expected to thrill arcade spectators with such Grand Guignol spectacles of death. In effect, then, a player can technically win a match, but still feel a sense of failure (and thus a strong desire to redeem themself by playing again) by not performing fatalities when prompted by the prominent message "Finish Him/Her!"

Video Game Violence and the Birth of the ESRB

During 1992–1993, *Street Fighter II* and *Mortal Kombat* partisans debated the relative merits of their preferred title, with Midway's game frequently criticized as a money-making gimmick aimed at adolescent gorehounds. Unlike *Street Fighter II*'s depth of play, *Mortal Kombat*'s detractors considered it little more than a *killing* game cynically disguised as a proper fighting game. This sentiment has remained difficult for the *Mortal Kombat* series to shake, even to this day, not least because the series' first game became a high-profile target for the National Coalition Against Television Violence and US politicians, aghast at its interactive displays of blood and gore at a moment when photorealistic violence in digital games seemed to increasingly converge with the aesthetic qualities of film and television.

Ironically, though, controversy did not erupt until September 1993, when *Mortal Kombat* was first ported to 16-bit home consoles, its sensationalistic violence suddenly earning nationwide press coverage because of its visibility in family homes. Arcades and other coin-operated amusement spaces have long had a low cultural reputation in North America, frequently associated with (male) juvenile delinquency and unseemly pleasures (Kocurek, 2015; Skolnik & Conway, 2017). Only when brought under parents' watchful eyes did *Mortal Kombat*'s violence merit a moment of moral concern, not only because home consoles were marketed as creating a masculine "third space" of dreamlike escapism upon invading the domestic sphere (Flynn, 2003), but also because 16-bit consoles could more closely approximate the graphical capabilities of arcade machines than earlier 8-bit consoles. Appearing amid an industrial "console war" between the Sega Genesis and Super Nintendo Entertainment System (SNES) (Harris, 2014), *Mortal Kombat* thus threatened to contaminate the private home with the public arcade's air of cultural disrepute. Indeed, when it came under US congressional scrutiny, console developers Sega and Nintendo were called to defend themselves, rather than the designers of the game, Midway (C-SPAN, 1993).

Once *Mortal Kombat* had been slated for a September 1993 release on Sega's Genesis and Game Gear systems, Sega preemptively formed its own Videogame Ratings Council (VRC) in May 1993—a self-regulatory move modeled after the Motion Picture Association of America's ratings system. Unlike movies, however, video games were not yet considered a form of "protected speech" under the US Constitution (a right finally recognized by the US Supreme Court in *Brown v. Entertainment Merchants Association* [2011]), hence Sega's desire to create an age-based classification system that would hopefully forestall governmental intervention over risqué content. *Mortal Kombat*, for example, earned an MA-13 rating (akin to the PG-13 rating for movies) for mild violence—though players could easily input a not-so-secret cheat code to unlock the game's blood sprites and fatality moves. Conversely, Nintendo had long maintained a policy of kid-friendly content for its games, so even as the SNES port boasted overall superior graphics, *Mortal Kombat*'s red blood sprites were instead rendered as gray "sweat," and several of its gorier fatalities were reanimated as bloodless finishing moves. Critical reviews in gaming magazines thus underscored the differences between the Genesis and SNES ports via questions about whether faithfully translating the arcade experience into the home meant more closely emulating the quality of gameplay (a debate framed by each console's technological capabilities) or the gimmickry of gore (a debate over the cultural value of Midway's original coin-op game). Nevertheless, Sega's port vastly outsold Nintendo's expurgated version, lending credence to long-standing suspicions that Midway's game would be little without the blood factor (Church, 2022).

Responding to the spreading parental outcry, on December 9, 1993, legislators Joseph Lieberman and Herbert Kohl convened a joint hearing of two US Senate subcommittees, seeking testimony from representatives of Sega and Nintendo in response to the legislators' co-sponsorship of a bill that would force manufacturers to adopt industry-wide labels on games with violent or sexual content (C-SPAN, 1993). The senators targeted not only *Mortal Kombat*, but also Konami's rail-shooter *Lethal Enforcers* (1992) and Digital Pictures' interactive movie *Night Trap* (1992)—three games from vastly different genres, but whose collective release in October 1992 seemed to herald an uncanny new blend of filmic and gamic violence. Indeed, it is no coincidence that all three games have photorealistic graphics that more closely resemble cinema—from the pixilation in *Mortal Kombat* and *Lethal Enforcers* to the full-motion video in *Night Trap*—compared to games like *Street Fighter II*, whose far more cartoonish sprites raised no concerns.

According to Lieberman (C-SPAN, 1993), the industry had one year to take substantial action, not only because CD-ROM-based games (such as *Night Trap*) allowed cinema and video games to increasingly converge (Russell, 2012), but also in order to have a mandate in place before the September 1994 home-console release of *Mortal Kombat II* (1993), which boasted twice as many fatality moves. Rather than adopting arch-rival Sega's existing VRC ratings system, Nintendo and other industry leaders reached a compromise via the creation of a new industry lobbying group, the Interactive Digital Software Association (renamed the Electronic Software Association in 2003). At a follow-up congressional hearing on March 4, 1994, industry representatives reported on plans for a system that would require game designers to submit potentially objectionable content to a ratings board—soon named the Electronic Software Rating Board (ESRB)—and major retailers agreed that age restrictions would be enforced at point of sale (C-SPAN, 1994; Harris, 2014). Endorsed by federal lawmakers in July 1994, the ESRB went into effect in time for *Mortal Kombat II*'s September release. Now freed from its prior kid-friendly policy, Nintendo's uncensored port of *Mortal Kombat II* helped confirm the superiority of the SNES console, while sociopolitical concerns over video game violence soon shifted from fighting games to first-person shooters like *DOOM* (1993).

By the time *Mortal Kombat 3* premiered in April 1995, Midway's franchise had spawned spin-off films, soundtrack albums, comic books, merchandise, and over 100 other licensed products—though most of these goods remained far more kid-friendly than the games themselves. While the *Mortal Kombat* craze would wane after 1995–1996, the series—still headed by Ed Boon at the time of writing—has remained a major player during the fighting genre's evolution, allowing it to vastly expand its narrative universe and, of course, its gory spectacles of death.

David Church

References

Ali, R. (2019). *NBA Jam*. Los Angeles: Boss Fight Books.
Church, D. (2022). *Mortal Kombat: Games of death*. Ann Arbor: University of Michigan Press.

C-SPAN. (1993, December 9). *Video Game Violence* [Video]. C-SPAN. org. Retrieved September 2, 2021, from https://www.c-span.org/video/?52848-1/video-game-violence

C-SPAN. (1994, March 4). *Video Game Violence* [Video]. C-SPAN.org. Retrieved September 2, 2021, from https://www.c-span.org/video/?55034-1/video-game-violence

Flynn, B. (2003). Geography of the digital hearth. *Information, Communication, & Society, 6*(4), 551–576.

Goto-Jones, C. (2016). *The virtual ninja manifesto: Fighting games, martial arts, and gamic Orientalism*. London: Rowman & Littlefield.

Harper, T. (2014). *The culture of digital fighting games: Performance and practice*. New York: Routledge.

Harris, B. J. (2014). *Console wars: Sega, Nintendo, and the battle that defined a generation*. New York: Dey Street.

Kocurek, C. A. (2015). *Coin-operated Americans: Rebooting boyhood at the video game arcade*. Minneapolis: University of Minnesota Press.

Russell, J. (2012). *Generation Xbox: How videogames invaded Hollywood*. East Sussex, UK: Yellow Ant.

Skolnik, M. R. & Conway, S. (2017). Tusslers, beatdowns, and brothers: A sociohistorical overview of video game arcades and the *Street Fighter* community. *Games and Culture, 14*(7–8), 742–762.

Further Reading

Hunt, L. (2003). *Kung fu cult masters: From Bruce Lee to Crouching Tiger*. London: Wallflower Press.

Hutchinson, R. (2007). Performing the self: Subverting the binary in combat games. *Games and Culture, 2*(4), 283–299.

Kent, S. L. (2001). *The ultimate history of video games: from PONG to Pokémon and beyond—The story behind the craze that touched our lives and changed the world*. Roseville, CA: Prima Publishing.

Kocurek, C.A. (2015). Who hearkens to the monster's scream? Death, violence, and the veil of the monstrous in video games. *Visual Studies 30*(1), 79–89.

Schott, G. (2016). *Violent games: Rules, realism, and effect*. New York: Bloomsbury Academic.

DOI: 10.4324/9781003199205-28

NEED FOR SPEED III: HOT PURSUIT (1998)

By the early 1990s, video game consoles were beginning to see the limitations of the classic video game cartridge. CD-ROM peripherals for home systems appeared and experimented with superior audio and video quality. Games such as *Star Wars: X-Wing* (released for the PC in 1993 by LucasArts Entertainment) and various flight simulators (such as *Falcon 3.0* in 1991 for PC by Spectrum HoloByte and MicroProse) signaled the potential for polygon-based gaming: three-dimensional renderings of realistic vehicles and full-motion video to fill in the narrative context.

On this backdrop, Electronic Arts (EA) founder Trip Hawkins was among the many developers pushing video game consoles to shift toward CD-ROM gaming and the ill-fated 3DO console technology. Although the console left few lasting impressions on gaming culture and development, at least one set of tire marks laid down in 1994 are still scorching hot and as fast as ever, nearly thirty years from ignition: the *Need for Speed* (*NfS*) franchise.

Authentic Cars, Arcade Driving

First released on the 3DO in 1994 and ported to the personal computer in 1995, *The Need for Speed* was lauded for offering superior graphics and sounds as well as offering authentic cars and driving mixed with full-motion video narratives (*Electronic Gaming Monthly*, 1995). The initial game was released as a collaboration with *Road & Track* magazine (the magazine was included in the title of the first *NfS* game), and this partnership likely fostered the franchise's early focus on "a driving game that immersed you in the perfect drive, that gave you a window into what the best road cars could actually do, and how" (*NfS* producer Hanno Lemke, as cited by Hogan, 2020). That said, high-end sports cars are difficult to drive and providing near-perfect replications of those experiences is unlikely to appeal to a broad set of gamers. Although other franchises (such as Sony's *Gran Turismo*) were focused on presenting realistic driving and racing, *NfS* focused on authentic cars being playable for even novice gamers—some refer to this as the "drive 'em up" genre. This was described by Sciarrino (2015) in reviewing a later entry to the franchise:

> [The game's] physics are intentionally rubbery and much appreciated that way because that's why we play *Need for Speed* games. We come back over and over again because we love drifting [street cars] around hairpins and know that, if we tried pulling that off in real life, it's more likely to end with us needing a tow truck and a chiropractor.
>
> (para. 4)

Unlike most racing games that took place on closed circuits, *NfS* driving took place on open roads—somewhat reinforcing the developer's vision for simulating the experience of racing a Ferrari or a Porsche down a long stretch of highway rather than running laps on an international raceway. This open-road racing is critical to *NfS* for another reason, as it also sets up the player's eventual (and long-standing) battles with police and highway patrol, presented as an ever-present and inconvenient foil in the player's efforts to overtake their opponents while weaving through oncoming traffic and other obstacles. Should a police cruiser catch up with the player—either by out-driving them or by setting up a set of road spikes or roadblock—the player's arrest is imminent.

Playing as the Police

Street races and law enforcement (or rather, law avoidance) are common features of many *NfS* games (and similar games released by EA, such as the motorcycle racer *Road Rash* [1991]). Yet, law enforcement was central to the third game of the *NfS* franchise, *Need for Speed III: Hot Pursuit* (EA Seattle and Electronic Arts Canada, 1998; now called *Hot Pursuit*). First released for the Sony PlayStation in 1998, the game expanded on the previous entry's focus on realistic sports cars and illegal street racing, but with one seemingly small but incredibly impactful addition for those who played on PC (and later, on consoles): players could also assume the role of the police, pacing and running down speeders using a variety of customized and exotic police interceptors.

Playing from the perspective of law enforcement marked a dramatic shift in how the game was engaged with, as the fundamental goal of all open racing games—driving quickly from start to finish—is less relevant in *Hot Pursuit*. Instead, police pursuits are marked by the player-cum-officer actively and aggressively pursuing illegal street racers. Racers are not so much apprehended as wrecked into submission using a combination of tire spikes, electromagnetic pulse strikes, roadblocks of police vehicles, or by simply using one's police car as a makeshift battering ram (in order of least to most potentially injurious). In these hot pursuits, the drivers of the vehicles are made invisible (often obscured behind the dark-tinted glass of the in-game vehicles) and the vehicles themselves are front and center. Gameplay is a battle of cars and speed, and human bystanders, drivers, or police officers are rarely present (perhaps as a mechanism for moral disengagement; Hartmann, 2017) as the human cost of street racing is never made salient in *Hot Pursuit*. When cars are stopped (that is, wrecked), the game shifts to slow-motion renderings and replays of the crash, so that the player can enjoy the satisfaction of having busted yet another racer.

Perhaps natural for a game franchise built around illegal street racing, police officers were commonly presented as the primary antagonists for players. In the very first *NfS* game, police officers often presented themselves at the most inopportune times for players attempting to overtake other racers and claim their cash prizes. On top of oncoming traffic and other road hazards, remarkably aggressive cops ruthlessly pursue by attempting to bash and block the player into submission. Those unlucky enough to be stopped were treated to full-motion videos of a not-so-subtle stereotypical portrayal of a Caucasian highway patrol officer, shotgun in hand, making wisecracks at the player (e.g., "Congratulations, you just won an all-expenses paid county vacation!") before applying more-than-necessary force to handcuff and detain the racer.[1] Later *NfS* games were even more aggressive with respect to police officer cut-scenes—in *High Stakes*, officers pull their handguns on players stopped for arrest, and in *Underground*, they kick detained players while handcuffed and lying on the ground.[2]

We see a noticeable shift in how police are portrayed in *Hot Pursuit*, which features players as officers. In these games, cut-scenes of officers behaving badly are replaced with dramatic crash sequences and cars pulled to a stop, with later *Hot Pursuit* games increasing their use of cut-scenes and dramatic camera angles for maximum effect. In the most recent releases, shards of metal and glass are strewn across the screen as seemingly driverless (and thus, victimless) cars are spun and flipped to a full stop. Rather than officers themselves making arrests, a graphic "Busted!" or similar is displayed on screen, providing an immediate quantification of the player's performance—racers arrested, elapsed time—with more elaborate "Bounty" systems in later games that awarded points for driving and pursuit skills, and the use of force and other notes. There is more than a bit of irony associated with aggressively patrolling the highways for street racers while earning points for risky driving (players earn additional points for driving into oncoming traffic, driving around sharp turns, nearly missing collisions with other cars, and riding in the slipstream of other vehicles) with slogans such as "To Protect and Serve" emblazoned on the back of their patrol cars.

Without a doubt, *Hot Pursuit* cast players as police in name only. In a sense, these games invite players to digitally cosplay as highway patrolpersons—there is a bit of a nostalgic thrill in driving a Ford "Crown Vic" police car, reminiscent of the late eighties and early nineties US law enforcement, and the exotic thrill of racing a police-spec Lamborghini highway patrol car. Yet, this cosplay is less focused on role-playing elements of police work, as even later missions in the series (such as a rapid response mission to be the first responder to an unspecified emergency) feature all the thrills of a street race with none of the context of a life-or-death emergency scenario (save arriving on the scene as quickly as possible, with bonus points for doing so while driving as riskily as possible). Although fundamentally a street racing game, *Hot Pursuit* plays more like an arcade-style fighting game. Players are required to really harness and focus on the cognitive and physical demands of the gameplay mechanics rather than on the emotional and social demands of engaging other players or characters (Bowman, 2021). In many ways, this battle-like focus on gameplay is what sets *Hot Pursuit* apart from other *NfS* games—and racing games more broadly.

Hot Pursuit and similar games were a concern for scholars worried that players would engage with the games and then engage in risky driving behaviors (Hull et al., 2012; Vingilis et al., 2013; Stollberg & Lange, 2020). Police pursuits as portrayed in *Hot Pursuit* are highly stylized but share little in common with the reality of police work, in which high-speed chases are inherently dangerous (Hill, 2002); some suggest that pursuits involve "police use of the deadliest weapon in their arsenal: the motor vehicle" (Alpert & Anderson, 1986, p. 2). To this end, *Hot Pursuit* does not purport to be an authentic simulation of police work, but rather presents players with the novelty of "the other side" of the street-racing scene. Related to this and given renewed social concern around police brutality and the role of police in society in the twenty-first century (Eaglin, 2021), the portrayal of police as (mostly White male) aggressors in *Hot Pursuit* could be further unpacked (Pautz & Warnement, 2013).

Sustained Success

Speaking to the staying power of *Hot Pursuit*, the game was remastered and re-released twice: first in 2010 for the PlayStation 3 and Xbox 360 (and various other console and mobile devices); and again in 2020 for the PlayStation 4, Xbox One, and Nintendo Switch. The 2010 release sold over 400,000 copies in the US alone, just two weeks after its release (Graft, 2010) and global sales are estimated to have topped more than 5 million units. As of writing, the 2020 remaster is still available for digital download in most retail venues, and the *Hot Pursuit* entries in the *NfS* franchise are consistently rated higher than other *NfS* games.[3]

The *Need for Speed* franchise will hit thirty years running in 2024. Along with more than two dozen iterations, a collection of *NfS*-inspired Hot Wheels toy cars, and a 2014 film distributed by Walt

Disney Studios that grossed over $200 million against a production budget of only $66 million, the franchise shows no signs of halting. It might have gotten off to a slow start, but *Hot Pursuit* continues to keep players pursuing speeding perps in wide-brimmed police sunglasses and souped-up police interceptors, and the popularity of the chase is unlikely to stall anytime soon.

Nicholas David Bowman

Notes

1. https://www.youtube.com/watch?v=mc8bJmTfsO0
2. https://www.youtube.com/watch?v=qwmKKcaAEMI
3. https://www.metacritic.com/search/all/need%20for%20speed/results

References

Alpert, G. P., & Anderson, P. R. (1986). The most deadly force: Police pursuits. *Justice Quarterly, 3*(1), 1–14. doi.org/10.1080/07418828600088761

Bowman, N. D. (2021). Interactivity as demand: Implications for interactive media entertainment. In C. Klimmt & P. Vorderer (Eds), *Oxford handbook of media entertainment* (pp. 647–670). Oxford, UK: Oxford University Press.

Eaglin, J. M. (2021). To "Defund" the Police. *Articles by Maurer Faculty. 2987*. Retrieved June 10, 2021 from https://www.repository.law.indiana.edu/facpub/2987

Electronic Gaming Monthly. (1995, April) The Need for Speed. *Electronic Gaming Monthly, 69*, p. 38.

Graft, K. (2010, December 10). New Need for Speed sells 417K at U.S. retail in November. *Gamasutra*. Retrieved August 30, 2021, from https://www.gamasutra.com/view/news/31974/New_Need_For_Speed_Sells_417K_At_US_Retail_In_November.php

Hartmann, T., (2017). The "moral disengagement in violent video games" model. *Game Studies*. Retrieved September 28, 2021, from http://gamestudies.org/1702/articles/hartmann

Hill, J. (2002). High-speed police pursuits: Dangers, dynamics, and risk reduction. *FBI Law Enforcement Bulletin, 71*, 14–19.

Hull, J. G., Draghici, A. M., & Sargent, J. D. (2012). A longitudinal study of risk-glorifying video games and reckless driving. *Psychology of Popular Media Culture, 1*(4), 244–253. doi.org/10.1037/a0029510

Hogan, M. (2020, November 3). How 'Need for Speed' became the world's biggest racing game. *Road & Track*. Retrieved August 30, 2021, from https://www.roadandtrack.com/car-culture/a34554081/history-of-need-for-speed/

Pautz, M. C., & Warnement, M. K. (2013). Government on the silver screen: Contemporary American cinema's depictions of bureaucrats, police officers, and soldiers. *Political Science & Politics, 46*(3), 569–579. doi.org/10.1017/S1049096513000516

Sciarrino, J. (2015, December 2). Why Need for Speed is the Fast and Furious Game we Never Got. *The Drive.* Retrieved August 30, 2021, from https://www.thedrive.com/gear-up/1081/why-need-for-speed-is-the-fast-and-furious-game-we-never-got

Stollberg, E., & Lange, K. W. (2020). The effects of video racing games on risk-taking in consideration of the game experience. *PLoSOne.* doi.org/10.1371/journal.pone.0240367

Vingilis, E., Seeley, J., Wiesenthal, D. L., Wickens, C. M., Fisher, P. & Mann, R. E. (2013). Street racing video games and risk-taking driving: An Internet survey of automobile enthusiasts. *Accident Analysis & Prevention, 50,* 1–7. doi.org/10.1016/j.aap.2012.09.022

Further Reading

McCully, W. (2017). Gran Turismo. In R. Mejia, J. Banks, & A. Adams (Eds), *100 greatest video game franchises* (p. 71–73). Lanham, MD: Rowman & Littlefield.

Khan, I. (2020, June 12). Video Games Have to Reckon with How They Depict the Police. *Kotaku.* Retrieved September 28, 2021, from https://kotaku.com/video-games-have-to-reckon-with-how-they-depict-the-pol-1844013471

Lott, M. R. (2006). *Police on screen: Hollywood cops, detectives, marshals, and rangers.* Jefferson, NC: McFarland & Company, Inc.

Posey, J. (2013). Tastes Like Chicken: Authenticity in a Totally Fake World. *Game Developers Conference Vault.* Retrieved June 10, 2021, from https://www.gdcvault.com/play/1018003/Tastes-Like-Chicken-Authenticity-in

DOI: 10.4324/9781003199205-29

NO MAN'S SKY (2016)

"EVERY ATOM PROCEDURAL." This was the opening salvo in Hello Games' remarkably successful promotional campaign for its most successful title to date, *No Man's Sky.* The 2013 trailer video started with nothing but a blank screen and its central pitch: an essentially infinite universe of explorable planets.[1] Each planet is unique in terms of climate, flora, fauna, and topography, because all of it is created on the spot by a gaming machine.

The graphically beautiful trailers seemed to promise the high-quality exploration, combat, and crafting of polished, big-budget, open-world games familiar at the time—titles like *Red Dead Redemption* (Rockstar, 2010) or *The Elder Scrolls V: Skyrim* (Bethesda, 2011)—but with no boundaries. Each promotional image and interview built up the hype surrounding *No Man's Sky*, which led to widespread disappointment and even anger when the final release did not meet all the expectations. Professional reviews were tepid; gamer reviews were scathing, pointing to apparently broken promises and missing features (Klepek, 2016). And while sales were massive, reports of game returns were also widespread.

Six years later, it is worth revisiting this game and considering how it has been one of the most important titles of the past decade. After the rocky release, the developers embarked on a long-term process of fixing and enhancing the game; today's iteration is substantially different to the release version. It has a large, active, and loyal community of players. But why, exactly, is *No Man's Sky* so notable? Its gameplay was not unprecedented. Open-world games with exploration, survival, crafting, combat, and more had all been done before 2016. Procedural generation in video games was not new. Even its development arc of pre-release hype, disappointment on release, and eventual rehabilitation was not a first. What makes *No Man's Sky* worth discussing is both the scope and scale of its core selling point—procedurally generated, open-world gaming—even if the initial release did not quite live up to the hype, and its role in stabilizing and cementing the games industry model of games as constantly updated platforms.

An Effectively Limitless Galaxy to Explore

No Man's Sky is a science-fiction-themed open-world game that houses a bunch of interrelated mechanics. The core part of the game is exploration: players can travel between galaxies, star systems, and individual planets. Once on those planets, they can fly through the atmosphere, and travel over land and through caves or underwater spaces where they can discover and catalog the flora, fauna, and minerals unique to that location. Other core activities include mining, harvesting, crafting, and base building. There are dozens of different materials that can be processed and used for the creation of livable structures, ground vehicles, technology upgrades, decorations, food, and more. In addition, the game allows players to exchange goods for currency in space stations. Players can also engage in spaceship or ground combat.

It is possible to ignore the game's narrative, but its universe has a backstory and alien races whose politics impact play. Completing quests gives a variety of rewards, and it is possible to learn the alien languages of the robotic hive-mind Korvax, the commercial-minded lizard-like Gek, and the fierce warrior Vy'keen, at space stations, ports, and research stations. Like many sandbox games, outside of the explicitly narrative elements in the opening stages, it does not have a singular goal. In fact, it eschews role-playing game elements like experience points and levels—although the player is likely to effectively level up by continuously improving gear and technology.

Players can play solo or multiplayer. The universe of the game is so large that it is quite easy to play for a long time without seeing another player-controlled character. But many *No Man's Sky* players work together in the same manner, as players do on *Minecraft* (Mojang, 2011) servers. There are communities where players build bases together and even galaxies that feature warring factions of players (Marshall, 2021). This is, in short, a very big and complicated game with many possibilities. The graphics are highly realistic, and just about every element in the game not produced by a player is designed by an algorithm. Each star system is randomly generated, and the flora, fauna, minerals, and topography of each planet are created as the player discovers them for the first time.

The other key element of the game worth mentioning is not part of the game itself, but its development and business model. *No Man's Sky* uses the traditional games industry model of selling copies of the game; it does not have any in-game purchasing or ongoing subscription fees. Yet the game is in continual development in the same manner as titles like *Minecraft, Fortnite* (Epic, 2020), and *League of Legends* (Riot, 2013). Every few months since the launch, Hello Games has dropped a significant update that adds new features, activities, game modes, graphic upgrades, and more. Early updates added base building and planetary vehicles, for instance, while later ones added multiplayer modes, different spaceship classes, greatly enhanced underwater and cave environments, the capacity to play in virtual reality, a variety of technologies, various quests, and much more. The most recent version of the game is quite different from the original release in both subtle and very noticeable ways.

Procedural Generation and Its Limits

Procedurally generated game levels date back to the early stages of computer game history. In the early 1980s, the popular game *Rogue* (Wichman & Toy, 1980) spawned an entire genre of combat-oriented games with computer-generated levels that never play the same way twice. Other early strategy games, like *Seven Cities of Gold* (Ozark Softscape, 1984), had computer-generated maps. In the first decade of the 2000s, games like *Dwarf Fortress* (Bay 12, 2006), *Spore* (EA, 2008), and *Minecraft* all deployed algorithms extensively. *No Man's Sky* launched at a time when titles using these techniques and ideas were proliferating rapidly, including the quirky survival game *Don't Starve* (Klei, 2013), the serene transportation puzzler *Mini Metro* (Dinosaur Polo Club, 2014), and the rhythm rogue-like title *Crypt of the NecroDancer* (Brace Yourself Games, 2014).

The difference between *No Man's Sky* and earlier titles was the scope and apparent quality of the procedural generation. It promised a massive universe of explorable planets—up to 18 quintillion unique worlds (Kharpal, 2016)—full of visually impressive, procedurally generated elements, which was basically unprecedented. This combination of visuals and scope suggested to players in 2016 that the game was going to be a harbinger of a new era in gaming, featuring the detailed, gorgeous, open worlds of games like *Skyrim*, with the limitless boundaries of *Minecraft*.

But does *No Man's Sky* actually fulfill this promise? The answer seems to be no—at least, not yet. The issue hinges on our perception of creative works. When artistic elements are created by computer algorithms, we can often perceive a lack of direct human involvement. One of the reasons is creative variability. Paintings have more than one color and songs have more than one note, and the artistic elements can be present in a variety of patterns. Computer creations often display a mechanical repetition that we do not typically expect in art created by humans—even in highly formulaic human work.

Borrowing from Lev Manovich's (2001) terminology, digital objects and processes work according to the logic of *modular* variability, whereas human creators practice *organic* variability. Modular variability is the kind of mathematically calculable range of possibilities that occur when component parts have set, defined, discrete variables. For example, LEGO studs limit the number of possible interactions between blocks, though there are still many possibilities. Mathematician Søren Eilers (2005) discovered that six standard two by four stud LEGO blocks can be combined in 915,103,765 different ways. The key point here is: since all digital objects are quantified, they can *only* display modular variability.

Organic variability, on the other hand, is the kind of imprecise range of possibilities that occur when component parts are messily defined and structured by organic life. It has the potential for far more chaos, even if that potential is often unrealized. The patterns in the roots of a plant are very difficult to map and predict. So is human creativity. Organic life is not *completely* unpredictable: roots cannot (easily) grow through rocks, and even jazz tends to fall into a kind of repetitiveness. But organic life frequently has a range of variable behavior that exceeds our capacity to calculate it precisely.

Limited modular variability is often easy to detect. The programmed rules of the Rogerian therapist variant of the famous ELIZA 1960s chatbot program become obvious when the user says something unusual. Complex modular variability is much harder to distinguish from organic variability. The algorithms can become so elaborate that the patterns are not easy to see. Computer researchers are currently trying to train machines to create sophisticated art or jazz music. This is the dream for procedurally generated games. If a game's engine is complicated enough, a player will not be able to determine whether the game's world was created by a human design team or by an algorithm, meaning the narratively or artistically rich, infinite fictional universe is a reality.

This vision has not yet been fully realized in *No Man's Sky*. The planets of the game are remarkable, both in their appearance and scale, and in the capacity to surprise players with odd flora, fauna, and minerals. However, just a little exploring reveals similarities across this supposedly infinite universe. Rather than truly unique planets, the game gives variations on themes. Many planets, for instance, have a kind of bracket fungus, or dog-like creatures, or weird flying worms. The planets come in only a handful of ecosystem types, with similar color palettes, which produces predictable gameplay and isn't a universe of infinite creative possibility. In short, the game falls into easily detectable patterns. The game's narrative can explain why a universe might have a limited range of possibilities—but that does not change the reality of gameplay.

It is an open question whether *No Man's Sky*—or any other procedurally generated game—will ever reach a point where players will be unable to tell if it is authored by a human or an algorithm. But with its ambitious deployment of the technology, this title certainly is a significant step in the quest to reach that future.

An Infinite Universe in a Never Finished Game

No Man's Sky's business model is directly related to its core technology. The way Hello Games funds its development is not unique: it sells copies of its game, which is the traditional way of making money from games. Its practice of perpetual development, while relatively new, is not unprecedented. The combination of the two *is* somewhat unusual. Most long-running titles that continually release new content either sell downloadable content modules (DLC) or rely on some version of a free-to-play business model (a handful of titles like *World of Warcraft* [Blizzard, 2004] are still supported by subscriptions, and streaming services may effectively reintroduce this practice). Titles like *Clash of Clans* (Supercell, 2012) allow players to level up faster through in-app purchases, and many games, like *Fortnite*, offer various cosmetic skins and other forms of decoration for sale. Even *Minecraft* features in-app purchases of player-created content.

No Man's Sky has no such ongoing revenue stream: once a player purchases a copy, it is free from then on. Obviously, this business model has supported the big-budget, Triple-A game production model for decades—this is primarily how a game like *Mario Party Superstars* (Nintendo, 2021) or *Sid Meier's Civilization VI* (Firaxis, 2016) make money. *No Man's Sky* continues to develop its game with regular releases, much as titles like *League of Legends* or *Among Us* (Innersloth, 2018) do, but it is funded by a one-time purchase.

The game's technology makes this possible. Because every element in the universe is procedurally generated, rather than handcrafted by a set of artists and designers, the company has been able to keep its development team much smaller than a traditional Triple-A developer producing graphics-intensive games. Hello Games's lean team allows revenue from game sales to stretch further; many games could not generate enough revenue from this business model to stay afloat and keep its core audience engaged. As such, *No Man's Sky* is an important part of the shift to games as perpetual communities of play. The traditional model of game production encourages movement from one title to the next. Some of today's biggest game franchises—and, in fact, entire genres like e-sports and massively multiplayer online games—are designed to be perpetually available and adding new content. In short, games are becoming less like movie franchises and more like serial television series or social media platforms. *No Man's Sky*, with its unique take on the never-ending game, suggests that as procedural generation becomes more refined, even games with a more traditional style of gameplay and business model might be able to transition to this approach.

A Continuing Universe?

All game history is iterative. Every game builds on its predecessors in some way, so even the great ones are not truly unique. The importance of a game, then, typically lies less in novelty, and more in how it shifts design paradigms and gaming culture. On those counts, *No Man's Sky* is very important. It really has integrated the technology of procedural generation into its design to a far greater degree than its predecessors, and it has demonstrated that a traditional business model can work with the new form of perpetual development. A rocky launch can still result in some interesting possibilities.

Kevin Schut

Note

1. Hellogamestube (2013, December 8). *No man's sky* [Video]. YouTube. Retrieved November 22, 2021 from https://www.youtube.com/watch?v=RRpDn5qPp3s&ab_channel=HelloGamesTube.

References

Eilers, S. (2005). *A LEGO counting problem*. Københavns Universitet. Retrieved November 20, 2021, from http://web.math.ku.dk/~eilers/lego.html
Kharpal, A. (2016, August 11). 'No Man's Sky': Would You Play a Game that takes 584 Billion Years to Explore? *CNBC*. Retrieved November 20, 2021, from https://www.cnbc.com/2016/08/10/no-mans-sky-release-would-you-play-a-game-that-takes-584-billion-years-to-explore.html
Klepek, P. (2016, August 18). Inside the Nasty Backlash Against 'No Man's Sky'. *Vice*. Retrieved November 22, 2021, from https://www.vice.com/en/article/9bk3mz/inside-the-nasty-backlash-against-no-mans-sky
Manovich, L. (2001). *The language of new media*. Cambridge, MA: MIT Press.
Marshall, C. (2021, May 11). A No Man's Sky Galaxy is Embroiled in an Ongoing War: Fighting among the Stars. *Polygon*. Retrieved November 20, 2021, from https://www.polygon.com/22430818/no-mans-sky-first-intergalactic-war-roleplay-fan-creation-regicide-campaign

Further Reading

Bogost, I. (2006). *Unit operations: An approach to videogame criticism*. Cambridge, MA: MIT Press.

DOI: 10.4324/9781003199205-30

THE OREGON TRAIL (1971)

An Educational Adventure

Let's start with the most obvious aspect of *The Oregon Trail* in its inclusion here in *Fifty Key Video Games*: it is the only game in this volume developed as a pedagogical tool for school children. *The Oregon Trail* originally came about as an adaptation of history lessons and a student teacher's board game concept in the very early days of interactive computer pedagogy. It was developed by a small group of teachers who sought to familiarize their students with the material realities of the nineteenth-century settlers who traveled to the western United States in search of the American dream of a better, more prosperous life. Though a text adventure, *The Oregon Trail* was a complex game that required players to manage resources and cope with incidents as their settlers journeyed further with each turn.

The core gameplay mechanics remain engaging to this day and appear, with minor variations, across all subsequent iterations of the game. From the 1971 text adventure to the contemporary iOS game, the world of *The Oregon Trail* is a lively game space filled with the adventures of obtaining and managing resources by organizing one's trail party, trading, purchasing items at purveyors, hunting, and monitoring the health of one's party, the weather and trail conditions, and interacting with historical recreations of characters one might have met while traveling West. There is a lot to do on *The Oregon Trail*, with opportunities for players who excel at different gameplay modalities, from resource management to skilled interactive hunting of prey. It is quite common for players and their characters to die on *The Oregon Trail*, an occurrence that allows a player to travel again, make different choices, and learn more nineteenth-century history along the way. Indeed, actually making it to Oregon is far less common for players than rerouting and retraveling the trail in a myriad of ways and still having one's party "die of dysentery," one in-game death scenario beloved by fans, so much so that it comprises the title of the nostalgic fan tome ... *And Then You Die of Dysentery: Lessons in Adulting from The Oregon Trail* (Reeves, 2018). Playing *The Oregon Trail* offers an opportunity to appreciate the challenging conditions of the historical route, which is exactly what its designers intended in 1971.

The Oregon Trail Began in Minnesota

Development of *The Oregon Trail* did not occur in a vacuum, but in the context of a larger endeavor in mainframe computing in Minnesota that had begun several years earlier. Joy Lisi Rankin's *A People's History of Computing in the United States* (2018) looks at the user-generated development of the MECC (Minnesota Educational Computing Consortium), developer of *The Oregon Trail*. The three Minneapolis Public Schools student teachers (and college students) who created *The Oregon Trail*, Don Rawitsch, Bill Heinemann, and Paul Dillenberger, participated in the thriving and collaborative networked computing culture in Minnesota, an environment that fostered and enabled their development of *The Oregon Trail* as a teleprinter game to enliven eighth grade American history lessons. In Minneapolis in 1971, both educators and major corporations (Engineering Research Associates, Control Data, Honeywell, Sperry-Rand UNIVAC, IBM, and even Pillsbury) were deeply engaged in time-shared computing for both professional and personal uses (Rankin, 2018, p. 141).[1] Rawitsch (a history major teaching American history) introduced his students to the first version of the game. These eighth graders, as well as a few other students at their school, were able to play *The Oregon Trail* via commands, notably entering "BANG" or "POW" when hunting, and the speed of their command entry affected the outcome of their hunt. The developers' access to the computer terminal was limited and, initially, the game's code was written out on paper, which is how they saved their original source code once their student teaching term was up in December 1971. Then, as Rankin and others have noted, *The Oregon Trail*, while a success with the small groups of students who initially played it, was set aside until the MECC was established in 1973, enabling the development and distribution of *The Oregon Trail*.[2] Rawitsch, then a new college graduate, was hired by the MECC and the organization was eager to develop its software library of content for schools. Rawitsch still had his paper copy of *The Oregon Trail* source code, which he reentered in the teletype, building upon and expanding the student teacher version of 1971 into the MECC's 1974 title, *The Oregon Trail*, which was distributed to Minnesota public schools, to the delight of many young students (Lussenhop, 2011). When the MECC purchased its first round of personal computers for Minnesota public schools in 1978, they were early adopters of the Apple II.[3] The MECC later developed variations of the game, including *The Amazon Trail* (MECC, 1993) and *The Yukon Trail* (MECC, 1994).

The entire history of *The Oregon Trail*'s development is remarkable and evidence of a deep cultural investment in educational computing in the late 1960s and early 1970s. The game's developers wanted to address the complex historical legacies of Western expansion for all peoples along the historical Oregon trail.[4] Later versions represented the different class positions of travelers and included interactions with a variety of non-player characters, including Native Americans and African-American trail guides, indicating an effort to populate the game's world with a variety of peoples while still relying upon tropes from Western films in its setting and tone. But in its earliest iteration, gameplay simply included encountering either hostile or friendly parties on the trail, varying weather conditions, hunting, and the management of supplies, elements found in all versions of the game across its history. When designer Don Rawitsch shared an overview and sample run of *The Oregon Trail* in *Creative Computing* in May 1978, he included a bibliography of the primary and secondary sources consulted during the game's design (Rawitsch, 1978, p. 133). The game schematic in *Creative Computing* includes the same misfortunes on the trail found in later versions, such as broken wagon axles, inclement weather, and attacks by wild animals. Programming in these narrative elements as probable and likely occurrences within the game, Rawitsch, Heinemann, and Dillenberg adeptly translated their own board gaming and American history expertise into a highly playable text adventure. In nearly every iteration that followed the initial teleprinter game of 1971, playing *The Oregon Trail* has involved an engaging set of gameplay elements that allow players to succeed through a combination of strategy and skill. As a text adventure game, small groups of students could play *The Oregon Trail* together, with one student entering commands decided upon by the group, a modality made necessary by the limited number of computers in classrooms.

With Each Turn, Challenges Emerge

One begins *The Oregon Trail* in Independence, Missouri, by assembling a party of travelers and procuring provisions for the journey. Once travel begins, settlers must manage their supplies (food, ammunition, clothing, cash) while encountering different obstacles and opportunities. In this sense, *The Oregon Trail* presents Western expansion as a series of decisions, each affecting the outcome of their character's successful travel to Oregon, as they face high river water, animal attacks, storms, or other hostile conditions or people along the way. Players who succeed in *The Oregon Trail* end the game when they arrive over 2,000 miles away in the Willamette Valley, though this is hardly a guaranteed player outcome. While players of later iterations of the game might experience these pivotal gameplay decisions fairly quickly, dying and starting over as needed, in the earliest teleprinter version of the game, after entering a command, student players had to wait "up to half an hour" for the game to process a command (Lussenhop, 2011). Conveyed in a matter-of-fact tone, the game convincingly communicated the stakes for nineteenth-century wagon train settlers to twentieth-century school children. Despite the technical challenges of teleprinter play, these narrative components of *The Oregon Trail* have endured, as generations of students played later versions of the game distributed by the MECC and via a partnership in the 1980s with Apple Computer, which invested heavily in the educational computing market during the early years of the personal computing industry.[5] In short order, the MECC produced versions of *The Oregon Trail* for the then-popular Atari 8-bit computers and many other computer and video game platforms.

Upon its induction into the World Video Game Hall of Fame in 2016, The Strong National Museum of Play described *The Oregon Trail* "as the longest-published, most successful educational game of all time."[6] Initially, *The Oregon Trail* was a single game in a library that many educators and programmers collaborated on for the MECC, over time the game became a major source of income for the educational computing organization and, by 2011, long after the MECC ceased operations in 1999, over 65 million copies of the game had been sold (Lussenhop, 2011).

The Oregon Trail was produced during a period when Westerns were thriving, even in family-friendly media. In 1954, Disney's hit television series *Davy Crockett* premiered and when Disneyland opened the following year, its Frontierland attractions enabled park visitors to encounter nineteenth-century-themed scenarios that included Conestoga wagons, trails, trading posts, and saloons. Airing on television just as the MECC began distributing *The Oregon Trail* to Minnesota schools, *Little House on the Prairie* (1974–1983), adapted from Laura Ingalls Wilder's 1932–1943 books of the same name, depicted the life of a farming family in nineteenth-century Minnesota.

Playing Through the Western

The Oregon Trail allowed its players to partake in an adventure that was not just lessons adapted from textbooks, but was also part of a broader interest in the story of the nineteenth-century American West. In the decades since the game's introduction, its popularity is evident in its many iterations, including its adaptation into a 2018 card game and the way the now-familiar blocky graphics of the 1980s Apple version of covered wagons are part of the cultural imaginary. It is evident that *The Oregon Trail* is part of American popular culture, as it appears in twenty-first-century card game iterations, console and mobile versions, and everything from T-shirts to memes. It also picked up on 1970s nostalgic sentiment about the nineteenth-century American West. In 2021, one can even purchase an artist's rendition of the MECC game's screen glitching as decor. *The Oregon Trail*'s mediated version of the historical settlement of the Western United States is now its own historical (and beloved) narrative for those who once played it at school or at home or play it now with younger generations.

The Oregon Trail's legacy is arguably even more significant to the history of computers and gaming than its popularity and surrounding fandom implies. The development and distribution of *The Oregon Trail*, along with its enduring game world and captivating modalities of play, demonstrate its importance as an artifact in the history of computing and American pedagogy. *The Oregon Trail* proved how computers could be playfully imagined as tools for learning at a time when personal computers were first being imagined. The dedicated labor of student teachers and computing enthusiasts in Minnesota is an early example of text adventure gaming and of early pedagogical computing. Both these legacies, as well as the game's inherent replayabilty, seemingly guaranteed by the vast array of potential hazards of wagon train migration that its programmers could incorporate, merit its place here. *The Oregon Trail* is more than simply "the most successful educational game of all time," it is a window into computing history and a key game, period.

Sheila C. Murphy

Notes

1. Rankin's history illuminates how invested Minnesota was in computing at the time *The Oregon Trail* was invented; when Pillsbury sold mainframe computing time to local Minneapolis schools in the late 1960s and various computer companies sold minicomputer time to the Minneapolis Public Schools, which had time-share terminals installed. Rawitsch, Heinemann, and Dillenberger worked as student teachers in a school with these time-sharing terminals. Their access to these technologies and their participation in Minnesota's computing culture crucially enabled them to envision *The Oregon Trail* as a computer game.
2. While these developments obviously situate *The Oregon Trail* as a very early entry in the history of computing games, the game's development and distribution is also notable as a very early example of computer education and the investment of educational resources in computing.
3. Shortly before the MECC became an Apple customer, Rawitsch (1978) published the source code for the already very popular game, *The Oregon Trail*.
4. In between its initial development when they were student teachers and the MECC's rollout of the game in 1974, Rawitsch was drafted to serve in Vietnam but was excused as a conscientious objector, while Dillenger and Heinemann began working full-time as teachers (Lussenhop, 2011).
5. Most later versions of *The Oregon Trail* replicate the original gameplay and narrative structure that begins with assembling a party and gathering supplies, and continues as that party travels westward, encountering different conditions. Across many different computing and video game platforms, gameplay of *The Oregon Trail* remains remarkably consistent, with only the Nintendo Wii game (2011) significantly altering the gameplay so that players gain supplies via different mechanisms, like unlocking goods via movement. Instead, most iterations involve some variation upon the first game's narrative mode, in which players respond to inquiries with commands or utilize keyboard actions to move through the game.
6. Also cited in Rankin (2018, p. 139 and 272). "*The Oregon Trail.*" *The World Video Game Hall of Fame*, Strong National Museum of Play, inducted 2016 (https://www.worldvideogamehalloffame.org/games/oregon-trail).

References

Lussenhop, J. (2011, January 19). Oregon Trail: How Three Minnesotans Forged its Path. *Star Tribune*, Retrieved August 19, 2021, from https://web.archive.org/web/20110123012937/http://www.citypages.com/content/printVersion/1740595/

Rankin, J. L. (2018). *A People's history of computing in the United States*. Cambridge, MA: Harvard UP.

Rawitsch, D. (1978, May-June). Oregon Trail. *Creative Computing*, 132–139.

Reeves, L. (2018) ....*And then you die of dysentery: lessons in adulting from The Oregon Trail*. Boston: Mariner Books.

Slater, K (2017, Winter). Who gets to die of dysentery?: Ideology, geography, and *The Oregon Trail*. *Children's Literature Association Quarterly* 42(4), 374–395.

Further Reading

Lipinski, J. (2013, July 29). The Legend of *The Oregon Trail*. *Mental Floss*.

Wong, K. (2017, February 15). The Forgotten History of *The Oregon Trail*, As Told by Its Creators. *Vice 15*. Retrieved August 20, 2021, from https://www.vice.com/en_us/article/qkx8vw/the-forgotten-history-of-the-oregon-trail-as-told-by-its-creators

DOI: 10.4324/9781003199205-31

PAC-MAN (1980)

The Birth of an Icon

In the decades since it was first released into arcades across the world, much has been written about the origins of Namco's *Pac-Man* (1980), much of it apocryphal. By way of example, the game's designer, Toru Iwatani, has claimed on numerous occasions that the inspiration for the game's titular character came during a business lunch in the shape of a partly-eaten pizza. However, while the designer has since been photographed recreating this apparently seminal moment for publicity purposes and this story has passed into gaming folklore (Kent 2001), in other interviews Iwatani revealed a rather more complex relationship between the character's name and the visual design which relate, respectively, to the onomatopoeic sound of the mouth moving in quick succession (*paku paku*) and a (rounded) version of *kuchi*, the Japanese character for mouth (Lammers, 1986). That said, it is worth noting that, neat though this explanation is, it omits an important detail that reminds us of the transnational flows of media and meanings, as well as the public nature of arcade game play. For its initial Japanese release, the game and its lead character were actually called Puck-Man and it was only after Namco's US subsidiary intervened to note this was something of an invitation to arcade-going vandals that the tweaked sobriquet we know today was born.

Mazes

At its heart, *Pac-Man* places the player in a maze filled with 240 pellets (sometimes known as dots). The aim of the game is to clear stages by consuming each pellet. Four monsters (often referred to as ghosts) serve as antagonists and hunt down Pac-Man along the corridors of the maze. Consuming one of the special "Power Pellets" turns the tables by giving Pac-Man the temporary ability to devour the monsters, while every object consumed, including bonus items such as cherries, strawberries, or keys, adds to the player's score. Among the game's innovations are its "coffee break" sequences that punctuate the action between stages. Brief though these animations might be, they are often considered the first cut-scenes (Loguidice and Barton, 2009).

From a design perspective, being a product of what is sometimes known as the "golden age" of technological innovation and wider cultural penetration in arcade video games (Kent, 2001), it is tempting to simply lump *Pac-Man* with its contemporaries such as *Asteroids* (Atari, 1979), *Space Invaders* (Taito, 1978) or Namco's own *Galaxian* (1979). However, even though this era was still in its infancy in 1980, *Pac-Man*'s design and ethos self-consciously bucked trends in a number of important ways. As Iwatani recalls, *Pac-Man* was, in part, a reaction to the games that dominated the arcade at that time: "All the computer games available at the time were of the violent type—war games and space invader types" (Lammers, 1986). And so, borrowing from Popeye the ability to become more powerful by eating (MoMA, 2013) and by placing consumption at its center, Iwatani's response to these dominant tropes in game design can be read as a literal reversal as shooting becomes eating (Mateas, 2003). More technically, as Wardrip-Fruin (2020) notes, this can be understood as an inversion of the meaning of objects colliding in a game's world and so, what might be seen as bullet and explosion in *Space Invaders*, is reconceived as food and consumption in *Pac-Man*.

While Iwatani explicitly rethought some aspects of contemporary arcade design, *Pac-Man* was not willfully contrary and followed the trend toward accessibility and immediacy that was, at least in part, a consequence of the received wisdom that Nolan Bushnell and Nutting Associates' failure to commercialize *Computer Space* had been due to the complexity of its controls (Pescovitz, 1999). At first sight, *Pac-Man* does seem an enticingly straightforward proposition.

Of course, this is not quite the same as saying the game is easy, and *Pac-Man's* economical, audiovisual, and hardware interface belies the complexity of gameplay opportunities that lurk beneath its colorful, inviting surface. As Wade puts it, "Pac-Man is a simple game to learn but difficult to master. … the rules are straightforward and all of the requisite information about the game's status is available to the player at any given point in time" (2014, p. 3). *Pac-Man's* clear objective, deep gameplay, and what might initially appear to be the inscrutability of its monster AI routines do, indeed, contrive to create a game of considerable difficulty. Moreover, while the maze does not conceal any part of its spatiality and is unchanging within and across all levels, its multiple paths and passages render the game extremely accommodating—and perhaps even demanding—of considered tactics and strategies in place of haphazard, ad hoc play.

Monsters

There can be no doubt that the maze is an important feature of *Pac-Man* and provides a literal frame for the gameplay. However, it is clear that the core challenge to the player comes from the monsters. Where the maze can lead the player into danger, it is also the route out of it. The monsters, on the other hand, are singularly focused on Pac-Man's demise. As Iwatani notes:

> Well, there's not much entertainment in a game of eating, so we decided to create enemies to inject a little excitement and tension. The player had to fight the enemies to get the food. And each of the enemies has its own character. …I wanted the monsters to surround Pac Man at some stage of the game. But I felt it would be too stressful for a human being like Pac Man to be continually surrounded and hunted down. So I created the monsters' invasions to come in waves.
>
> (Lammers, 1986)

It is for these reasons that contemporary analyses, such as the encyclopedic investigations presented by Hodges ([2007] 2017) and in Pittman's (2009) "Pac-Man Dossier," dedicate so much time and expend so much labor dissecting the AI and behaviors of the monsters. Rather than reading the behaviors from the screen, these investigations look inside the code to learn the routines that set out how the monsters will behave. As Mateas (2003) notes, the pathfinding rules that define the movement through the maze are actually surprisingly simple, and yet, because they are each different and operate in tandem, there is a richness and dynamism that not only gives rise to the perceived "waves" of attack and retreat that Iwatani speaks of, but also imbues each monster with its own character. While the blue, orange, and pink monsters seem to take circuitous routes to variously get in front of or behind Pac-Man, the red monster, known as Shadow/ Blinky in the English localization, is guided by a pathfinding rule that has it take the most direct route. As such, the monsters appear to work as a team, mounting coordinated attacks to head off Pac-Man, with Shadow often seen as the "leader".

Whether it is because they add the "excitement and tension" that make *Pac-Man* a game with challenge, because the choreography of their behaviors variously coordinates and differentiates them, or because they can transform from enemy to prize, we might reasonably assume that the game of *Pac-Man* is ultimately concerned with unraveling the algorithms that dictate the readable personalities, movements, and responses of the monsters. After all, as Mateas (2003, p. 4) puts it, "Without the ghosts there is no challenge in clearing a maze of pellets, and hence no game".

Memorization

With this in mind, a look at guides to playing *Pac-Man* published throughout the 1980s reveals something rather surprising. Ken Uston's "Mastering *Pac-Man*" is one of a number of paperback volumes published in the 1980s that were dedicated to providing guidance on "winning at" or "beating" video games (e.g. Kubey, 1982; Giguette, 1981; Sullivan, 1982) or *Pac-Man* in particular (Mulliken, 1982; Zavisca & Beltowski, 1982). Given their publication dates, we might not expect to find the term AI used to describe the monsters' movement, but it would surely be more than a little surprising to find almost no reference to the monsters at all. Yet, as we leaf through page after page of these books, we do find countless carefully drawn illustrations mapping out pathways through the maze, but these do not describe the movements of the monsters. Rather these "patterns," as they are known, document tried-and-tested maneuvers the player can use to negotiate the maze and gobble up every pellet, while avoiding the monsters. The introduction to Uston's book (in which over 120 of the 150 pages are dedicated to illustrating successful patterns) outlines the methodology:

> I diagrammed and tested all the patterns and gleaned those that, with the minimum of effort, would permit the novice to develop

into what we call a "PAC-Master," a player who can consistently score 150,000 or higher. I tested all the patterns on many machines to ensure they were universally applicable.

(Uston, 1982, p. 11)

To be clear, the AI routines remain as effective as ever; it is simply that successful patterns ensure that the monsters never catch Pac-Man. Indeed, given the deterministic nature of the AI model, the monsters will never catch Pac-Man as long as the pattern is executed "without hesitation". The flawless execution of the patterns is key and is a point made most emphatically in the guides.

> Speed and timing cannot be overemphasized as crucial requirements for the success of these patterns. A slight delay when rounding a corner could throw off the rest of the pattern for the board...Remember: Practice is the key to success.
>
> (Zavisca & Beltowski, 1982, p. 24)

Through these books, we see an altogether different construction of *Pac-Man* not based around understanding, predictions, and battling against the AI, but centering on the memorization of patterns derived through trial-and-error that allow the AI to be effectively ignored in exactly the same way each time. By overlaying these assiduously-mapped and notated singular routes, to be followed without deviation or hesitation, guides like Uston's show us how players in the 1980s transformed the multicursality of the maze into the processional unicursality of the labyrinth. The game is rendered controllable and relatable. As long as the pattern is executed perfectly, every element in the system and, thereby, every movement and personality trait of each monster, will play out in precisely the same way, forever and ever.

Or at least that is what was understood in the 1980s. In the pages of these archival documents of 1980s play, *Pac-Man* is unequivocally presented as a game with an infinitely cycling structure that will continue to serve up new levels ad infinitum (if not ad nauseam as both Uston [1982, p. 123] and Kubey [1982, p. 52] note that players may choose to step away from the machine with *Pac-Man* lives still intact!). Kubey's book, for instance, describes a pattern that is "the near-perfect way to deal with all the tables from the Ninth Key to infinity," (Kubey, 1982, p. 50) while Mulliken (1982, p. 4) similarly observes, "Note: The chart stops at the 9th Key; this is because at this point, the machine keeps giving you the same pattern."

A Game of Two Halves

What makes these descriptions of an infinitely cycling game so intriguing is the revelation that: "In 1999, at the Funspot arcade, celebrity player Billy Mitchell performed the first recorded perfect score of 3,333,360" (Burnham, 2003, p. 235). Quite simply, although we might reasonably assume that Iwatani had intended Pac-Man to be an infinitely cycling game that potentially continued forever, a programming glitch means that it crashes at level 256 (Hodges, [2007] 2017). It then presents a maze with garbled graphics on the right side of the screen and insufficient onscreen pellets for Pac-Man to consume in order to progress to the next level, so the game becomes resolutely completable and, crucially, finite. By completing all 256 available levels, consuming every pellet and all four monsters with every Power Pellet, *Pac-Man* reveals itself to be a game with a maximum score of 3,333,360. It is simply not possible to exceed this score without cheating or modifying the game in some way. Though it does not literally write it onscreen, the fatal flaw that gives rise to the split screen effectively adds a "Game Over" message to *Pac-Man*.

Importantly, there is no suggestion that discussion of this "killscreen", or "split screen" as it has become known among aficionados (reflecting the garbled nature for the maze graphics), was omitted from the documentation of *Pac-Man* in the 1980s guides we have seen. Rather, the assertions about the game's endlessly cyclical structure indicate that the existence of the split screen was simply not known. And so, just as the split screen divides the maze in two, its discovery marks a dividing line in our understanding of the game. Despite its apparent simplicity, *Pac-Man* must be seen as a game that supports two distinct ways of playing (differently constituted around the maze and the monsters). More than this, these ways of playing are keyed to particular historical moments and the availability of insight and knowledge of the game's operation.

James Newman

References

Burnham, V. (2003). *Supercade: A visual history of the videogame age 1971–1984*. Cambridge, MA: MIT Press.

Giguette, R. (1981.) *How to win at video games*. Torrance, CA: The Martin Press.

Hodges, D. ([2007] 2017). Splitting Apart the Split Screen. *Donhodges.com*, Retrieved October 4, 2021, from http://www.donhodges.com/how_high_can_you_get2.htm

Kent, S. L. (2001). *The ultimate history of videogames*. New York, NY: Three Rivers Press.

Kubey, C. (1982). *The winners' book of video games.* New York, NY: Warner Books.
Lammers, S. (1986). *Programmers at work: Interviews.* New York, NY: Microsoft Press. Interview with Toru Iwatani. Retrieved October 4, 2021, from https://programmersatwork.wordpress.com/toru-iwatani-1986-pacman-designer/
Loguidice, B., & Barton, M. (2009). *Vintage games: An insider look at the history of Grand Theft Auto, Super Mario, and the most influential games of all time.* Burlington, MA: Focal Press.
Mateas, M. (2003, November, 4-6). 'Expressive AI: games and artificial intelligence', in *Proceedings of Level Up: Digital games research conference.* Utrecht, Netherlands. Retrieved October 4, 2021, from http://www.digra.org/digital-library/publications/expressive-ai-games-and-artificial-intelligence/
Mulliken, J. D. (1982). *Pac-Man: The ultimate key to winning.* Philadelphia, PA: Running Press.
Sullivan, G. (1982). *How to win at video games.* New York, NY: Scholastic.
Pescovitz, D. (1999, June 12). 'The Adventures of King Pong', *Salon,* Retrieved October 4, 2021, from http://www.salon.com/1999/06/12/nolan/
Pittman, J. (2009, 23 February). 'The Pac-Man Dossier'. *Gamasutra,* Retrieved October 4, 2021, from http://www.gamasutra.com/view/feature/132330/the_pacman_dossier.php
Uston, K. (1982). *Mastering Pac-Man* (revised Eds). New York, NY: Signet.
Wade, A. (2014, August, 3-6). Dots, fruit, speed and pills: The happy consciousness of Pac-Man. In *Proceedings of DiGRA 2014.* Utah: Snowbird. Retrieved October 4, 2021, from http://www.digra.org/digital-library/publications/dots-fruit-speed-and-pills-the-happy-consciousness-of-pac-man/
Wardrip-Fruin, N. (2020). *How Pac-Man Eats.* Cambridge, MA: MIT Press.
Zavisca, E., & Beltowski, G. (1982) *Break a million at Pac-Man, New York.* NY: Delair Publishing Company.

Further Reading

Newman, J. (2016) Mazes, monsters and multicursality. Mastering Pac-Man 1980–2016. *Cogent Arts & Humanities,* 3(1). Retrieved October 4, 2021, from https://www.tandfonline.com/doi/pdf/10.1080/23311983.2016.1190439
Terpstra, A. and Lapetino, T. (2021) *Pac-Man: Birth of an Icon.* Amsterdam: Cook and Becker.
Wade, Alex (2018) *The Pac-Man principle: A user's guide to capitalism.* Abingdon: Zero Books.

DOI: 10.4324/9781003199205-32

POKÉMON GO (2016)

A Location-Based Game Breaks Through

In July 2016, something unprecedented happened. Around the world, crowds of people were suddenly walking outside, mobile phones in their hands, knowingly nodding or grinning to others doing the same:

playing a game. The media took note, too. Headlines marveled at the phenomenon and highlighted both the benefits and the dangers it posed. One of the biggest mobile games of the era, *Pokémon Go*, had launched. Within its first quartile, it had reached 500 million downloads.[1] The biggest hype was short-lived, but after a steep drop in active players, the game has gradually found new popularity. In 2020, the game had an estimate of 166 million active players (compared to the first year's 232 million)[2] and reached record-breaking revenue, surpassing $1 billion.[3] What lies behind these numbers? What made *Pokémon Go* the incredible success that it is, and even more, how has *Pokémon Go* changed games, technology—and us?

In *Pokémon Go*, the player takes on the role of a Pokémon trainer, whose mission is to collect Pokémon creatures. The game and its concept have their roots deep in an existing franchise. Pokémon (short for Pocket Monsters) originated in the 1990s with Game Boy games, but quickly grew into one of the biggest multimedia franchises with anime series, movies, collectible cards, manga, toys, even theme parks. The fandom and nostalgia connected to this franchise are crucial to *Pokémon Go*'s popularity (Alha et al., 2019). The friendly theme and cartoon characters also easily attracted people not familiar with the franchise.

What differentiates *Pokémon Go* from previous Pokémon games is that it is location-based: the game world is parallel to the physical world, showing a map overlay depicting the player's surroundings. The game tracks the device's GPS and, to move the player characters, the players must move themselves. The distance traveled is further calculated and utilized in the game. The game tracks movement speed, and when the speed limit is exceeded, game content no longer appears on the screen and the distance is not calculated. In this way, the game encourages exercising instead of staying still or driving around. The concept of going outside to walk and play a video game made *Pokémon Go* stand out, even if it was not the first game to include such features. Many research prototypes, artistic experiments, and commercial games with locative elements had existed before.[4] However, while some of the earlier games can be considered successful or impactful, none of them had really reached such mainstream status.

Pokémon Go is often described as an augmented reality (AR) game:[5] Pokémon can be seen in the player's physical surroundings through the smartphone screen. AR is more of an extra feature than a core gameplay element, as this view is present only in specific parts of the game. Even then, most players turn the AR feature off when possible (Paavilainen et al., 2017), as using AR makes interactions more cumbersome and drains the battery faster. Still, the importance of the feature is not to be underestimated. It has served as a way to take amusing or artistic pictures: having an egg-like Pokémon resting on a frying pan or showing a whale-like creature jumping from the ocean creates interesting and playful mixes between the real and the digital. This proved to be a well-functioning viral tactic for the game, as social media was swamped with these pictures.

The central goal in the game is catching and collecting Pokémon. When the player is near such a creature, it appears on the map, and the player can tap it to begin a minigame. The player then uses the touch screen to aim and throw Poké Balls toward the Pokémon, trying to catch it inside the ball and consequently as a part of their collection. The player can also visit various PokéStops to receive items and Gyms to battle Pokémon left there by other players. These locations are based on existing points of interest in the environment: parks, statues, buildings, or other landmarks. *Pokémon Go* incorporates information about these locations in the game, which makes it a useful companion app when getting to know one's surroundings, whether in one's own neighborhood or exploring a new place.

While these core mechanics have stayed relatively the same, in other regards, *Pokémon Go* has changed and evolved considerably since its launch. The game started with 146 catchable creatures, while at the time of writing there are over 650 Pokémon, with new ones still being added regularly. New alternative variants have also been added, such as very rare "shiny" Pokémon. The game has introduced a variety of new activities, including events, sending gifts, trading Pokémon, player-versus-player leagues, and raid bosses. Compared to its earliest iteration, the current version is complex, with much more to achieve. Simplicity was important in the beginning as it made the game approachable, but as active players keep reaching the initial goals, more content needs to be added to maintain players' interest. The increasing amount of content keeps demanding more from players, while the goal to "catch 'em all" might start to feel unreachable for players starting out later or playing more casually. This is a challenge not unique to *Pokémon Go* but common in service-based games in general: how to balance the experience between players in different phases of the game.[6]

From Random Encounters to More Strategic Cooperation

Although the game did not have many real multiplayer features at launch, players have always existed in the same world, both virtually and physically. Even if players cannot see each other inside the game, they are very visible to each other outside of it. Importantly, the content in the game is shared by all players: in addition to the shared PokéStops and Gyms, the Pokémon themselves appear in the same location for everyone. During the first summer, a rare Pokémon was an event shared by all nearby players. Stampedes happened and dinners were interrupted with shouts of urgency as people rushed to the streets to catch the creature before it disappeared. In crowded areas, hundreds, even thousands of players might run in the same direction. A passerby might ask what was happening, getting an excited response of a Snorlax being spotted on the other side of the park.[7] Depending on whether the person was a *Pokémon Go* player or not, they would then hurry to join the hunt or shake their head in confusion.

In some locations, several PokéStops happened to exist near each other, meaning that there would be both more Pokémon spawning and more resources dropping from the stops themselves. These spots quickly turned into hubs for players. This created a different kind of play experience: suddenly the optimal strategy was not to walk, but to stay in one place. Families arrived together, friends organized picnics, and passersby came to wonder what was going on. Opportunities for emergent sociality arose: players had a common interest to talk about, making it easier to break the ice between strangers. Even without talking, sharing something with those around you brought a feeling of togetherness. These aspects created a shared feel of a game world that non-players were oblivious of, strengthening the sense of belonging (Vella et al., 2019).

In addition to increasing sociality between strangers, the game also strengthened existing social relationships. Families often play together, which in some cases may be the first time the parents have taken a close interest in their children's gaming hobby. The game also transformed social relationships, as children can suddenly be the experts and advise their parents (Koskinen & Meriläinen, 2021). For some children, Pokémon hunts may form the earliest gaming memories and create shared experiences and nostalgia for a whole generation.

Many of the social dimensions were made possible by the popularity of the game. Encounters were frequent due to the sheer number of players, seeing others playing the same game. As the player population crashed after the first summer, the chance encounters and the sense of community also decreased. New social interactions were facilitated through raids: battles against Pokémon often so powerful that no individual player could beat them alone. The raids were timed to attract players to a certain area at a certain time. This has given rise to cooperation between players, and increased the threshold for participation. Outside the raids, players do not have to actively play together and can choose whether they want to communicate with those around them, whereas raids often include organizing and sharing information. Some of the most powerful legendary Pokémon are locked exclusively behind raids, making them a mandatory step toward completing the collection. The forced sociality has pushed some players away from the game, while for some initially hesitant players they have created an empowering experience of building up the courage and skill to play together.

Breaking the Norms of Play and Gaming

One of the legacies of *Pokémon Go* is that location-based games are now part of mainstream gaming, but it is not easy for individual games to get there. Countless games have followed this path, but most have either failed or had only moderate success. While new hits do appear, the kind of success *Pokémon Go* reached in 2016 is difficult to replicate and is the result of many things that went right: the popularity and suitability of the franchise, hype around the game, viral marketing, positivity for encouraging outdoor activities, technology that felt new, and novel gameplay that was simple and flexible yet offered enough to do for more dedicated players.

Even if we do not see a similar craze again, its impact remains. *Pokémon Go* helped diversify player populations, brought families together, enabled random encounters and connections, created a feeling of belonging, got many interested in walking and learning about their surroundings, and provided meaningful, memorable experiences for countless people. That impact on our society is not trivial. The leaps in location-based technology and AR have created new and more widely available experiences which continue to evolve. We might not yet be in a world where AR is properly utilized, but we are a step closer to it.

While many of the game's impacts are positive, there are other sides to a game with popularity of this caliber. Especially during its peak months, players could take over locations such as parks or graveyards and disrupt their intended use, or trespass in private spaces. Some players or crowds focusing on their mobiles in traffic created dangerous, in some cases even fatal, incidents. It is further important to remember that not all players have equal opportunities to partake in playing the game. *Pokémon Go* is notorious for its lack of content in the countryside, and in some countries it is not even available. For people of color, playing the game, especially during nighttime or in unsafe areas, can be more dangerous, even life-threatening (Salen Tekinbaş, 2017). The game has problems with accessibility, as it is based on moving to various locations, sometimes inaccessible, for instance, with a wheelchair, and does not offer accessibility options for people with vision impairments either. There are also questions of fairness and ethics in how the game makes its money, whether from microtransactions or with the data it collects from its users.[8]

Even though *Pokémon Go* is still extremely successful, it is not without its future challenges. Frequent events and new content might tire out players, while finding more ways to monetize the remaining crowd could turn away others. It is also unclear how *Pokémon Go* will fare in post-pandemic times. During the COVID-19 pandemic, significant changes were made to support playing from home and avoiding larger gatherings. As these changes are retracted, it remains to be seen how willing players are to return to the pre-pandemic gameplay, especially as some of the temporary changes improved the game's accessibility and safety.

Pokémon Go has evolved since its launch and managed to remain highly popular, but the first months of the game were the most impactful for our society. Suddenly, playing a video game was not only okay, but it was beneficial, and not only for children, but also for people of all ages. Never have we seen such a global social phenomenon in games, where so many people around the world visibly and shamelessly played a video game, regardless of age or status. While the beneficial effects of outdoor activity and exercise are significant, it is important to note that a playful mindset, cross-generational gaming, and the joys of playing a game were suddenly shared by a massive, diverse audience. We are a playful species, but we tend to regulate and gatekeep the partaking in gaming and playful activities, while determining what is considered acceptable behavior. Breaking these norms, at least for a little while, is one of the biggest impacts of *Pokémon Go*.

Kati Alha

Notes

1. https://press.pokemon.com/en/pokemon-go-exceeds-500-million-downloads-worldwide
2. https://www.businessofapps.com/data/pokemon-go-statistics/
3. https://sensortower.com/blog/pokemon-go-one-billion-revenue-2020
4. For a recap of location-based games history, see Leorke (2018, pp. 17–44).
5. AR refers to technology where a real-world environment is altered or enhanced with digital technology in real-time.
6. 'Service-based games' refers to a model where games are offered as a service that the player has access to instead of a product that is owned by the player.

7. A Snorlax was one of the rare Pokémon in 2016.
8. Microtransactions are in-app purchases that the player can choose to buy with real money to enhance the experience. In *Pokémon Go*, players can purchase or earn in-game currency that can then be used to buy several types of benefits: increasing storage space; acceleration for gaining experience or hatching eggs; items to attract more Pokémon or to heal Pokémon after battles; and Poké Balls.

References

Alha, K., Koskinen, E., Paavilainen, J., & Hamari J. (2019). Why do people play location-based augmented reality games: A study on Pokémon GO, *Computers in Human Behavior*, *93*, 114–122.

Koskinen, E., & Meriläinen, M. (2021). Social playfulness—Memorable family co-play experiences with Pokémon GO. In A. Spanellis & J. T. Harviainen (Eds), *Transforming Society and Organizations through Gamification: From the Sustainable Development Goals to Inclusive Workplaces* (pp. 247–270). Cham: Palgrave Macmillan.

Leorke, D. (2018). *Location-Based Gaming: Play in Public Space*. Singapore: Springer.

Paavilainen, J., Korhonen, H., Alha, K., Stenros, J., Koskinen, E., & Mäyrä, F. (2017). The Pokémon GO experience: A location-based augmented reality mobile game goes mainstream. *In Proceedings of the 2017 CHI Conference on Human Factors in Computing Systems*, 2493–2498.

Salen Tekinbaş, K. (2017). Afraid to roam: The unlevel playing field of Pokémon Go. *Mobile Media & Communication*, *5*(1), 34–37.

Vella, K., Johnson, D., Wan Sze Cheng, V., Davenport, T., Mitchell, J., Klarkowski, M., & Phillips, C. (2019). A sense of belonging: Pokémon GO and social connectedness. *Games and Culture*, *14*(6), 583–603.

Further Reading

Geroimenko, V. (2019). *Augmented reality games I: Understanding the Pokémon GO phenomenon*. Cham: Springer.

Montola, M., Stenros, J., & Waern, A. (2009). *Pervasive games: Theory and design*. Burlington: Morgan Kaufmann.

DOI: 10.4324/9781003199205-33

PONG (1972)

Was *PONG* First?

The significance of *PONG* can be simply stated in as few as three words: it was first. This claim alone should be sufficient to stake a claim to a place among the fifty key video games, but it begs a more important question: first at what? Certainly not the first video game. In summer 1972, when Al Alcorn installed the first version of *PONG* at Andy Capp's Tavern, a bar located not far from Atari in Sunnyvale, California, one could already count a handful of predecessors, from Higinbotham's *Tennis for Two* (1958), to *Spacewar!* (Steve Russell, Martin Graetz, Peter Samson and Wayne Witaenem, 1962) and on to Ralph Baer's *Brown Box* and the Magnavox Odyssey based on Baer's machine.

Baer himself directly answered the question of whether *PONG* was first, whether it counted as the first game and accordingly whether Nolan Bushnell, Atari's founder, could be considered its inventor. In his book *Videogames in the Beginning*, Baer presented documents and recollections about his own role in the history of video games, centered on his work at Sanders Associates that led to the first patent for what he called a "TV gaming display" in his original notes, dated September 1, 1966, nearly six years before *PONG*. He anointed himself "the Father of Videogames by definition," thinking himself to be the first to file for a patent. What did that conclusion leave for Bushnell and *PONG*? According to Baer, *PONG* might not have been the first video game, but Bushnell could nonetheless claim to be the inventor of something else; he "had the vision to introduce videogames into the arcade environment." From Baer's perspective, *PONG*'s status in video game history was not about inventing the video game; it was about inventing the video game industry (Baer, 2005, pp. 3–24).

Soon after Nolan Bushnell and Ted Dabney founded Atari, Inc. (originally Syzygy) in June 1972, they hired an engineer named Al Alcorn. The three engineers had worked together in the Videofile group at Ampex, a San Francisco Bay Area company that played a crucial role in the invention and commercialization of audio and video recording technologies, beginning in the late 1940s. The deft combination of analog and digital engineering they took from Ampex and brought to Atari would become the foundation for the new game company's products and profits.

The first assignment Bushnell gave to Alcorn was to design an electronic ping-pong game that could be played in game arcades. Alcorn later learned that the project Bushnell gave him was a ruse, "a simple video game which we now know was just an exercise" to break him into game design (Alcorn 2008, p. 10). Alcorn delivered *PONG*, which, after successful testing in a local bar called Andy Capp's Tavern, became the first successful, mass-produced, commercial arcade video game. Describing *PONG* even in this more constrained fashion as "first" is at once both accurate and misleading. Even if as a finished game *PONG* probably struck most players as anything but problematic, the origins of this simple game raise questions about the "video game" as occupying a space straddling contemporary computer and television technology. *PONG* is a key game for video game *history*; its status as "first" game or, following Baer, as the progenitor of an industry, requires that we understand what kind of game it was.

What Kind of Game Was *PONG*?

The complex history of this simple game begins with its connection to computer-based games. The *PONG* arcade console betrays few obvious connections to computer technologies of the early 1970s. Widespread adoption of the microprocessor as the central component of home computers and television consoles had not yet occurred. The *PONG* prototype's cabinet and circuitry required only a modest investment in electronic components, a modified television set, and some ad hoc wiring and parts. *PONG*'s game mechanics and graphics depended on Alcorn's knowledge of how transistor-transistor logic (TTL) and television circuitry could be deployed to decode video signals to produce the images and sounds of the game, as well as game control functions. It did not use a microprocessor or a custom integrated circuit; rather, it was made from components familiar to an engineer who understood the various ways an oscillating wave could be manipulated. The original game ran not one line of program code.

And yet, *PONG* has been depicted as a product of the computer age or even as an artifact of computer technology. One of the earliest critical studies of video games, Loftus & Loftus' *Mind at Play* (1983), described *PONG* as being "entirely under the control of a computer," and their version of the video game's "family tree" showed arcade games and digital computing as its parents (pp. 6–7). Michael Malone (1985), in his excellent history of Silicon Valley, wrote that *PONG* was put together by a "computer programmer" (p. 343). These mischaracterizations of *PONG* reflect a natural, if perhaps careless, assumption about the dawn of the video game. If much of its past and, as we now know, its future was bound to the computer, we are tempted to see computer code in every video game and a processor inside every game machine. Alcorn's original *PONG* console was not a computer game.

This is not to say that *PONG*'s creators were not influenced by computer technology. The game that set Bushnell on the path to *PONG* was *Spacewar!*, developed at MIT about a decade earlier. Video game patents, many of them linked to Ralph Baer's claim discussed above to having first documented the idea of a television console game in 1966, have challenged claims that *PONG* or Bushnell's prior game, *Computer Space*, amounted to inventing game technology based on the raster scan graphics of television displays. Legal arguments defending licenses based on Baer's patents also occasionally depicted computer games such as *Spacewar!* as prior art for *Computer Space* (Lowood, 2009, pp. 15–17). Perhaps more than any other company of the early video game era, Bushnell and his colleagues at Atari negotiated contradictions and convergences of computer and television technology in producing arcade games (beginning with *PONG*), dedicated home consoles (also beginning with the home version of *PONG*), programmable game machines, and home computers, all within less than a decade of the company's founding.

The Development of *PONG*

While Alcorn designed *PONG*, Bushnell provided the impetus for Atari's early projects. His entrepreneurial imagination responded forcefully to the environment that awaited him when he moved to California after graduation from the University of Utah in 1968 to take an engineering position at Ampex. He was now in the hotbed of high-technology entrepreneurship, at the southern boundary of the region Don Hoefler (1971, p. 1) had just begun calling "Silicon Valley U.S.A." in 1971. Surrounded by first-rate research engineers and product development teams at Ampex, he developed a vision for games like *Spacewar!*—which by the late 1960s had become a fixture of computing in university and industrial laboratories—that situated them as the main attractions in a new entertainment format: electronic game arcades. This was the practical insight Baer attributed to Bushnell. However, the first step was not *PONG*. Rather, Bushnell began this project by designing a modestly priced computer arcade game inspired by *Spacewar!*, a lineage he acknowledged by calling his first game *Computer Space*.

Bushnell's departure from Ampex in March 1971, his partnership with Ted Dabney, his decision to join Nutting & Associates, which acquired and manufactured *Computer Space*, and the founding of Atari, have been recounted by numerous writers (e.g., Herman, 2001, pp. 11–15; Kent, 2001, pp. 28–40; Goldberg & Vendel, 2012). While Bushnell worked on *Computer Space* during 1971, he may have been aware of other projects inspired by *Spacewar!*, notably the summer project of a recently graduated Stanford AI Lab (where Bushnell presumably played *Spacewar!*) student, Bill Pitts, and his friend, Hugh Tuck. Their *Galaxy Game* was installed in the Stanford student union in September 1971. Like Pitts and Tuck, Bushnell intended to program a version of *Spacewar!*, but using raster graphics on a cheap, off-the-shelf television set, not on the kind of expensive vector graphics monitor one would find in a computer lab around that time. When this configuration of computer and television sets proved unworkable, Bushnell built a system without the computer. Dedicated circuits controlled all aspects of *Computer Space*, from game logic to player controls. After sculpting a futuristic cabinet for the arcade console, Bushnell sold his game to Nutting and joined the firm as chief engineer to oversee the final design, manufacturing, and distribution.

The historical verdict on *Computer Space* has generally been negative, whether with respect to sales, gameplay, or the complexity of its controls. These assessments miss its general significance for the video game as a technological construct. Specifically for *PONG*, *Computer Space* was the negative example for Bushnell and Al Alcorn. It provided the learning experience that would shape Atari's first product as a less complicated machine and game. Even more important, it pushed Atari's design philosophy and general technical configuration for arcade consoles and moved Bushnell's attention from the world of laboratory-based computer games (*Spacewar!*) to a stable arcade console format. Now he could realize his vision of the video game as an arcade experience and basis for a new entertainment industry, which Atari extended a few years later into the domain of consumer products.

There was also some good news financially. Dabney and Bushnell invested $500 in royalties from *Computer Space* after leaving Nutting to fund Atari as a startup. When Alcorn was hired, he understood the application of transistor logic and integrated circuits to analog problems such as television video. Concerned that he could not expect Alcorn to go from not knowing what a video game was to designing a game, Bushnell told his new hire that General Electric had contracted with Atari to produce a video game based on ping-pong. Alcorn learned later that "this was simply an exercise that Nolan gave me because it was the simplest game he could think of" (Kent, p. 40). The ruse eased Alcorn into electronic games. Assigning Alcorn a design problem simple enough to provide context for on-the-job training simultaneously, if unknowingly, addressed criticism that the complexity of *Computer Space* explained its limited appeal, while also giving Alcorn a manageable engineering task. *PONG* would be a simple game.

Alcorn produced the *PONG* prototype within a few months. The successful installation in Andy Capp's Tavern, with eager bar patrons lining up to stuff quarters into the game, might generously be called the consumer testing phase of the project. After acquiring funding for a production facility, Atari began marketing to arcades before the end of 1972, and by the next year *PONG* was in international distribution. A home version, which could be connected to television sets, would follow in 1975.

PONG's Success

PONG's success as the game that launched the electronic arcade industry has been credited to the unrepentant simplicity of its design. Three short sentences on the cabinet's faceplate told players everything they needed to know: put a quarter into the machine, a "ball" will be served; move the paddle to hit the ball back and forth. As I have argued, *PONG*'s success reversed the failure of *Computer Space* by stepping away from the complexity of computer games. Unlike *Computer Space*'s beautiful fiberglass cabinet, the *PONG* prototype was set in an ugly square box covered with orange paint and wood veneer, and the simple plate for control knobs and instructions. As game and as aesthetic design, *PONG* and *Computer Space* were opposites. As an engineering design, however, *PONG* followed *Computer Space* in its modularization and optimization of hardware. Prepared by experience and inclination, Alcorn was in a favorable position to build an efficiently engineered arcade console in three respects: (1) he built his game from the ground up, without first having to wrestle a complicated computer game to the ground; (2) he could use digital components to solve the analog problem of mastering television output, precisely Alcorn's special domain of engineering knowledge; and (3) the images required for the game were relatively simple—unlike the oddly shaped objects such as the spaceships in *Computer Space* that required ad hoc memory solutions such as diode arrays—and the ball, paddle, and other images in *PONG* were all based on simple rectangles that television circuits could generate on the fly. This last point was especially important. It is worth emphasizing again that not one line of software code was involved in the construction of *PONG*. Like *Computer Space*, *PONG*'s game logic and control operations were paced by synchronization signals for the rasterized television display, except that Alcorn understood perhaps more intuitively than Bushnell how to work with these signals during every cycle through the television circuits. Since every image was based on rectangles, he could generate them by gating counters, even the seven segments of the score display. Alcorn was thus able to build *PONG* optimally from a modest number of integrated circuits, which fed his obsession with reducing the parts count, eliminating unnecessary parts not only to make the game run more efficiently, but also to reduce the cost of the final product.

The technological lineage leading from *Spacewar!* through *Computer Space* to *PONG* is one way to narrate the complicated historical relationships embedded in the "video game." *Computer Space* and *PONG* were both *television* games in the sense that their designers applied techniques of television engineering to make them, and in fact they required actual televisions to operate. Yet, the vision and the initial impulse behind Bushnell's project emerged from the computer space of academic laboratories and large-scale computers. *PONG* was cut loose from this mooring in a way that produced a compelling arcade game. In this telling of the story, arcade consoles, the home game foreshadowed in Alcorn's original *PONG* design and finally home consoles created during the mid-1970s—Atari's home version of *PONG* (1975), General Instruments AY-3-8500 "TV game on a chip" (1976), and the microprocessor- and ROM-based Atari 2600 (1977)—addressed Bushnell's self-imposed problem of reducing the computer game to a configuration suitable for delivery as an entertainment product to mass markets. And yet, Atari never gave up on the computer game. The company's early marketing literature characterized games like *PONG* as "video computer games" and claimed that they revolutionized the industry "when we harnessed digital computers and video technology to the amusement game field with *PONG*." (Atari, 1972). In its marketing and advertising, Atari thus encouraged later verdicts that video games began as an ambitious coupling of complex computer and video technology, when in fact they began, like PONG, as simple television games.

Henry Lowood

References

Alcorn, A. (2008). *Oral History of Allan (Al) Alcorn*. Computer History Museum. Mountain View, CA. Retrieved August 15, 2021 from http://archive.computerhistory.org/resources/access/text/2012/09/102658257-05-01-acc.pdf

Atari (1972). Atari Expands Worldwide. Advertising flyer. *Arcade Flyer Database*. Retrieved February 2022, from https://flyers.arcade-museum.com/?page=flyer&db=videodb&id=3303&image=1

Baer, R. (2005). *Videogames in the beginning*. Springfield, NJ: Rolenta.

Herman, L. (2001). *Phoenix: The fall and rise of videogames*, 3rd ed. Springfield, NJ: Rolenta.

Hoefler, D. (1971, January 11). Silicon Valley USA, *Electronic News*, 1, 4.

Kent, S. (2001). *The ultimate history of video games*. New York: Three Rivers Press.

Loftus, G. & Loftus, E. (1983). *Mind at play: The psychology of video games*. New York: Basic.
Lowood, H. (2009, July-September). Video games in computer space: The complex history of *Pong*. *IEEE Annals in the History of Computing* 31, 5–19.
Malone, M. (1985). *The big score: The billion-dollar story of Silicon Valley*. Garden City, NY: Doubleday.
Goldberg, M., & Vendel, C. (2012). *Atari Inc: Business is fun*. Carmel, NY:Syzygy.

Further Reading

Guins, Raiford (2020). *Atari design: Impressions on coin-operated video game machines*. New York: Bloomsbury.

DOI: 10.4324/9781003199205-34

PORTAL (2007)

An Orange Drop in the Gaming Ocean

Portal's (Valve, 2007) success story began at the end of spring 2005 when eight graduating students from the DigiPen Institute of Technology showcased their game *Narbacular Drop* under the team name Nuclear Monkey Software at a job fair organized by the university. When Valve representatives saw this innovative 3D puzzle-platformer based on magical portals, the team was hired in July 2005 to develop their idea in the Source Engine (Swift, Wolpaw, & Barnett, 2008, p. 8). After two years in development, *Portal* was published for Windows, Xbox 360, and PlayStation 3 through *The Orange Box* (Valve, 2007). With nearly 4 million physical copies sold worldwide, excluding Steam sales (Rose, 2011), *Portal* became a landmark video game crowned with more than seventy industry awards and thirty Game of the Year Awards. To delineate the value of *Portal* as a key video game, it is essential to outline its unique experience, its influence on the puzzle and FPS (first-person shooter) genres, and its various layers of meaning.

The Portal Experiment: A Successful Test Report

Portal is a story-driven and physics-based, first-person puzzler set in the military-industrial universe of the *Half-Life* franchise (Valve, 1998–). Players embody Chell, a non-white woman of ambiguous ethnicity waking up in an enclosed relaxation vault of the Aperture Science Enrichment Center. The protagonist is welcomed by the computerized female voice of GLaDOS (voiced by Ellen McLain), an apparently benevolent AI that puts her through a series of nineteen test chambers where "fun and learning are the primary goals" (Valve, 2007). Upon progression, small narrative cues scattered in the lab gradually force players to question the educative purpose of the experiment and piece together a sinister story filled with dark and cynical humor.

Portal's groundbreaking gameplay mechanic relies on the Portal Gun, a device that can shoot two interconnected portals to open new passages that cut through space. The core puzzling and platforming experience revolves around placing portals on surfaces of the gamespace to transport weighted cubes onto big red buttons, to jump on elevated and mobile platforms, to get out of deep pits, and to cross huge gaps. As things get harder, the game design introduces various obstacles such as deadly toxic water, walls that cannot receive portals, screens of particles that remove all portals when crossed, and shooting turrets. These components are combined to form mind-bending challenges. Players have to overcome puzzles that require synchronized and coordinated portal (dis)placements to redirect flying energy balls into their receptacle, the accumulation of momentum to execute high velocity jumps, and the management of portals between isolated sectors through careful memorization and planning; all of this often coupled with time-pressure elements like timed doors and time-critical jumping sequences on automated platforms moving along rugged courses.

A Puzzling Generic Legacy

To grasp *Portal*'s cultural impact, it is necessary to situate its unique ludonarrative proposition in the context of its generic affiliations. In his history of the puzzle genre, Mora-Cantallops (2018) analyzes games like *Loco-Motion* (Konami, 1982), *Tetris* (Pajitnov, 1984), *Lemmings* (DMA Design, 1991), and *Myst* (Cyan, 1993), and theorizes nine generic components forming the structural backbone of the genre. The paradigmatic configuration organizes a series of puzzles with a given solution in which players have to manipulate pieces while being restricted to certain moves. Typically, there is no time pressure, chance is absent or minimal, dexterity requirements remain trivial and some scoring systems are often included. Most puzzle games are played in single-player mode from an extradiegetic position, while storytelling is optional or secondary.

Following this model, *Portal* transforms the genre on the levels of dexterity, player role, and narration. The game breaks from the classic disembodied cognitive challenge based on 3D still images found in

Myst and *The 7th Guest* (Trilobyte, 1993). Instead, the puzzle-solving experience entails a non-trivial kinesthetic choreography based on agile maneuvering of Chell's navigational affordances, acrobatic control of the first-person camera, precise aiming abilities, execution of time-critical jumps, and mastery of objects' physics. For instance, the last section of chamber eighteen requires the skillful use of the double flinging technique, a boosted jump exploiting gravity to dive into an entry portal, be catapulted via the exit portal with augmented velocity, and falling back again into another portal to double the momentum. In this vertically oriented puzzle, players face a series of three, relatively small and disconnected, square-shaped platforms placed at radically different heights above a pit of toxic water. To climb their way up, they have to execute an uninterrupted sequence of double flinging jumps. While in midair, players have to quickly aim at the next visible platform to reshoot each portal and then control Chell's spatial trajectory to land right back in the newly placed entry portal and be propelled through the new exit.

Moreover, *Portal* breaks with the ornamental narrative template that positions players outside the game world. Instead, it relies on the first-person embodiment into a cryptic character entangled in a complex story. As Chell starts the tests in the aseptic and cold-blue atmosphere of the Aperture Science lab, she notices surveillance cameras tracking her movements and vacant offices behind blurred glass. While suspicions might be eased by GLaDOS's humorous guidance, motivation, and the appetizing promise of a cake as final reward, the eventual inclusion of life-threatening dangers reveals the AI's true evil nature. For instance, when Chell arrives in chamber sixteen, GLaDOS has replaced the test with a "live-fire course designed for military androids" and sarcastically "apologizes for the inconvenience" and wishes Chell "the best of luck." Upon entrance, the character is attacked by turrets programmed to shoot her. Halfway through, players can find a removable wall blocked by cubes, near the word "help" written in red on the floor. Behind the wall lies the secret hideout of a mentally troubled Aperture Science former employee named Doug Rattmann, as revealed in the official comic *Portal 2: Lab Rat* (Valve, 2011). The refuge contains traces of Rattmann's desperate attempt to run away from GLaDOS and warn others about her malicious intentions with sinister scribbles on the wall indicating that "the cake is a lie," thus revealing the rogue AI narrative trope. The elegance of *Portal*'s story lies in the mutual enrichment of ludic and narrative elements. On the one side, the harshness of puzzle-solving fuels the surveillance and imprisonment atmosphere of the lab. On the other, the environmental storytelling produces a puzzling mystery to be deciphered by gathering clues through attentive listening, appropriation of diegetic tools and puzzle-solving skills acquired inside the main narrative arc.

While the puzzle genre settled itself in the casual mobile gaming market at the turn of the 2000s (Adams, 2014, p. 78), *Portal* kickstarted a niche in the indie scene which motivated other designers to experiment with a similar assemblage of generic components. Aside from *Portal 2* (Valve, 2011) and countless mods for the *Portal* franchise, notable titles are *Q.U.B.E.* (Toxic Games, 2011), *Quantum Conundrum* (Airtight Games, 2012), *Antichamber* (Demruth, 2013), *The Talos Principle* (Croteam, 2014), *The Turing Test* (Bulkhead Interactive, 2016), *Superliminal* (Pillow Castle, 2019), and *Manifold Garden* (William Chyr Studio, 2019). All these games work within *Portal*'s lineage by further bending the laws of physics, stretching visuo-spatial requirements, and designing unique methods to manipulate the gamespace and its objects.

Aiming Down: A Non-Combative Lineage

Portal also left its mark on the FPS genre beyond the inclusion of a portal mechanic in a conventional multiplayer shooter as with *Splitgate: Arena Warfare* (1047 Games, 2019). According to Pinchbeck (2013, p. 159), the main contribution of *Portal* rests on its non-combat orientation. For instance, even the neutralization of turrets in chamber sixteen is a puzzle to solve rather than a gun fight. Players need to find a way to push the machine on its side, either by shooting a portal underneath it, dropping a cube on its head, charging it with a cube, or by sneaking up from behind to drag it on the floor. This design paradigm moves away from the environmentally destructive, fast-paced, run-and-gun, and reactive gameplay that characterizes traditional shooters. Rather, it proposes a spatially constructive, slow-paced, tactical-oriented, and proactive FPS experience, focused on the ingenious avoidance of direct conflict, crafty navigation, and thoughtful reflection and planning. This legacy persists in FPS crossovers like *Mirror's Edge* (EA DICE, 2008), *Dishonored* (Arkame Studios, 2012), *Story About My Uncle* (Gone North Games, 2014), *DeadCore* (5 Bits Games, 2014), *SUPERHOT* (SUPERHOT Team, 2016), *Valley* (Blue Isle Studios, 2016), and *The Turing Test*.

On a discursive level, *Portal* also subverts the FPS archetypes established around 2000 when the genre embraced photorealistic militarism as the new norm following successes like *GoldenEye 007* (Rare, 1997), *Medal of Honor* (DreamWorks Interactive, 1999), *Half-Life: Counter-Strike* (Valve, 2000), *Operation Flashpoint: Cold War Crisis*

(Bohemia Interactive, 2001), *Battlefield 1942* (DICE, 2002), and *Call of Duty* (Infinity Ward, 2003). The game discards the trope of the militarized, hypermasculine, and obedient white male soldier mindlessly dominating others through armed conflict while gazing at sexually objectified women. Instead, it develops the rich story of a non-hypersexualized and rebellious non-white woman, resisting objectification from a militarized system of oppression and striving for emancipation through kinesthetic prowess and creative spatial-temporal reasoning.

Throughout the series of tests to which she is subjugated, Chell undergoes a process of empowerment leading her to fight for retaliation and liberation. Upon entering chamber nineteen, it becomes more than clear that GLaDOS surreptitiously conducts scientific experiments on humans used as lab rats. This last puzzle is literally designed to kill Chell in a fire pit. Before being burned alive, the protagonist has to hijack the Portal Gun to jump on a nearby walkway and escape in the sinuous backstage of the lab to locate and destroy her nemesis. Combined with the game's critical discourse about the precariousness of human life in relation to existential risks from AI, this "feminist critique of the FPS genre" (McNeilly, 2011) situates *Portal* in a wave of contemporary shooters that explore deeper themes such as "utopia and free will (*BioShock*), the futility of war and loss of innocence (*Far Cry 2* [Ubisoft, 2008]), antiglobalism and civic dissent (*Mirror's Edge*)" (Pinchbeck, 2013, p. 160).

Flinging Through *Portal*'s Layers of Meaning

Many game scholars dedicated their efforts to unraveling the cultural significance of *Portal*. Some explore questions about human struggles in a society of control, where power and governance operate through gamified algorithmic machines (such as video games) that sculpt how individuals self-discipline, perceive, think, and behave (Nohr, 2015). Other contributions study the narrative experience of the transmedia franchise to analyze how the loose plot threads motivate fans to partake in the playful excavation and extension of the (para)text to coalesce their personalized interpretations within the core narrative (Mittell, 2012; Wendler, 2014).

Authors also explore the complexity of the characters. DeWinter & Kocurek (2015) look at Chell's popularity among female players and conclude that her muteness, visual absence, obscure backstory, and racial ambiguity have opened a space of appropriation for marginalized players to identify with a protagonist that mirrors their struggle within the male-dominated landscape of gaming culture. Harkin (2020) articulates a feminist-oriented psychoanalytic analysis of GLaDOS's patriarchal codification as a castrating mother, to contextualize this monstrous figure as a masculine-coded cultural reaction to the demographic shift toward adult women following the casual gaming revolution in the 2000s.

In addition, researchers reflect on the metaludic nature of the game. For Grewell, McAllister, & Ruggill (2015), GLaDOS's empty gratifications and hostile humor produce a metacommentary on the role of ridicule as a fundamental game mechanic operating in every game to persuade play, test players' tenacity, and generate pleasure when the pain of failure is overcome. Ouellette & Ouellette (2015) conceptualize the interactions between GLaDOS, Chell, and the lab structures as a nexus of *mise-en-abîme* that mirrors ontological elements of games and play, such as key game design processes (tutorials, feedback systems, rewards, playtesting, etc.), the conditioning of participants through monitoring and behavioral techniques, the shared ludic contract between designer and players, and the transgressive impulse to bend the rules and beat the system at its own game.

There Is Still Research to Be Done

In light of its innovative experience, generic legacy, and complex layers of meaning, *Portal* offers multiple keys to study how the art of video games can push the boundaries of its medium by reflecting critically on its own materiality, design structures, discursive apparatus, and sociocultural context. *Portal*'s heritage therefore opens precious portals to a unique gaming laboratory to conduct new ludic experiments. Minding this gap can only lead to better video game design and science...and cake.

Hugo Montembeault

References

DeWinter, J., & Kocurek, C. A. (2015). Chell game: Representation, identification, and racial ambiguity in PORTAL and PORTAL 2. In B. Neitzel, T. Hansel, & R. Nohr (Eds.) *"The cake is a lie!": Polyperspektivische Betrachtungen des Computerspiels am Beispiel von PORTAL* (pp. 31–48). Münster: LIT. doi.org/10.25969/mediarep/14996

Grewell, G., McAllister, K. S. & Ruggill, J. E. (2015). "You really do have braindamage, don't you?": Ridicule as game mechanic in the portal-series. In B. Neitzel, T. Hansel, & R. Nohr (Eds.) *"The cake is a lie!": Polyperspektivische Betrachtungen des Computerspiels am Beispiel von PORTAL* (pp. 323–348). Münster: LIT. doi.org/10.25969/mediarep/15011

Harkin, S. (2020). "The only thing you've managed to break so far is my heart": An analysis of *Portal*'s monstrous mother GLaDOS. *Games and Culture*, 15(5), pp. 529–543. doi.org/10.1177/1555412018819663

McNeilly, J. (2011, March 21). Portal is the Most Subversive Game Ever. *Games Radar*. Retrieved May 21, 2021, from https://www.gamesradar.com/classicradar-portal-is-the-most-subversive-game-ever/

Mittell, J. (2012). Playing for plot in the Lost and Portal franchises. *Eludamos*, 6(1), pp. 5–13. Retrieved May 21, 2021, from https://www.eludamos.org/index.php/eludamos/article/view/vol6no1-2

Mora-Cantallops, M. (2018, August 7–10). *Transhistorical perspective of the puzzle video game genre* [paper presentation]. Proceedings of the 13th International Conference on the Foundations of Digital Games. Malmö, Sweden. doi.org/10.1145/3235765.3235768

Nohr, R. F. (2015). "Now let's continue testing". PORTAL and the Rat in a Maze. In T. Hensel, B. Neitzel, & R. F. Nohr (Eds), *"The cake is a lie!" Polyperspektivische Betrachtungen des Computerspiels am Beispiel von PORTAL* (pp. 199–223). Münster: LIT. doi.org/10.25969/mediarep/15004

Ouellette, M. E., Ouellette, M. A. (2015). Make lemonade: The pleasantly unpleasant aesthetics of playing PORTAL. In T. Hensel, B. Neitzel, & R. F. Nohr (Eds), *"The cake is a lie!" Polyperspektivische Betrachtungen des Computerspiels am Beispiel von PORTAL* (pp. 259–280). Münster: LIT. doi.org/10.25969/mediarep/15007

Pinchbeck, D. (2013). *DOOM: SCARYDARKFAST*. Ann Arbor: The University of Michigan Press.

Rose, M. (2011, April 20). Portal sells 4 million excluding steam sales. *Gamasutra*. Retrieved May 21, 2021, from http://www.gamasutra.com/view/news/34204/Portal_Sells_4_Million_Excluding_Steam_Sales.php

Swift, K., Wolpaw, E., & Barnett, J. (2008, January). Thinking with Portals. *Game Developer*, 15(1), 7–12.

Valve. (2011). *Portal 2: Lab Rat*. Retrieved May 21, 2021, from https://www.thinkwithportals.com/comic/

Wendler, Z. A. (2014). "Who Am I?": Rhetoric and narrative identity in the Portal series. *Games and Culture*, 9(5), pp. 351–367. doi.org/10.1177%2F1555412014543517

Further Reading

Adams, D. M., Pilegard, C., & Mayer, R. E. (2016). Evaluating the cognitive consequences of playing Portal for a short duration. *Journal of Educational Computing Research*, 54(2), pp. 173–195. doi.org/10.1177/0735633115620431

Burden, M., & Gouglas, S. (2012). The algorithmic experience: Portal as art. *Game Studies*, 12(2). Retrieved May 21, 2021, from http://gamestudies.org/1202/articles/the_algorithmic_experience

Ruberg, B. (2019). *Video games have always been queer*. New York: New York University Press.

Schiller, N. (2008). A Portal to student learning: what instruction librarians can learn from video game design. *Reference Services Review*, 36(4), pp. 351–365. doi.org/10.1108/00907320810920333

DOI: 10.4324/9781003199205-35

RESIDENT EVIL (1996)

Few are the games that can claim to be the source of the labeling of a subgenre and of a whole gaming trend. This is the case with *Resident Evil* (Capcom, 1996) regarding the action-adventure "survival horror" genre. Yet, *Resident Evil* was not an innovative game. Rather, the designer Shinji Mikami and his team have used the elements of prior works for their own ends as well as the technological limitations of the PlayStation One. And the game has set the characteristic features of horror video games. It has literally opened doors to a new emotional experience, and this chapter explains how. Insofar as *Resident Evil* has been discussed a lot, I'll solely be backtracking here and collecting all the relevant aspects that make it a key video game.

An Interactive Horror Movie

Resident Evil might never have made it into history and remained hidden in the shadow of another famed zombie video game released the same year, the arcade light gun rail shooter *House of the Dead* (Sega AM1 R&D Division, 1996). Indeed, asked to make a horror videoludic work to follow Capcom's role-playing game *Sweet Home* (1989) on the Nintendo Famicom, and rather than deploying the same top-down view on a maze-like manor, Mikami first wished to design everything in full 3D with a first-person perspective.[1] However, the PlayStation hardware could not render everything in 3D without sacrificing the quality of the graphics, and this was working against his original intention. As Mikami stated:

> [W]hat I really wanted to do was make a horror movie where you could become the main character and experience all the fear and you could decide what to do. I was aiming for the type of horror entertainment that is not possible in the form of a movie.
> (EGM Editors, 1996, p. 60)

The opening cut-scene is, as a matter of fact, filmed in live-action footage, and is well known for not being very good. Through dark and shaky images, mostly close-ups and medium shots, the Alpha team from the Police Department's Special Tactics And Rescue Service (STARS) is attacked by ferocious beasts in the forest northwest of Raccoon City while looking for a previous team gone missing during an inquiry about cannibal attacks. The team is forced to escape into a nearby mansion and to investigate the premises. Although it was created during a time where the interactive movie genre was developing, *Resident Evil* is not a Full-Motion Video game. It did not propose a branching structure and interactivity reduced to limited and punctual decisions. Opportunely, Mikami went for another design.

Blind Space, Blind Spots and Doors

Resident Evil's protagonists, monsters, and items were modeled in real-time 3D, while the environment was pre-rendered. This allowed the creation of detailed, gruesome, and sinister locations suitable to the horror genre. Furthermore, Alex Aniel asserts: "*Resident Evil* is considered at the time of its release as a Michelangelo's ceiling" (2021a, p. 25, freely translated)[2]. But such a technique was not new. Although Mikami denied it for nearly twenty years (he did admit it in a *Le Monde* interview in 2014; see Audureau), journalists and reviewers of the time did not fail to underline the resemblance: *Resident Evil* was actually a replication of the schema of *Alone in the Dark* (I-Motion Inc. & Infogrames). This action-adventure, French video game, designed by Frédérick Raynal in 1992, had groundbreakingly merged 3D polygons for characters, enemies, and items, and pre-rendered 2D images for backgrounds. It had deployed filmic predefined camera angles. It had given the choice between a female or a male protagonist (as *Resident Evil* will), locked in a mansion full of deadly creatures and surprises and in need of managing an inventory to get out alive. That being said, *Resident Evil* will not be a simple clone. It will make the videoludic proposition of *Alone in the Dark* much scarier.

The pre-rendering of the settings had two implications: first, the position of the camera presenting the scenes had to be predefined; and second, the virtual space had to be shown in different parts, inasmuch as no camera was (yet) continuously moving around. Consequently, it is by means of film montage that the spatial articulation had to take place. Like a good movie buff (George A Romero's zombie flicks were his references), Mikami has used these constraints to his advantage with the aim of exploiting the possibilities of framing and shot-assembling. He did it perfectly in a moment now canonical in the annals of scary video games. When Jill Valentine or Chris Redfield—the two playable characters with some variations in their path[3]—cross a corridor at the beginning of their search of the mansion, a change in angle shows them moving away from the camera, while a dog bursts from a window along with loud shattering, wisely framed on the right side and in the foreground of the image. If the player continues running and turns the corner of the corridor, a second dog will appear in a similar fashion, but from the left and with Jill or Chris coming from the back and walking toward it.[4] These two jump scares have set the stage for what it means to play *Resident Evil*.

As one will understand, if there is one term that has been employed to qualify Capcom's game, it is well and truly "cinematic" (and not just due to the presentation of the cut-scenes in letterbox format, one of the first featuring a gruesome zombie turning around in close-up toward the player).[5] Similar to the moment just described, and not always from the best position to face a hazard, the camera viewpoints are varied, showing the premises from different distances, the front and the back, the right and the left, a low and a high camera angle, the side and a top-down view, and so on. For the player, this entails not knowing how the next location will be visualized and where Jill or Chris will stand in the frame. They therefore were constantly required to scan the new shot and to be attentive; in fact, they had to stay alert.

There is one film technique that Mikami will greatly bring into play, namely what Pascal Bonitzer called the "blind space." Insofar as a frame inherently leaves its surrounding unseen, the offscreen space became as important as the onscreen. According to Bonitzer, "The enemy is virtually everywhere if the vision is partial" (Bonitzer, 1982: 96, freely translated). The zombies and other bioweapons populating the manor and threatening the STARS agent could effectively spring unexpectedly from any side of the frame. To add to this tension, Mikami went further:

> Even if you knew before looking round a corner that a zombie was going to be there, we set up blind spots so that players wouldn't be able to see the zombies [immediately] and that in turn produced an uneasy feeling that caused players to feel afraid.
> (in Davies, 2009, p. 53)

In an opposite manner, the living dead could also be heard before being seen, so as to let the player anticipate a harsh encounter.

Another limitation linked to the rendering of the gameworld has been used in a significant way: the loading screens between areas were presented as movements through the different doors of the mansion or as taking the stairs. In place of a simple time-out, these transitions built a constant foreboding. In addition to not knowing where the threat could come from, the player never knew what was waiting ahead. Following Poole: "Perhaps the greatest reason for the game's success is its virtuosic tempo: periods of wandering through deserted environments with a gnawing sense of unease are interrupted by startling high-adrenaline events" (2000, p. 201). This tempo is due to the fact that *Resident Evil* is an action and adventure game. Items (such as keys, emblems, and crests) must be located and collected to be able to progress.

Lack of Control, Power, and Means

Although Mikami will lean toward a more action-oriented style of play in his later works (for instance with *Resident Evil 4*, Capcom, 2005), he has undoubtedly put the player in the shoes of a protagonist of a horror movie. He has given them agency, but not in a purely fluent way. Even though the controls of the game were responsive, they have been described as clumsy and cumbersome because they were tank controls. These refer to movements mapped to the player-character's orientation. The four-way directional buttons of the PlayStation One controller had to be used straightforwardly: pressing up to go forward, down to go backward, left and right to turn in that direction. To the extent that camera placements changed the position of the player-character in space, and that the movements were not adapting to the view, it was not making navigation that easy. As for an army tank, it is necessary to stop to rotate and change direction; and pressing down does not make them spin around, but only back off. By holding the square button, they could run forward, but not in the opposite direction. What's more, using the R1 button to draw a weapon would freeze them on the spot. More than flaws, these constraints rendered encounters with monsters more stressful and unsure. The tank controls were a design choice to do just that.

The heroes may be members of an elite police unit, but they are not put in a position to make full use of force; on the contrary, Jill starts the game with a gun and Chris with a survival knife. They will have to come across the four powerful weapons (five, if we count the rocket launcher received during the final battle). Ammunition will not be found in abundance in the manor, and even the common zombies won't go down on the first shot. To restore their health, the player also has to look for a variety of herbs that can be mixed (green, red, and blue). This will be essential because their inventory is limited: Jill can carry eight items and Chris only six; once an item is taken, it cannot be dropped. This restriction requires some management and, often risky, back-and-forth trips between an item and the box set near save points, allowing one to deposit and store things that could be recovered later in any of the boxes. As if that wasn't enough, the player could not save the game as they pleased. They had to find ink ribbons to be placed into a typewriter to do so. Since there are no automatic checkpoints in *Resident Evil*, dying signified a return to the latest saved game, which could have been a long while ago. The player had to be very thoughtful.

As rightfully noted by Reed, the game took a different approach to the question of empowerment of the player, normally given through bigger firepower:

> Instead, *Resident Evil* opts for psychological empowerment. It doesn't want you taking down every enemy. It doesn't even want you engaging with every enemy. It wants to scare you, but it also forces you to confront and push through fear. …*Resident Evil* is designed to make you panic, but it teaches you not to. If you do, you will die.
>
> (2020, p. 29)

You had to learn to use flight and unlearn to just fight. The whole experience was intense. This was not made for, or aimed at, young players (as many players recalled playing it as kids, the game has left its mark on many). Donovan explains:

> The maturation of video games from toys to home entertainment was aided by game developers' increasing attempts to cater for older teenagers and adults. These attempts were only partially a response to the popularity of the PlayStation. …And it was Capcom's 1996 horror game *Resident Evil* that was the most significant of all these adult-orientated games.
>
> (Donovan, 2010, p. 274)

In the end, mainly through the gameplay, Mikami has reached his objective of making horror entertainment more frightening than a zombie movie, if not at least as blood-curdling.

To Keep Surviving the Horror

By means of the labeling on the covers of the trial version of the first release, as well as through a loading screen, Capcom has coined the expression "survival horror". Aniel observes: "Yes, there will be fear, tension, but above all, the player's goal will be at first…to simply survive. Survival and horror become the key words of a genre of which *Resident Evil* is the founding father, and which will give birth to many descendants" (2021a, p. 24; freely translated).[6] To form a genre in itself (*survival horror* came to refer to all scary video games), there will indeed be several works based on the features and strategies put forward by Mikami and his team. Some of them, like *Silent Hill* (Konami, 1999) and *Fatal Frame* (Tecmo, 2001), have given rise to a further refinement of the formula. Above all, *Resident Evil* has become a popular franchise, with a large number of games, spin-offs, and remakes, as well as movies, TV series, comics, novelizations, and stage plays. The saga goes on. With each new opus, it is a question of surviving until the next variation of the virus.

Bernard Perron

Notes

1. With its first-person perspective, and playable in virtual reality using the PlayStation VR headset, *Resident Evil VII: biohazard* (Capcom) will fulfill such a wish in 2017.
2. As the French translation of the book (2021a) is much livelier than the original version (2021b), I prefer referring to it.
3. It was not the case in *Alone in the Dark*. Emily Hartwood and Edward Carnby live the same adventure.
4. There is a resemblant eruption in *Alone in the Dark*, but it falls short since the window is small, visible far back in the attic, and it is possible to catch a glimpse of the fiend just before it breaks the glass.
5. There is a similar moment during an encounter with a living-dead in *Sweet Home*.
6. As we have noted, *Alone in the Dark* would be the founding father and *Resident Evil* the influential paradigmatic work.

References

Aniel, A. (2021a). *Resident Evil: de l'autre côté du mouroir*. Houdan: Pix'n Love.
Aniel, A. (2021b). *Itchy, tasty: an unofficial history of Resident Evil*. London: Unbound.
Audureau, W. (2014, October 10). Shinji Mikami, 'Resident Evil' et la source du jeu d'horreur. *Le Monde.fr*. Retrieval October 15, 2014, from http://www.lemonde.fr/pixels/article/2014/10/14/shinji-mikami-aux-sources-du-jeu-d-horreur_4502400_4408996.html
Bonitzer, P. (1982). *Le champ aveugle. Essais sur le cinéma*. Paris: Cahiers du cinéma and Gallimard.
Davies, J. (2009, February). The making of *Resident Evil*. *Retro Gamer*, 61, 50–55.
Donovan, T. (2010). *Replay: The history of video games*. East Sussex: Yellow Ant.
EGM Editors (1996, March). The developers of resident evil spill their guts. *Electronic Gaming Monthly*, 80, 60–61.
Poole, S. (2000). *Trigger happy: The inner life of video games*. London: Fourth Estate.
Reed, P.J. (2020). *Resident Evil*. Los Angeles: Boss Fight Books.

Further Reading

Farhaly, N. (Eds) (2014). *Unraveling Resident Evil. Essays on the complex universe of the games and films.* Jefferson, NC: McFarland.

Perron, B. (2018). *The world of scary video games: A study in videoludic horror.* New York: Bloomsbury.

DOI: 10.4324/9781003199205-36

RIVEN (1997)

Cyan's *Myst* (1993), created by brothers Rand and Robyn Miller, held the title of best-selling video game until 2002, when it was passed by *The Sims* (Maxis Software, 2000). Cyan's *Riven: The Sequel to Myst* (1997) was an even larger project, released on five CD-ROMs instead of *Myst*'s one, and requiring ten times the budget of *Myst*. *Riven*'s relationship to *Myst* was described by the Miller brothers as being like what *The Lord of the Rings* (1954–1955) was to *The Hobbit* (1937) (Harrold, 2005; Carroll, 1997). *Riven*'s graphics are beautiful and elegant, with a variety of lush textures, plays of light and shadow, and a variety of moods evoked through design, composition, lighting, and the ambient soundtrack. Despite being initially stored only on CD-ROMs, *Riven* contained over three hours of video and almost five thousand still images. Even today, in the realm of video games it remains an exemplar of a game that gracefully integrates story, world, and interaction, weaving them together in a seamless whole that provides an alluring and satisfying experience for players, even down to the packaging in the images on the CD-ROM sleeves.

Embedded Story

Although the game is a sequel to *Myst*, and takes place after *The Book of Atrus* (1995), which provides backstory for the game's events, the game stands on its own as a story, and no prior knowledge of the storyline or world is required to play it. At the game's beginning, Atrus sends the player from D'ni to the world of *Riven* through the use of a Linking Book. The story concerns members of the culture of the D'ni, who write Descriptive Books that each contain the description of a world (known as an "Age"), and associated Linking Books, which are capable of taking people into the world of the associated Descriptive Book when they place their hand on the first page of the Linking Book. Atrus sends the player into D'ni to find his imperious father Gehn, who has imprisoned Atrus's wife Catherine. Atrus also gives the player a Trap Book, which looks like a Linking Book, but is really a one-man prison. The player's goal is to trap Gehn, free Catherine, and then signal Atrus who will bring a Linking Book so everyone can leave Riven, which is slowly deteriorating and becoming unstable.

The world of Riven, which is made up of five interconnected islands, is unstable due to errors Gehn made as the author of the Descriptive Book for Riven. Gehn's design aesthetic, and love of the number five, is apparent throughout the world, even down to the indigenous five-lobed fruit that grows there. Whereas Myst Island was like an empty world devised to contain puzzles, the Age of Riven is a lived-in world, with puzzles closely integrated into purposeful objects and places. On Jungle Island, the largest island of Riven, there is also a village of natives, whom Gehn has been lording over, and they are fearful of visitors, but provide the player with an ally against Gehn. They, in turn, have written their own world, Tay, to which the player will also go. The player's journey also includes the 233rd Age, Gehn's small, private world, where the player discovers more about Gehn in his office and bedroom, including details that make him a bit more sympathetic.

Thus, the worlds experienced in the game are supposedly devised and designed by the character themselves. The worlds and characters are inextricably intertwined and interdependent for the experience of the game. Having written the Riven Descriptive Book, Gehn has an advantage over the player that is immediately evident very early in the game; upon arriving at Riven, the player is immediately captured in a cage, and the Trap Book is taken away by one of Gehn's minions (some villagers who do his bidding). But moments later, another, differently dressed native, whom the player will later learn is a Moeity scout, darts Gehn's minion, knocking him out. He takes the book, and releases the player from the cage, dashing off before we can catch him; the player is freed, but no longer has the needed Trap Book. The Moeity turns out to be a native resistance movement against Gehn, so in the first moments of the game the player encounters natives from both sides of the conflict before even starting to wander Riven's islands.

World and Interaction

Likewise, the world and player interaction are also tightly interwoven. The design of the world supports the game's puzzles, and Gehn's security measures and ruling of the world give them a reason to be, so that they are naturalized into the surroundings, as is the information the player must learn in order to solve the puzzles and gain access to places. In some cases, one cannot learn how to use a machine until the machine is receiving power, and then sending power to the machine becomes a sub-goal. While clues are sometimes necessary to figure out how to use machines, sometimes the use of the machines or mechanisms is also what provides clues. For example, in the village schoolroom, there is a toy gallows in which two wooden villagers, Moiety rebels, are suspended over a wooden wahrk (an animal that is a combination of a whale and a shark) ready to eat them. Depending on the symbol showing in a small window, the villagers will be lowered a number of times until eaten by the wahrk. The player learns the D'ni numbering system by using the toy, which at the same time demonstrates how schoolchildren are simultaneously taught both numbers and the punishment that awaits them if they turn against Gehn.

In other places, the design of the world is used to provide clues, some of which require the right vantage point, and a sense of geography and the lay of one's surroundings is a crucial part of understanding the game. Even the tiniest details, like a scarab beetle seen briefly on a wooden post, or the sounds that certain animals make, have meaning and connection to things elsewhere. The player, then, must be keenly aware of the islands' rich environment, the geography, biology, and culture of Riven, as well as some sense of the struggle going on between Gehn, his minions, and the Moiety. Only by knowing these things can the player solve puzzles, learn to work the machinery of Riven, and determine how to interact with the game's characters when such exchanges occur.

Finally, interaction and story are interwoven, and although the story is not entirely linear, certain events need to be accomplished in a particular order if one is to be successful (for example, one needs to get the Trap Book back before it can be used against Gehn, and conditions are set up in such a way so that one must trap Gehn before Catherine can be freed). The order that the player visits the five islands may vary, but knowledge of all five is needed for the solving of certain puzzles. While the irreversible moments of choice are relatively few, choosing the right options is important as it determines which of the ten endings of *Riven* one will encounter, with only one of them being truly favorable. Although the villagers are wary of visitors, a few interactions with them remain, and noticing their doings is important as well (for example, when an imprisoned Moiety seems to disappear from a prison cell without having left through the cell door, which indicates another passage leading out of the cell). Moments of interaction, and even seeing characters doing things at a distance, provide a feeling that the place is inhabited, while still giving the player much contemplative time alone.

Besides its human inhabitants, the Age of Riven has a variety of animals and wildlife that the player encounters and can occasionally interact with in a limited way, and there are vehicles the player can enter and ride (elevators, a mine car, a submarine, and several MagLev cars). While many games of the twenty-first century now provide detailed worlds populated with animated flora and fauna, and a wide variety of usable machines and vehicles, the Miller brothers' *Riven* is indeed a part of their lineage and was ground-breaking for its time, extending and refining many of the ideas and designs presented in *Myst*. Few games can claim to give meaning to the intricate details of the game's world to the degree that *Riven* does; the *Myst*-inspired game *The Witness* (Thekla, 2016) has environmental puzzles woven into its world, but its look is more stylized, and there is barely any narrative or purpose for most of the puzzles populating the island. *Riven* integrates things as well, and more naturally, and most players will not even absorb everything on the first time through the game.

A Perfect Marriage of Form and Content

The form and content of *Riven* are thematically related and analogous. Just as a Descriptive Book contains within it the description of a world that can be entered, the CD-ROM contains the code that describes a world that can be visited vicariously; at the same time, the player's diegetic hand (the cursor is shaped like a hand at this point) is placed on the linking panel within a Linking Book to be transported to the world of the associated Descriptive Book, the player is simultaneously pointing to and clicking on the on-screen image, which vicariously takes them into the game world. The imaginary worlds of the game are diegetically said to be devised by the game's characters, acting as subcreated subcreators (to use Tolkien's term), and the D'ni write worlds just as the Miller brothers write game worlds; in fact, Rand Miller even plays Atrus within the game, taking the overlap even further. No other games thematically connect their form and content at such a high level.

Despite being released rather late in the year (October 28, 1997), *Riven* went on to be the second-best-selling software title of 1997, with 640,000 units sold by the year's end; it was beaten only by Microsoft's Windows 95 CD Upgrade which sold 659,000 units (Scally, 1998). *Riven*'s sales reached 1 million units by April 1998, and by 2001 over 4.5 million units had been sold (Staff, 1998; Pham, 2001). Other games would appear in the *Myst* franchise, but none would reach *Riven*'s heights of expressive integration. Versions of *Riven* are now available for the iPhone and iPad, bringing the game to a new generation of twenty-first century players.

Riven became the heart of a franchise that included a series of video games, novels, a board game, a comic book, conventions, and more. It also represents the pinnacle of the point-and-click adventure genre. Even though the genre has now evolved into three-dimensional, freely-explorable environments, with increasingly photoreal graphics, none of them were as great a leap ahead of its predecessors as *Riven* was, and many owe their existence and inspiration to games like *Myst* and *Riven*. The close marriage of theme, form, and content, and the tight interweaving of story, world, and interaction, is occasionally attempted by these games, but, arguably, the outcomes never quite measure up to what *Riven* was able to do in 1997. Regardless of how the genre continues to advance, *Riven* has earned its place in video game history —as a key game in the development not only of its genre but also of the medium—and a place in the long tradition of the building of imaginary worlds as well.

Mark J. P. Wolf

References

Carroll, J. (1997, September). (D)RIVEN, *Wired* Magazine, p. 172.

Harrold, C. (2005, November 13). The Legacy of Myst: A Link to Other |Worlds, *The Skyline View*. Retrieved October 14, 2021, from https://www.theskylineview.com/uncategorized/2005/11/13/the-legacy-of-myst-a-link-to-other-worldsbr/

Pham, A (2001, May 17). Game Design; Adding Texture, Detail to Miller Brothers' Legacy, *The Los Angeles Times*, page T4. Archived from the original on February 3, 2013.

Scally, R. (1998, March 9). "PC, Video Game Software Sales Hit Record High in 1997", *Discount Store News*. Retrieved October 14, 2021, from https://indexarticles.com/business/discount-store-news/pc-video-game-software-sales-hit-record-high-in-1997/

Staff, (1998, September). Player stats: Top 10 best-selling games, 1993—present, *Computer Gaming World*, 170, p. 52.

Further Reading

Wolf, M. J. P. (2011). *Myst & Riven: The world of the D'ni*, Ann Arbor, MI: University of Michigan Press.

DOI: 10.4324/9781003199205-37

SID MEIER'S CIVILIZATION (1991)

Roots of a Franchise

Sid Meier's Civilization (Microprose, 1991; hereafter *Civilization*) kicked off one of the most successful and influential series in game history. As conceived by legendary game developer Sid Meier, over 33 million copies of this turn-based strategy game franchise have been sold since its release and it has won numerous awards, ranking #1 on a list of "150 Best Games Of All Time" in the magazine *Computer Gaming World* (Schreier, 2013). Designed first for MS-DOS, then coming to the Commodore Amiga 500/600 and Atari ST, Apple and Windows, and Nintendo platforms, its game mechanic aims for a balance of building, research, economics, culture, and war.

Although its visuals and gameplay evolved over time, the basics remained the same: guide a people from the early stone age through human history to the present day and into a future of colonizing new planets (Edwards, 2007). The player starts with one village in 4,000 BC, chooses a leader for their tribe, and aims to conquer the world; for a new village, the player picks whether to go with a settler, a scout, or a warrior, and each unit selected can change the balance between expansion and preservation, offense and defense. The isometric perspective is a world map with menus for building, diplomacy, science, and the arts, to grow your area of influence bigger, stronger, and richer than the competition. The option *not* to resemble our Earth is available, but the rhomboid plots (or later the hexagonal, as in *Civilization V* [Firaxis Games, 2010]) of sea, forest, desert, hills, and so on, always touch at the edges, making it possible to circumnavigate the game-world as a cylindrical playscape (Pitts, 2013).

Influences

When Sid Meier and Bruce Shelley appeared at the 2017 Game Developers Conference to reflect on their first *Civilization* game, they acknowledged borrowing from *SimCity* (Will Wright for Maxis, 1989) and the British war game *Empire* (Walter Bright for Interstel, 1971), as well as classic board games like *Risk* (Parker Bros, 1959) and the Avalon Hill board game named *Civilization* (Hartland Trefoil 1980). Its light-hearted portrayal of politics pits nations against each other, with leaders who are not even from the same era—Genghis Khan and Caesar, Napoleon and Cleopatra. In opting for a turn-based game rather than the flow of a real-time simulator, Meier and Microprose had a hit on their hands.

The story of Microprose, the American video game company founded by Bill Stealey and Sid Meier, began with the flight simulators *Hellcat Ace* (1982) and *Solo Flight* (1983); at the time, games and simulations were considered isolated markets. Commentators argue that simulations and games may have technical similarities but serve different aims (Friedman, 1999). We call global strategy/simulation games those that afford a player control not just over individual units, armies, or cities, but also over an entire state competing with other states (Dor, 2014). The *Civilization* franchise gave rise to a new label as it unfolded over three decades of development and twelve editions, not to mention expansion packs and spin-offs (such as the so-called 4X, where you pursue victory through four routes—explore, expand, exploit, and exterminate). One inches closer to a win-condition or end-state as one explores the map, expands one's region of influence, exploits cultural achievements and technologies, and exterminates the competition. This type of game is not just a numbers generator but acts as a simulation of a half-dozen millennia of human history, as both a model *of* civilization and a model *for* civilization. This aspect provoked vigorous debate among fans and critics: should *Civilization* be understood as an accurate representation or as a speculative sandbox? Does it sacrifice historical verisimilitude in the name of fun, or does it betray ideological bias? These debates may have contributed significantly to the ongoing fascination with *Civilization*.

Modeling

One can distinguish between a model *of* something and a model *for* something: the former helps us render a question or problem tractable, whereas the latter implies an exemplary or normative role (Geertz, 1973, p. 93). Both are exercises of the imagination and are important in game design. A model is more than a hypothetical description of a complex entity or process. In modeling integrated systems, what you can model can add up to very complex interactions, assuming your observations and implementations of relations or mechanisms are transferable. A model can confirm theoretical hypotheses, or it can violate them and question implicit assumptions; some argue that modeling succeeds intellectually when it results in failure (McCarty, 2004). Still, how does one scale from model trains or an educational model of the solar system, for instance, to an interactive model of a complex open world where human agency meets the artificial intelligence of non-player characters?

Sid Meier is often quoted (though his own memoir concedes there may not have been a canonical moment to quote) defining a game as "a series of interesting decisions," and pledging to focus on fun aspects of a simulation and to discard anything that undermines fun (such as pandemics or earthquakes). Interestingly, Meier rejected interactive fiction gaming because its dialogues offered "only one right answer, which was bad, but they also had an infinite number of wrong answers, which was worse" (Meier, 2020). His choices in developing this groundbreaking title can be telling; for instance, *Civilization* ignores the strategic and tactical potential of weather, of seasons, and of climate change (Krapp, 2019). Despite omitting what insurance companies call acts of God, *Civilization* models a range of other highly complex and dynamic systems, such as science, exploration, economy, agriculture, and warfare (Chen, 2008). The game associates the discovery or development of certain technologies with certain cities, which can see "passive growth" through proximity, trade, and cultural connections (Gillen, 2008). Buildings count as achievements in the categories of culture and of science, and that can benefit a civilization's happiness (Totilo, 2010). Governmental, legal, labor, and economic factors enrich the menu of your options, inflecting your diplomatic choices that, in turn, change how the game's AI-controlled leaders perceive you and each other. Arguably, *Civilization* models not just historical, but also sociological and anthropological processes (Uricchio, 2005).

Civilization does not insert your avatar in the action, it affords players a god-like perspective and so the phrase "god game" entered the game genre lexicon. In retrospect, modeling culture, science, religion, and economics as competition was no big leap. Sid Meier's train simulator *Railroad Tycoon* (Microprose 1990), which likewise fomented a franchise and influenced countless other business simulators, already featured commodity trade and terrain challenges. Just as Meier started on *Railroad Tycoon*, Will Wright released *SimCity*, a major influence not just for what would become *Civilization*. Reportedly, the idea of responding with a game about "the entire history of human civilization" came to Meier on an Amtrak ride to New York in 1990, and he described the first draft of *Civilization* as "more like *SimCity* on a global scale" (Meier, 2020). Notably, later attempts to expand *Civilization* for online interactive multiplayer modes did not succeed to the extent realized by other titles.

Hypotheticals

Historians ask what games and simulations contribute to understanding. While offering an escape from our lived reality, they also refer us back to power structures and social control outside those fictional worlds. Simulations are particularly suited to exploring complex chains of alternate past or future scenarios where nothing is preordained: counterfactual and hypothetical worlds. To offer playful engagement with historical figures that improves on access to a textbook account of their lives, as Meier's memoir notes, Microprose hired the Princeton doctoral student Ed Bever (who was writing strategy game reviews in his spare time) to mine history for *Civilization*. But in *Civilization* one never plays a menial laborer, office worker, or middle manager, one's task is to lead an entire tribe to victory. Potential identification with historical figures is constrained to a few leaders who never face internal challenges to their rule. However, if games illustrate history from a contemporary perspective and omit enough to make things causally stringent in retrospect, this is owed not just to a blinkered view of how we got here, but also to the logic of a program seeking to entertain (Squire & Barab, 2004, p. 511). Although games tell things differently from books or films, players are aware of the dual nature of their choices as not only embedded in a programmed environment, but also subject to individual enactment. Between backstory and enacted campaigns, cut-scenes and challenging missions, the emphasis is on making experience of time meaningful.

One of the most blatant historical discontinuities in *Civilization* is that you might play as leader of the Aztecs and nonetheless build Chateau Versailles or a Saturn V rocket. The nation-state really only bloomed in the nineteenth century, but in the game it takes root in the Bronze Age. Storytellers take liberties, for instance, in the Asterix comics (1959-present), the Gauls battle Caesar's legions in the Colosseum in Rome in the year 50 BC. This could not have taken place because the Colosseum was built a century later. But the graphic novel opts to show a Rome as readers expect it, featuring the Colosseum. In computer games we often get a similar pastiche. When Sid Meier's game *Pirates!* (Microprose, 1987) set the scene for European expansion into the early modern Caribbean with baroque clothes and etiquette, it did not feature murder or slavery, opting instead for a pirate mythology built up by Hollywood (Chapman, 2013, p. 61). Despite piracy's influence on warfare, economics, and diplomacy, we do not find it in *Civilization*.

Even as Meier welcomed the criticism *Civilization* drew from historians, he maintained that history revealed a clear progression through anarchy, despotism, monarchy, communism, republic, and democracy (Brooks, 1994). However, most theories of history do not stipulate a teleology that inexorably leads to certain outcomes. Designing the game so that a cultural victory is possible requires a theory of culture that allows for this to become a game mechanic. Designing the game so that scientific progress follows certain steps implies a linear theory of science. Designing the game so that trade routes are advantageous or disadvantageous discloses a theory of markets and their function over historical periods. In *Civilization*, we recognize a pronounced US-centric view of the globe and its politics (Poblocki, 2002).

Conclusion

Combining the pyramids, Elvis, and nuclear warfare, *Civilization* plays fast and loose with history and, in doing so, it raises questions about our image of history (Kapell & Elliott, 2013, p. 2). Superficial use of games in teaching may be worse than none, and perhaps worse than using cinematic or belletristic samples, but judicious use can engage students in ways few other materials do (Mitgutsch, 2009). This is due to an appetite for interactive entertainment, a sense of responsibility for actions unfolding on screen, and opportunities to discuss a game's structure and strictures with other players. *Civilization* cannot avoid clichés in representing several millennia; to play it well means to explore how it codes historical success, lest it remain an abstract open-world simulation without paths to a win-condition. Visual, auditive, and haptic immersion perfects a projected continuity of historical experience that differs radically from our actual lived experience of history; nonetheless, many historians value the hypotheticals games explore. *Civilization* is not only a successful (though productively debatable) model of world history, but it also evolved into an influential model for game development—both in charting new boundaries between strategy and simulation gaming, and in maintaining the momentum of a world-class franchise of sequels and spin-offs.

Peter Krapp

References

Brooks, E. (1994, May). Pachyderm Platoon. *Computer Gaming World #118, 166–168.* Retrieved October 31, 2021, from http://www.cgwmuseum.org/galleries/index.php?year=1994&pub=2&id=118

Chapman, A. (2013). Affording history: *Civilization* and the ecological approach. In Matthew Kapell & Andrew Elliott (Eds), *Playing with the past. Digital games and the simulation of history* (pp. 61–69). New York: Bloomsbury.

Chen, A. (2008, September/October). Architect of Civilizations, *Stanford Magazine*. Retrieved October 31, 2021, from https://stanfordmag.org/contents/architect-of-civilizations

Dor, S. (2014). Strategy. In Mark J. P. Wolf & Bernard Perron (Eds), *The Routledge companion to video game studies* (pp. 275–281). New York: Routledge

Edwards, B. (2007, July 18). The History of Civilization. *Gamasutra*. Retrieved October 21, 2021, from https://www.gamasutra.com/view/feature/1523/the_history_of_civilization.php?page=5

Friedman, T. (1999). Civilization and its discontents: Simulation, subjectivity, and space. In Greg M. Smith, (Eds), *On a silver platter: CD-Roms and the promises of a new technology* (pp. 132–150). New York: NYU Press.

Geertz, C. (1973). *The interpretation of cultures*. London: Fontana.

Gillen, K. (2008, February 20). Making of: Soren Johnson on Civ 4. *Rock Paper Shotgun*. Retrieved October 21, 2021, from https://www.rockpapershotgun.com/2008/02/20/making-of-soren-johnson-on-civ-4/

Kapell, M. & Elliott, A. (2013). To build a past that will stand the test of time. In Matthew Kapell & Andrew Elliott (Eds), *Playing with the past. Digital games and the simulation of history* (pp. 132–148). New York: Bloomsbury.

Krapp, P. (2019). Realism: Civilization. In Nina Hunteman & Matt Payne (Eds), *How to play videogames* (pp. 44–51). New York: New York University Press.

McCarty, W. (2004). Modelling: A study in words and meanings. In: Schreibman S, Siemens R and Unsworth J (Eds) *Companion to digital humanities*. Oxford: Blackwell, ch. 19. Retrieved October 31, 2021, from http://www.digitalhumanities.org/companion

Meier, S. (2020): *Sid Meier's Memoir! A life in computer games*. New York: WW Norton.

Mitgutsch, K. (2009). Gaming the schools. *Medienimpulse* 2, Retrieved October 31, 2021, from http://www.medienimpulse.at/pdf/Medienimpulse_Gaming_the_Schools._Mitgutsch_20091208.pdf

Pitts, R. (2013, June 27). Knowing History: Behind Civ V's Brave New World. *Polygon*. Retrieved Oct 31, 2021, from http://www.polygon.com/features/2013/6/27/4453070/civ-the-making-of-brave-new-world

Schreier, J. (2013, June 26). Sid Meier: The Father of 'Civilization'. *Kotaku*. Retrieved October 31, 2021, from https://kotaku.com/the-father-of-civilization-584568276

Poblocki, K. (2002). Becoming-State: The bio-cultural imperialism of Sid Meier's Civilization. *Focal - European Journal of Anthropology* 39, 163–172.

Squire, K. & Barab, S. (2004, June). Replaying history: Engaging urban underserved students in learning world history through computer simulation games. *ICLS '04: Proceedings of the 6th International Conference on Learning Sciences* (pp. 505–512). doi/10.5555/1149126.1149188

Totilo, S. (2010, April 20). God was a Math Problem. *Kotaku*. Retrieved October 31, 2021, from https://kotaku.com/god-was-a-math-problem-5521052

Uricchio, W. (2005). Simulation, history, and computer games. In Joost Raessens & Jeffrey Goldstein (Eds), *Handbook of computer game studies* (pp. 327–338). Cambridge MA: MIT Press.

Further Reading

Ausubel, J.H. and Robert Herman (1988).: *Cities and their vital systems: Infrastructure past, present, and future.* Washington, DC: National Academies Press.

Juul, J. (2001). Games telling stories? *Game Studies. The International Journal of Computer Game Research* 1(1). Retrieved October 31, 2021, from http://www.gamestudies.org/0101/juul-gts/

Lewin, C.G. (2012). *War games and their history.* Stroud: Fonthill Media.

Putra, A. (2016). Civilization through the ages: 25 years of evolution. *GameAxis.* Retrieved October 31, 2021, from https://www.gameaxis.com/feature/civilization-ages-25-years-evolution/

DOI: 10.4324/9781003199205-38

SIMCITY (1989)

Before the global phenomenon that became *The Sims* (Electronic Arts, 2000; discussed on p. 239-243), there was *SimCity*. The brainchild of game developer Will Wright, this game would come to define the city-building genre and span a series of games for the personal computer, game consoles, and mobile platforms. It also inspired a slew of spinoff "sims" games with which developer Wright experimented under the Maxis label: from the ant simulation of *SimAnt: The Electronic Ant Colony* (Maxis, 1991) to the quirky *SimCopter* (Maxis, 1996), which allowed players to fly around the cities created in *SimCity 2000* (Maxis, 1993).

This chapter is divided into three main sections. First, it charts the making of *SimCity*. The second section looks at the main gameplay features of the game and its critical reception upon release. The third is dedicated to the exploration of how the model of the game has been critiqued by scholars and how *SimCity* became one of the first games to be included in school programs. It concludes by presenting how, up to this day, the game is still considered an interesting tool for teaching, despite its many flaws.

A Brief History of *SimCity*

The creation of *SimCity* takes roots in Wright's first game, *Raid on Bungeling Bay* (1984). While creating new maps, the developer realized that it was more fun to design and create new environments rather than play the actual game. This, in turn, gave him the impulse to build a new game from scratch that would enable the player to plan, create, and maintain a large megapolis. It would include concepts about urban planning, specifically those found in the book *Urban Dynamics* by Jay Forrester (Moss, 2015). A computer engineer from MIT, Forrester laid the groundwork of modern urban economics by creating a model with 150 equations and 200 parameters that could, in theory, predict the growth of modern cities (Baker, 2019). This appealed to Wright, who saw an opportunity to use the model in the game thus making it more interesting than a spreadsheet (Donovan, 2011).

At first, the game was called *Micropolis* and was judged to be unpublishable by Wright's publisher, Brøderbund Software. The main problem was that it lacked any real ending or objective "win" conditions and the publisher felt that it would repel potential gamers. The absence of a clear ending in *Micropolis* was a conscious choice by Wright who claimed, in different interviews, that the game was more of a toy than a video game. As such, *Micropolis* could leverage different models (i.e., those of Jay Forrester) with which players could experiment. Rather than imposing set scenarios, Wright wanted players to use their imagination and set themselves some goals to explore the full potential of the toy (Friedman, 1999).

Not discouraged by Brøderbund Software's refusal, Wright found a partner, Jeff Braun, who shared his vision for *Micropolis*, so together they founded Maxis to publish the game. However, they still needed extra help and successfully won over Brøderbund Software who agreed to publish the game on the condition that pre-defined scenarios be added (Wilson, 1989). Renamed *SimCity* and available on multiple platforms (Amiga, Macintosh, IBM PC and Commodore 64), the game was a smash hit. Reviewers raved about the gameplay mechanics that allowed players to make decisions and visually perceive the effect of those actions on the game world (Wilson, 1989). Others commented on the challenge players faced, but insisted on the game's fun factor (McCandless, 1989). In the end, despite Brøderbund's fears, reviewers did not complain about the lack of a real endgame outside the predefined scenarios.

Players seemed to agree with reviewers as the game sold well and sales didn't dwindle after a few months; they even increased two and three years after release (Donovan, 2011). The game was rapidly inducted in multiple "halls of fame" (*Computer Gaming World*, 1991) and is still considered one of the greatest games of all time. However, the attention *SimCity* received was not limited to computer and games publications, and it became one of the first games to appear in mainstream media when it was featured in *The New York Times* and had a proper review in *Time* magazine (Moss, 2015).

Main Gameplay Features

SimCity uses an oblique projection, which, appropriately, is primarily used in technical drawing and illustrations. The frame isn't anchored to the screen as players can freely move the camera around the map and multiple menus depict information for the player. This helps players understand how their decisions affect zoning, services, and facilities in their city. Two game modes are available: infinite building, where the only limit is monetary availability (which in itself is not a big deal as one can choose to embezzle funds to keep the city afloat) (McCandless, 1989); while a second mode of play tasks players to win specific scenarios and to take the reins of different real-world cities, such as San Francisco or Boston.

The map presented to the player is randomly generated on each new game and covers a ten by ten mile space. Players edit the map using the in-game editor, which takes inspiration from MacPaint (Donovan, 2011). A "brush" the size of a three by three grid is used to define the characteristics of the different zones and enables the player to set taxes for each one. At first, a new city needs power, either coal or nuclear (which is more efficient, but with a risk of reactor meltdown), for three types of zone: residential (housing, religious centers, etc.); commercial (local businesses); and industrial (manufacturing).

As the city grows, more infrastructure can be added, as the virtual mayor sees fit, to support the objective of keeping citizens (the sims) happy: police and fire stations are essential to stave off crime and fire; while roads and railroads help the virtual citizens go about their daily lives and improve commerce. Eventually, when the city crosses a certain population threshold, the player can add airports and seaports to open its metropolis to the outside world and to improve foreign trade. A last addition to the gameplay mechanics is disasters, which can be added to the game by the player or they can be completely deactivated. Disasters range from simple earthquakes and floods to a giant lizard, akin to Godzilla, that terrorizes the player's cities.

The Influence of *SimCity* on City-Building Games

SimCity has had a lasting influence in different spheres, notably on city-building games (CBG), but also outside of gaming, in education. Even if *SimCity* is the most recognizable CBG, it was not the first—two early examples of the genre are *Hamurabi* by David H Ahl (1973) and *Santa Paravia and Fiumaccio* by George Blanks (1978). *Hamurabi* allowed players to manage the city of Sumer and was more of a managerial sim, as you could not build any new structures. *Santa Paravia* included most of the features now commonly associated with CBG, such as screens that informed the player of progress, and it was possible to build new infrastructure to support a bustling city. However, those games still felt more like adapted board games with a predefined rules set and less like a simulation (Moss, 2015). This is where *SimCity* distinguished itself. Partly because technology had evolved to allow full graphical representation (as opposed to being text-based), and by using a precise model, Wright allowed players to invest in the possibility space and honored their choices in a form of emergent gameplay (Soler-Adillon, 2019) but players remained confined to the black box of the simulation (Ashley, 2021). It is the affordance provided by the model that made *SimCity* such a hit and enabled it to gain traction outside of gaming circles. As a game series, *SimCity* would hold the title for best CBG until *SimCity 4* (Maxis, 2003), which proved to be too complex for many players, and the disastrous launch of *SimCity* (Maxis Emeryville, 2013) with its always-online requirement, which put off players. This also marked the end of major new releases on PC and console, and currently only a mobile version (*SimCity: BuildIt* [TrackTwenty, 2014]) is actively being supported.

SimCity Critiques and Educational Use

This chapter previously addressed how *SimCity* was one of the first games to break into mainstream media and brought about scrutiny by scholars and educators. The first aimed to better understand the nature of the black box at the heart of the simulation, while the second was more interested in the pedagogical implications of game-based education and catering to a new generation of students growing up with video games. To measure the influence of *SimCity* outside of gaming circles, one can look at the number of academic discussions it generated, notably around the nature of its black box (systems where inputs and outputs are known but the underlying model is not) (Kolson, 1996). Scholars critiqued the shortcomings of the model, such as the absence of pollution, or the fact that *SimCity* only simulated the typical North American city (Starr, 1994). The discourse has now switched from an actual critique of the model to the ongoing influence of the game on politicians, city planners, and the like (Ashley, 2021; Baker,

2019). This attests to the enduring influence of the game and solidifies its place as an important landmark in the history of video games.

For Wright, *SimCity* was never meant to be taken seriously or as a tool that teachers could use in the classroom. Playing the game was simply more interesting than reading a book about urban planning or trying to understand complex models about how cities grow (Donovan, 2011). However, even considering all its shortcomings, *SimCity* managed to carve a niche in several training programs as a way to experience city development (Baker, 2019; Rufat & Minassian, 2012). It still remains an interesting example of how video games can be useful as a teaching tool for two main reasons. First, it opens a possibility space that students must explore to find solutions to the various problems that can emerge from the player or be assigned by teachers. In turn, this could lead to the development of problem-solving skills, which are frequently cited as an interesting feature of video game-based teaching (Gee, 2007). The second reason *SimCity* is interesting is the black box at the heart of its simulation. While it is impossible to fully take it apart, it is still possible to dissect it, discuss it, critique it, and endeavor to have an epistemic discussion with students (McCall, 2012). The use of *SimCity* and other CBG has been the subject of many discussions, but few studies systematically address their impact on student learning (Boutonnet, 2018).

SimCity and Beyond

This chapter charted the history of *SimCity* through its inception up to the various critiques of its model and the possibilities the game can have as a tool for education. The impact of *SimCity* can still be felt today, even if the series is now more or less dormant. The CBG genre is still thriving with games such as *Cities: Skylines* (Colossal Order, 2015) and evolving with games like *Banished* (Shining Rock Software, 2014) or *Frostpunk* (11bit Studios, 2018), which bring new elements to the traditional formula, and others like *Buildings Have Feelings Too!* (Blackstaff Games, 2021) or *Dice Legacy* (DESTINYbit, 2021), which bring about new twists and keep the genre fresh (Livingtson, 2021).

Alexandre Joly-Lavoie

References

Ashley, C. (2021). *The Ideology Hiding in SimCity's Black Box*. Polygon. Retrieved July 7, 2021, from https://www.polygon.com/videos/2021/4/1/22352583/simcity-hidden-politics-ideology-urban-dynamics

Baker, K. T. (2019). Model metropolis. *Logic*, 6. https://logicmag.io/play/model-metropolis/

Boutonnet, V. (2018). Interprétations historiques et constructions de mondes virtuels au temps de Civilization, SimCity et Minecraft. In M.-A. Éthier, D. Lefrançois, & A. Joly-Lavoie (Eds), *Mondes profanes: Enseignement, fiction et histoire* (pp. 161–177). Québec: Presses de l'Université Laval.

Computer Gaming World. (1991, October). On silvery disks of splendor. *Computer Gaming World*, 87, 112.

Donovan, T. (2011). The Replay Interviews: Will Wright. *Gamasutra*. Retrieved August 29, 2021, from https://www.gamasutra.com/view/feature/134754/the_replay_interviews_will_wright.php?page=3

Friedman, T. (1999). The semiotics of Sim City. *First Monday*, 4(4). doi.org/10.5210/fm.v4i4.660

Gee, J. P. (2007). *What video games have to teach us about learning and literacy*. New York: Palgrave MacMillan.

Livingtson, C. (2021). City Builders with a Twist are my New Favorite Genre. *PC Gamer*. Retrieved July 22, 2021, from https://www.pcgamer.com/city-builders-with-a-twist-are-my-new-favorite-genre/

McCall, J. (2012). Historical simulations as problem spaces: Criticism and classroom use. *Journal of Digital Humanities*, 1(2). Retrieved July 22, 2021, from http://journalofdigitalhumanities.org/1-2/historical-simulations-as-problem-spaces-by-jeremiah-mccall/

Moss, R. (2015). *From SimCity to, Well, SimCity: The History of City-building Games*. Arstechnica. Retrieved July 20, 2021, from https://arstechnica.com/gaming/2015/10/from-simcity-to-well-simcity-the-history-of-city-building-games/

Rufat, S., & Minassian, T. (2012). Video games and urban simulation: New tools or new tricks? *Cybergeo European Journal of Geography*. doi.org/10.4000/cybergeo.25561

Soler-Adillon, J. (2019). The open, the closed and the emergent: Theorizing emergence for videogame studies. *Game Studies the International Journal of Computer Game Research*, 19(2). Retrieved July 20, 2021, from http://gamestudies.org/1902/articles/soleradillon

Starr, P. (1994). Seduction of sim: Policy as a simulation game. *The American Prospect*, Spring (17), 19–29.

Wilson, J. L. (1989, May). What do the "Sim"ple folk do. *Computer Gaming World*, 59, 16–17.

Further Reading

Lauwaert, M. (2007). Challenge everything? construction play in Will Wright's SimCity. *Games and Culture*, 2(3), 194–212. doi.org/10.1177/1555412007306205

DOI: 10.4324/9781003199205-39

THE SIMS 4 (2014)

The Sims (Maxis, 1989–present) is an unusually long-running franchise introduced by Maxis and Electronic Arts in 2000 with console, PC, online, and mobile versions and over seventy-five expansion packs. Its latest title, *The Sims 4* (2014), had over 36 million unique players as of May 2021. The appeal, according to its creators and many scholars, is the ability to "play with life" (Favis, 2020). Players create characters—called sims—and their homes, and, along with an artificial intelligence system that influences sim actions, they lead characters through careers, relationships, and shopping sprees. As a sandbox game, *The Sims 4* has few built-in goals, and its design provides considerable freedom to set up player-designed scenarios, challenges, and stories.

In its early editions, *The Sims* provided a set of options to design characters' hair, skin tone, shape, and clothing that were robust compared to other games of the time. These character design capabilities—quickly identified as a core appeal of the game—expanded to include more nuance, and in 2016 a patch to *The Sims 4* dramatically increased flexibility and openness in character gender by decoupling it from appearance options that are traditionally associated with gender, such as clothing, walk, voice, hair (including facial hair), and accessories. By removing the standard gender-based limits on appearance design, the game separated avatar gender from its gender performance. This was a major step in the game's long tradition of enhancing the diversity of their character options and has been followed by other changes, such as adding more non-Western clothing options, including hijabs, kufi caps, and saris, although access to many of these requires purchasing expensive additional downloadable content.

The built-in base game gender options are extensive and carefully considered. The developers worked on the update with the LGBTQ+ advocacy group GLADD to design how gender choices are presented (Handrahan, 2016). Once players select a gender by clicking one of the symbols for male or female, a button opens options to customize the sim's physical frame, clothing preference, whether or not it can become pregnant or get others pregnant, and if it can use the toilet standing up. The initial gender symbol selection determines the gender pronoun used by the game. Importantly, unlike most, this game allows players to alter avatar characteristics at any time during gameplay, including changing any of its gender, body, skin tone, and movement characteristics.

The gender customization options in *The Sims 4* set the bar high and responded to the message many people had long been sending: players want to see themselves in games. The range of gender and relationship options in *The Sims* franchise has been at the forefront of diverse representation options since its inception, and its breadth of affordances makes the game unusual, but not alone, in the video game landscape. It is joined by games where characters have no gender designation, such as the US edition of *Animal Crossing: New Horizons* (Nintendo, 2020), and ones such as *Saints Row IV* (Volition, 2013), where players can select any voice, clothing, or hairstyle for any gender. The LGBTQ Games Archive (Shaw, 2016) lists twenty explicitly and ten implicitly trans or non-binary characters in games (although many are non-playable) and sixty-six that are gender non-conforming, although only eleven are games that allow for non-binary gender customization.

The Sims 4 does not fare as well in other areas of representation, however, especially for designing a character's race or disabilities. Players have responded to these shortcomings by using *The Sims 4's* "custom content" modding capabilities, which allow players to add options to the appearance and actions of their sims, such as the nuanced black hair, clothing, and skin tones from creators EbonixSims and AfrosimtricCCFinds. Other content creators have developed items to represent disabled sims, such as hearing aids, prosthetic limbs, a nasal oxygen tube, wheelchairs, and even service dogs.

How to Play: Invitations to Transgression and Multiplicity

Gameplay in *The Sims 4* is based on the interaction between player commands and sim personalities. When players are not actively controlling them, sims follow preferences determined by the traits and aspirations chosen in the character creation process. A sim designated as a cheerful bookworm who loves exercise will perform independent actions—including resisting player commands at times—that follow its personality, such as setting out for a jog instead of going to work. Neglecting a sim for too long results in game-controlled behavior that often departs from the sim's optimal duties, creating a dynamic narrative that serves as the core challenge of the game. However, appearance choices, including gender and race, do not change how sims behave in the game. A female sim is no less likely to get a Tech Guru job than a male sim, and straight sims are not more likely to be welcomed at the neighbor's house than gay ones; race has no bearing on who a sim befriends or where it lives. The game studiously avoids Othering characters based on these identities, which makes it stand out among games that offer a range of gender, sexuality, and race options.

Although its default settings and mechanics largely encourage creating nuclear, heteronormative families who pursue material and social success (Crocco, 2011), sims can easily be guided to follow stories that oppose the dominant narrative: they can seek a dramatic death instead of a long life; reject materialism; or configure their household with any number of sims in any configuration of relationships. Its developers embrace this approach and the game explicitly invites play that transgresses societal norms with character options such as vampires or a "criminal" career track, and personality options such as meanness or "evil." Shaw (2017) suggests that understanding games requires understanding how players take up, adapt, and resist the meanings and structures designed into them, especially in relation to a game's mechanics and interface. Although players have always found ways to exploit existing options to tell the stories they want to tell (Evans, 2018; Shaw, 2017), the gender affordances in *The Sims 4* make playing with gender and sexuality easier and more accessible for those seeking to find themselves represented in games as much as for those exploring representations different to their own.

Distinct from most other games with player-generated characters, *The Sims* requires the creation of, and control over, multiple characters. For example, when playing a household with two adults and a teenager, the player must select each sim in turn to ensure it makes dinner, practices the piano, or does homework. This design emphasizes creating a *cast* of characters that can also generate a range of relationships between players and their avatars, including using a sim to represent the self, as a symbiote to explore different identities, or even as an Othered foil to experiment with challenges from personal enemies (Banks, 2015). Scholars have pointed to this multiplicity of roles as a core appeal of games that fulfill "a human need to express the plural aspects of themselves" (Stenros & Sihvonen, 2020).

This multiplicity is also present in how individual characters can be played as sim appearance options can be changed at any point during gameplay. Although many games provide mechanisms for character growth via skills and abilities, they rarely, if ever, allow alterations to gender and racial identities once avatar design is complete. By moving beyond a fixed character design approach, *The Sims 4* adds a dimension of identity play that reinforces notions of flexibility and spectrums in terms of representation, thus de-essentializing identity to permit shifts from straight to gay, male to female, or dark- to light-skinned as part of the narrative players pursue.

By designing multiplicity as well as character growth into the game, *The Sims 4* breaks away from a fixedness inherent in most games, even open ones such as sandbox games. Beyond providing a spectrum for character gender performance, the game rejects the notion that performed identities are fixed and permanent once developed. This detachment literalizes the emergent and contextual performativeness of gender and sexuality, disrupting what Judith Butler calls "settled knowledge and knowable reality" (2004, p. 27). Representation in the stories players can tell in *The Sims 4* moves beyond the politics of identity into the politics of performance (Stenros & Sihvonen, 2020), and allows the player to examine the self and its relation to the social by creating their own exclusions and concealments. The ideologies encoded in the game via its interface options explicitly depart from hegemonic norms surrounding fixed, binary gender through what Bogost (2010) terms the "procedural rhetoric" generated by its built-in affordances.

Identity-Blindness or Transgressive Freedom?

As much as *The Sims 4* has been acclaimed by players and scholars for its gender identity affordances, the franchise has also been critiqued for its structure of egalitarian, identity-blind meritocracy that reinforces hegemonic assumptions about society (Crocco, 2011). For example, where personality, career, age, and relationship choices have a significant effect on gameplay via the AI that controls sim behaviors, other identity markers have no such impact. Black and white, trans and cis-gendered, gay and straight characters all experience the sim neighborhoods in identical ways. The historical and institutional forces that shape offline lives have no built-in equivalent in the sims' worlds. *The Sims 4* gives players the options to be trans in individual sim performance, for instance, but provides no built-in way to connect this identity to an historically grounded social world—such identities are literally only skin deep. This neutrality formulates an identity-blind politic that contributes to a kind of post-racial, post-gender, post-sexuality social universe. Because the game draws explicitly on the white, heteronormative idealization of suburban life (Consalvo, 2003), its very lack of Othering results in a lack of critique of this idealization, thus straightwashing and whitewashing the gameplay experience. As TL Taylor (2003) points out, ignoring the structural aspects to historically marginalized identities in games is ignoring issues pertaining to those identities as subject to debate, critique, and confrontation.

But as much as *The Sims 4* draws on realism for many aspects of its design, it is ultimately a game for creating fantasy worlds designed by the player, more akin to dollhouses than reality simulations. Stenros and Sihvonen (2020) argue that gameplay in such spaces is oriented around narrative engagement that allows players to design an escapist world that does not require built-in structures to explore. Fung (2017) suggests that despite the limitations of a sexuality-blind design, games such as *The Sims* do offer important avenues for experimental play that destabilizes essentialisms and heteronormative views on gender and sexuality. Numerous scholars have pointed to the importance of video games' capacity to allow for identity play, including with gender (McRae, 1996), race (Nakamura, 2008), sexuality (Fung, 2017), body type (Harper, 2020), and physical abilities (Farris, 2020). In particular, because the options for disrupting gender performance norms are built into the game, its invitation to transgress is made more accessible to those who might not otherwise have explored them. These opportunities are important for white, heterosexual, cis-gendered, and/or typically abled players as much as for others (Shaw, 2009). *The Sims 4* is thus ideally suited for "queering play" by consciously creating otherness and transgressions, heightening players' freedom to self-insert, to correct stereotypes and assumptions, or to subvert existing structures (Ruberg, 2019).

Final Thoughts: Normalizing Disruptions

Ultimately, *The Sims 4* allows players to experiment with identities in a context where the only consequences of their race, gender, or sexuality are those the players themselves create. As a result, a multiplicity of adaptable genders, races, and sexualities are normalized in this game, which serves as a powerful statement in a medium that has long been critiqued for its white, heteronormative assumptions. By integrating fluidity and flexibility of gender and sexuality, *The Sims 4* offers a politic that normalizes players' own perspectives and stories. What is it like to develop relationships that completely disregard gender? What does it look like when all mothers have jobs and all fathers stay home? When children all have three parents instead of two? When no one in the whole city is cisgender? The interface affordances in *The Sims 4* allows players to create—or disrupt—their own versions of "normal" to explore such questions in ways no other game allows. Its character customization and gameplay set a standard for gender performance in games and, while far from perfect, its power to normalize fluid and complex gender expressions makes such performances feel more possible, both in other games and in the life we play with outside our video games.

Rosa Mikeal Martey

References

Banks, J. (2015). Object, me, symbiote, other: A social typology of player-avatar relationships. *First Monday 20*(2). Retrieved July 25, 2021, from https://journals.uic.edu/ojs/index.php/fm/article/view/5433

Bogost, I. (2010). *Persuasive games: The expressive power of videogames.* Cambridge, MA: MIT Press.

Butler, J. (2004). *Undoing gender.* New York: Routledge.

Consalvo, M. (2003). Hot dates and fairy-tale romances: Studying sexuality in video games. In B. Perron & M.J.P. Wolf (Eds), *The video game theory reader* (pp. 171–194). New York: Routledge.

Crocco, F. (2011). Critical gaming pedagogy. *Radical Teacher, 91*, 26–41.

Evans, S. (2018). Queer(ing) game studies: Reviewing research on digital play and non-normativity. In T. Harper, M.B. Adams & N. Taylor (Eds), *Queerness in play* (pp. 17–33). London: Palgrave.

Farris, A. (2020). The player and the avatar: Performing as Other. *Storytelling, Self, Society, 16*, 177–199.

Favis, E. (2020, February 4). How The Sims Navigated 20 Years of Change to Become one of the Most Successful Franchises Ever. *The Washington Post.* Retrieved July 25, 2021, from https://www.washingtonpost.com

Fung, C. (2017). Playing with identities: Queering digital narratology and the exploration of gender and sexual identities. *Digital Humanities Quarterly, 11*(3). Retrieved July 25, 2021, from http://www.digitalhumanities.org/dhq/vol/11/3/000331/000331.html

Handrahan, M. (2016, June 3). Maxis and GLAAD Collaborate to Remove Gender Restrictions from The Sims. *Gamesindustry.biz.* Retrieved July 25, 2021, from https://www.gamesindustry.biz/

Harper, T. (2020). Endowed by their creator: Digital games, avatar creation, and fat bodies. *Fat Studies, 9*, 259–280.

McRae, S. (1996). Coming apart at the seams: Sex, text and the virtual body. In L. Cherny & E.R. Weise (Eds), *Wired women: Gender and new realities in cyberspace* (pp. 242–263). New York: Seal Press.

Nakamura, L. (2008). *Digitizing race: Visual cultures of the internet.* Minneapolis, MN: University of Minnesota Press.

Ruberg, B. (2019). *Video games have always been queer.* New York: New York University Press.

Shaw, A. (2009) Putting the gay in games: Cultural production and GLBT content in video games. *Games and Culture, 4*, 228–253.

Shaw, A. (2016). LGBTQ Game Archive. Retrieved July 25, 2021, from https://lgbtqgamearchive.com/

Shaw, A. (2017). Encoding and decoding affordances: Stuart Hall and interactive media technologies. *Media, Culture & Society, 39*, 592–602.

Stenros, J. & Sihvonen, T. (2020). Like seeing yourself in the mirror? Solitary role-play as performance and pretend play. *Game Studies: The International Journal of Computer Game Research, 20*(4). Retrieved July 25, 2021, from http://gamestudies.org/2004/articles/stenros_sihvonen

Taylor, T.L. (2003). Multiple pleasures: Women and online gaming. *Convergence: The International Journal of Research into New Media Technologies, 9*, 21–46.

Further Reading

Shaw, A. (2014). *Gaming at the edge: Sexuality and gender at the margins of gamer culture*. Minneapolis, MN: University of Minnesota Press.

Gray, K. (2014). *Race, gender, and deviance in Xbox Live: Theoretical perspectives from the virtual margins*. New York: Routledge.

DOI: 10.4324/9781003199205-40

SPACE INVADERS (1978)

Few games revolutionized the video game landscape like *Space Invaders* (Taito, 1978), and even fewer games have created such a long-lasting legacy. While *Computer Space* (Syzygy Engineering, 1971) launched the coin-op industry in the early seventies and *PONG* (Atari, 1972) raised awareness of video games in pop culture, the truth is that the commercial viability of coin-op gaming was in a slump until *Space Invaders* revitalized the scene (Mental Floss UK, 2018). The game literally propelled a niche novelty into a large-scale industry.

Tomohiro Nishikado

Space Invaders was created by Tomohiro Nishikado, an electronics engineer employed at Pacific Industries Ltd., a subsidiary of Taito Trading Company. He never set out to make video games, but an old friend and trusted colleague recruited him. Initially, Nishikado created the over-sized electro-mechanical game *Sky Fighter* (Taito, 1971) and its scaled-down version, *Sky Fighter II* (Taito, 1971).

Nishikado spent half a year reverse-engineering Atari's *PONG* and, as a result, developed a series of ball and paddle knock-off titles: *Elepong* (Taito, 1973), *Soccer* (Taito, 1973), and *Davis Cup* (Taito, 1973), that became some of Japan's earliest-produced video arcade games. Since Nishikado was the only employee experienced in integrated circuit (IC) technology, while also being familiar with solid-state electronics, he found himself working with transistor-transistor logic (TTL)—a high-speed, low-cost technology solution that his superiors believed to be the future of the arcade industry (Sambe, 2013). In fact, *Space Invaders* originated from an evaluation tool to assess a programmer's skills with hexadecimal numbers (Thomasson, 2012).

Development

Development on *Space Invaders* began in 1977. Nishikado affirms, "For the invader game, I was inspired by Atari's *Breakout* game." He noticed that players gained significant gratification from clearing an entire screen of blocks. Further discussing *Breakout* (1982), Nishikado states, "It was a game that made you want to play it again and again. I thought to myself, 'how can I make this into a new game?' We thought maybe a battle-based game would be good. Initially we considered tanks, planes, ships, and then we considered various targets." Unlike Atari's *Breakout*, Nishikado imagined a game where the targets fired back. "We tried it with soldiers and it was great fun, but people shouldn't be shot." Taito, as a company, decided that they did not want its games to present "an image of war."[1]

With humans and war machines out, Nishikado decided to pursue a science fiction angle. Originally, he was inspired by the popular anime *Space Battleship Yamato* (1974–1975). Nishikado continues, "about that same time in the U.S. there was talk of *Star Wars* (George Lucas, 1977) coming out, so we decided to go with something like a droid—which moves like a human, but isn't a human. But the game didn't really click, and I wasn't convinced."

The droids were too human-like and didn't work, but Nishikado still believed that the sci-fi theme could be salvaged. At the time, the song *Space Monster* by the Japanese female pop music duo Pink Lady topped the music charts, and this became the game's working title. Since the cabinet artwork was designed during this period of development, it explains why the side of the cabinet displays colossal human-like monsters that are absent from the actual game.

Next, Nishikado considered the addition of marine life, something very important to Japanese island culture. He reveals,

> When I was little, *War of the Worlds* by author H.G. Wells was very popular. So having grown up seeing that, I thought that aliens were octopuses. I looked up at the sky and wondered whether aliens may come and attack us. That's why we used octopus as the biggest enemy in *Space Invaders*. I drew a monster like an octopus. Then I thought about a squid as another sea creature. Then there's the crab, although it looks a bit weird… and a UFO.[2]

While Nishikado had worked with fellow team members on previous projects, he designed *Space Invaders* solely on his own. He fabricated all the hardware in its entirety, including engineering the microcomputer from the first step through to completion. As a result, Nishikado is truly the "Father of *Space Invaders*."

Taito executives did not have big expectations for Nishikado's game and initially the title received little fanfare. A successful coin-op at the time moved a few thousand machines, so the industry took notice

SPACE INVADERS (1978)

when Taito manufactured more than half a million cabinets in the first year alone.

In *Space Invaders*, players attempt to protect planet Earth from an advancing alien armada. Stacked in six columns consisting of eight aliens each, the intruders move back and forth in an organized manner, marching down a row at a time until ultimately landing on Earth and ending the game. The player slides in a horizontal manner, shooting invaders while dodging enemy fire and hiding behind any of the three shields before they are damaged and penetrated. With each enemy movement, the machine produces a thumping sound; one of four notes that some consider the first time that music in a video game was in sync with the actions taking place on screen (The Strong Museum, 2019). The audio and video working in tandem lured players deeper into the arcade experience. As enemy ranks are diminished, the alien's encroachment gains momentum and the audio track speeds up, making for a very dramatic effect—one of much urgency to the player. While such an effect could be chalked up to solid game design, it was actually the result of technical limitations and luck. As the enemy count was reduced, the maxed-out central processing unit (CPU) had less work to compute, which freed up memory space and allowed the game to run more efficiently. Recognizing the value the happy accident offered, Nishikado left it unchanged.

Prior games simply moved static graphic sprites about the video screen. Nishikado alternated the sprites to give movement to the enemies' appendages and as a result the game was the first to feature fully-animated characters. *Space Invaders* is often incorrectly credited with being the first game to display "high scores", but *Sea Wolf* (Midway, 1976) recorded and displayed top scores two years earlier. *Speed Race* (Taito, 1974), also awarded extra driving time when a pre-determined score was reached. *Space Invaders* may not have been the first, but its creator certainly advanced the concept. Nishikado expands, "if you see the high score, it encourages people to want to beat those scores and do better. It's what's called a 'replay appeal'."[3]

Reception

Competing for the high score became a global phenomenon. In an attempt to become top dog, obsessed players learned to exploit the game's programming. For instance, a randomly appearing UFO usually awarded those that shot it 50, 100, or 150 points. However, players eventually learned that if the UFO was destroyed using the twenty-third shot, then the game would award 300 points for its destruction every fifteenth shot thereafter.[4]

Another programming bug allowed for a "safe spot" directly below a bottom row invader. Nishikado recalls,

> One day I saw a really good player putting up some high scores around 150k. When I looked closely at what he was doing, I saw that the very bottom row of invaders' shots seemed to pass right through his ship. It's because I programmed it so that their shots would come out just a little bit in front of the invaders (in Duval, 2020).

Space Invaders became so popular that Japanese corner fruit stands converted to makeshift arcades, dubbed "invader houses." There is an often-repeated urban legend declaring that *Space Invaders* shut down Tokyo for more than a week. Supposedly, so many 100-yen coins were trapped in the machines that wannabe travelers found themselves stranded as the shortage brought the subway system to its knees. However, official government records tell another tale, stating that 100-yen coin production was actually lower in 1978 and 1979 than in preceding years. It is possible that the release of *Space Invaders*, in combination with fewer coins being manufactured and circulated, could have contributed to the difficulties (Paradis, 2014).

The phenomenon did not relegate itself to Japan. Midway licensed *Space Invaders* from Taito to release the game in North America. Unparalleled in popularity, the game could pay for itself in less than a month.[5] This encouraged storefronts to carry other coin-ops, helping the industry to grow substantially very quickly.

Fallout

Of course, everything *Space Invaders* was not always rosy. Long before the term "Nintendo Thumb" was ever uttered, people who played arcade games for long periods developed "Space Invaders Wrist," a stiffness in the hands, wrists, and elbows. This form of repetitive strain injury (RSI) was named by the *New England Journal of Medicine* (Duval, 2020).

In addition to potential physical harm, *Space Invaders* was often accused of causing social unrest. Many teenagers eager to play engaged in panhandling, robbery, and other crimes to fund their "fix." Such inappropriate behaviors were the start of public outcries against the video game industry. Parent groups and government organizations argued that video games harmed minors, and the residents of Texas brought a case all the way to the United States Supreme Court in an effort to ban the games outright (De Maria & Wilson, 2002, p. 46).

Expansion

With the world mesmerized by the coin-op hit, it wasn't long before its reach expanded to home consoles. The premier port of *Space Invaders* was released in 1979 for the relatively obscure Bally Professional Videocade, often referred to as the Bally Astrocade. This release was not official and was quickly renamed *Astro Battle* (Bally, 1979) when Atari officially licensed the game for its video computer system (VCS) in 1980. It marked the first time that an arcade game had been legitimately permitted by another company to be ported to a home video game console.

While Bally's version was representative of the arcade hit, Atari's version added more bells and whistles, providing much more variety. In total, the VCS version had 112 variations, including for size and speed, moving shields, zig-zagging laser bombs, and invisible aliens to hunt.

Prior to *Space Invaders* being published on Atari's console, the company's warehouses were full of unsold VCS inventory. However, once *Space Invaders* landed on the console in 1980, people lined up at retailers to purchase a VCS just to play the game in their own homes. As a result, sales of the units quadrupled and had to be rationed out to department stores to meet the demand, while console production was increased. *Space Invaders* became the first "killer app" when it sold over a million copies, doubling Atari's gross income to $145 million. Warner Communications, the parent company of Atari, found its stock rise a whopping thirty-five percent, which resulted in Atari becoming the fastest-growing company in history (Herman, 2016, p. 76).

The game has appeared on just about every video game console and computer platform since, and is likely to reappear indefinitely on future generations of gaming platforms. This is truly a sign of a far-reaching key video game. *Space Invaders* was recognized as the "highest-grossing entertainment product" during its heyday, surpassing $1 billion in sales in only nine months. By the end of 1982, *Space Invaders* machines had consumed the equivalent of 8 billion coins.[6]

Of course, there is more to *Space Invaders*' legacy than just sales numbers. Since the game launched the golden age of video arcade games, the creatures have become symbols and icons for the industry worldwide. Many prominent video game designers, including John

Romero and John Carmack—the creators of *DOOM* (id Software, 1993)—and Shigeru Miyamoto—the father of Donkey Kong, Mario, and Zelda—point to *Space Invaders* as their introduction to the field. Today, *Space Invaders* is considered one of the most influential video games of all time.

Michael Thomasson

Notes

1. "Boom & Bust." *High Score*, created by France Costrel, season 1, episode 1, Great Big Story for Netflix, August 19, 2020.
2. Ibid.
3. Ibid.
4. Space Invaders Wiki: in Enemies, Space Invaders Characters, UFO. Retrieved June 14, 2021, from https://spaceinvaders.fandom.com/wiki/UFO
5. Ultimate Pop Culture Wiki (2018). *Space Invaders*. Retrieved September 22, 2021, from https://ultimatepopculture.fandom.com/wiki/Space_Invaders
6. Gartner, H. (1982, November 23). "Making millions, 25 cents at a time". *The Fifth Estate*. Canadian Broadcasting Corporation.

References

De Maria, R. & Wilson, J. (2002). *High score: The illustrated history of electronic games*, Berkeley, CA: McGraw-Hill.

Duval, N. (2020). *Space Invaders: 15 Mind-Blowing Facts About the Arcade Classic*. Retrieved April 6, 2021, from https://www.thegamer.com/space-invaders-facts/

Herman, L. (2016). *Phoenix IV: The history of the videogame industry*. Springfield, NJ: Rolenta Press.

Mental Floss UK. (2018). *10 Fascinating Facts about Space Invaders*. Retrieved Sept. 22, 2021, from https://www.mentalfloss.com/article/91107/10-fascinating-facts-about-space-invaders

Paradis, C. (2014). *Insert Coin to Play: Space Invaders and the 100 Yen Myth*. Retrieved Sept. 22, 2021, from https://www.academia.edu/3672374/Insert_Coin_to_Play_Space_Invaders_and_the_100_Yen_Myth

Sambe, Y. (2013). *A Brief History of Arcade Game Display Technologies*. Retrieved May 14, 2021, from https://www.jstage.jst.go.jp/article/syntheng/6/2/6_94/_pdf

Space Invaders Wiki: *Enemies, Space Invaders Characters, UFO*. Retrieved June 14, 2021, from https://spaceinvaders.fandom.com/wiki/UFO

The Strong National Museum. (2019). *Composing Classics: A History of Video Game Music* Retrieved Sept. 22, 2021 from https://artsandculture.google.com/exhibit/composing-classics-a-history-of-video-game-music-the-strong/JwJi0uNkq_X8IQ?hl=en

Thomasson, M. (2012). Space Invaders. In Mark J.P. Wolf (Eds), *Encyclopedia of video games: The culture, technology, and art of gaming* (pp. 609–612). Westport, CT: Greenwood Press.

Ultimate Pop Culture Wiki (2018). *Space Invaders*. Retrieved Sept. 22, 2021, from https://ultimatepopculture.fandom.com/wiki/Space_Invaders

Further Reading

Thomasson, M. (2019). Space Invaders: The story of how Tomohiro Nishikado revived the early coin-op industry and inadvertently helped save Atari's home VCS console. *Old School Gamer Magazine*, (12), 24–25.

DOI: 10.4324/9781003199205-41

STARCRAFT (1998)

StarCraft is a real-time strategy (RTS) game where the player takes control of a Terran, Zerg, or Protoss faction. Terrans are militaristic humans, Zergs are insectoids infesting other species, while Protoss are psionic and technologically developed aliens. The player must amass resources to create units and buildings to destroy their opponent(s) on a battlefield. Developed by Blizzard Entertainment with Chris Metzen and James Phinney as senior designers, *StarCraft* was released globally for Windows on March 31, 1998. *Brood War*, its expansion, quickly followed in November 1998 and a Mac version was launched in March 1999.

StarCraft hit the shelves during the golden age of RTS games and represents one of its classic iterations. It is also one of the most prominent games to contribute to the early e-sports scene. While Blizzard was an American company, the fame of the game is mostly linked to its legacy in South Korea, where e-sports, as we know them, emerged. The goal of this chapter is to show how *StarCraft* contributed to contemporary e-sports through its creative specificities, its technological context, and its sociocultural adoption in South Korea.

Creative Decisions

Real-time strategy games in 1998 were mostly divided into two modes with very few common points: a campaign mode and a skirmish mode. Skirmish is a fight between two or more players, whether they are AI or human opponents, while campaigns involve a series of maps organized in a storyline to be played against an AI. Playing *StarCraft* in campaign mode, or even in single-player skirmish, is very far from the multiplayer mode. I argue that they follow different gameplay paradigms: a decoding paradigm for solo play; and a foreseeing paradigm for multiplayer mode (Dor, 2014).

The decoding paradigm is a way to play campaigns and most solo skirmish games. In most campaign scenarios, the enemies' strategies are already coded in the game and superficially interact with the player's actions. They are designed so that the player faces a specific challenge. Playing a specific scenario or level means optimizing one's own strategy and anticipating the opponent's AI patterns.

The foreseeing paradigm implies that the opponent's actions are predictable according to game rules. In multiplayer matches, each player starts with roughly equivalent units. They can grow their armies, technologies, and economy using the same rules. Thus, the game is not to predict a pattern in the AI's actions, but to anticipate an opponent's moves according to the same rules as the player's own moves. Game development decisions led *StarCraft* to being a key video game in the transition between decoding and foreseeing paradigms.

It is as a foreseeing game that *StarCraft* is almost unanimously praised as a balanced asymmetrical game. Terran, Zerg, and Protoss are seen as almost equivalent in terms of game cost and benefits, even though they are vastly different in game feel. Of course, it does not mean that every faction is equivalent, but it signifies that their strengths and weaknesses must be considered when playing. For instance, the Zergs can muster fast units early in the game, so other factions must wall their base if they want to have a chance to counter an early "rush." An equilibrium between technology, economy, and defense is necessary. If a player invests their resources to climb in the technology tree or to build another base, their army will be smaller than their opponent's, and thus will be a little weaker for some time. That is why information is crucial, so the player can scout their opponent's base to see a building indicating a progression on the tech tree, and anticipate which units or strategies are unfolding. Hiding buildings, armies, and even bases to play with the opponent's expectations and lead them to make bad decisions is the whole strategic aspect of foreseeing games. It fosters strategic depth and naturally builds suspense for an audience. When a player hides a building for a sneak attack, their opponent could know and prepare accordingly, since it is among a set of possible actions in the game. Foreseeing is a key of e-sport design and strongly depends on timing and deception.

Games that only focused on foreseeing were quite rare in 1998, since online and even modem play were not commonplace. *StarCraft* was not seen as especially original in 1998. It was initially meant to be released in 1996, one year after *Warcraft II: Tides of Darkness* (Blizzard Entertainment, 1995), but the company decided to completely change the original design after they realized it would not be very different from most RTS games that were flooding the market. Rather than being a top-down "*Warcraft* in space" with mirrored factions, the visual perspective switched to an axonometric one and the three factions of the game were designed to be asymmetrical. While some RTS turned to 3D graphics, the *StarCraft* game engine was still in 2D, although it used 3D models to render game unit sprites (Andreadis, 2018). Its visual clarity and the relatively low number of units makes it easier for strategic play and for an audience to follow.

The game mechanics span two different scales: micro- and macro-management (or simply called micro and macro). Macro actions are those related to economic or technological advantages in the game, while micro actions are unit control, especially in combat. Competitive players must multitask macro and micro actions very quickly, to the point where their actions can be as fast as 300 clicks per minute. Control was voluntarily limited to focus on micro: only twelve units can be selected at a time, which means that players cannot simply select all their military units and attack blindly. Mechanics open a possibility space to virtuosity for professional players. For instance, looking at their battle statistics and their common competitive usage, three Zerglings should beat one Zealot, but Protoss player Bisu (Kim Taek Yong) showed in a Proleague match against Jaedong (Lee Jae-dong) that he can eliminate seven Zerglings with two Zealots and save both of them (nevake, 2010, 12:30–12:50). E-sports spectatorship relies on both the virtuosity opened by the mechanics and the ingenuity of strategic play.

Technological Context

Balance as an ideal of fair play—which made *StarCraft*'s fame—is an abstract concept and wholly depends on the dynamics between players and their strategies in a specific place and time, often called the "metagame" (Boluk & LeMieux, 2017, p. 14). When one specific strategy emerges as an always successful one—a "dominant strategy"— the balance is broken. "Zerg rush" was often seen as a game-breaking strategy near the release date, before patching altered the game and fixed it. However, in 1998 game patches were very difficult to implement and rely on. The support for game patches was possible through the centralization of gameplay on Blizzard's server, Battle.net.

Battle.net launched with the release of *Diablo* in 1996. It would be a key for *StarCraft* development for two reasons. First, it was meant to be the only way to play *StarCraft* online as every player had to connect to the servers.[1] It would thus limit piracy, ensure that the community was not dispersed on different servers, and spread common strategies. Second, new patches were mandatory to play online. Battle.net would automatically download and install the newest patches, forcing new versions of the game on every player. If the Zerg rush is still a famous strategy rooted in geek culture, these technical decisions ensured *StarCraft* would be renowned as a balanced rather than a broken game.

This centralization of online play also meant that competitive players were mixed with more casual players. Blizzard supported a ranking system through its "ladder" mode, and the most ranked players earned their place to the first tournaments. There was a huge diversity of game maps on Battle.net, thanks to the complexity of the map editor. Map makers could create new campaigns by linking different maps together, adding new sound for dialogs, and using a trigger system that would make the game react to specific player's actions. The editor was used to add "observer" players on competitive maps. When joining a new game on Battle.net, it would automatically download the map if needed. New maps could easily spread if they were appreciated.

Many players valued the "Use Map Settings" mode, which often led to anything but RTS games. By using triggers cleverly and by customizing game units, users created role-playing games and various mini-games. The map "Aeon of Strife", for instance, was arguably an early iteration of the Multiplayer Online Battle Arena (MOBA) genre now prominent in e-sports (Boluk & LeMieux, 2017, p. 234-235). While the campaign editor was quite powerful as a creating tool, specific hacks pushed it even further (Johnson, 2009, p. 54). Those hacks were essential for e-sports, since most competitive maps make use of them.[2] In 2019, Blizzard officially stopped supporting their own editor to endorse an unofficial map editor that integrated these hacks, ScmDraft 2 (Sherman, 2019).

Sociocultural Context

Of course, any cultural manifestation such as e-sports comes not only from technical or creative choices, it must also be anchored in a sociocultural context. What made *StarCraft* such an important game for e-sports comes from a cultural conjuncture and institutional decisions in South Korea. At the end of the 1990s, South Korea was facing a financial crisis and its youth faced massive unemployment. The government accelerated its strategic plan to rehaul the connectivity of the country; in the meantime, "PC Bangs" emerged as a popular pastime. PC Bangs are Internet cafés where you could play computer games for a relatively cheap hourly fee (Chee, 2006). *StarCraft*'s distributor HanbitSoft offered free copies of the game to PC Bangs

(Huhh, 2009, p. 107), and it became a hit to the point where it accelerated the growth of broadband connections and Internet cafés from 100 in 1997 to more than 23,000 by 2001 (Jin, 2010, pp. 20–25).

The years after the release of *StarCraft* saw the emergence of organized tournaments supported by both public initiatives and private corporations (Taylor, 2012, pp. 19–25). The first World Cyber Games sponsored by Samsung were held in 2000, as arguably the "first real international eSports tournament" (Scholz, 2019, p. 22). That same year, the Ministry of Culture, Sports, and Tourism founded the Korean eSports Association (KeSPA) to support and regulate e-sports in their territory. One of their responsibilities was to authorize third-party companies to broadcast e-sports tournaments held in South Korea. Thus, OnGameNet and MBCGame received a license to organize their own "StarLeagues" (SL), shortened to OSL and MSL, and to broadcast them on their TV channels entirely dedicated to e-sports.

KeSPA also regulated the status of "progamer" by authorizing players to participate in tournaments, provided they met the prerequisites to be promoted to "pro" and "semipro", or by revoking their status, such as when match-fixing scandals surfaced in 2010. The top few progamers had the social status of pop stars, with mostly female fandoms (Hjorth et al., 2009, p. 255). Progamers play in teams sponsored by major South Korean corporations (Samsung, SK Telecom, CJ Corporation, etc.) and have a strict lifestyle, where they train together for hours a day. Some metagame changes were linked to progamer innovations, such as when Bisu popularized a strategy in Protoss vs Zerg where, in the air, Corsairs would repel Overlords to limit their detection ability, so that the invisible Dark Templars could sneak an attack on the ground. Other progamers are famous for how they managed to surprise their opponents with strategies completely outside the meta, such as when BoxeR (Lim Yo Hwan) defeated his opponent by supporting an early attack with his worker units. Others like Flash (Lee Young Ho) were renowned for their consistent wins. South Koreans dominated most of *StarCraft* international tournaments in the 2000s.

Even though the national model of regulation and promotion of e-sports was never exported from South Korea, the professionalization of *StarCraft* in the country showed how e-sports could play a major cultural role. Creative decisions from Blizzard and a technological infrastructure were facilitators, but the emergence of an organized and systematic institutionalization of e-sports also needed a specific sociocultural conjuncture. The key role South Korea played in e-sports is of utmost importance to understanding today's competition in gaming, to decentralize game studies from the West, and to show how games in culture go far beyond the location and moment they were designed. *StarCraft* was the perfect playground for e-sports to emerge.

Simon Dor

Notes

1. Although Blizzard enforced this decision through legal means, third-party servers to play the game still exist today.
2. Since the game is in 2D, the use of ramps to change altitude in the original game is only possible from one angle. The hacked editors allowed the use of "reversed" ramps, which have been since integrated into the *Remastered* edition (Lefebvre, 2018).

References

Andreadis, K. (2018). 20 years of StarCraft: An IGN Retrospective. *IGN*. Retrieved August 1st, 2021, from https://ca.ign.com/articles/2018/12/03/20-years-of-starcraft-an-ign-retrospective

Boluk, S., & LeMieux, P. (2017). *Metagaming: Playing, competing, spectating, cheating, trading, making, and breaking videogames*. Minneapolis: University of Minnesota Press.

Chee, F. (2006). The games we play online and offline: Making Wang-tta in Korea. *Popular Communication*, 4(3), 225–239.

Dor, S. (2014). A history of real-time strategy gameplay from decryption to prediction: Introducing the actional statement. *Kinephanos*, special issue, 58–73. Retrieved August 1, 2021, from http://www.kinephanos.ca/2014/real-time-strategy/

Hjorth, L., Na, B., & Huhh, J.-S. (2009). Games of gender. In L. Hjorth & D. Chan (Eds), *Gaming cultures and place in Asia-Pacific* (pp. 251–272). New York/London: Routledge.

Huhh, J.-S. (2009). The "bang" where Korean online gaming began. In L. Hjorth & D. Chan (Eds), *Gaming cultures and place in Asia-Pacific* (pp. 102–116). New York/London: Routledge.

Jin, D.Y. (2010). *Korea's online gaming empire*. Cambridge, MA: MIT Press.

Johnson, D. (2009). "StarCraft" fan craft: Game mods, ownership, and totally incomplete conversions. *Velvet Light Trap: A Critical Journal of Film & Television*, 64, 50–63.

Lefebvre, E. (2018). Starcraft Remastered Shows off New Ramps and Plans for Group Matchmaking. *Massively Overpowered*. Retrieved August 1st, 2021, from https://massivelyop.com/2018/06/17/starcraft-remastered-shows-off-new-ramps-and-plans-for-group-matchmaking/

nevake. (2010). SPL Bisu vs Jaedong 2010-07-06 @ Judgment Day. Retrieved August 1, 2021, from https://youtu.be/26-YW4Qcj-o?t=750

Scholz, T. (2019). *eSports is business: Management in the world of competitive gaming*. Basingstoke: Palgrave Macmillan.

Sherman, M. (2019). StarEdit Deprecation in Patch 1.23.0. *Starcraft Forums*. Retrieved August 1, 2021, from https://us.forums.blizzard.com/en/starcraft/t/staredit-deprecation-in-patch-1-23-0/223

Taylor, T. L. (2012). *Raising the stakes: E-sports and the professionalization of computer gaming*. Cambridge: MIT Press.

Further Reading

Galloway, A. R. (2007). StarCraft, or, balance. *Grey Room*, 28, 86–107. doi.org/10.2307/20442767

Jin, D. Y., & Chee, F. (2008). Age of new media empires. A critical interpretation of the Korean online game industry. *Games and Culture*, 3(1), 38–58. doi.org/10.1177/1555412007309528

McCrea, C. (2009). Watching *StarCraft*, strategy and South Korea. In Hjorth, L. & D. Chan (Eds), *Gaming cultures and place in Asia-Pacific* (pp. 179–193). New York/London: Routledge.

DOI: 10.4324/9781003199205-42

SUPER MARIO 64 (1996)

From 1985 to 1995, Nintendo had delivered eight games featuring their mascot (in Super form) that defined and popularized the platform genre. Their successful formula of the linear 2D game had evolved over the years to feature new characters, abilities (power-ups), and richer visuals. But in 1996, with the release of Nintendo's new console dawning (the Nintendo 64 or N64), the idea that Super Mario was now going to be in 3D was met with apprehension as well as excitement. How would a 3D Mario game work, given that the proven 2D formula would be incompatible with 3D space? Many speculated that the idea would not work, but as we would learn, the predictions were themselves two-dimensional. As *Edge* magazine put in the opening of their review in August 1996:

> If Nintendo aimed to set itself a tough task, choosing to make the first Nintendo 64 title a continuation of the most legendary series of videogames in history must rank as the most demanding one imaginable. Mario's lineage, after all, is a concertedly two-dimensional one, and hardly ideal material upon which to base what was destined to the be most intensely scrutinised 3D videogame of all time.

(p. 68)

As we would learn, Nintendo were not going to simply transfer an old design into 3D, they were going to redefine the game and the genre in the same way as the original.

The Next Generation

Nintendo had already ventured into 3D on the Super Nintendo (SNES) with the introduction of the Super FX chip in order to deliver *Star Fox* (Nintendo, 1993), a 3D rail shooter. Shigeru Miyamoto, Mario's creator, upon seeing *Star Fox*, conceived the idea of a 3D Mario game. As the internal name of the Super FX chip was referred to as Super Mario FX or the Mario Chip, there was speculation that *Super Mario 64* began as a SNES title; it had not (*Star Fox* programmer Dylan Cuthbert confirmed this to be false). Design on a 3D Mario platformer began in 1993, development began a year later and it was released as intended in 1996 as the N64's launch title. There was a clear intention that Nintendo's successor to the Super Nintendo would be a 3D console and that Nintendo would scale back 3D development on the SNES to create a distance that would aid that distinction. This ultimately resulted in *Star Fox 2* (Nintendo, 1996) not being released at the time, even though it was completed.

Nintendo was not going to be the first to introduce a true 3D platformer to the world; that honor (Guinness World Record) belongs to *Jumping Flash!* (Sony Computer Entertainment, 1995), albeit in first-person perspective. A year later, in 1996, we would see three further 3D platformers arrive on Sony's PlayStation in order to compete with Nintendo's mascot—*Crash Bandicoot* (SCE, 1996), *Floating Runner* (THQ, 1996), and *Bubsy 3D* (Accolade, 1996). *Crash Bandicoot* definitely looked the part. It had the hallmarks of a Mario game with the introduction of a new cartoony character that Sony would use to compete with Mario and Sonic, and the game even featured a level select map reminiscent of *Super Mario World* (Nintendo, 1990). Though *Crash Bandicoot* was a success, its 3D implementation was somewhat lacking. The game was composed of linear 3D levels and traditional side-scrolling, this was not really Sony's equivalent of *Super Mario 64*, but it was seen as the main competitor. *Floating Runner* lacked depth and quality. *Bubsy 3D* was criticized for its inappropriate controls and for its overall poor transition from 2D to 3D. It had unintentionally demonstrated the very thing that Nintendo wanted to avoid and that players and critics were worried about.

A Whole New World

Super Mario 64 takes a completely new approach to its predecessors and competitors. Whereas the 2D games featured an array of linear levels with the sole goal of reaching the end, *Super Mario 64* delivered

SUPER MARIO 64 (1996)

a range of arenas for the player to freely explore and complete a series of tasks/puzzles to collect Power Stars, which are the player's reward and a means of progression in the game. The game wants you to go on a journey of discovery and experimentation, which is indicative of Miyamoto's design philosophy. There are many secrets and Easter eggs to be discovered, but a lot of these involve feeding your curiosity. For example, as early as the first stage, you are introduced to a cannon that you can launch yourself from. It is there for a specific reason, for you to progress toward the level's goal. Yet, you find yourself asking what if I fire myself over there or at that thing? By exploring and asking such questions throughout, the game ultimately results in rewards, and it was this game that gave us the clear notion that Miyamoto knew what we were going to do almost as if he was with us as we played. This deep understanding of players and play is one of the things that makes this and subsequent Nintendo games so special.

The tasks themselves are where this game really comes into its own and not only stands apart from previous games but also sets a standard for future 3D platformers. From racing a Koopa, finding a snowman a new body, or rescuing a baby penguin, there's a lot more for the player to do than just collect coins and stomp on Goombas (who are here in giant and micro form). Each arena is like a zone in a theme park—categorized by its environmental setting (e.g., snowy mountains, sandy deserts, oceans, or volcanoes)—and inviting the player to explore and accomplish the tasks. In doing so, the player is rewarded with new tasks and the discovery of secrets. The countdown timer, a prominent feature in previous games, has now been omitted. Nintendo is clearly stating their intention that these levels are to be savored. Each arena is effectively a sandbox for the player to explore. There are enemies confined to their biomes, such Mr. Blizzard (a snowman that throws snowballs), Klepto (a condor located in the desert), and a shark (ironically called Sushi, unironically located in water). Each environment plays differently, and not just for aesthetic purposes; for instance, water in cold climates is harmful. Each arena offers something different, never feeling repetitive, and there is genuine excitement and intrigue as you venture into each one.

The game's plot is all too familiar—Princess Peach has been captured by Bowser (interestingly, this is the first time outside of Japan that the princess goes by Princess Peach rather than Toadstool). On this occasion, the princess has been imprisoned in her own castle, where Mario must venture to enact a rescue. The castle itself provides the player with more than a fitting and pleasing aesthetic, it is a hub for all the levels of the game, with wall paintings representing the doors that the player jumps into to begin a level. This new addition is an innovative approach to the map screen introduced in *Super Mario Bros. 3* (1988), allowing the player to select their path of progression and making the level select feature essentially a level in itself. The hub world would continue to be a core feature in the series and influenced other games, such as *Banjo Kazooie* (Rare, 1998).

Avatar and Player Evolution

Mario himself also changed. With the introduction of 3D, we get to see him in even more detail, and we get to hear his voice (provided by Charles Martinet) for the first time. Mario's movement now makes use of an analog stick that, in addition to controlling direction (360 degrees), also determines speed. The days of holding the B button to run are gone as Mario can go from tip-toeing to a dash by how far the stick is pushed. The analog stick, or more specifically the analog thumbstick, and its successful application would influence all subsequent consoles. Digital buttons, previously used for movement, now controlled the camera, and controlling the camera would prove to be a fundamental component in any third-person 3D game, which *Super Mario 64* delivered (albeit, temperamentally, with poor perspectives at times that hamper gameplay, but it was revolutionary nonetheless). Nintendo would improve upon this key feature, not only in the sequel (*Super Mario Sunshine*, Nintendo, 2002), but more importantly for the first 3D Zelda game, *Ocarina of Time* (Nintendo, 1998), highlighting the importance of the camera system.

Mario's existing catalog of actions were added to with the ability to Double Jump, Triple Jump, Wall Jump, Flip Jump, Backflip, Ground Pound, Punch, Kick, Dive, and Crawl. Nintendo had moved away from making Mario feel inadequate when not in a Power-Up form by empowering him with a range of abilities to add more variety to the level design and to provide options for how a player could traverse obstacles. The addition and evolution of Mario's movements further developed the platforming genre, showcasing innovative design in its use of 3D space. Nintendo did not shy away from exploring a variety of structures and biomes—pyramids, mountains, and oceans, to name a few. In terms of Power-Ups, the ability to fly returned (introduced in *SMB3*) in the form of Wing Mario, with new additions in the form of Vanish Mario (Mario becomes semi-transparent in order to go through objects), Metal Mario (tough and heavy), and finally, Mario can make use of a Koopa shell to surf his way through levels.

Super Mario 64's Legacy

Nintendo managed to deliver a magical place to explore and experience when playing *Super Mario 64*. The new open, non-linear gameplay demonstrated the benefits of freedom, as long as there are things to see and do. Shigeru Miyamoto, the game's director, showed his philosophy of rewarding exploration and consistently providing the player with a sense of accomplishment. The levels invite repeat play-throughs to obtain all 120 Power Stars—you don't need them all, seventy will finish the game, but you will be pulled in to trying to get them all. The game is engaging to play and, unlike previous games, is not just about making it through to the end. Sometimes you just want to spend time in the game and run around like a child in a park playground. Through the third dimension, Nintendo has created a happy place to escape to.

The reviews were universally positive, and the game received high praise and high scores across the board. Japan's leading game magazine *Famitsu*, awarded it 39/40, *Edge* gave it 10/10, *Electronic Game Magazine* 9.5/10, *IGN* 9.8/10, and *GameSpot* 9.4/10. Delaying the game (and console launch) was vindicated as Nintendo achieved another killer application on Day 1.

From this game onward, Nintendo had successfully transferred a popular franchise from 2D to 3D, paving the way for others from the era to do the same, proving it can be done despite requiring significant changes, which in this case included evolving the genre from a platformer to include action-adventure. Dan Houser from Rockstar (responsible for the *Grand Theft Auto* series) freely admits to borrowing from the game and there are numerous references made in the *Assassin's Creed* games—a realistic take on the platform action-adventure genre. *Assassin's Creed IV: Black Flag's* (Ubisoft, 2013) Director Ashraf Ismail specifically adds:

> The best reference I can say for this is effectively like *Mario 64*. Think about it. You have the castle, which is the ocean [in *ACIV*], and you have these portals that take you to these really unique worlds where you can come back to these worlds and do a bunch of things. Do collectibles, find stuff that has value for you. That's effectively what it is, but we've taken a much more credible approach to it, obviously. This was the world we decided to build. We wanted a hub world with pockets of maps and it's really different for [*Assassin's Creed*].

Epilogue

Though the 2D franchise would continue to evolve, Nintendo now had a new stream in this open, non-linear game design. *Super Mario 64* would be followed by *Super Mario Sunshine* (2002), *Super Mario Galaxy* (2007), *Super Mario Galaxy 2* (2010), and *Super Mario Odyssey* (2017). *Sunshine* essentially polishing its predecessor and the following sequels improving on the genre even further. The original was re-released on the Nintendo DS (Nintendo, 2004), Wii U Virtual Console (Nintendo, 2015), and as part of a collection for the Nintendo Switch, as *Super Mario 3D All Stars* (Nintendo, 2020).

At present, *Super Mario 64* is the N64's most successful game, selling 11.9 million copies. For Shigeru Miyamoto, this would be the last Super Mario game he would direct. The game that took his creation to 3D and to a new level of play fulfilled his focus of exploratory gameplay while also delivering on Nintendo's mission statement of putting a smile on people's faces.

Mario Michaelides

References

Aziz, H. (2013, October 8). *How Super Mario 64 Influenced Assassin's Creed IV*. Retrieved November 15, 2021, from https://www.destructoid.com/how-super-mario-64-influenced-assassins-creed-iv/

Editor (1996, August). Super Mario 64. *Edge, 35*, 68–71.

Suellenstrop, Chris. (2012, November 9). Americana at Its Most Felonious. *The New York Times*. Retrieved November 15, 2021, from https://www.nytimes.com/2012/11/10/arts/video-games/q-and-a-rockstars-dan-houser-on-grand-theft-auto-v.html

Further Reading

Matsui, S. (2018). *Super Mario Encyclopaedia*. Milwaukie: Dark Horse.

Ryan, J. (2011). *Super Mario: How Nintendo Conquered America*. New York: Penguin.

Winter, J. (2015). *Shigeru Miyamoto*. New York: Bloomsbury.

DOI: 10.4324/9781003199205-43

***SUPER MARIO BROS.* (1985)**

Nintendo's *Super Mario Bros.* wasn't the first video game starring Mario, but it is one of the most notable. When it was released in 1985, the console market in North America had collapsed and many thought video games were just a fad. By 1987, the North American console market had rebounded and Nintendo was in control of seventy percent of that market (McGill, 1988). The games released for its console were one of the main reasons why Nintendo was able to capture so much of the market, with *Super Mario Bros.* chief among them. In the years since its release, the game has sold more than 40 million copies (due in no small part to its being bundled with the NES, starting in 1988). It has been remade and updated several times and had numerous sequels and spin-offs. Among its accolades are being named one of the greatest video games of all time by numerous publications, including *Time Magazine* and *Game Informer* (Fitzpatrick et al., 2016; Game Informer, 2010). While there are countless reasons why *Super Mario Bros.* has had such a lasting impact, some of the biggest are the way the game combined elements from previous games in new ways, the design of the game itself, and its impact on the video game industry.

Design and Gameplay

While Nintendo ended up releasing cartridge-based games long after, *Super Mario Bros.* was meant to be the last cartridge-based game released before switching to floppy disk-based games and "a grand culmination of other games" ("Super Mario Bros. 25th Anniversary: 5. Original Super Mario Developers," 2010). Therefore, *Super Mario Bros.* borrowed elements from earlier games like: *Mario Bros.*'s (Nintendo, 1983) coin collecting, green pipes, and turtle-like enemies; *Excitebike*'s (Nintendo, 1984) ability "to scroll part of the screen;" and *Devil World*'s (Nintendo, 1984) capability to have "characters twice as big as characters in the previous games" ("Super Mario Bros. 25th Anniversary: 5. Original Super Mario Developers," 2010). However, rather than just taking elements from previous games, *Super Mario Bros.* took those elements and combined them in new and unprecedented ways. As Nathan Altice writes, none of the individual aspects of *Super Mario Bros.* were revolutionary, "but in combination they served as the architectural foundation for tile-based worlds tailored to character-based platforming" (2015, p. 6).

Part of what made *Super Mario Bros.* stand out was the fact that, rather than static screens like earlier Mario games including *Donkey Kong* (Nintendo, 1981) and *Mario Bros.*, its world seamlessly scrolled as the player moved Mario. In a game such as *Pitfall!* (Activision, 1982), the character moves across the screen from left to right while the backgrounds remain stationary. But in *Super Mario Bros.*, the character typically stays in the middle of the screen and the background moves from right to left. This gives the impression that the level is one continuous scene rather than individual sets. *Super Mario Bros.*

wasn't the first to do this as other games, such as *Defender* (Williams Electronics, 1981), had continuous scrolling (Altice, 2015, p. 118). Nonetheless, it combined this and other technical accomplishments with the personality of Mario, the memorable graphics, and other elements to create something notable.

In addition to scrolling backgrounds, *Super Mario Bros.* had levels that were alive with their own enemies, environments, and music. Mario's first games, including *Donkey Kong* and *Mario Bros.*, all took place against black backgrounds. *Super Mario Bros.* had multiple locations, each with its own settings. The first level was bright and colorful, with a blue sky in the background and fluffy white clouds. The second level may have seemed like a throwback, with its black background, but this was because it took place underground. Later levels replaced the ground with platforms that seemed to be high up in the sky, or they took place entirely underwater.

This variety also extended to the enemies, which came in several shapes and sizes, and with creative names like Koopas, Goombas, Hammer Bros, Bloopers, or Piranha Plants. Each enemy had a different play mechanic for defeating them. Moreover, in *Super Mario Bros.*, Mario had actual facial features and a personality. Games for earlier systems may have had human characters but they tended to be little more than stick figures. Mario had distinct clothes and a moustache. When he jumped, he raised his arm as if in victory and a bouncy chime played. These all combined to make Mario seem upbeat and energetic.

More than just bouncy sound effects, *Super Mario Bros.* had memorable music throughout the game. There were earlier games with music in them, but few have become as iconic as composer Koji Kondo's *Super Mario Bros.* soundtrack. The theme song is so well known that when Paul McCartney met Koji Kondo, "Paul started singing the overworld [background music]" ("Legend of Zelda Series Super Best—Interview with Koji Kondo—Music, Kondo, Game, Songs, Mario," 2010). Each of the four environments of the game has its own theme, and yet the entire soundtrack to *Super Mario Bros.* is less than three minutes long (Schartmann, 2015, p. 1). Despite its overall brevity, the music of *Super Mario Bros.* has been performed by numerous orchestras around the world, has appeared in many subsequent Nintendo games, and has had academic articles and at least one book devoted to it (Schartmann, 2015).

In addition to these aesthetic elements, the gameplay of *Super Mario Bros.* is also engaging and full of secrets and surprises. It is deceptively simple. The player controls Mario (or, as a second player, his brother, Luigi) and moves him from left to right as he jumps over or onto enemies and environmental obstacles—such as chasms, fire, and falling objects—to achieve the final goal of rescuing Princess Peach from the evil King Koopa. The game's controls are limited to just three buttons: a plus-shaped one moves the character; a round one makes the character jump; and a second round one makes him jump or throw fireballs (there is also a select and start button but those are not used while playing the game). If that was all *Super Mario Bros.* consisted of, it might have been enough to make the game a hit, but the game also uses these controls in multiple ways to present various challenges and surprises.

One of the biggest surprises players encounter for the first time comes at the end of the fourth level. Previous games often had a small number of levels. For example, *Donkey Kong* had four levels that repeated, and *Mario Bros.* just had different colored versions of the same level. So, it seemed logical that when the player reached the end of the fourth level in *Super Mario Bros.* and defeats King Koopa, the game would either end or perhaps cycle back to the first level. Instead, the player learns that not only have they not defeated the final boss and that Princess Peach is in another castle, but also that it was not the end of the game, just the end of the first of eight worlds, each with four levels.

The game is full of many other surprises, such as invisible floating blocks, pathways that could be discovered by breaking bricks, and special pipes that could be entered to reveal bonuses or alternate paths that skipped a section of the level or even warped to other levels. These "warp zones" also made the game easier to replay because it allowed a player to skip to a later level without having to grind through earlier levels. So, if a level was frustrating the player, one quick trip through the warp pipe would skip past that level and let the player continue the game. These features rewarded players for exploring and encouraged them to keep replaying the game.

In the days before the Internet or walkthroughs, these secrets and tricks became a kind of folklore that spread from person to person, largely by word of mouth and magazines. Like traditional folk stories, some of the "secrets" were exaggerated or totally wrong. Because of this, players could never be sure which secrets or tricks were real and so they had to replay the game to see for themselves. In this way, an informal network of players was created who would talk about the game and speculate whether there were still more secrets to discover. This helped the reputation of *Super Mario Bros.* grow and kept people thinking about the game.

Impact

Of course, the success of *Super Mario Bros.* extended far beyond the quality of the game itself and the secrets it was alleged to contain. The game was also a financial success. That success seemed unlikely when *Super Mario Bros.* was released because, whereas in 1983 the video game market in North America had $3 billion in sales (including both home and arcade game sales), by 1985 the market had crashed to only $100 million (Adler, Rogers, Brailsford, Gordon, & Quade, 1989, p. 65). Nintendo faced an uphill battle when they entered the North American console market, but they succeeded and, by 1988, sales of video games and cartridges had rebounded to $2.3 billion, due largely to Nintendo (Adler et al., 1989, p. 66).

Mario led the charge and by 1990, "was more recognized by American children than Mickey Mouse" (Sheff, 1993, p. 9). This popularity led to companies releasing an incredibly large number of products with Mario's name and likeness on them. A Nintendo book from 1991 bragged, "You could spend an entire day using Mario products" and listed a range from clothes to clocks (Tilden, 1991, p. 26). Name a product and there is a good chance that they have made a Mario-branded version. In fact, there are so many Mario-branded products that in 2010, one collector had over 5,400 items with Mario on them (Glenday & Guinness World Records Limited, 2017, p. 83).

The popularity of Mario and *Super Mario Bros.* was more than a fad. The enduring appeal can be seen in the fact that Nintendo has released versions of *Super Mario Bros.* for every one of their home consoles and handheld systems, except for the Nintendo 64, the Game Boy, and the Nintendo DS. Mario himself has appeared in over 200 games, ranging from cameos to starring roles, and in practically every genre, from platforming to puzzle and side-scrolling to sports (Glenday & Guinness World Records Limited, 2017, p. 82). Up to this time, *Super Mario Bros.* is still being played, not only by the generation who were kids in the 1980s, but also by the current generation.

Conclusion

With all the achievements and accomplishments of *Super Mario Bros.*, it is little wonder that it has been named one of the best video games by so many. After all, it was a milestone of game design, sold millions of copies when the North American console industry was thought to be dying, led to a marketing blitz of thousands of items, and continues to entertain and inspire a whole new generation of players. To this day, new players are discovering the game and experienced players are coming back to it. It seems certain that *Super Mario Bros.* will continue to influence video games for a long time to come.

Bryan-Mitchell Young

References

Adler, J., Rogers, M., Brailsford, K., Gordon, J., & Quade, V. (1989, March 6). The Nintendo Kid. *Newsweek*, pp. 64–68.

Altice, N. (2015). *I am error: The Nintendo family computer/entertainment system platform*. Cambridge, MA: MIT Press.

Fitzpatrick, A., Pullen, J. P., Raab, J., Grossman, L., Eadicicco, L., Peckham, M., & Vella, M. (2016, August 23). Best Video Games of All Time: TIME's Top 50, *Time*. Retrieved July 31, 2021, from https://web.archive.org/web/20190526164501/http://time.com/4458554/best-video-games-all-time/

Game Informer. (2010, January). The Top 200 Games of All Time. *Game Informer*, (200).

Glenday, C. & Guinness World Records Limited. (2017). *Guinness world records: Gamer's edition*. London: Guinness World Records.

Legend of Zelda Series Super Best - Interview with Koji Kondo - Music, Kondo, Game, Songs, Mario. (2010, November 16). *Zelda Power*. Retrieved July 16, 2021, from https://web.archive.org/web/20101116161356/https://zeldapower.com/index.php/features/interviews/legend_of_zelda_series_super_best_-_interview_with_koji_kondo.php

McGill, D. C. (1988, December 4). Nintendo Scores Big. *The New York Times*, p. 1.

Schartmann, A. (2015). *Super Mario Bros.* New York: Bloomsbury Academic.

Sheff, D. (1993). *Game over: How Nintendo zapped an American industry, captured your dollars, and enslaved your children*. New York, NY: Random House Inc.

Super Mario Bros. 25th Anniversary: 5. Original Super Mario Developers. (2010, September 13). *Nintendo.co.uk*. Retrieved July 16, 2021, from https://www.nintendo.co.uk/Iwata-Asks/Super-Mario-Bros-25th-Anniversary/Vol-5-Original-Super-Mario-Developers/1-Using-the-D-pad-to-Jump/1-Using-the-D-pad-to-Jump-212727.html

Tilden, G. (Eds). (1991). *Mario Mania: Nintendo player's guide*. Redmond, WA: Nintendo of America.

Further Reading

Horowitz, K., & McFerran, D. (2020). *Beyond Donkey Kong: A history of Nintendo arcade games*. Jefferson, NC: McFarland & Company, Inc., Publishers.

Ryan, J. (2011). *Super Mario: How Nintendo conquered America*. New York, NY: Penguin.

Super Mario Bros. 25th Anniversary: 1. Bringing Video Games Home. (2010, September 13). *Nintendo.co.uk*. Retrieved July 21, 2021, from https://www.nintendo.co.uk/Iwata-Asks/Super-Mario-Bros-25th-Anniversary/Vol-2-NES-Mario/1-Bringing-Video-Games-Home/1-Bringing-Video-Games-Home-215978.html

DOI: 10.4324/9781003199205-44

TETRIS (1984)

There are several key scenes in *The Queen's Gambit* (2020) on Netflix where chess prodigy Elizabeth Harmon (Anna Taylor-Joy) imagines statuesque pawns, bishops, and knights sweeping across the ceiling, analyzing countless possibilities for games in her head. Harmon is depicted as obsessively fascinated with the elegant movement of the pieces: practicing, refining, and committing strategies to memory. While viewers may not have had this kind of connection to the game of chess, many of them are likely to recall a similar experience with the video game *Tetris*—imagining the tetriminos endlessly rotating in midair and falling gently into neat rows behind one's eyelids, afterimages of hours of compelling play set to the game's captivating musical loops.[1]

Tetris is ubiquitous and influential, a household name known to gamers and non-gamers alike; the popularity of this falling block puzzle has been consistently credited to the addictive qualities of its satisfying, challenging, yet irreducibly simple gameplay (for example, Lincoln, 1992). The game has sold over 500 million copies according to the official *Tetris* website, and earned a Guinness world record for the most ported video game in October 2010, with versions on sixty-five platforms. However, it was not Alexey Pajitnov's 1984 prototype that catapulted *Tetris* to its unassailable place in the gaming pantheon, but the versions accompanied by Russian-tinged graphics and music that were commercially released for the Nintendo Entertainment System (NES) and the Game Boy in 1989, which allowed a wide range of players to access and experience a sleek, polished version of the original idea. *The Top 47,858 Games of All Time* podcast, for instance, unequivocally ranked the 1989 Game Boy release as the greatest game of all time.[2] While this argument complicates the notion of "the game" as a single entity in a volume such as this, *Tetris* remains remarkably stable in its core game design across various iterations.[3] I would argue that the game owes its continuing cultural resonance and relevance not only to this constancy and sense of timelessness, but also to its added music and graphics, which imparted a distinctive personality to the game and transformed it into a lasting icon. In this brief chapter, I describe not only the ludic merits of *Tetris*, but also how the music transformed the puzzle game and solidified its status as a transcendent pop cultural icon, before situating the game within academic discourse.

Alexey Pajitnov developed *Tetris* on an Electronika 60 terminal in June 1984 while working for the Soviet Academy of Sciences, programming in Pascal in his spare time (Sheff, 1994; Plank-Blasko, 2015).[4] The original version had black and white graphics (with the pieces represented by square brackets instead of the patterned squares and colors of later iterations), and no sound. However, as *Tetris* made its way to the United States, it acquired distinctively Soviet graphics and music that exoticized the game for US audiences and added a purported glimpse behind the Iron Curtain (Plank-Blasko, 2015). The 1988 release by Spectrum HoloByte was the first to introduce the Russian aesthetic to entice North American players to play "The Soviet Challenge".[5]

From Folk Tune to Fandom: The Music of *Tetris*

Nintendo also chose to draw upon the game's Soviet origins for its NES and Game Boy releases, with music complementing the images of St. Basil's Cathedral that adorned both title screens. For example, the NES version incorporated Tchaikovsky's "Dance of the Sugar Plum Fairy" from *The Nutcracker* (Gibbons, 2009). The selections in the Game Boy version, identified only as Tetris A, Tetris B, and Tetris C in the game's options menu, present an unlikely assortment of musical accompaniments to the gameplay. Tetris A is a re-creation of the nineteenth-century Russian folk tune "Korobeiniki", which became a "musical metonymy" for *Tetris* itself (Plank-Blasko 2015, p. 8). Tetris B was newly composed by Nintendo's Hirokazu Tanaka, and Tetris C presents an abridged version of the Menuet from Bach's French Suite no. 3 in B minor, BWV 814. While the three tracks seem incongruous at first, with origins spanning several centuries of music history, they share common elements of musical language that create cohesiveness in the score and a unified effect on the player: all are in minor keys at a brisk tempo of about 140 beats per minute; with compact forms conducive to looping, utilizing occasional or pervasive sharped seventh scale degrees; and presenting an overall sense of rhythmic density and momentum that motivates the player in the flow-state processes of play.

A YouTube search for "the Tetris song" brings up thousands of hits, from re-uploads of the original game audio to covers featuring a variety of traditional and nontraditional instruments. I found clever covers of "Korobeiniki" or "Tetris A" on YouTube for violin, accordion, timpani, marimba and vibraphone, ocarina, Otamatone, music box, calculators, electric toothbrushes, and even an apartment building's intercom system. The most successful of these tribute videos have millions of views, such as Smooth McGroove's multi-tracked *a cappella* vocal cover of Tetris A, which had 9.8 million views at the time of writing. These videos attest to the power of the game music in the popular imagination.

"Perfection in Motion:" The Gameplay

The music of *Tetris* complements gameplay that can best be described as "perfection in motion" (Matthewmatosis, 2013). The set of seven different tetromino pieces represents a Goldilocks-esque "just right" with regard to gameplay complexity (styled in *Tetris* games as "tetriminos," to better match the game's title and allow for a trademark on the term); triominoes only have two permutations, which lack challenge for the player, whereas the twelve permutations of pentomino shapes would be too complicated to manage well. Further, the gameplay has a universal appeal that does not require mediation from language, narrative, or culture (which also makes it easier for new players to understand quickly), and every player will be challenged by the game at some point as it progresses (Matthewmatosis, 2013). Other pieces have used similar descriptions, such as "airtight," "bulletproof," and "impenetrable" to espouse the intuitive perfection of the gameplay and its difficulty curve. Jordan (2009) explored the game's mechanics in detail, examining elements such as the algorithms that pseudo-randomly select tetriminos for the player to create a finely-tuned difficulty curve, and the introduction of color, sound, and visual interface design to "enhance gameplay cognition." Additionally, part of the game's appeal lies in its constructive impulse—creating lines and tidying up the game space instead of going on a destructive rampage. Stafford (2012) frames *Tetris* in light of the Zeigarnik effect, a phenomenon in which human beings have a better memory of tasks that they have not yet completed or that were interrupted. *Tetris* is endlessly incomplete and thus intensely and psychologically absorbing, addictive, and memorable.

Beyond the Game

The influence of *Tetris* has reached far beyond popular culture and game design into academia. It was central in one of the foundational methodological arguments in the field of game studies between ludologists—who wanted to focus on the game's interactivity, its unique and sophisticated simplicity—and narratologists—who suggested a narrative experience for those playing, overlaid on the game with the player as the protagonist in a story of their own creation (Murray, [1997] 2016; Eskelinen, 2001). Some narratologists created specific narratives for *Tetris*, connecting the anxiety of play to real-world analogues, such as modern workaholic culture in the United States or Western assumptions about harsh experiences of life in a communist society (Murray [1997] 2016; Roe, 2011). Although many researchers now engage in a hybrid approach, the debate illuminated fundamental questions about the role of game studies in either connecting video games to their predecessors in other media or in highlighting their unique differences with regard to ludic construction.

Psychological and neurological research on *Tetris* persists to the present day; the game creates such a deep impact on the player that images of the game pieces can persist, even in patients with amnesia who cannot recall actual gameplay, a phenomenon known as the "*Tetris* effect" or Game Transfer Phenomena (Ortiz de Gortari, 2019). Other research focuses on potential therapeutic applications, suggesting that playing the game as an early intervention after trauma may serve as a "cognitive vaccine" to help reduce flashbacks from PTSD by interfering with memory consolidation (Hagenaars et al., 2017; Butler et al., 2020). *Tetris* gameplay may even decrease food, alcohol, and drug cravings in real-world settings (Skorka-Brown et al., 2015).

Although players often become hooked the moment they begin to play, the Russian-themed music and graphics of *Tetris* helped to differentiate the puzzle game in the US market in the late 1980s and drew in players of all ages, in essence helping it to transcend a mere fleeting popularity and take its place as an enduring cultural icon. That the music contributes so strikingly to the experience of the game—mimicking, aligning with, or even creating the musical experience of the flow state of play—was echoed by the game's creator in a 1994 interview for *Wired*. When asked if *Tetris* was akin to an electronic drug or a "pharmatronic", Pajitnov responded: "Many people say that, but my feeling is it's more like music. Playing games is a very specific rhythmic and visual pleasure. For me, *Tetris* is some song which you sing and sing inside yourself and can't stop" (Goldsmith, 1994).

Dana Plank

Notes

1. Although the spelling "tetromino/tetrominoes" is standard in mathematics to describe geometric shapes composed of four orthogonally-connected squares, The Tetris Company always uses "tetrimino/tetriminos," terms they have trademarked. The imprint or afterimage is popularly known as "the *Tetris* effect," or more generally as game transfer phenomena (Ortiz de Gortari, 2019).
2. It has appeared on at least forty other such lists of the greatest games of all time, too many to list here.
3. Throughout the game's thirty-seven-year history, several game mechanics have evolved behind the scenes. However, many versions maintain a

similar enough look and feel that the changes may be imperceptible to the average player. For example, block distribution in the original game was truly randomized, which could lead to awkward gameplay if players were unlucky enough to field the same shape over and over from the game's random number generator (RNG). Modern versions place boundaries on this randomness by having the game draw from a limited set and then replenishing it once it has been depleted—almost as if the tetriminos were being drawn one by one from a bag and dropped into the field of play.
4. David Sheff's *Game Over: How Nintendo Conquered America* (1994) is the most exhaustively-researched source on the complicated history of *Tetris*'s journey from the Soviet Union to the United States. Programmers initially shared copies on floppy disc across Europe, and many unsanctioned versions appeared on the market. Sheff documents the legal battles around various competing ports of the game, and Henk Rogers's eventual deal with Pajitnov and the Soviet Ministry of Software and Hardware export, known as ELORG (Elektronorgtechnica), to license the game to Nintendo of America.
5. As I wroite in 2015, these elements included: "red box art complete with images of St. Basil's Cathedral, a Soviet hammer and sickle…the Cyrillic letter Ya in place of every R, and Russian music" (Plank-Blasko, 2015, p. 13). Spectrum HoloByte CEO Gilman Louie confirmed that these elements were deliberately chosen to appeal to players in the US. Pajitnov also speculated that the Russian elements helped with marketing the game, increasing interest and sales (Nutt, 2010).

References

Butler, O., Herr, K., Willmund, G., Gallinat, J., Kühn, S., & Zimmerman, P. (2020). Trauma, treatment and *Tetris*: Video gaming increases hippocampal volume in male patients with combat-related posttraumatic stress disorder. *Journal of Psychiatry & Neuroscience, 45*(4), 279–287. doi:10.1503/jpn.190027

Eskelinen, M. (2001). The gaming situation. *Game Studies,* 1(1). Retrieved November 4, 2021, from http://www.gamestudies.org/0101/eskelinen/

Gibbons, W. (2009). Blip, bloop, Bach? Some uses of classical music on the Nintendo Entertainment System. *Music and Moving Image, 2*(1), 40–52. Retrieved November 4, 2021, https://www.jstor.org/stable/10.5406/musimoviimag.2.issue-1

Goldsmith, J. (1994, May 1). This is your brain on *Tetris*: Did Alexey Pajitnov invent a pharmatronic? *Wired.* Retrieved November 4, 2021, from http://www.wired.com/wired/archive/2.05/tetris_pr.html

Hagenaars, M.A., Holmes, E.A., Klaassen, F., & Elzinga, B. (2017). *Tetris* and word games lead to fewer intrusive memories when applied several days after analogue trauma. *European Journal of Psychotraumatology, 8*(sup 1), 1386959. doi:10.1080/20008198.2017.1386959

Jordan, W. (2009). Morphology of the Tetromino-stacking Game: The Design Evolution of *Tetris*. Paper presented at DiGRA'09: *Breaking New Ground:*

Innovation in Games, Play, Practice and Theory, Digital Games Research Association Conference, London, United Kingdom, 1–4 September. Retrieved November 4, 2021, http://www.digra.org/wp-content/uploads/digital-library/09291.05226.pdf

Lincoln, S. (1992, November 3). The Nintendo Trap. *The Washington Post*. Retrieved November 1, 2021, from http://www.washingtonpost.com/archive/lifestyle/1992/11/03/vignette/39fbb497-6c74-4bf2-9676-91761000fe8f/

Matthewmatosis. (2013, July 11). *Tetris—A perfect game?* [Video]. YouTube. Retrieved November 1, 2021 from https://www.youtube.com/watch?v=Tnztj1UlkQs

Murray, J.H. ([1997] 2016). *Hamlet on the holodeck: The future of narrative in cyberspace*. New York: The Free Press.

Nutt, C. (2010, June 28). Alexey Pajitnov—*Tetris*: Past, present, and future. *Gamasutra*. Retrieved November 4, 2021, from http://www.gamasutra.com/view/feature/134248/alexey_pajitnov__tetris_past_.php

Ortiz de Gortari, A. B. (2019). Game Transfer Phenomena: Origin, development, and contributions to the video game research field. In A. Attrill-Smith, C. Fullwood, M. Keep, & D. J. Kuss L. (eds), *The Oxford handbook of cyberpsychology* (pp. 531–556). New York: Oxford University Press.

Plank-Blasko, D. (2015). From Russia with fun: *Tetris*, Korobeiniki, and the ludic Soviet. *The Soundtrack*, 8(1+2), 7–24. doi:10.1386/st.8.1-2.7_1

Roe, E. (2011). *Tetris* and the Fall of the Soviet Union. *Super Game Theory*. Retrieved November 4, 2021, from https://web.archive.org/web/20120429041226/http://supergametheory.com/2011/12/27/tetris-and-the-fall-of-the-soviet-union/

Sheff, D. (1994). *Game over: How Nintendo conquered the world*. New York: Vintage Books.

Skorka-Brown, J., Andrade, J., Whalley, B., & May, J. (2015). Playing *Tetris* decreases drug and other cravings in real world settings. *Addictive Behaviors* 51, 165–170. doi.org/10.1016/j.addbeh.2015.07.020

Stafford, T. (2012, October 29). The Psychology of *Tetris*. *Mind Hacks*. Retrieved November 1, 2021, from http://mindhacks.com/2012/10/29/bbc-future-column-the-psychology-of-tetris/

Further Reading

Helmuth, L. (2000, October 13). Video game images persist despite amnesia. *Science, New Series*, 290(5490), 247–249. doi.org/10.1126/science.290.5490.247a

Jana, D. (2015, February 2). Why is *Tetris* a Mathematically Perfect Game Design that Requires no Tutorial? *Gamasutra*. Retrieved November 1, 2021, from https://www.gamasutra.com/blogs/DevJana/20150202/182335/Why_is_Tetris_a_mathematically_perfect_game_design_that_requires_no_tutorial.php

Juul, J. (2001). Games Telling Stories? A Brief Note on Games and Narratives. *Game Studies*. Retrieved November 4, 2021, http://www.gamestudies.org/0101/juul-gts/

Stickgold, R., Malia, A., Maguire, D., Roddenberry, D., & O'Connor, M. (2000). Replaying the game: Hypnagogic images in normal and amnesics. *Science 290*(5490), 350–353. doi:10.1126/science.290.5490.350

Temple, M. (director). (2004). *Tetris—From Russia With Love.* United Kingdom: BBC Four.

DOI: 10.4324/9781003199205-45

THIS WAR OF MINE (2014)

War as a Topic

It is not easy to classify *This War of Mine*—a Polish game released by 11Bit Studios in 2014—using a single genre description. The game's theme has led authors to use the term "war game" (Bjørkelo, 2018; House, 2019; Kampe, 2019), which is rather surprising as it is very unusual to classify games solely on the basis of their topic. It seems that the main advantage of invoking the "war game" category was that it enabled the authors to make a distinction between *TWoM* and previous games that depicted war. The reason why researchers felt the need to single out *TWoM* is that previous "war games" presented war from the military perspective. This is true even of games with a strong anti-war message, such as *Valiant Hearts* (Ubisoft Montpellier, 2014). In contrast, *TWoM* is a game that focuses only on the perspective of civilians trying to survive in a war-torn city.

The theme of the game was originally inspired by the siege of Sarajevo (Gieba, 2019), but the developers continued their research looking at conflicts in other countries such as Iraq, Ukraine, Syria, Chechnya, and Kosovo (House, 2019). Some of the developers were also influenced by the tales of family members who lived through the Warsaw Uprising. The resulting setting is a deliberate amalgam of modern urban civil wars. Some aspects, such as the names of the characters, point to the Balkans, while others, such as the names of the sides in the conflict, are more reminiscent of Syria. The city's architecture makes it look like Eastern Europe, while the in-game radio plays Polish songs.

War as Game Mechanics

From a ludic perspective, *TWoM* can be seen as a model product of its time, that is, a combination of mechanics that gained popularity on the independent game scene in the early 2010s, such as crafting, permadeath, and random level generation. What is novel is how all these elements are used to emphasize the game's anti-war message and the fact that the game achieves this using mostly mechanics instead of traditional narrative.

TWoM is a survival game in the most literal sense—the goal of the game is that at least one of the characters survives. The task of the player is to micromanage the actions of the survivors, gather materials, craft new items, and make decisions during many random events, such as encounters with other survivors. The environments are semi-randomized: the structure of the game stays the same on the general level, but differs in detail, for example, in the subset of locations the player can visit, their layouts, and the objects that can be gathered there.

The reliance on randomness strengthens the game's emergent narrative. First, the player does not know when the conflict will be over. This is important as it simulates the uncertainty of survival and determines a different strategy, as the player must always use their resources responsibly. This aspect was recognized by Elisabeth Toma (2015), who described uncertainty as one of the mechanics of the game. Recognizing the limits of emergent narratives, the developers decided to add two especially challenging situations that guaranteed that the players encountered difficult ethical dilemmas. One of them gives the player the chance to save a woman who is being raped by a soldier. The other enables the player to sacrifice an elderly couple for the benefit of the player's group of survivors.

Apart from occasional comments made by the characters, the player must discover the game's mechanics by themselves. This is not unusual for independent survival games, but in this case, it connects with the game's message: in wartime, people are constantly disoriented and must quickly adapt. The player has to pay close attention to their surroundings, as even the early stages of the game may be vastly different after a restart.

In addition to this, *TWoM* features permadeath—another staple of contemporary independent game design. As pointed out by De Smale, Kors and Sandovar, permadeath enables the developers to simulate "the precariousness of life in war and the psychological trauma that occurs to survivors of war" (2019, p. 388). The high difficulty level of *TWoM* means that it is extremely likely most players will experience the death of at least one character. As shown in House (2019), even a small misstep can initiate a chain reaction that leads to an unexpected, shocking finale.

The game is divided into two alternating stages. During the day, the survivors stay in their base where they can craft materials, cook, and heal. The player can control one character at a time and changes between them. At night, the player can choose one of the characters and scavenge the surrounding buildings. This split was directly influenced by the experience of real survivors who emphasized how different a siege felt during the day and at night.

Everything the characters collect is automatically transferred to a common pool and may be immediately used by others, sometimes at the cost of realism. For example, even though the player must physically move a character to a certain room so they can craft a shovel, the item created is then immediately available to all the characters in the building. On the surface, this design choice could be dismissed as a simple "quality of life" solution. And yet, as argued by Radosław Bomba (2015), even such a small detail is not devoid of meaning as it suggests that the players identify with the whole group and not with individual members. This message is further strengthened by the interface, which calls the inventory "our things."

The gameplay is very deliberate and slow paced, showing the differences in the experience of time during war and peace. Days can be filled with boredom as, due to the lack of resources, there is often little to do. This may lead players to skip the day phase very early. On the face of it, this may look like a design flaw. But once again, it shows how the game's message is strengthened by its mechanics. As mentioned by civilian survivors of war, boredom was an everyday experience and survivors sometimes tried to hasten the time by sleeping (Białoszewski, 1970).

The Aesthetics of *This War of Mine*

TWoM is also very distinctive from the aesthetic perspective. It is a 2D side-view game that pulls the camera back, presenting cross-sections of whole buildings. This makes *TWoM* look like a digital dollhouse—a solution rarely seen in games. One notable game that shares this look is a rather forgotten Commodore 64 game, *Little Computer People* (*LCP*) (Activision, 1985), released in 1985 (Bjørkelo, 2018). The association of *TWoM* with *LCP* is worth pointing out, as the latter was a direct inspiration for *The Sims* (Maxis, 2000)—a game that has been compared to *TWoM* by both reviewers and the developers themselves (who called it *The War Sims* during development).[1]

Still, *LCP* can be seen as the ideological antithesis of *TWoM*. In the former, the player has no control over the titular "little human" inhabiting the digital house. The only thing they can do is to provide water, food, and entertainment. These resources are infinite, and the simulation depicts the monotony of a happy life of consumption—it functions like a "human aquarium."

The very subdued color palette of *TWoM* uses mostly different shades of gray and black. This foreshadows the ethical message of the game, as we could say that everything the player observes happens in the "gray zone." The artists used a "live pencil" effect inspired by the famous a-ha music video *Take on Me* (1985). This effect seems to suggest that whatever happens on the screen is being painted before the player's eyes; it is history in the making. Music and the interface point at another source of inspiration—the post-apocalyptic games which were gaining popularity at the time *TWoM* was released. Both are very reminiscent of *The Last of Us* (Naughty Dog, 2013)—another game famous for its adult representation of moral choices.

Is *This War of Mine* Realistic?

During their interview for Ars Technica, the developers revealed that from the beginning, they did not want the game to be realistic because they wanted the player to focus on game mechanics. On the other hand, *TWoM* strives for realism when it comes to the depiction of characters, using real-life, raw photos of the developers and very detailed life-like animation. In addition, the character portraits are not completely static—they blink from time to time, adding to the realism.

The best way to make sense of this and other superficial incongruities is to use Holger Pötzsch's notion of *selective realism* (Pötzsch, 2017). As he argues, even games advertised as realistic representations of war are typically very selective when it comes to the aspects that they portray. For example, they very rarely represent civilians, let alone allow the player to kill them. *TWoM* is selective as well, but it selects and realistically represents aspects other games ignore.

TWoM sacrifices realistic environments for the realism of its characters—their depiction and, most importantly, their social relations and psychological states. The player must look after the wellbeing of the characters, as being depressed affects speed of movement and can lead to alcoholism or even suicide. The developers tried their best to achieve the desired emotional impact without using cheap emotional narrative tricks. For instance, even though the first DLC introduced children, it is not possible to kill underage characters. This careful combination of realistic and conventional elements serves a higher purpose. As the developers explained in an interview, their main goal was to achieve "emotional realism" (De Smale et al., 2019). They wanted the player to go through an approximation of some of the emotional states of the characters. The result of this is that the experience of playing *TWoM* has been described as "positive negative"—a thought-provoking process that is emotionally draining, maybe even unpleasant, but at the same time deeply compelling.

TWoM can be seen as a critique of triple-A war-themed games, as its marketing tagline "In War, Not Everyone Is a Soldier" was a direct response to the slogan "There's a soldier in all of us" used to promote *Call of Duty: Black Ops* (Treyarch, 2010). At the same time, it can be seen as a critique of the thematic safety of independent survival games that focus on fantastic apocalyptic scenarios such as zombie invasions. The military conflict represented in *TWoM* is deliberately unspecified. What we learn is that it is a civil war in which the government is fighting a group of rebels and that the characters do not side with either group. This can still, to some extent, be compared to zombie games, where civilians are often a side of their own, struggling with both monsters and hostile militant groups.

As pointed out by Bomba (2015), the conflict in *TWoM* is very different from the wars in former Yugoslavia which inspired the game. In those conflicts, the societal cracks that led to the war, such as differences between nationalities, have also been reflected in the civil community. The result of this is that it would have been very unlikely for a random group of survivors to get over their differences so easily and cooperate. This observation can be generalized—in most cases of civil conflicts, whatever led to them, be it religion, nationality, or class tensions, and so on, would have been visible within the civil population and, by extension, in the group controlled by the player. Bomba argues that the game tacitly assumes that community and cooperation are intrinsically positive phenomena. On the other hand, the idealized picture that the developers decided to present allowed for an unprecedented focus on the domestic environment during the war. This led scholars to call it the first feminist war game (Kampe, 2019).

Using *This War of Mine* in Education

It is not often that a computer game spawns such discussions, so it should not come as a surprise that several authors recognized it as having educational potential, as observed by Toma (2015) and Byrd, the latter stating that "one could easily imagine it being incorporated into the classroom to function as an interactive supplement alongside books like 'All Quiet on the Western Front' or 'Dispatches'" (2014) Another article suggested that *TWoM* could be used as a tool to counter the pedagogy of war or function like the poverty simulators used in nurse training to elicit empathy and improve understanding of the poor (Kampe, 2019).

The developers, who were very interested in using *TWoM* in schools, suggested that the teachers should strive to take advantage of medium-specific elements of *TWoM*, such as the use of randomness. Unlike traditional readings, different students engaging with a game could go through completely different experiences. Comparing these differences and, especially, the choices made by students enables the teachers to use *TWoM* to generate ethical dilemmas (Tłuchowski, 2021).

This potential has been recognized by the Polish government, which decided to add it to the official high-school reading list.[2] Even though *TWoM* has not been classified as a mandatory reading, it remains the first computer game to be listed alongside such works of culture as Joseph Conrad's *Lord Jim* (1899) or Sophocles' *Oedipus Rex* (429BCE).

Paweł Grabarczyk

Notes

1. See Ars Technica interview at https://www.youtube.com/watch?v=FNrCAWVKVQ0
2. The process was initiated in 2020 and at the time of writing has not yet been finished. The developers of *TWoM* suggested that the game should be part of the reading canon in 2022.

References

Białoszewski, M. (1970). *Pamiętnik z powstania warszawskiego*. Warsaw: Państwowy Instytut Wydawniczy.

Bjørkelo K. A. (2018).It feels real to me: Transgressive realism in *This War of Mine*. In K. Jørgensen, F. Karlsen (eds), *Transgression in games and play*, (pp. 169–186). Cambridge, MA: MIT Press.

Bomba, R. (2015). "Simowie" na wspak. "Gra This War of Mine" w perspektywie retoryki proceduralnej. *Wielogłos*, (25), 87–95.

Byrd, Christopher, (2014, December 8), *This War of Mine* Deals with the Horrors of War Without the Gore, *Washington Post*. Retrieved March 2, 2022 from https://www.washingtonpost.com/news/comic-riffs/wp/2014/12/08/this-war-of-mine-review-a-game-that-appeals-to-hearts-and-minds/

De Smale, S., Kors, M. J. & Sandovar, A. M. (2019). The case of *This War of Mine*: A production studies perspective on moral game design. *Games and Culture*, 14(4), 387–409.

Gieba, K. (2019). Territory of Agon. Civilian perspective in a besieged city in the computer game *This War of Mine*. *Future Human Image*, (12), 22–27.

House, R. (2019). Reframing the domestic experience of war in *This War of Mine*: Life on the battlefield. In J. Saklofske, A. Arbuckle, J. Bath (eds), *Feminist war games? Mechanisms of war, feminist values, and interventional games*, (pp. 53–63). New York: Routledge.

Kampe, C. (2019). Seven dimensions of a feminist war game: What we can learn from *This War of Mine*. In J. Saklofske, A. Arbuckle, J. Bath (eds), *Feminist war games? Mechanisms of war, feminist values, and interventional games*, (pp. 132–149). New York: Routledge.

Pötzsch, H. (2017). Selective realism: Filtering experiences of war and violence in first- and third-person shooters. *Games and Culture*, 12(2), 156–178.

Tłuchowski, W. (2021). Przewietrzymy skostniały kanon, *PolskiGamedev.pl*. Retrieved August 19, 2021 from https://polskigamedev.pl/tag/magazyn/

Toma, E. (2015). Self-reflection and morality in critical games. Who is to be blamed for war? *Journal of Comparative Research in Anthropology and Sociology.* 6 (1), 209–224.

Further Reading

Demick, B. (2012). *Besieged: Life under fire on a Sarajevo Street*. London: Granta.
Maček, I. (2011). *Sarajevo under siege. Anthropology in Wartime*. Philadelphia: University of Pennsylvania Press.

DOI: 10.4324/9781003199205-46

ULTIMA IV: QUEST OF THE AVATAR (1985)

Many factors influenced game designer Richard Garriott to create the computer role-playing game (CRPG) *Ultima IV: Quest of the Avatar* (1985). Garriott reported feeling "bored" with the conventional "pillaging and plundering" game designs of *Ultima I, II, and III* (Herz, 1997, p. 157). He was dismayed by reports of *Ultima III* players who achieved victory by "killing all of the villagers in town because it was the fastest way to advance" (Donovan, 2010, p. 147). He felt "surprised" that players "did not play with the moral compass they followed in the real world" (Garriott & Fisher, 2017, p. 93). At the same time, cultural watchdogs branded him "the satanic perverter of America's youth" (Donovan, 2010, p. 147), inflamed by a moral panic about *Dungeons & Dragons* (Gary Gygax and Dave Arneson, 1974) and other role-playing games. In response, Garriott decided to design a game which would "hold a mirror up to the player's behavior" (Garriott & Fisher, 2017, p. 94). He believed that the right game design could "incorporate a player's own value system," forcing the player to "emotionally invest in the game" (p. 94). Fueled by his conviction that "role-playing can be a powerful experience and has the profound ability to teach" (p. 94), Garriott viewed his work on *Ultima IV* as an attempt "to further develop an emerging art form" (p. 99): a CRPG with "ethical or spiritual underpinnings" (Bub, 2002, p. 60).

ULTIMA IV: QUEST OF THE AVATAR (1985)

Playing with Ethics in *Ultima IV*

Video game researchers identify *Ultima IV* as the first CRPG to design gameplay for ethical action and reflection. Donovan (2010) writes that the "moral backbone and quest for enlightenment" of *Ultima IV* represents a "major departure from every other role-playing game created up until that point" (p. 148). Barton (2008) describes *Ultima IV* as "almost philosophical, encouraging gamers to think about the good life and ponder age-old questions of good and evil" (p. 115). In this way, *Ultima IV* aspires "to reach themes that had previously been solely in the domain of literature or cinema, and thereby reflects the maturity of digital games as an expressive medium" (Mäyrä, 2008, p. 81). Other researchers note the same innovation (Herz, 1997; King & Borland, 2003). This consensus bolsters Garriott's own suggestion that *Ultima IV* is "the first video game in history to focus on morality rather than killing" (Garriott & Fisher, 2017, p. 99).

From start to finish, the gameplay of ethical action and reflection permeates *Ultima IV*. The fictional land of Britannia summons the player into the game to lead its people out of the Age of Darkness into an Age of Enlightenment. To accomplish this, the player must complete the Quest of the Avatar, thereby embodying the life of virtue for Britannia. The Quest of the Avatar consists of attaining enlightenment in eight virtues, discovered gradually across the gameplay: Honesty, Compassion, Valor, Justice, Sacrifice, Honor, Spirituality, and Humility. The game begins as the player generates a character by ranking the eight virtues in a brief quiz about ethical dilemmas. Next, the player traverses Britannia in search of traveling companions, lost lore, and wise advisors who can assist in the Quest of the Avatar. Finally, having attained perfect enlightenment in all eight virtues, the player enters the Great Stygian Abyss to win the game by defeating monsters, bypassing dungeon traps, and passing a final test about the virtues.

Ultima IV's gameplay intertwines the conventional with the subversive. As a conventional CRPG, it presents the player with a predictable system of tactical combat, inventory management, spatial navigation, experience points accrual, leveling up, and randomized encounters (Barton, 2008). Throughout gameplay, the player monitors a familiar CRPG interface of hit points, food points, and gold points. At the same time, unknown to the player, *Ultima IV*'s system monitors a hidden, statistical "internal karma counter" (Spector, 1992, pp. 369–370) to track the player's practice and progress in the eight virtues. Often, the quest for wealth and power interferes with the quest for enlightenment. For example, if the player attacks a wild animal such as a bear to gain experience and gold, they also suffer loss in the virtues of Compassion, Honor, and Justice. In contrast, fleeing from a wild animal achieves virtuous, though not monetary, gains. Thus, the virtuous Quest of the Avatar subverts the conventional CRPG quest for wealth and power.

The statistics of *Ultima IV*'s virtue system remain inaccessible to the player throughout the game. Instead, the player depends upon the qualitative feedback of Hawkwind the Seer for guidance toward enlightenment. Hawkwind can "see" the hidden values of the virtue system when queried about the player's progress in a specific virtue. However, he offers only oblique advice such as "Strive to know and master more of thine inner being. Meditation lights the path!" or "Thou art doing well on the path to inner sight. Continue to seek the inner light." His advice forces the player to contemplate the consequential links between virtues and actions through inductive reasoning, gradually coming to understand the Quest of the Avatar. For example, the player must ask, "Which of my specific gameplay actions, and in what amount, have led Hawkwind to confirm or dismiss my general progress in Spirituality? Or Compassion? Or Humility?" The player also gains some insight into virtue from Lord British—the Sovereign Lord of Britannia—as well as from the citizens of Britannia. The hiddenness of the *Ultima IV* virtue system provokes sustained critical and ethical reflection throughout the Quest of the Avatar.

Ultima IV as Philosophical Quest

Howard (2008) argues that "a search for meaning is not analogous but rather intrinsic to the design of quests because of the literary history of quest narratives and their associations with religion and mythology" (p. 2). In literary history, the quest narrative often begins in an open-ended and undefined manner. Howard notes, for instance, that in the Arthurian quest for the Holy Grail, "each knight deliberately sets off alone into the forest at a point where there is no path" (p. 7). Although Arthurian knights know that they seek the Holy Grail, they do not know precisely what it is, where it is, what will be required to gain it, or what will occur upon its discovery. Through its association with the Last Supper of Christ, furthermore, the Holy Grail functions as a spiritual object of transcendence and mystery. In this way, the Holy Grail holds forth a promise of revelatory meaning which will surpass the current understanding of those who seek it. Action (seeking the Holy Grail) generates meaning (discovering the Holy Grail). Thus, Howard contends that well-designed quests "conjoin meaning and action in gameplay rather than putting them into conflict" (p. 21). Through game actions, players embark upon a quest for game meanings. These game meanings are constituted by a "progressively greater understanding" (p. 26) of rules, narrative, and world; a "drive to overcome difficulties and better oneself" (p. 27) as both player and avatar; and the uncovering of "symbolic correspondences" (p. 28) embedded in the game's backstory and theme.

As in Arthurian legend, the Quest of the Avatar begins in an open-ended, ambiguous manner. Depending upon their answers to the opening virtue quiz, the player may begin as one of eight classes in one of eight towns. Many towns are in remote locations, hidden within mountain ranges or forests or swamps, offering no clear path from one to the next. The non-player characters which populate each town offer only fragmentary insights about the Quest of the Avatar. Hidden shrines promise enlightenment if the player can first uncover their locations and learn their mantras. Bit by bit, the player pieces together the meaning of the Quest of the Avatar, gradually coming to know not only the meanings but also the applications of the virtues. In a surprising twist, the player must eventually assume the burden of atoning for sins already committed during the initial, unfamiliar hours of *Ultima IV* gameplay. Although some scholars suggest that *Ultima IV* gameplay is reducible to mere puzzle solving (e.g., Myers, 2010, pp. 90–94), the story, theme, and symbols of *Ultima IV* lend themselves to an "unfolding revelation" (Hayse, 2010, p. 38) of richer, philosophical meaning.

The Quest of the Avatar in *Ultima IV* corresponds to the moral philosophy of the medieval quest. To MacIntyre (2007), the medieval quest demands the social practice of virtue for the sake of a larger community and its tradition. Put simply, two ethical questions guide the medieval quest: "What is the good for me?" and "What is the good for (others)?" (p. 218). These questions, intertwined and complementary, comprise a "unity of life" (p. 218) for the questing hero. To live virtuously is to live for the good of others. MacIntyre also recalls two "key features" (p. 219) of the medieval quest in addition to the two ethical questions which guide it. First, it must begin with a "partly determinate conception of the final *telos*" (p. 219). In other words, the questing hero needs to understand the goal of the quest, at least in part. Second, the questing hero must pursue the medieval quest not as a search for the certain or known, but as a search for the uncertain and unknown. MacIntyre explains:

> It is in the course of the quest and only through encountering and coping with the various particular harms, dangers, temptations,

and distractions which provide any quest with its episodes and incidents that the goal of the quest is finally to be understood. A quest is always an education both as to the character of that which is sought and in self-knowledge.

(2007, p. 219)

Put another way, the hero cannot fully grasp the end or means of the medieval quest from its start. Instead, the quest itself will teach the hero what to seek and how to seek it. To MacIntyre, the virtues are those personal and social "dispositions" which "enable" and "sustain" the "quest for the good" (p. 219). The medieval quest both requires and bestows the necessary virtues for success.

As in MacIntyre, the Quest of the Avatar begins with questions about a social context. The land of Britannia has emerged from a feudal Age of Darkness. Now, the newly united land of Britannia stands on the cusp of an Age of Enlightenment. Britannia needs the player to show the way forward by pursuing the higher calling of virtue. Britannia needs an exemplar—an Avatar. Throughout gameplay, the player must ask not only, "What makes me stronger and richer?" but also "How do I practice virtue for the sake of Britannia?" As MacIntyre suggests, the player begins with an incomplete understanding of the Quest of the Avatar. As gameplay unfolds, however, the player gradually begins to construct an operational framework for practicing virtue and achieving the enlightenment of Avatarhood. Due to the hidden nature of *Ultima IV's* virtue system, the player can succeed only through an ongoing cycle of experimentation, reflection, and theorizing throughout gameplay. A player who has been boastful or robbed others in early gameplay, for example, must recognize and atone for those misdeeds through new game actions. By trial and error, the player comes to uncover and assemble a practical model of *Ultima IV's* virtue system that is tied to the "socially local and particular" (MacIntyre, 2007, p. 127) of Britannia.

Contributions

Ultima IV: The Quest of the Avatar stands as a prototype of the philosophical game. Garriott designed *Ultima IV* after the fashion of a medieval quest for the elusive but alluring idea of the Good. *Ultima IV* forces its player to engage in critical reflection on the nature of virtue, thereby gaining the enlightenment of Avatarhood within a simulated social milieu. By intentionally concealing the calculations of virtue, Garriott thrusts the player into Bogost's (2006) "possibility space" (p. 85). Bogost defines the possibility space as a gameplay occasion which provokes mental dissonance and tension within the player's understanding of the game, an experience of "self-reflection, debate, dispute, and a host of other contentious activities" (p. 122). The concealed nature of virtue in *Ultima IV* sustains the possibility of ethical reflection rather than reducing ethical decision-making to mere mathematics.[1] Garriott's innovations are many, not least his popularization of the term "avatar" in gameplay (de Wildt et al., 2019). *Ultima IV* opened the door to a CRPG future marked by the data visualization of morality meters and reputation gauges. Nevertheless, if the moral economy and internal karma counter of *Ultima IV* are Garriott's greatest innovations, their hiddenness is Garriott's genius.

Mark Hayse

Note

1. In *Ultima V: Warriors of Destiny* (1985), however, Garriott allows for the CTRL-K keystroke to open a visual display of all virtue scores tracked by the karma counter.

References

Barton, M. (2008). *Dungeons and desktops: The history of computer role-playing games*. Wellesley, MA: A K Peters.

Bogost, I. (2006). *Unit operations: An approach to videogame criticism*. Cambridge, MA: MIT Press.

Bub, A. S. (2002, May). Game with God. *Computer Games Magazine, (2002)*138, 60–62.

de Wildt, L., Apperley, T. H., Clemens, J., Fordyce, R., & Mukherjee, S. (2019). (Re-)orienting the video game avatar. *Games and Culture, (15)*8, 962–981. doi.org/10.1177%2F1555412019858890

Donovan, T. (2010). *Replay: The history of video games*. East Sussex, England: Yellow Ant.

Garriott, R., & Fisher, D. (2017). *Explore/create: My life in pursuit of new frontiers, hidden worlds, and the creative spark*. New York: William Morrow.

Hayse, M. (2010). Ultima IV: Simulating the religious quest. In C. Detweiler (Eds), *Halos and avatars: Playing video games with God* (pp. 34–46). Louisville, KY: Westminster John Knox.

Herz, J. C. (1997). *Joystick nation: How videogames ate our quarters, won our hearts, and rewired our minds*. Boston, MA: Little, Brown and Company.

King, B. & Borland, J. (2003). *Dungeons and dreamers: The rise of computer game culture from geek to chic*. Emeryville, CA: McGraw-Hill/Osborne.

Howard, J. (2008). *Quests: Design, theory, and history in games and narratives*. Wellesley, MA: A K Peters, Ltd.

MacIntyre, A. C. (2007). *After virtue: A study in moral theory* (3rd Eds). Notre Dame, IN: University of Notre Dame Press.
Mäyrä, F. (2008). *An introduction to game studies: Games in culture.* Thousand Oaks, CA: SAGE Publications.
Myers, D. (2010). *Play redux: The form of computer games.* Ann Arbor, MI: University of Michigan Press.
Spector, C. (1992). A conversation with Richard Garriott. In R. DeMaria & C. Spector (Eds), *Ultima: The Avatar adventures* (pp. 363–389). Rocklin, CA: Prima Publishing.

Further Reading

Sicart, M. (2009). *The ethics of computer game design.* Cambridge, MA: MIT Press.

DOI: 10.4324/9781003199205-47

WII SPORTS (2006)

Minimalist Lessons

When it comes to the influence and legacy of key video games, *Wii Sports* stands as a unique example of how to achieve more with less, that is, how to reach greatness through minimalism. Currently, when the "less is more" perspective of many indie titles has permeated game culture as a whole, influencing the mainstream with retro aesthetics and arcade nostalgia, it is commonly accepted that there are multiple paths to create memorable games without top-notch engines, photorealistic graphics, or convoluted plots. But when Nintendo released its highly anticipated new console, the Wii (November 2006), using a bundled sports simulator with childlike visuals and super-simple game dynamics, few people imagined the revolutionary impact that *Wii Sports* would end up having. With its two biggest competitors, the Xbox 360 and the PlayStation 3, betting everything on faster, bulkier, and more powerful hardware, which reinforced the games industry's "super-pumped" race toward anthropocentric realism, flashy cut-scenes, and bigger-than-life narratives, Nintendo was certainly going against the tide (while remaining true to its brand). Precisely because everyone else was giving players more of the same, launching their new console with a bundle of five mini-game sports simulations (tennis, baseball, bowling, golf, and boxing) that required players to move awkwardly in front of their TVs and control doll-like avatars using motion sensors, was a bold move, an unprecedented risk that the designers themselves were aware of, as they retell how they were preparing for the Electronic Entertainment Expo (E3) showcase to the public:

> *Yoshikazu Yamashita* (Game designer, Nintendo EAD): During E3, games with unbelievable graphics using an incredible number of polygons were lined up in the surrounding booths, and I could barely contain my excitement just thinking about putting *Wii Sports* next to them.
>
> *Katsuya Eguchi* (Creator of the *Animal Crossing* series and Producer of *Wii Sports*, Nintendo EAD): Rather than spend the money trying to pursue a photorealistic game experience, I would rather focus on conveying the freshness of the Wii experience to our customers ... After seeing the response at E3 it became apparent to us that users were enjoying it in the same way we thought they would. From that point on, we were able to continue development without hesitation.[1]

The consequences of that design strategy in game history are well known. *Wii Sports* became a hugely successful title (according to Nintendo, worldwide sales were 82.90 million units) that encouraged a gradual shift toward more inclusive and accessible game design, becoming a key component of what Jesper Juul called "the casual revolution." It defied the limits between hardcore/casual video games and questioned the prejudices implied in such broad categorizations, thanks to a juicy, intuitive, and addictively mimetic interface that brought people of all ages and genders together: "fun in new ways, because players can learn from watching each other, because failure becomes an enjoyable spectacle, and because they become more immediately social" (Juul, 2009, p. 112). But before going deeper into those social and performative aspects, it is important to underline that Nintendo's self-conscious embrace of a "less is more" design path, opting out of the hyper-realistic and graphics-focused race of its competitors, was a radical choice that carried cultural and sociological implications as well as economic and creative ones.

Nintendo and the Ethics of Casual Fun

A decade before designers like Jenova Chen started to talk at GDC conferences about the need to slow things down in game design—that is, the need to limit the power-drive logic of unbounded enhancements (play with less) in an increasingly consumerist society that is draining the planet's resources with greedy and unsustainable exploitation (live with less)—*Wii Sports* was already pushing the boundaries of what game culture was and could be, opening the mainstream to new experiences, broader accessibility, and a friendlier *ethos* beyond the all-or-nothing mentality of many other games. Going against the grain has certainly been part of Nintendo's philosophy since its origins, with their traditional approach of "lateral thinking with seasoned withered technology" to quote Gunpei Yokoi's expression, but the release of the Wii pushed things further at a moment where the competition (and the tension) with other Japanese game companies was fierce, and the stakes couldn't be higher. Genyo Takeda, the general manager of Nintendo's Integrated Research and Development Division at the time, explicitly underlined why his team chose to diverge from the established technological roadmaps (to just want more) during the Nintendo Wii's design process.

> This may sound paradoxical, but if we had followed the existing roadmaps we would have aimed to make it "faster and flashier!". In other words, we would have tried to improve the speed at which it displays stunning graphics ... It must have been about a year after we started developing Wii. After speaking with Nintendo's development partners, I became keenly aware of the fact that *there is no end to the desire of those who just want more*. Give them one, they ask for two. Give them two, and next time they will ask for five instead of three. Then they want ten, thirty, a hundred, their desire growing exponentially. Giving in to this will lead us nowhere in the end.
> (Takeda in Iwata, 2006, emphasis mine)

From Martin Heidegger's writings on technology (1977), to Donna Haraway's *Cyborg Manifesto* (1991) and Sianne Ngai's *Theory of the Gimmick* (2020), key thinkers and philosophers have underlined how technological developments within capitalist societies have a critical impact on the way we live, reflecting political issues, social inequalities, and historical junctures. With his tech-focused and to-the-point discourse, Genyo Takeda highlighted that exact same *ethical* problem: the need to transcend "the desire of those who just want more" in order to expand, instead, both the horizons of game design and the experiences of players. That was, in hindsight, the greatest achievement of *Wii Sports*: in an increasingly individualistic world, where playing games was becoming more of a self-centered experience, or a multi-player one but based on online virtual relations instead of physical in-person ones, and which often revolved around wanting—and having—more (speed, graphics, power), this "little" sports simulator retook the social camaraderie of early arcades, where gathering different players together around a screen, in a shared space, was key. When almost everyone in the games industry was obsessed with *more*, Nintendo seduced players all over the world with *less*, forgetting perfect graphics for a second to simply play, and move.

Playing for Laughs: Gestural Comedy

Just as Frank Capra defined silent comedies as "movies that moved," emphasizing the kinetic and physical qualities of cinema, real-life movements and gestures lay at the core of *Wii Sports* from its very conception: "gestural interfaces alter the space and the role of the body, shifting the focal point of interactivity from a predominantly screen-based environment to a more hybrid relationship between digital and physical bodies and spaces" (O'Grady, 2012, p. 260). In line with Miyamoto's motto of designing gameplay around motion verbs (Jenkins, 2005, p. 175), *Wii Sports* reclaimed the real-world player space (as opposed to virtual screen space) as the center of game culture, making the best of the fact that millions of players already knew the basic rules of tennis or bowling, and could therefore focus on the fun and often hilarious movements of their bodies in front of—and not just inside—the screen: kids, parents, and grandparents played and laughed together on a scale unprecedented in game history. But beyond the numerous scientific studies about the game's social and health benefits (Schell et al., 2016), one of its most original aspects is how it heavily relied on comedic performance, that is, fostering laughter through gameplay.

While physical comedy and visual gags have always been part of Nintendo's imagery (Garin, 2014), *Wii Sports* went a step further by refusing to use well-known characters like Mario or sign licenses with famous athletes, allowing players instead to personalize their own caricatures in the style of Japanese *kokeshi* dolls. Going back to previous company software like the 64DD Mario Artist and unreleased games such as the Gamecube Manebito project, the possibility of creating a customized parody of yourself through the Mii Channel was key, because it encouraged players to fool around with their clownish avatars inside the game and consequently emphasized the comedic performativity of their own *real* bodies (weird postures, unexpected clashes, funny bloopers) in front of the screen. This design choice brings to mind what the French philosopher Merleau-Ponty called bodily intentionality: a kind of understanding of spatial qualities like distance and orientation naturally sensed by our body and not mediated by reflection, in terms of its capacities to act, its dispositions, its projects and purposes (Carroll, 2007, p. 127), which had reached unparalleled aesthetic heights in the masterpieces of silent film comedy during the 1920s.

On that note, it doesn't seem a coincidence that the designers responsible for the game, from Miyamoto to Eguchi himself, or the programmers, all mention funny anecdotes and gags when remembering how *Wii Sports* was created and tested: executives comically running toward the screen while swinging their remotes during a Board of Directors meeting; visitors at the E3 using their free left hand to toss an imaginary ball up for a serve; a grandmother making an impossible catch in baseball with the whole family cheering; the sound of spontaneous laughter filtering out of the internal testing rooms in Kyoto; and debates about whether table tennis should or should not be played in a Japanese *onsen*, etc. Far from being a collateral effect, the emphasis on such humorous and comedic instances was essential for both the design and the success of the game, with simplicity and brevity (less is more) at the core of it all:

> Not every game has to be like an encyclopedia. There is nothing wrong with magazines or comics. If the idea is good enough, it's ok to keep it simple ... You can guarantee that anyone playing the game will be wearing a huge smile. There aren't many games you can say that about.
>
> (Eguchi in Iwata, 2006)

That mixture of movement, simplicity, and laughter came naturally, because *Wii Sports* was designed in parallel to the Wii Remote, the console's revolutionary controller, not as a separate product but as a blend of different mini-games that had previously served to test efficiency and playability with the motion sensor and the accelerometer. So the social, experimental, and comedic aspects of the design process emphasized by its creators ended up being part of the game itself, its flavor.

In terms of its precedents, and beyond Nintendo's 8-bit sports simulators like *Baseball* (1983) or *Tennis* (1984), the game's unique celebration of diversity through failure, for comedic purposes, links *Wii Sports* with a longstanding tradition of visual humor that goes back to *commedia dell'arte*, pantomime, and slapstick (Garin, 2022). Not by chance did the great silent clowns like Chaplin, Lloyd, and Keaton release immensely popular movies making fun of the very same sports featured in Nintendo's game, although the most Wii-like parody of tennis takes place in *Monsieur Hulot's Holiday* (Jacques Tati, 1953). Both in the game and the films, the gestures and movements of real people are repurposed, humorously, inside the screen. An overtly harmless and simple game was capable of doing the most difficult thing as far as game history is concerned: bringing to life earlier cultural practices and aesthetic modes (the past) while reshaping the playing habits and creative horizons of game culture as a whole (the future).

A Friendlier Game Culture

As proven by Seán Crosson in his analysis of sports and film (2013), mocking sport via different kinds of parody enables audiences to question the cultural capital and power dynamics so deeply rooted in contemporary societies. Therefore, in terms of its impact on the future of game history, *Wii Sports* can be read not only as a humorous and socially empowering take on bodily performance and gestural interfaces (O'Grady, 2012), but also, more importantly, as a critique of the competitive, patriarchal, and agonistic culture of hardcore sports games that

> turn the unquantifiable into rationalized calculations and code, to give the gamer the sensation of control and direction they lack in relation to the sports they follow, as well as other aspects of the capitalist society in which they live.
> (Crawford, 2015, p. 587)

Perhaps the game's true lesson was not to make us move or laugh thanks to visual interactions, but to question some of the clichés and hierarchies of gamer culture (power, speed, masculinity) that existed back in the day, helping us imagine a friendlier, less dominant, way to play. Against the male-centered power drive of other sports games and its narrow-mindedness, playing *Wii Sports* will always be an alternative form of resistance, where the score is measured not in points but in laughs.

Manuel Garin

Note

1. All quotes from Nintendo's game designers and programmers come from interviews within the *Iwata Asks* archive, available online at https://iwata-asks.nintendo.com/

References

Carroll, N. (2007). *Comedy incarnate*. Malden MA: Blackwell Publishing.
Crawford, G. (2015). Is it in the game? Reconsidering play spaces, game definitions, theming, and sports videogames. *Games and Culture*, 10(6), 571–592.
Crosson, S. (2013). *Sport and film*. New York: Routledge.
Garin, M. (2014). *El gag visual. De Buster Keaton a Super Mario*. Madrid: Cátedra.
Garin, M. (2021). On Nintendo's visual humour: Slapstick cinema and comic theatre in super smash bros. In K. Rutter, T. Z. Majkowski, J. Svelch (Eds), *Video games and comedy* (pp. 86–102). London: Palgrave MacMillan.
Haraway, D. (1991). *Simians, cyborgs and women: The reinvention of nature*. New York: Routledge.
Heidegger, M. (1977). *The question concerning technology and other essays*. New York: HarperCollins.
Iwata, S. (2006). *Iwata Asks*. Retrieved August 1, 2021, from https://iwataasks.nintendo.com/
Jenkins, H. (2005). Games, the new lively art. In J. Raessens, J. Goldstein (Eds), *Handbook of computer game studies* (pp. 175–192). Cambridge MA: The MIT Press.
Juul, J. (2009). *A casual revolution. Reinventing video games and their players*. Cambridge MA: The MIT Press.
Ngai, S. (2020). *Theory of the gimmick*. Cambridge MA: Harvard University Press.
O'Grady, D. (2012). Gestural interfaces. In M. J. P. Wolf (Eds), *Encyclopedia of video games: The culture, technology and art of gaming* (pp. 257–262). Santa Barbara: ABC-Clio.
Schell, R. et al. (2016). Social benefits of playing wii bowling for older adults. *Games and Culture*, 11(1–2), 81–103.

Further Reading

Barthes, R. (2007). *What is sport?* New Haven: Yale University Press.
Chess, S. & Paul, C. A. (2019). The end of casual: Long live casual. *Games and Culture*, 14(2), 107–118.
De Schutter, B. (2011). Never too old to play: The appeal of digital games to an older audience. *Games and Culture*, 6(2), 155–170.
Garin, M. (2015). Super Mario, the new silent clown: Video game parodies as transformative comedy tools. *International Journal of Cultural Studies*, 18(3), 305–309.
Jones, S. E. & Thiruvathukal, G. K. (2012). *Codename revolution. The Nintendo Wii platform*. Cambridge MA: The MIT Press.
Garin, M. (2022). On Nintendo's Visual Humour: Slapstick Cinema and Comic Theatre in *Super Smash Bros*. In K. B. Rutter, T.Z. Majkowski, J. Svelch (Eds), *Video games and comedy* (pp. 93–112). London: Palgrave MacMillan.

DOI: 10.4324/9781003199205-48

WING COMMANDER III: HEART OF THE TIGER (1994)

Wing Commander III: Heart of the Tiger (ORIGIN Systems, 1994) is the third installment of the popular *Wing Commander* space-combat series. Initially released for the home computer (MS-DOS/MacOS), it was subsequently ported over to consoles, including the ill-fated 3DO, and the newly launched Sony PlayStation. While previous titles in the *Wing Commander* series used 2D sprite-based graphics, *Wing Commander III* used a combination of source media often composited into the same scenes, including 3D graphics (texture-mapped polygonal models) and full-motion video (FMV). With its big budget production and Hollywood cast, *Wing Commander III* demonstrated what the interactive movie game was capable of (and what some of its limitations were), at the height of the genre's popularity.

Interactive Narrative Structures

Wing Commander III's futuristic narrative centers around the human Terran Confederation's continuing battle with the alien Kilrathi Empire. Based on the carrier ship *TCS Victory*, players lead a series of space battles against the Kilrathi, leading up to an attack on the aliens' homeworld. The gameplay is structured primarily into a narrative mode, which is presented in full-motion video (FMV), and a combat simulation mode presented using a combination of 2D and 3D graphics. In the narrative mode, players follow Col. Christopher Blair, the titular Wing Commander, in live-action video sequences (featuring *Star Wars* actor Mark Hamill). These sequences take the form of a choice-based branching narrative: players decide where to go next on the ship, who to speak to and what to say during conversations with characters, typically from a binary set of choices. The sequences ramp up into a series of space battles, which players experience in first-person perspective. This combat simulation mode is set up through configurative play (players choose their ship and weapons through a 2D interface, and their wingman in live-action video), with the combat itself taking place as real-time, arcade-style target shooting, viewed through a cockpit interface.

The narrative is directed by both the player's explicit choices (primarily conversation choices with the crew of the *Victory*), the outcome of their space battles, and indirectly through a "morale" score that applies to both individual non-player characters (NPCs) and the entire crew. For example, players have the option of pursuing a romantic relationship with chief fighter technician Rachel or pilot Lt. Flint; if they fail too many missions, they can end up in an unwinnable final battle resulting in the death of Blair. Morale can be impacted by both the conversation choices made by players (and/or their decision to engage at all), and choices in battle (a character with high morale may perform better).

Branching interactive narrative structures often create significant information processing and data storage demands. Even branching structures designed to prune the exponential expansion of possible paths create a lot of narrative content, much of which players never see (except through replay). This is further complicated in a game using rich media like video. *Wing Commander III* was made possible by the four CD-ROMs on which it was released. As Jonathan Lessard notes, the CD-ROM was a transformative technology for media-rich interactive content, with the unprecedented capacity and data speed of CD-ROMs, and the ability to call up media, including pre-recorded and/or pre-rendered content, in response to player input (Lessard, 2009, p. 197). But such technology often pushed the boundaries of what computers of the era could do and did not come cheap. Even given the relatively static nature of the video sequences in *Wing Commander III*, the game still necessitated high-end home computer or console hardware, with an advanced processor that would allow it to manipulate large media files and 3D graphics fluidly. The game would serve as a technology driver: both a way to justify the increased expenditure of a high-end system, and a way to demonstrate what a high-end system could do.

The Cinematic Video Game

With one of the largest development budgets of the era,[1] *Wing Commander III* has been referred to as the first serious FMV shoot, released at the peak of the interactive movie game's popularity, in advance of its subsequent decline in the late 1990s/early 2000s. The game was promoted as a multi-million-dollar production "professionally scripted and filmed in Hollywood" (Perron, 2007). Advertising rhetoric heralded this convergence between blockbuster film and video games, with taglines such as "Lights, camera, action. Made in Hollywood. Directed by you" (*Wing Commander CIC*, n.d.). *Computer Gaming World* would pronounce *Wing Commander III* the "first successful interactive movie" (1996). As Dominic Arsenault and Bernard Perron note, positioning games as interactive movies often formed part of the genre's branding and legitimation practices (2015, p. 2), positioning them as an up-and-coming successor, or at least worthy competitor, to feature films.

Cinematic cut-scenes are common instruments to convey and hold together a game's narrative structure, as well as elements of spectacle reward (Howells 2002, p. 113). But *Wing Commander III* was more than just a series of battles with narrative video clips interspersed throughout. It was simultaneously a "Movie with a game inside it. Or a game with a movie inside it" (Assistant Producer Rob Irving, in Barton, n.d.). Far from being static "cut-scenes" simply contextualizing the combat sequences, the video media supported interactive narrative gameplay that, most notably through the morale scoring, could, in fact, impact the dynamic space battles. Reviews noted the game struck a good balance between these segments, with the FMV enhancing the gameplay, rather than substituting for it (Imagine Media, 1995).

Yet as noted in Therrien et al., "Where the dynamic worlds of animated games could realize the full potential of the medium, games incorporating less dynamic, less interactive cinematic media were positioned (both explicitly and implicitly) as suspect and retrograde" (2020). At a time when video games were still finding their footing as a cultural form, movie–game hybrids like *Wing Commander III* could be seen as a threat: part of a "colonizing" attempt from cinema (Aarseth, 2001; Arsenault and Perron, 2015) on one hand, and a mark of what Eric Zimmerman decried as "cinema envy" (2002) on the part of game developers on the other. Interactive cinema games became a poster child for radical ludology arguments, bolstered by voices like Espen Aarseth and Markku Eskelinen who argued such works were an affront to the true nature and potential of video games (Klevjer, 2002, p. 1).

Commenting on the eventual failure of the FMV genre, Tanine Allison highlights how the compositing of live-action video and the relatively primitive 3D graphics of the era was "awkward at best" (2020, p. 282). Lessard remarks that such games:

> ... offered a much richer visual content than what was previously available and seemed to finally achieve video games' long-time ambition: to provide an experience that combines the audio-visual quality of movies with the freedom of action of games. These great expectations lead [sic] to a general disappointment as the public discovered games that usually combined B-grade cinematographic productions with very restrictive gameplay.
>
> (2009, p. 198)

Linking the restrictive gameplay with the available technology infrastructure, Jimmy Maher (*Digital Antiquarian*, n.d.) argues that, "agency is sharply circumscribed by the inherent limitations of pre-shot, static snippets of video and the amount of storage space said video requires ...". Even on a high-end system, video had to be tortured into the formatting constraints, and accessing data from CD-ROMs, while faster than floppy disks, was still far too slow (Russell, 2012, p. 95), particularly for gamers just getting a taste for the emergent, real-time play of the first-person shooter. As a result, rather than the movie-like spectacle promised, players were instead often irritated by slow load times, faced with overly compressed and artifacted images, watching second-rate performances on media that would occasionally crash their systems.

Possibilities of Captured Media

While it's easy to focus on what didn't work, it's important to also note how the design of the game *did* work with the constraints and opportunities that it had. *Wing Commander III* illustrates core FMV design strategies (Therrien et al., 2020) that game designers used to work with the affordances of the media: in particular, material constraints on how such media could be used. For example, video lacks the radical mutability of computer animation, which constrains what you can do with it in an interactive context. Branching narrative structures can easily accommodate and frame periods of static linearity, so this mode of gameplay can serve as a design solution for games incorporating video.

The *Wing Commander* franchise was in some ways uniquely suited for an interactive movie treatment. As in previous games in the series, the action (fight sequences) is primarily viewed through a flight cockpit interface, providing a conceptual bridge between live action and animated graphics. This allows for the actions players perform to be nearly identical to what they might see and do in an actual cockpit, which presents a highly mediated interface even outside the gameworld. By combining arcade gameplay in real time with interactive branching in static filmed sequences, the design could cleverly incorporate both dynamic and static gameplay. This was neatly consistent with the *Wing Commander* series, which had already distinguished itself among combat simulators by the way it combined arcade-style shooting missions with a narrative context.

The use of captured media also allowed the game makers to capitalize on video's indexical affordances. Video is commonly perceived as having privileged status in representing real people, even in the context of a fictive narrative. As such, video encouraged players to connect with characters in a way that the 8-bit characters of the era did not. As Digital Pictures president Tom Zito offered: "There are certain human, gut reactions that can only be triggered by seeing another human ... Real people produce real reactions" (Russell, 2012, p. 76). Critics felt the use of recognizable actors in the FMV sequences enhanced "realism, emotional delivery and suspense" (Imagine Media, 1995). And by incorporating live-action performances, ORIGIN could market *Wing Commander III* as starring recognizable (albeit affordable) genre actors, including Hamill and sci-fi stalwarts such as Malcolm McDowell, John Rhys-Davies, and François Chau.[2] While the performances may be stilted and at times laughably corny (indeed weak acting performance is one unfortunate reputation that FMV games acquired), the presence of recognizable actors helped market these games to non-gamer audiences more comfortable with TV than "cartoons." Actors also offered expanded promotion opportunities, through television and magazine interviews, "behind the scenes" production footage, and other paratextual media.

The Legacy of *Wing Commander III*

Interactive cinema games are often viewed with derision, yet the design conventions they employed and the desires they embodied still sit at the foreground of contemporary game design (Lessard, 2009). Video games may have largely abandoned FMV, but the "cinematic" affect is still prominent in video game titles (Arsenault & Perron, 2015), presented largely through photorealistic animated sequences, and borrowing extensively from the feel of blockbuster films. The indexical affordances of captured media are still called upon to present "real" performers, but in forms more conducive to seamless integration with animation, for example through voice acting[3] and performance capture. Following Rune Klevjer, such games "are rhetorical-ludological bastards because we want them to be" (2002), and games continue to engage both cinematic and ludic elements in order to capitalize on the strengths of both. Bringing things full circle, game engines and virtual production techniques pioneered in these early interactive cinema games are more popular in feature film and television production than ever, with productions like *The Mandalorian* (2019) heralded as the future of cinematic production (Axon, 2020).[4]

Wing Commander III: Heart of the Tiger continues to have lessons to teach us about both video games and virtual production, particularly relating to captured media: the value of real performances, capture's computational intensity and use as a technology driver, the design challenges inherent in static versus dynamic media, and the ways in which interactive cinema design patterns address some of these challenges. But more so, as Jamie Russell argues, "The FMV fad's historical importance lies in the way it suggested an alternative kind of video game: a more adult, less twitch-based entertainment experience that could hold its head up high among its more cinematic peers" (2012, p. 104).

Cindy Poremba

Notes

1. The game was produced for just over $3.5 million (Perron, 2007).
2. In line with the genre's tendency toward titillation, porn star Ginger Lynn Allen was cast as a possible love interest.
3. Hamill remaining a prominent voice-actor for such games.
4. In a 1994 production documentary, actor Malcom McDowell presciently describes *Wing Commander III* as the future of filmmaking, with its hybrid virtual production presenting a way of managing escalating production costs and bringing to life increasingly imaginative storyworlds (Foshko, 1994).

References

Aarseth, Espen. (2001). Computer game studies, Year one. *Game Studies*, 1(1). Retrieved March 1, 2022, from http://gamestudies.org/0101/editorial.html

Allison, Tanine. (2020). Losing control: *Until Dawn* as interactive movie. *New Review of Film and Television Studies*, 18(3), 275–300.

Arsenault, D., & Perron, B. (2015). De-framing video games from the light of cinema. *G|A|M|E: The Italian Journal of Game Studies* (4). Retrieved August 1, 2021, from http://www.gamejournal.it

Axon, S. (2020). The Mandalorian was Shot on a Holodeck-esque Set with Unreal Engine, Video Shows. *Ars Technica*. Retrieved August 1, 2021, from https://arstechnica.com/gaming/2020/02/the-mandalorian-was-shot-on-a-holodeck-esque-set-with-unreal-engine-video-shows

Barton, M. (n.d.). *Matt Chat 329: Rob Irving on Wing Commander III*. Retrieved August 1, 2021, from https://www.youtube.com/watch?v=6D4vPbXKfLM

Computer Gaming Weekly (1996). *Computer Gaming Weekly 148* (72).

Foshko, A. (1994). *The Making of Wing Commander 3: Heart of The Tiger [VHS]*. Retrieved August 1, 2021, from https://www.youtube.com/watch?v=bsI0y2DncAM

Howells, S. A. (2002). Watching a game, playing a movie: When media collide. In G. King & T. Krzywinska (Eds), *Screen play: Cinema/videogames/interfaces* (110–121). London: Wallflower Press.

Imagine Media. (1995, October). *NEXT Generation (10)*. Retrieved August 1, 2021, from http://archive.org/details/nextgen-issue-010

Klevjer, Rune. (2002). In defense of cutscenes. In F. Mäyrä (Eds), *Proceedings of the computer games and digital cultures conference* (191–202). Tampere: Tampere University Press.

Lessard, J. (2009). Fahrenheit and the premature burial of interactive movies. *Eludamos. Journal for Computer Game Culture, 3*(2). Retrieved November 16, 2021, from https://www.eludamos.org/index.php/eludamos/article/view/vol3no2-5

Maher, J. (n.d.). Wing Commander III. *The Digital Antiquarian*. Retrieved August 1, 2021, from https://www.filfre.net/2021/03/wing-commander-iii/

Perron, Bernard. (2007). Genre profile: Interactive movies. In M. J. P. Wolf (Eds), *The video game explosion: A history from PONG to PlayStation and beyond* (127–134), Westport, CN: Greenwood.

Russell, J. (2012) *Generation Xbox: How videogames invaded Hollywood*. East Sussex: Yellow Ant.

Therrien, C. (2017, July). From Video Games to Virtual Reality (and Back). Introducing HACS (Historical-Analytical Comparative System) for the Documentation of Experiential Configurations in Gaming History. *Proceedings of the 2017 DiGRA International Conference*. DiGRA 2017, Melbourne, Australia. Retrieved August 1, 2021, from http://www.digra.org/wp-content/uploads/digital-library/57_DIGRA2017_FP_Therrien_HACS.pdf

Therrien, C., Poremba, C., & Ray, J.-C. (2020). From dead-end to cutting edge: Using FMV design patterns to jumpstart a video revival. *Game Studies, 20*(4). Retrieved August 1, 2021, from http://gamestudies.org/2004/articles/therrienporembaray

Wing Commander CIC. (n.d.). Retrieved August 1, 2021, from https://www.wcnews.com/

Zimmerman, E. (2002). Do independent games exist? *Game on: The history and culture of videogames*. Retrieved August 1, 2021, from http://www.ericzimmerman.com/texts/indiegames.html

Further Reading

Cobbett, R. (2015). FMV isn't Dead: A Second Chance for Video in Video Games. *PC Gamer (July 28)*. Retrieved October 25, 2021, from https://www.pcgamer.com/fmv-isnt-dead-a-second-chance-for-video-in-video-games/

Voll, C. S. (2020, September 30). How Real People Became Video Game Characters Again. *Medium*. Retrieved August 1, 2021, from https://superjumpmagazine.com/how-real-people-became-video-game-characters-again-6c02857ec5ba

DOI: 10.4324/9781003199205-49

WORLD OF WARCRAFT (2004)

World of Warcraft (WoW) is a Massively Multiplayer Online Role-Playing Game (MMORPG) with a persistent gameworld that also evolves when you are not logged in. *WoW* is more than a game, noted for its complex social and economic society, and cultural online communities, as well as its extraordinary mixture of art, design, and technologies. With roots in the earlier *Warcraft* games, *WoW* was launched in 2004 in the US and 2005 in Europe and China by Blizzard Entertainment. Within the first few months the game had one million players and it continued to grow to a peak of about 12 million players by 2010. This enormous interest among players is one of the notable features of *WoW*. The game also became widely known among non-players, making it a target for much of the criticism of video gaming, including excessive gaming. Its popularity has not only given rise to a productive online fan culture, with portrayals of the game as well as players of *WoW* in popular culture and literature, but has also enticed researchers from a wide range of academic disciplines to explore the game with a particular interest in understanding the worldliness of *WoW* (Corneliussen & Rettberg, 2008), gameplay (Ducheneaut et al., 2006), and gamers (Williams et al., 2006). The way that the complex social communities of *WoW* in many ways reflect communities of the real world has inspired an interest in the lessons we can learn from *WoW*, for instance in terms of leadership and collaboration (Rapp, 2020).

Still the most popular MMO in 2021, *WoW* has large player bases in Asia, the US, and Europe. Although we recognize the international and multicultural aspects of *WoW* as important, this chapter is based on information and research mainly presented in English.

World of Warcraft, the Basics

WoW is a fantasy game of strange creatures and magic. Playing the game has been compared to "an animated fairytale" within which you have an active role (Nardi, 2010). The planet Azeroth is your first meeting with the *WoW* universe. It is a world at war where you need to choose whether to become a champion for the Horde or the Alliance. The two enemy factions are separated through the narratives and quests driving the gameplay, each holding power in certain regions and cities. They are also divided by the game's mechanics which prevent easy communication between the two factions.

The original playable Alliance races were the human, dwarf, night elf, and gnome, and the original Horde races "a ragtag batch of peoples" (Langer, 2008, p. 87), including the orc, tauren, undead, and troll. Player-characters joining the Alliance soon outnumbered the Horde two to one (Ducheneaut et al., 2006). Langer suggests that the original Alliance races reflected a Western whiteness, while the Horde races borrowed features and symbols from "real-world cultures that have themselves been marginalized and colonized" (Langer, 2008, p. 87).

While this might inspire notions of good and evil, such a simple divide is misdirected, challenged by the visual presentations, symbolism, and narratives of the two factions. The game design has been criticized for employing stereotypes about real-world people; however, some of the same stereotypes are also criticized *within* the game, suggesting that the game design "is a tricky, complex construction of cultural meaning [that] is both racist and antiracist, frequently at the same time" (Langer, 2008, p. 105).

After deciding faction and race, the player needs to choose class. Playing as a warrior or paladin will give a different experience than a warlock, monk, or druid, as the class guides which role a character will have, in particular, in group play: tanks attract the enemy's attention and take the major parts of their hits, DPS (damage per second) are characters that are specialized to do damage but are not equally sturdy to withstand the enemy's attack, while a healer keeps the fighting characters alive. This system of character roles and tasks involves a process of learning not only the game mechanics but also the unwritten rules for gameplay and collaboration.

Playing the Game

WoW presents many goals for players, the most obvious being to level their character from 1 to the top level. The top level expanded with each new game expansion until level 120. In 2020 with the expansion *Shadowlands*, the levels were compacted to a total of 60. Characters at level 120 would overnight find their new status to be level 50 with yet another 10 levels to go. This also made it quicker to move new characters through the lower levels and to reach the more exciting end-game activities.

Each race has its own starting area where the player will gradually learn the game, pick up quests from a quest giver with an exclamation mark, solve the quest, and return to the quest giver. This builds players' technical gameplay skills and introduces the character's combat and survival techniques, like knowledge about weapons, while building inventory with useful equipment, healing potions, and more. Gradually the characters become better prepared for survival in a hostile world. The quests are an important tool for narrating the history of the game. However, it is not necessary to engage with the narrative. A more common strategy is to skip directly to "accept" the task. Such a superficial relationship is encouraged by many quests being repetitive, making it more like training for tedious work rather than a fun activity. This has been criticized among players, and more recent updates of the game have a wider variety of quest structures. Certain quests will, for instance, take the players to dedicated areas, for experiences and cinematics that can only be seen while performing the quest.

Beyond quests and leveling there are many other goals that players can pursue. Some goals are defined by the chosen server type. Characters on player vs. player (PvP) servers are in constant combat mode, as characters can attack any member of the opposite faction of Horde or Alliance. On player vs. environment (PvE) servers, PvP is optional, while the main faction battles are fought in the various battlegrounds. Role-playing servers, either in combat or the more peaceful mode, add another element to the gameplay as staying in the character role can affect gameplay. *WoW*'s environment is, moreover, poorly designed for role-playing and proper role-players are often "playing another game entirely" (Williams et al., 2006).

Some goals of the gameplay have lost their initial attraction in parallel with a growing body of players who have collected in-game wealth that can be transferred from one character to another. One such goal was that of acquiring a ground mount, an important marker for the character's success in the early days of *WoW*, before most players had built a gold reserve. The mount gave a major speed boost, saving many long walks across Azeroth, which was particularly helpful when moving across the landscape on a server set to combat mode. New goals have developed in the game in order to keep the interest of deeply engaged gamers. Players have also developed strategies, such as theorycrafting, to more skillfully engage with the game. This refers to the practice where players test different features of the game, report to other players, and collaboratively create an overview of player-characters' performance statistics with the goal of mastering the game mechanics.

Expanding the *WoW* Universe

WoW has gone through major changes following a total of eight major expansion packs since the first, *The Burning Crusade*, in 2007. The expansions have substantially altered the original gameworld and gameplay in many ways. The changes are motivated through the developing game narrative, but the far more notable differences for the average player are likely to be those that change the landscape, present new land areas, planets, and playing areas underground or in the afterlife; new quests, dungeons, raids, and battlegrounds providing a massive number of new tasks and activities; new playable races and classes; new functionalities in the game mechanics, and improved animations and visual details. Following requests from *WoW* fans, Blizzard Entertainment released *WoW Classic* in 2019, in which players can revisit the original Azeroth including most of the original gameplay mechanics.

Players and Player Culture

Although *WoW* has been a target for critiques of gaming as an asocial and time-consuming activity, it has also challenged these ideas, for instance by pushing an understanding of gaming as a social activity. After nearly two decades and literally millions of gamers logging in, a substantial proportion in Asia, *WoW* also challenges the image of the stereotypical white, young player, although it has a more male-dominated player base than most other MMOs (Yee, 2017). While the game design has been perceived as highly feminist, the player culture has been found to be more masculinist, which might indicate one reason for fewer women participating.

WoW has been compared to a "capitalist fairytale in which anyone who works hard and strives enough can rise through society's ranks and acquire great wealth" (Rettberg, 2008, p. 20). It has been suggested that this can lead to ideas of equality of opportunity. However, "gold miners" who make grinding a profession, selling in-game gold to pay their real-life expenses, while other players buy in-game gold to level a successful character, suggest that real-world inequalities are also reproduced in *WoW*. This includes crime, and players have experienced the theft of their accounts, finding their in-game bank accounts emptied.

What Made *WoW* Successful?

Lowood and Krzywinska pointed out in 2006 that increased access to broadband was important for the success of *WoW*, a point nearly forgotten today when WiFi is ubiquitous in the Western world. There are, however, other aspects of *WoW* that can explain the success it has had in Asia, the US, and Europe, and we will point to some of these.

While the *Warcraft* series might have prepared the ground, *WoW*'s ability to enroll millions of players reflects a pedagogical system for gradually easing players' knowledge and skills about the game already from the starting area. The cartoon graphic style of the *WoW* universe had a similar effect of appearing inviting for a diverse group of players, giving the game its multicultural success (Aarseth, 2008). But it is also designed as a "rich text" where many references and allusions to real-world culture employ players' knowledge to create depth in the gameworld (Krzywinska, 2008). The non-player character calling out "How can you have any pudding if you don't eat your fish?" is easily recognizable for Pink Floyd fans. *WoW* also built on recognizable mechanics from older multiplayer games such as the chat commands from multi-user dungeons (MUDs), combining the imagery from well-known graphic games with tested text-based player interaction systems (Mortensen, 2006). This meant that a horde of players were ready to move into *WoW* to explore Azeroth.

A continuous stream of new content ensures that *WoW* never ends. A multitude of different goals target a diverse player base, making the gameplay as interesting for the casual gamer playing alone as for the more advanced player enjoying a mythic raid. Recent developments, for instance offering new content that needs to be unlocked by earning in-game achievements, reveals Blizzard Entertainment's strategy of targeting current players. *WoW Classic* invites those who ran the older game on private servers to return to the familiar landscapes of the original.

Coming Home to *WoW Classic*

Long queues made servers crash when *WoW Classic* was launched. It revealed that several of the older game mechanics that had fallen by the wayside as *WoW* developed still held value for many players. For instance, in *Classic WoW*, "kill-stealing" is still possible, that is, stealing the reward from a mob where other players had done the main work (Hernandez, 2019). Contemporary *WoW* does not allow this, in order to eliminate player conflict. In *WoW Classic*, this rather encouraged player collaboration and group effort to prevent such negative behavior. Thus, the queues for the original were not only reflecting nostalgic feelings for the game but also players who missed the collaboration and group efforts in a community of old friends, which is perhaps the most lasting impact of this large and enduring game.

Hilde G. Corneliussen and Torill Elvira Mortensen

References

Aarseth, E. (2008). A hollow world: *World of Warcraft* as spatial practice. In H. G. Corneliussen & J. W. Rettberg (Eds), *Digital culture, play, and identity: A World of Warcraft reader* (pp. 111–122). Cambridge, MA: MIT Press.

Corneliussen, H. G., & Rettberg, J. W. (2008). *Digital culture, play, and identity: A World of Warcraft reader*. Cambridge, MA: MIT Press.

Ducheneaut, N., Yee, N., Nickell, E., & Moore, R. J. (2006). Building an MMO with mass appeal. A look at gameplay in *World of Warcraft*. *Games and Culture*, 1(4), 281–317.

Hernandez, P. (2019). *World of Warcraft Classic* players are standing in long lines to finish quests. Retrieved July 2, 2021, from https://www.polygon.com/2019/8/27/20835116/wow-classic-queue-lines-blizzard-launch

Krzywinska, T. (2008). World creation and lore: World of Warcraft as rich text. In H. G. Corneliussen & J. W. Rettberg (Eds), *Digital culture, play, and identity: A World of Warcraft reader* (pp. 123–141). Cambridge, MA: MIT Press.

Langer, J. (2008). The familiar and the foreign: Playing (post) colonialism in World of Warcraft. In H. G. Corneliussen & J. W. Rettberg (Eds), *Digital culture, play, and identity: A World of Warcraft reader* (pp. 87–108). Cambridge, MA: MIT Press.

Mortensen, T. E. (2006). WoW is the new MUD. Social gaming from text to video. *Games and Culture*, 1(4), 397–413.

Nardi, B. (2010). *My life as a night elf priest: An anthropological account of World of Warcraft*. Ann Arbor: University of Michigan Press.

Rapp, A. (2020). An exploration of World of Warcraft for the gamification of virtual organizations. *Electronic Commerce Research and Applications*, 42, 100985. doi.org/10.1016/j.elerap.2020.100985

Rettberg, S. (2008). Corporate ideology in *World of Warcraft*. In H. Corneliussen & J. Rettberg (Eds), *Digital culture, play, and identity: A World of Warcraft reader* (pp. 19–38). Cambridge, MA: MIT Press.

Williams, D., Ducheneaut, N., Xiong, L., Zhang, Y., Yee, N., & Nickell, E. (2006). From tree house to barracks: The social life of guilds in *World of Warcraft*. *Games and Culture*, 1(4), 338–361.

Yee, N. (2017). *Beyond 50/50: Breaking Down The Percentage of Female Gamers by Genre*. Retrieved June 24, 2021, from https://quanticfoundry.com/2017/01/19/female-gamers-by-genre/

Further Reading

Bainbridge, W. S. (2010). *The Warcraft civilization: Social science in a virtual world*. Cambridge, MA: MIT Press.

Glas, R. (2013). *Battlefields of negotiation: Control, agency, and ownership in World of Warcraft*. Amsterdam: Amsterdam University Press.

Toft-Nielsen, C. (2019). Going home again? Fan nostalgia in anticipation of World of Warcraft Classic. *MedieKultur: Journal of Media & Communication Research*, 35(66), 3–17.

DOI: 10.4324/9781003199205-50

ZORK (1980)

When focusing on adventure games, we tend to think about early graphical video games on the Atari or Commodore 64. However, it is important to note that the genre goes back much further than that. *Zork* is a text-based interactive fiction computer game released between 1977 and 1979 for the DEC PDP-10 mainframe computer.

The game was developed by four members of the MIT Dynamic Modelling Group—Tim Anderson, Marc Blank, Bruce Daniels, and Dave Lebling—and was directly inspired by the second text language adventure game,[1] Will Crowther's *Colossal Cave Adventure* (1975)—considered the known work of interactive fiction (IF) (Anderson & Galley, 1985). *Zork* was later released as a commercial game for personal computers in three parts—split due to the memory limits of personal computers at the time. The three titles released were *Zork: The Great Underground Empire – Part I* (1980), *Zork II: The Wizard of Frobozz* (1981), and *Zork III: The Dungeon Master* (1982). The interpreter outputs the story textually, and the player types inputs (preceded by >). The game begins with the following text:

```
West of House
You are standing in an open field west of a white
house, with a boarded front door.
There is a small mailbox here.
>open mailbox
Opening the small mailbox reveals a leaflet.
>read leaflet
(Taken)
"WELCOME TO ZORK!
```

Early research in game studies sought to identify suitable theoretical frameworks and analytical methods to further the study of computer and video games. Scholars recognized immediately that most games have narrative potential—and indeed many games like *Zork* are heavily story driven—but that video games are also made up of mechanics and procedures that are written in code. The resultant narratology/ludology debate—in which games were initially viewed by some to be complex narratives and by others as complex systems of play (see, e.g., Frasca, 2003; Jenkins, 2004; Pearce, 2005; McManus & Feinstein, 2006)—highlights the interdisciplinary nature of games scholarship.

Gameworlds in Text

As the field grew alongside this emerging medium, game scholars came to acknowledge games as existing on a spectrum, where games can be understood as having both ludic and narrative properties to varying degrees (Pearce, 2005; Murray, 2005). As theories of games grew more robust, game scholars began to recognize novel narrative and ludic properties in games. For example, Jenkins writes about the potential for games to tell spatial or environmental stories, comparing them to elaborate theme parks where story elements are "infused into the physical space" (2004, p. 123). In the case of *Zork*, this physical space is represented entirely by text and is revealed to the player in bits and pieces in response to the commands entered by the player into the text parser.

Zork is inextricably linked to tabletop role-playing games, such as *Dungeons & Dragons* (*D&D*), published in 1974 (Tactical Studies Rules, Inc). Interestingly, *Zork* was originally called *Dungeon*, but the programmers were forced to change the name of the game after receiving notice from the publishers of *D&D* claiming that the name violated their trademark. *Zork* was a nonsense word that was commonly used by MIT hackers as the name for an unfinished program (Anderson & Galley, 1985), so the developers changed the name of the program from *Dungeon* to *Zork*.

Humor and Unconventional Commands

Zork is distinguished in the interactive fiction (IF) genre as an especially rich game—both in the quality of the storytelling and in the sophistication of its text parser.[2] The game opens with little to no instruction for the player, who has to either try typing different commands to see what works (what is afforded by the language processor of the game, as well as what their player character is physically capable of doing *in game*) or obtain a list of commands.[3] There were no graphics, platforms, or sprites—the gameworld and player actions were crafted entirely in text. Unlike other text-based games that were limited to simple verb–noun commands (e.g., "attack troll"), the text parser in *Zork* was able to parse more complex commands and was even prepared with a seemingly limitless supply of humorous responses in anticipation of unconventional commands from the player:

```
>attack the nasty-looking troll with the garlic
Trying to attack the troll with a clove of garlic
is suicidal.
The flat of the troll's axe skins across your
forearm.
```

Giappone (2015) underlines that as a genre, adventure games inherently play with metafictional humor, and frequently embed self-parody in both the resultant narrative and the affordances of the game's parser. As noted by Giappone, "Zork's developers saw the exploration of the useless as one of the most delightful features of the game"; as the developers later revealed in interviews, they took great pride in programming in clever or unexpected responses to unconventional player commands. For example:

```
>attack the mailbox with the elvish sword
I've known strange people, but fighting a small
mailbox?
```

Affordances

The concept of an affordance was coined by the perceptual psychologist James J. Gibson (1979) and was later introduced to the human–computer interaction (HCI) community by Donald Norman (1988). In computing, an affordance is the design aspect of an object which suggests how the object should be used, or "an action possibility available in the environment to an individual, independent of the individual's ability to perceive this possibility" (McGrenere and Ho, 2000, p. 179). This is a broad definition, but an important one when considering the variety of digital storytelling platforms available today (e.g., hypertext, video games, etc.) and the differences in how they support storytelling. As an interactive storytelling platform, games have the potential to position the audience in ways that passive media cannot.

As noted above, games scholars recognize interactive stories as complex artifacts that possess both ludic and narrative properties (Cardona-Rivera and Young, 2013). In referencing Norman's affordances, Mateas (2001) suggests that video games have two types of affordances: *material affordances* and *formal affordances*. Material affordances are defined as opportunities for action that are presented by the game to the player, either directly by prompting the player to action, or indirectly by allowing the action to take place. Formal affordances are a more complex matter and are defined as the players' motivation to perform one particular action out of all potential actions (Mateas, 2001).

However, Pinchbeck (2009) notes that it is important to understand gameplay itself as "a network of affordance relationships which define supported actions" (in the abstract). In this case, the theoretical focus is upon actions that are both supported by the game's algorithms and guided by the game's narrative elements. Furthermore, gameworlds do not exist in a vacuum—the aforementioned prevalence of humor and parody in the adventure genre also shape the affordance relationships in the game in terms of player expectations and gameplay mechanics.

Pinchbeck states that it is clear in interactive stories that balance both ludic and narrative elements that "story is used to manipulate player behaviour—that it serves a distinct gameplay function" (Pinchbeck, 2009, abstract). He asserts that gameplay must be understood as a network of affordances.

In the context of *Zork*, if we consider the text prompt—the ability to type commands into the game—as a *material affordance*, then the commands the user chooses to type into the text prompt, whether they choose commands intended to move the story forward or decide to test the parser's response to unconventional commands, are *formal affordances*. Both are supported by the game's algorithms and narrative elements and play with the metafictional conventions of the genre. Familiarity with the prevalence of self-parody in the adventure genre potentially invites this kind of playfulness early on in gameplay. However, even in moments of productive exploration, the game frequently deploys humor to break from a series of repetitive obstructions,[4] as seen in the exchange below between the player and the game. Here, the game deploys humor to mask the lack of true agency in a game whose natural language text parser affords the illusion of agency in a highly constrained text-based environment:

```
>west
Kitchen
On the table is an elongated brown sack, smelling
of hot peppers.
A bottle is sitting on the table.
The glass bottle contains:
 A quantity of water

>drink water
I'd like to, but I can't get to it.

>get bottle
Taken.

>drink water
I'd like to, but I can't get to it.

>open bottle
You open the glass bottle.
>drink water
Thank you very much.  I was rather thirsty (from
all this talking, probably).
```

Affordances and Agency

Player agency has been discussed in the context of its impact on storytelling in games (see, e.g., Adams, 1999; Jenkins, 2004). Game critics often note that true interactivity poses a potential threat to narrative design, where the alternative—stories "on rails"—can overly constrain the "freedom, power, and self-expression" associated with interactivity (Adams, 1999). In the context of this chapter, we understand the concept of "on rails" game design to refer to both the potential for physical movement (e.g., north, south, east, and west) within the environment to be pre-scripted or constrained, and the story elements and/or the users' progression through the game's narrative.

With more than 15,000 lines of game code, *Zork*'s text parser gives the illusion of agency within a highly constrained environment, often using humor to mask moments where agency is constrained. The text parser maps player input onto the following three variables: PRSA (action), PRSI (indirect object), and PRSO (direct object). Every object in the game has properties associated with it in the game's code, including its name, description, actions associated with it, and adjectives used to describe it. Each object also has a list of responses associated with it, based on the context in which the object was referenced by the player. The parser also supports synonyms (via a synonym table), clauses, and other aspects of natural human language (Ajdnik, 2020).

Conclusion

When we think about emerging digital poetics, it is important to consider the platform-specific storytelling affordances of each platform. Different platforms allow for different levels of player agency. Different platforms will also change the way we tell stories. *Zork* was highly influential in terms of its scope, use of natural language processing, and the ways in which the game playfully engaged with the genre of text-based adventure games. Arguably, *Zork* also laid the groundwork for the IF genre and Twine—a popular open-source tool for hypertext narratives and modern text-based games.

Victoria McArthur

Notes

1. Jacobi, G. (2017). Interacting with Words: Development of a text-based game on language.
2. In IF games, a text parser is part of the game code that takes the text typed by the player and simplifies it into something the game can understand.

3. Typing help provides the user with a short list of helpful command words and an explanation of how the game deals with directions, actions, prepositions, and ambiguity. However, external guides have been published with a more detailed overview of how those commands can be used in combination with other words or phrases (e.g., using words like IT, ALL, or AND in a command, as in >TAKE ALL THE TOOLS).
4. Even in graphical games there are always limitations on what players can do and where they can go. These are often set via invisible physical barriers and game mechanics or code. However, in text-based games, these barriers need to be communicated to the player through text. *Zork*, like other games in the genre, plays with these barriers by including a mix of typical error messages as well as pre-coded humor.

References

Adams, E. (1999). Three problems for interactive storytellers. *Designer's Notebook Column, Gamasutra, 144*. Retrieved August 1, 2021, from https://www.gamedeveloper.com/design/the-designer-s-notebook-three-problems-for-interactive-storytellers-resolved

Ajdnik, R. (2020). Zork: The great inner workings. *Medium*. Retrieved August 1, 2021, from https://medium.com/swlh/zork-the-great-inner-workings-b68012952bdc

Anderson, T., & Galley, S. (1985). The history of Zork. *The New Zork Times, 4*(1–3).

Cardona-Rivera, R. E., & Young, R. M. (2013). A cognitivist theory of affordances for games. *DiGRA '13 - Proceedings of the 2013 DiGRA International Conference: DeFragging Game Studies*. Retrieved August 1st, 2021, from http://www.digra.org/wp-content/uploads/digital-library/paper_74b.pdf.pdf

Frasca, G. (2003). Ludologists love stories, too: notes from a debate that never took place. *DiGRA '03 - Proceedings of the 2003 DiGRA International Conference: Level Up*, 4–6. Retrieved August 1st, 2021, from http://www.digra.org/wp-content/uploads/digital-library/05163.01125.pdf

Giappone, K. (2015). Self-reflexivity and humor in adventure games. *Game Studies, 15*(1). Retrieved August 1st, 2021, from http://gamestudies.org/1501/articles/bonello_k

Gibson, J. J. (1979). *The ecological approach to visual perception*. Boston: Houghton Mifflin.

Jenkins, H. (2004). Game design as narrative architecture. In Wardrip-Fruin, N. & Harrigan, P. (Eds) *First person: New media as story, performance, and game* (pp. 118–130). Cambridge, MA: The MIT Press.

Mateas, M. (2001). A preliminary poetics for interactive drama and games. *Digital Creativity, 12*(3), 140–152.

McGrenere, J., & Ho, W. (2000). Affordances: Clarifying and evolving a concept. In *Proceedings of Graphics Interface, 200*, 179–186.

McManus, A., & Feinstein, A. H. (2006). Narratology and ludology: Competing paradigms or complementary theories in simulation. In *Developments in Business Simulation and Experiential Learning: Proceedings of the Annual ABSEL conference, 33*, 363–372.

Murray, J. H. (2005). The last word on ludology v narratology in game studies. *DiGRA '05 - Proceedings of the 2005 DiGRA International Conference: Changing Views: Worlds in Play*. Retrieved August 1 2021, from https://inventingthemedium.com/2013/06/28/the-last-word-on-ludology-v-narratology-2005/

Norman, D. A. (1988). *The psychology of everyday things*. New York: Basic Books.

Pearce, C. (2005). Theory wars: An argument against arguments in the so-called ludology/narratology debate. *Digital Games Research Conference 2005, Changing Views: Worlds in Play*. Retrieved August 1, 2021 from http://www.digra.org/wp-content/uploads/digital-library/06278.03452.pdf

Pinchbeck, D. M. (2009). *Story as a function of gameplay in First Person Shooters and an analysis of FPS diegetic content, 1998–2007* (Doctoral dissertation, University of Portsmouth).

Further Reading

Ford, M. (2016). *Writing interactive fiction with Twine*. Indianapolis, IN: Que Publishing. Historical source *(2019) Zork I codebase*. Retrieved August 1, 2021, from https://github.com/historicalsource/zork1

Montfort, N. (2005). *Twisty little passages: An approach to interactive fiction*. Cambridge, MA: MIT Press.

DOI: 10.4324/9781003199205-51

INDEX

2D games 257, 258, 261, 262
3D games 257–258, 260, 261, 262
3D graphics 295
3D puzzle-platformer 209
3DO 173
7th Guest, The 211

AAA games *see* Triple-A games
accessibility 34, 59, 162, 191, 200–201, 288
Acorn Electron 88, 91
Acornsoft 90
action games (genre) 58, 77
action-adventure games (genre) 9–10, 12, 14, 77, 154, 216, 217, 261
action-RPG games (genre) 56
Activision 13
adaptation 9–10, 184, 188
Adventure (1979) 9–14, 154
adventure games (genre) 12, 145, 148–149, 150, 151, 154, 155, 157, 219, 305, 307; *see also* text-based adventure
Aeris G., death of, 115
aesthetic 1, 4, 5, 17, 21, 24, 44–45, 61, 105, 118, 124, 144–145, 148, 157, 159–160, 162, 167, 259, 264, 276, 290–291; of continuity 139–140; design 44–45, 207, 223; Gothic 56–57, 70; play 35; retro 286; Russian 269
affordances 11, 16, 18, 50, 52, 96, 107, 211, 236, 240–243, 296, 297, 307–309, 310

Age of Empires 29, 30
age ratings 118
agency 24, 83, 95, 118, 160, 219, 229, 230–231, 295, 309–310
AGI game engine 149
AI *see* artificial Intelligence
AI *see* GLaDOS
Alcorn, A. 202–208
algorithm 180–182, 193, 213, 270, 308–309
Aliens (film) 69
Alone in the Dark 217, 221
American Dream 123
Among Us 183
Ampex 203, 205
Android 34, 120, 162
Andy Capp's Tavern 203, 206
Angband 58–59
Angry Birds (film) 15
Angry Birds (game) 15–20, 99
Animal Crossing 21–26, 216, 240, 287
Animal Crossing: New Horizons 240
animation 57, 65, 73, 75, 76, 78–80, 162, 191, 277, 296, 297, 302
anthropocentrism 286
Antichamber 212
Apex Legends 122
appeal, to women 24
Apple 120
Apple Computer 186, 187
Apple II 90
AR *see* augmented reality
arcade 9, 10, 14, 34, 42, 50, 52–53, 54, 58, 63–64, 68, 75–76, 77, 79, 90, 148–150, 155, 166–170, 176,

INDEX

190–191, 195, 203–208, 216, 245, 247–249, 266, 286, 289, 293, 296; *see also* coin-op games
Arena 81–83, 86
artificial intelligence 135, 192–194, 210, 211, 213, 229, 239, 242, 251–252
Assassin's Creed (franchise) 261
Assassin's Creed Origins 26–32
assassins 27
Asteroids 67, 191
Astro Battle 249
Atari 9, 13, 203, 205–208, 249
Atari 2600 system 9, 66, 208
Atari VCS / 2600 9–14, 249
attract mode 168
augmented reality 197–198, 200
Autcraft 164
auteur 13, 38, 40, 42, 52, 94, 286; body 289–290
avatar 28, 63, 78, 94–96, 106, 118, 122, 148, 160, 161, 229, 239, 260, 285; customization 23, 241; *see also* character
AY-3-8500 chip 208

Bach, J.S. 269
Baer, R. 51, 203–205
balance 253–254
Bally Professional Videocade 249
Bandfuse: Rock Legends 130
Banished 237
Banjo Kazooie 260
Barrow, S. 3, 5
Baseball 290
battle 27, 45, 91, 95, 97, 111, 113, 115, 132, 154, 166, 167, 174, 176, 198, 199, 202, 291, 230, 246, 253, 266, 293–294, 295, 302; *see also* fighting
Battle Royale (film) 117
Battle.net 60–61, 253–254
Battlefield 1942 213
Battlefield 48
BBC Micro Model B 88, 90–91
Beat Saber 130
Beatmania 51
Bejeweled 32–38

Bejeweled Blitz 33
Bejeweled Champions 33
Bejeweled Stars 33
Bell, D. 88, 90–92
Bergensten, J. 163
Better Together update (*Minecraft*) 162
Bientôt l'été 143
Big Trouble in Little China (film) 168
Bioshock 140, 213
black box 236–237
Black Cauldron, The 149
blind space *see* offscreen space
Blizzard Entertainment 251, 253–254
Blood 138
Bloodsport (film) 168
Blow, J. 38, 40–42
Bluth, D. 79–80
Book of Atrus, The 222
Book of the Dead (book) 57
Boon, E. 167, 171
box *see* packaging
Braben, I. 88, 90–92
BRAID 38–44, 98
branching narrative *see* narrative
Breakout 245–246
Brood War 251
Brown Box 203
Brown v. Entertainment Merchants Association 170
Bubsy 3D 258
building *see* game mechanics
Buildings Have Feelings Too! 237
Bushnell, N. 191, 203–208
business models 20, 99–101, 121–122, 180, 182–183
Butler, J. 21, 24, 242

C418 161
Call of Duty (franchise) 44–48, 213
Call of Duty 2 45
Call of Duty: Black Ops 71, 278
Call of Duty: Black Ops II 48
Call of Duty: Modern Warfare 2 44–50, 98
Call of Duty: Modern Warfare 2 98
Call of Duty: World at War 45
camera angle 105, 140, 175, 217–218

314

INDEX

Candy Crush Saga 33, 35, 121
Capcom 166–167, 220
capitalism 48, 102, 105, 121, 288
Capra, F. 289
captured media 296, 297
caricature 289
cartridge *see* packaging
casual games 15–20, 33, 34, 35–37, 51, 54, 99, 101, 103, 212, 214, 287
casual players 17, 101, 254
CD-ROM 57, 93, 171, 172–173, 222, 225, 294
censorship 44, 48, 73
Centipede 64
CGA color images 150
Chaplin, C. 290
character: complexity 213–214; creation 82, 84–85; customization 94, 131, 239–241; diversity 239; leveling system 84–85, 115, 281, 302; *see also* avatar; player character
cheating 23, 61, 95, 170, 195
Chen, J. 143, 145, 287
cinema 289–291; Hollywood 48; silent cinema 290; *see also* film
Cities: Skylines 237
city-building games (genre) 233, 235
Civilization (board game) 227
Clash of Clans 182
classroom 28, 30–32, 187, 237, 278
cliffhanger 64–65
Coalition for App Fairness 120
Cobra MK III 88
coin-op games 63, 166, 169, 170, 245, 246, 248, 249; *see also* arcade
collision detection 11
Colossal Cave Adventure 14, 306
Columbine High School Massacre 73
Combat 10
comedy 288–292; physical 289; *see also* humor; slapstick
Commodore 64 system 90, 234, 276, 305
community, online 41, 94, 96, 100, 144, 156, 161, 163–164, 179, 199, 253, 283, 299, 304; autism 162; civil 278; deviant leisure 96;

pacifists 97; role play 97; social 300, 304
competition 22, 52–55, 105, 108, 227–229, 255, 289
computer history 89, 188–189
computer role-playing game (CRPG) 280–286; *see also* role-playing game
Computer Space 191, 204–208, 245
console generation: sixth 105; eighth 108
consumerist society, 287–288
controller, 17–18, 50–51, 54–55, 67, 140, 219, 290 *see* guitar
controls 17–18, 149, 157, 191, 206, 258, 265, 219
convention 9, 17, 58, 93, 94, 97, 101, 102, 111, 117, 124, 127, 138, 143, 144, 149, 151, 152, 157, 167, 168, 212, 277, 280–282, 297, 307–309; comic book 226; early cinema 64–65
copyright 13, 18, 117, 119
cosplay 175
Counter-Strike 135
COVID-19 30, 164, 201
crafting 143, 160, 162, 178–179, 274
Crash Bandicoot 258
Crash: video game 75, 262, 266
Creative Computing 186
creative mode 160–161
cross-franchise narrative 119
cross-generational gaming 199, 201
cross-play 119–120, 161
Crusader Kings 29
Crush the Castle 16
Crypt of the NecroDancer 180
culture: cultural reaction 214; fandom 93, 300; game culture 15, 17, 35, 54, 89–92, 103, 213, 286, 288, 289, 291; real world 303
customization *see* avatar, character
cute 21–24
cut-scene 45–46, 49, 57, 110, 111, 114–115, 119, 135–137, 139–140, 146, 175, 191, 216, 218, 230, 286, 295
cyborg 51, 138

315

INDEX

D'ni 222, 224–225
Dabney, T. 203, 206
Dance Central 54
Dance Dance Revolution 50–56, 129
Dance of the Sugar Plum Fairy 269
Dark Souls 89
Dark Wheel, The (book) 88
Dark Wheel, The 88
David/Goliath tale 88
Davis Cup 245
DeadCore 212
Dear Esther 143
Defender 264
Descriptive Books 222–223, 225
Destiny 2 122
Deux Ex: Human Revolution 138
Devil World 263
Devil World's 263
Diablo 56–63, 81, 253
Diamond Mine 33
Dice Legacy 237
difficulty 18, 43, 35, 59, 67, 85, 97, 131, 136, 141, 145, 155, 156, 158, 161, 192, 270, 275
Dillenberger, P. 185, 187
Diner Dash 35
Discord 165
Discovery Tour 27–28, 30–32
Dishonored 212
disk *see* packaging
Don't Starve 180
Donkey Kong 63–68, 88, 263, 264–265, 265; cereal 67; character 63–65; Game and Watch 67
DOOM 69–75, 92, 117, 135–136, 138, 171, 250
Dragnet (TV Show) 65; television theme 65–66
Dragon's Lair 75–81
driving games (genre) 173
Drop7 16
Dropzone 43
Duck Hunt 132
Duke Nukem 3D 138
Dungeon Master 58
dungeon-crawler (genre) 58, 81, 162
Dungeons & Dragons 9, 58, 81–82, 280, 307

Dwarf Fortress 180
Dyer, R. 76–77, 79
dynamic system 229

EA *see* Electronic Arts
Easter eggs 9, 13, 14, 168, 259
eco-criticism 102
economy 61, 94, 229, 285; game's 252; in-game currency 95; real world money 95; *see also* business models; free-to-play; microtransactions
educational game 184, 186–189
educational use of game 28, 32, 159, 228, 236–237, 278–279
EGA color images 148, 150
Eguchi, K. 287
Egypt 27–29, 31, 57
Elder Scrolls, The (franchise) 81
Elder Scrolls II: Daggerfall, The 81–87
Elder Scrolls V: Skyrim, The 178, 181
Electronic Arts 33, 105, 108, 174
Electronic Entertainment Expo E3 287
Electronic Football 79
Electronic Software Association 171
Electronic Software Rating Board 171
Electronika 60 terminal 268
Elepong 245
Elite 88–93
embodied gameplay 132, 134
embodiment 51, 211
emergent narrative 275; *see also* narrative
Empire 227
empowerment, process of 213, 220
English Premier League 109
Enter the Dragon (film) 168
environmental storytelling *see* storytelling
Epic Games 117, 118–121
e-sports 50, 53, 54, 104, 183, 251–256
ethics 275, 277, 280–286, 287–288; and in-game choices, 90, 275, 277, 279, 281–285; in game development, 120, 201, 280, 288;

of player behaviors, 62, 97; *see also* morality; philosophy
EVE Online 92, 93–98
Evil Dead II (film) 69
Excitebike 263
exergaming 53–54
exploration 27, 30–32, 82–83, 91, 137, 140, 153, 154, 155–156, 178–179, 229, 233, 261, 307, 309
Eye of the Beholder 58

F2P *see* free-to-play
Facebook 18, 98–101, 103
Falcon 3.0 172
Famicom 155; *see also* Nintendo Family Computer Disk System
family play 289, 290
fantasy (genre) 300
farming simulator 101–103; *see also* simulation
Farmville 98–104
Fatal Frame 221
female: audience 64; characters 64, 151, 217, 240, 241; fandoms 255; players 101, 213; soccer team 106
femininity 24, 37
feminist analysis 151, 213–214, 278
feminized players 17, 33, 35, 37
Ferrari 173
FIFA 14 104–110
FIFA Ultimate Team (FUT) 107
fighting 12, 45, 49, 89, 119, 138, 154, 278, 301, 308; *see also* fighting games
fighting games (genre) 111, 166–169, 171
film canon 1–3; admission 2; and politics of: the Academy 2; canon-making 2; selection 3
film: as influence 154; *see also* cinema
Final Fantasy VII 110–116
finishing moves 168–171
first-person puzzler 209
first-person shooter (FPS) (genre) 11, 44, 48, 49, 69, 70–71, 72, 74, 83, 117–118, 135–136, 138–140, 171, 209, 212–213, 296; archetypes 212; crossovers 212; *see also* military shooter
fitness *see* exercise
Flight Control 16
flinging technique 211
Floating Runner 258
flOw 143–144
flow 144
Flower 98, 144
FMV *see* full-motion video, live-action
Forden, D. 167
Forrester, J. 233
Fortnite Battle Royale 116–123, 180, 182
franchise 15, 22, 44, 45, 48, 106–107, 109, 111–112, 118, 119, 130, 131, 133, 134, 153, 154, 156, 171, 173–174, 176–177, 183, 197, 200, 202, 209, 212, 213, 221, 225–226, 227, 228, 231, 239, 240, 242, 261, 262, 296
free-to-play (F2P) 93, 100, 103, 119, 182; as business model, 19–20
Frogger 64
Frome, J. 4
Frostpunk 237
full-motion video (FMV) 171, 293–297; *see also* live-action video

gag 290
Galaga 67
Galaxian 63, 191
Galaxy Game 205
game analytics 100–101
game as a service 121, 198, 201
game balance *see* balance
Game Boy 197, 266, 268, 269
game canon 1–5, 91–92; *see also* film canon
game culture *see* culture
game design 1, 2, 13, 20, 41, 60, 63, 90, 102, 124, 134, 143, 144, 155, 186, 203, 210, 214, 228, 247, 262, 266, 268, 270, 275, 280, 286–292, 297, 300, 310; conventions 17, 150, 191; feminist 303; for casual games 17, 18; inclusive and accessible 287

INDEX

game mechanics 23, 33–34, 36–37, 44–45, 51, 53, 99, 117–118, 176, 185, 204, 234, 241, 253, 270, 271, 275, 277, 300–303, 308, 311; about time 38, 39; building 117–118
game testers 156
Game Transfer Phenomena *see* Tetris effect
game world *see* world: of the game
game's economy *see* economy
Gamergate controversy 102
games of empire 105
gamespace 51, 210
gaming culture *see* culture
Garriott, R. 280–281, 284–285
gatekeeping 93, 95, 97
Gauntlet 58
Gazzard, A. 91
gender 21, 24, 35, 37, 52, 101, 103, 124, 126, 287; performance 239–243
genres *see* action games, action-adventure games, action-RPG games, adventure games, city-building games, driving games, dungeon-crawler, fantasy, fighting games, first-person shooter (FPS), interactive fiction, interactive movie, massively multiplayer online game (MMOG), massively multiplayer online role-playing game (MMORPG), match-3 games, music games, platformer games, puzzle games, first-person puzzler, puzzle-platformer, racing games, real-time strategy games, rhythm games, roguelike, role-playing games (RPG), sandbox, shooter games, sport video games, strategy games, survival games, survival horror, text adventure games, walking simulators, western
German Bundesliga 109
gestures 16, 28, 142, 289, 290
Giger, H.R. 70

GLaDOS 209, 211, 213–214
God of War franchise 119
GoldenEye 007 212
Google 120
Gothic *see* aesthetics
Gough, J. 161
Gran Turismo 173
Grand Theft Auto (franchise) 83, 261
Grand Theft Auto III 21, 123–129; and race and racism, 125–128; gender and sexism, 125–126; parody and satire, 125–127; violence, 125–126, 128
Grand Theft Auto: San Andreas 124, 126
Grand Theft Auto: Vice City 126
graphics: photorealistic 172, 286, 297; raster 205; vector 89, 206
Graveyard, The 143
Greek history *see* history
griefing 61, 96
Guinness World Record 258, 266, 268
guitar controller 130–133
Guitar Freak 129
Guitar Hero 51–52, 55, 129–135

Half-Life 71, 135–140, 209
Halo franchise 119
Halo: Combat Evolved 21, 136
Hamurabi 236
Haraway, D. 288
hardcore games 15, 17, 19, 35, 36, 161, 287, 291
Hawkins, T. 173
Heidegger, M. 288
Heinemann, B. 185, 187
Hellcat Ace 228
Hip-hop, 125
historical literacy 32
historical thinking 30
historical video games 29–30, 32
history, erasure of 46–49; Greek 27–29, 31; in games 228–233; representation of 45–47, 49, 185; temporal distance from 44–45
Hobbit, The (book) 222

INDEX

Hollywood 48, 65, 124, 128, 230, 293, 294
Home PONG 207
horror movie 216, 219; *see also* film
Hot Wheels toy cars 176
House of the Dead 216
Howard, J. 282–283
HUD 45
humor 210–211, 214, 307, 308, 310; *see also* comedy

IBM PCjr 148
Ice Cube 67
identity 35, 240, 241, 243; gamer identity 17–19, 25, 101; identity markers 242; identity politics 242; player 101
ideological bias 228
immersion 18–19, 29, 110, 132, 231
in-app purchase *see* microtransaction
independent games 41, 144–145, 286
Indiana Jones (film franchise) 154
Indie Game: The Movie 38, 40, 41
indie scene 212
individualism 288
industry *see* video game industry
inequality 288, 291
Inferno (book) 57
Infiniminer 161
in-game store 119
instruction manual 154, 156, 163; *see also* packaging
interactive cinema *see* interactive movie
Interactive Digital Software Association *see* Electronic Software Association
interactive fiction (genre) 229, 305–307
interactive movie (genre) 170, 216–217, 294–298
interactive storytelling *see* storytelling
interactivity 45, 75–76, 80, 136, 137, 140, 217, 270, 289, 310

interface 5, 45, 50, 58, 61, 75, 83, 89, 148, 192, 241–243, 270, 276, 277, 281, 287; gestural 289, 291, 293, 296; mimetic 51, 54–55
International Superstar Soccer 105
Internet 56, 60, 72, 90, 93, 115, 254–255, 265
iOS 34, 120, 144, 162, 185
iPad 226
iPhone 16, 17, 226
Iron Curtain 269
Iwatani, T. 190–193, 195

Java 160
Jenkins, H. 306–307
Journey 141–147
Jumping Flash! 258
Jumpman/Mario 63–64, 66–67
Just Dance 54, 129
Juul, J. 9, 12, 17–18, 33–35, 51, 54, 101, 144, 287

Keaton, B. 290
kinesthetic experience 146, 210–211, 213
kinesthetic pleasure 145
King Kong (film) (1933) 65; (1976) 65
King of Kong: A Fistful of Quarters, The (film) 67, 68
King's Quest 148–152
Kissing Booth 2, The (film) 52–53
Kissing Booth, The (film) 53
Kohl, H. 170
Konami 53, 54, 105, 108, 109
Kondo, K. 157, 264
Korobeiniki 269

Lamborghini 175
Lands of Lore: The Throne of Chaos 58
laserdiscs 75–76
Last of Us, The 277
laughter *see* comedy
lay: popular history 28–30
League of Legends 98, 180, 183
Lee, B. 168
Legend of Zelda 10, 153–159

INDEX

LEGO 160, 181
Lemmings 210
Lethal Enforcers 170–171
Lieberman, J. 72, 170–171
linearity 46, 296
Little Computer People (LCP) 276
live-action video 216, 295, 296; see also full-motion video
Lloyd, H. 290
loading screen 119, 218, 220
location-based game 196–197, 200, 201
Loco-Motion 210
looping (musical) 269
Lord of the Rings, The (book) 222
lore 156
ludology 270, 295, 306
ludonarrative harmony 136–140, 219

MacIntyre, A.C. 283–284
Magnavox Odyssey 203
mainstream 287
Manifold Garden 212
map 22, 28, 86, 111, 149, 150, 197, 198, 227, 228, 235, 258, 260; editor 254; in game 154; in packaging 156; two-dimensional 142
Mario Bros. 263
Mario Party Superstars 183
Mario/Jumpman see Jumpman/Mario
Mario: character 21, 63, 66, 67, 249, 258, 260, 262, 264, 289; merchandising of, 266
marketing 15, 25, 43, 53, 90, 100, 106, 108, 119, 155–156, 157, 200, 207–208, 266, 271, 278
Martin, P. 4
masculinity, hegemonic 24 see patriarchy
massively multiplayer online game (MMOG) (genre) 93–97
massively multiplayer online role-playing game (MMORPG) (genre) 111, 299

masterpiece 4
match-3 games (genre) 33–34, 35, 36
maze 10, 12, 63, 191–195, 216
Maze War 71
MECC (Minnesota Educational Computing Consortium) 185–188, 189
Medal of Honor 212
Meier, S. 89, 227–230
Merleau-Ponty, M. 289
metacommentary see metaludic nature
metagame 253, 255
metaludic nature 214
Micropolis 234
Microsoft 33, 163
Microsoft Game Studios 160, 163
Microsoft Garage 162
Microsoft Xbox 360 42, 54, 176, 209, 286
microtransactions 100, 103, 201
Midway 166–171
Might & Magic 58
Mikami, S. 216–221
military shooters 44, 48; see also first-person shooters
Miller, R. 222, 225
Mills, S. 151
mimetic narration 138
Minecraft 83, 117, 159–166, 180, 183
Minecraft Realms 162, 164
MinecraftEDU 164
Mini Metro 180
mini-game 286
minimalism 286
minor key (music) 269
Mirror's Edge 212–213
mise-en-abyme see metaludic nature
Mission: Asteroid 150
Miyamoto, S. 42, 63–64, 153, 154, 155–156, 157, 250, 258–259, 261–262, 289; design philosophy 259, 261
MMORPG see Massively Multiplayer Online Role-Playing Game

320

INDEX

MOBA *see* Multiplayer Online Battle Arena
mobile games, 15–20, 43, 197
modding 71, 72, 86, 117, 135, 162–164, 240; sexuality 240–243
modeling 228–229
Moira 58
Mojang 160–164
momentum *see* kinesthetic experience
monetization 19–20, 100, 103, 201
monsters 18, 39–40, 61–62, 70, 72, 73, 135, 156, 191–195, 217, 218, 246, 278, 281
moral orientation 91
moral panic 121, 280
morality 280–286; good and evil 301
Mortal Kombat 72, 166–172
Motion Picture Association of America 170
motion sensor 286–292
movement *see* gestures
Ms. Pac-Man 64
multiplayer 56, 60–61, 71–72, 116, 117–118, 122, 132, 141, 146, 161, 180, 183, 198, 212, 229, 251–252, 288
Multiplayer Online Battle Arena (MOBA) 254
Multi-User Dungeons (MUDs) 304
Murray, S. 124
music 23, 38, 39, 51, 53–54, 55, 57, 63, 64, 65–67, 110, 112–115, 119, 129, 130, 133–134, 153, 154, 157, 160, 161, 182, 246, 247, 264, 268–270, 272, 277; and atmosphere 157; dance 54; in concert 157; in games 51; rhythm 51; *see also* soundtrack
music games (genre) 129, 130
musical composition 157
musical cue 157
Myst 210, 211, 222, 225–226
Myst franchise 225–226
Myst Island 223
Mystery Case Files: Ravenhearst 35
Mystery House 150

Narbacular Drop 209
NARC 167
narrative 38–41, 45–47, 106–107, 110–115, 136–140, 151, 153, 154, 156, 157, 240, 241, 243, 286, 300, 302, 306, 307, 309; branching 293–294, 296; *see also* lore
narratology 270, 306
National Coalition Against Television Violence 169
nature 24, 102, 155
navigation 31, 89, 139, 212, 219, 281
NBA Jam 167
Need for Speed III: Hot Pursuit 172–177
Nemesis: The Wizardry Adventure 81
Ngai, S. 288
NHL Hockey (franchise) 9
Night Trap 72, 170–171
nineteenth-century Western settlers: representation of 184–188
Nintendo 35, 63, 65, 67, 112, 153, 155, 157, 158, 170–171, 257–261, 262, 266, 269, 272, 286–292; "Nintendo thumb" 248
Nintendo Entertainment System (NES) 67, 111, 155, 268
Nintendo Family Computer Disk System (FDS) 67, 111, 155, 156, 158, 216
Nintendo GameCube 21, 23, 289
Nintendo Wii 17, 35, 54–55, 189, 286–292
Nishikado, T. 245, 247–248
No Man's Sky 92, 178–184
non-combat design paradigm 212
nonhuman animals 102
non-linearity 77–78
non-player characters (NPCs) 22, 28, 31, 86, 94, 95, 97, 101, 113, 114, 160, 186, 199, 229, 283, 293, 304
nostalgia 40, 51, 160, 188, 197, 286
Not All Fairy Tales Have Happy Endings (book) 151
Notch *see* Persson, M.
notgames 142–143
Nutcracker, The (film) 269

INDEX

Nutting & Associates 205–206

obsolescence, technological 99
Ocarina of Time 260
offscreen space 218
open-world games 88, 92, 117, 123, 178–179, 231
Operation Flashpoint: Cold War Crisis, 212
Orange Box, The 209
Oregon Trail, The 184–189 *see* computer history, nostalgia, pedagogical

packaging 88, 222; box 156; cartridge 155, 156, 158; disk 155, 156; instruction manual 158; *see also* map
Pac-Man 63, 64, 67, 190–196
Pajitnov, A. 268, 269
Palm Pilot 34
Paquette, D. 126
Pa-Rappa the Rapper 51
parody 125–127, 289, 291, 307, 308, 309; *see also* comedy
patriarchy 291; patriarchal codification 214
Paul, C. 36
pedagogical tool *see* educational game
performance 12, 44, 50, 51–53, 125, 132–134, 139, 175, 289, 291, 296, 297, 302
Perils of Pauline, The (film) 64–65
permadeath 59, 94, 274–275
Persson, M. 160, 163–164
philosophy 280–286; *see also* ethics; morality
photorealistic militarism 212
Pitfall! 66, 263
Pitts, B. 205
pixilation 167, 171
Plants vs. Zombies 99
platformer games (genre) 258, 259, 261
player character 10, 11, 22, 39, 69, 70, 127, 131, 180, 219, 300, 301; spaceship 94; *see also* customization

player versus player (PvP) 94–97, 122, 302
PlayerUnknown's Battlegrounds 117, 122
Pocket Monster *see* Pokémon
point-and-click games 57, 226
Pokémon (franchise) 197
Pokémon 197–199
Pokémon Go 196–202
police 27, 94, 174–177, 216, 219, 235
Police Quest 149
politics 1–3, 13, 28, 179, 227, 230–231, 242, 291; of technology 288
PONG 10, 11, 42, 202–209, 245
Porsche 173
Portal 2: Lab Rat (comic) 211
Portal 209–215; franchise 212–213
post-traumatic stress disorder (PTSD) 271
Pötzsch, H. 277
power dynamics 291
preservation: game 19
Pro Evolution Soccer (PES) 105, 109
procedural generation 59, 61, 77, 82–83, 160, 162, 179–183
productive play 36–37
progamers 255
protect-the-ball feature 108
puzzle 36, 38, 39, 149, 150, 153, 154, 156, 157, 209, 211, 213, 266
puzzle games (genre) 33, 36, 210, 212, 268, 271; *see also* first-person puzzler; puzzle-platformer
puzzle-platformer (genre) 38, 209
puzzle-solving 157, 210–212, 283
PvP *see* player versus player

Q.U.B.E. 212
Quake 139
Quantum Conundrum 212
Queen's Gambit, The (tv series) 268
quest 9, 12–13, 39, 57, 85, 148, 158, 182, 280–286, 300–302; fetch quests 22
quick-time event 76

race 113, 125–128, 240, 243
racial ambiguity 213

322

racing games (genre) 23, 173, 176
racism 125–128
Radar Scope 63–64
raid 198, 199–200, 302, 304
Raid on Bungeling Bay 233
Raiders of the Lost Ark (film) 78
Raiders of the Lost Ark 154–155
Railroad Tycoon 229
Raine, L. 161
Rawitsch, D. 185, 186
Ready Player One (book) 40
realism 76, 82, 105, 108–109, 118, 135, 167, 242, 276–277, 286, 297; historical 27
real-time 12, 22, 27, 57, 58, 86, 148–150, 201, 217, 228, 293, 296
real-time strategy games (genre) *see* strategy
Red Dawn (film) 47
Red Dead Redemption 178
religion 229, 278, 280–286
Rescue on Fractalus 88
Resident Evil 216–222
Resident Evil VII: biohazard 221
reviews and reviewers 28, 82, 85–86, 108, 170, 173, 178, 217, 230, 234–235, 257, 261, 276, 295
rhythm games (genre) 51, 52, 55, 129, 130
Ring Fit Adventure 55
Risk (board game) 227
Riven 222–226
Riven, Age of (world) 222–225
Road & Track magazine 173
Road Rash 174
Robinett, W. 9–14, 40
Rock Band 52, 129–131
Rocksmith 130
Rockstar 123, 125, 128, 261
Rogers, H. 272
Rogue 58, 180
roguelike (genre) 57–59, 180
role-playing games (RPG) (genre) 56, 58, 61, 81, 83, 111, 156, 179, 216, 254, 302, 307; *see also* computer role-playing game; massively multiplayer online role-playing game

Rosenfeld, D. 161
RPG *see* role-playing game
Run-and-gun game 212

safety 22, 50, 137, 155, 200, 201
Saints Row IV 240
Sakaguchi, H. 112
sandbox (genre) 81, 83, 95–96, 124, 128, 160, 179, 228, 239, 242, 259
Santa Paravia and Fiumaccio 236
satire 125–127
save: game progress 19, 59, 106, 107, 149, 155, 158, 219
SCI 149
scoop turn 108
score 11, 23, 42, 67, 85, 133, 191, 194–195, 207, 247, 291, 293
Scott Pilgrim vs. the World (film) 52
Sea Wolf 247
seasonal seriality 106–107
Sega 170–171
Sega Game Gear 170
Sega Genesis 169–170
service-based games *see* game as a service
Seven Cities of Gold 180
sexism 102, 125–126
Shariki 33
shooter games (genre) 167, 170–171; *see also* first-person shooters
shopping: as game mechanic 23
Sid Meier's Civilization 30, 227–233
Sid Meier's Civilization VI 183
Sid Meier's Pirates! 230
Sierra Adventure, The (book) 151
Sierra On-Line 148–149, 151–152
Silent Hill 221
Silicon Valley 204–205
SimAnt: The Electronic Ant Colony 233
SimCity 60, 227, 229, 233–238
SimCopter 233
SIMON 51, 79
Sims, The 146, 222, 233, 239–245, 276
simulation 16, 108, 117, 130, 132, 176, 228–231, 233, 236, 237, 242, 276, 285, 293; game 98–103
Sky Fighter 245

INDEX

slapstick 290
Slot Racers 1 9
Smooth McGroove 269
Soccer 245
social gameplay 131, 133
social gaming 99
social media 119, 126, 165, 183, 198
social networks 99
sociality 199–200; emergent 199; forced 200
society of control 213
Solo Flight 228
Sony 120
Sony PlayStation 110, 112–113, 144, 174, 258, 293
Sony PlayStation 2 123, 130, 132
Sony PlayStation 3 141, 143, 176, 209, 286
soundtrack 53, 57, 113, 133, 157, 171, 222, 264
South Korea 251, 254–256
Soviet Union 268–269, 272
Space Battleship Yamato (anime) 246
Space Invaders 63, 64, 67, 191, 245–250; "Space Invaders Wrist" 248
Space Monster (song) 246
Space Quest 149
Spacewar! 91, 203–205, 208
Spectrum HoloByte 269
Speed Race 247
spirituality 280–286
Spore 180
sport video games (genre) 104–109; sport simulators 290
sports commentary and broadcasting 105
sprites 57, 72, 89, 149, 167, 170, 171, 247, 253, 307
SSX 145
St. Basil's Cathedral 269
Staiger, J. 1–3
Star Fox 258
Star Raiders 88, 91
Star Wars (film) 15, 118, 172, 246, 293
Star Wars: X-Wing 172
StarCraft 251–256
stereotypes 37, 126, 127, 167, 175, 243; character 301; players 303

stereotypes *see* race, racism
Story About My Uncle 212
story *see* narrative
story-driven games 306; *see also* narrative
storytelling 64, 77, 201, 307, 308, 310; environmental 137–138, 211; interactive 308, 309
strategy 2, 24, 85, 89, 176, 187, 199, 231, 252, 255, 275, 301; business 108, 120, 121, 304; design 156, 287; dominant 253; real-time 251–253; *see also* strategy games
strategy games (genre) 58, 160, 227, 228, 231
Street Fighter II: The World Warrior 166–167, 169, 171
subcreation 225
Super Mario 3D All Stars 262
Super Mario 64 257–262
Super Mario Bros. 40, 42, 155, 157, 262–267; creation of 263–265; impact of 265–266; sales figures 263, 266
Super Mario Galaxy 262
Super Mario Odyssey 62
Super Mario Sunshine 260, 262
Super Mario World 258
Super Nintendo Entertainment System (SNES) 105, 111, 169
SUPERHOT 212
Superliminal 212
Superman 154
survival horror (genre) 216, 220
survival: games (genre) 275, 278; mode 160–161
Sweet Home 216
Syzygy 203

Taito 245, 246–247
Takeda, G. 288
Tale of Tales 142
Talos Principle, The 212
Tanaka, H. 269
tanooki suit 21
target audience 112, 134, 304; patterns and preferences of players 101, 103

INDEX

Tati, J. 291
Tchaikovsky, P.I. 269
team licenses: football 108–109
technology 40, 75, 76, 86, 91, 99, 102, 109, 148, 155–156, 173, 179, 182–183, 197, 200, 204–205, 208, 236, 245, 252, 289, 294, 298; tree 252
teleprinter game 185, 187
Tencent 120
Tennis 290
Tennis for Two 203
Terminator 2: Judgment Day 167
Terminator: Future Shock 83
Tetris 33, 210, 268–274; neurological study of 271; psychological study of 271
Tetris effect 268, 271
tetrominoes/tetriminos 268, 270
text adventure games (genre) 88, 149, 152, 184–185, 187, 189, 305, 307, 310–311
thatgamecompany 143–144
theorycrafting 302
This War of Mine 274–280
Thorn/EMI 90
Thumper 51
TIGsource 160, 163
Time Zone 150
time-critical jump *see* kinesthetic experience
Titanfall II 71
title screen 156, 269
Tobias, J. 167–168
Tolkien, J. R. R. 58, 225
Tony Hawk's Pro Skater 3 21
top-down: perspective 63, 154, 216, 252; view 218
tower defense 117
Transformers (film) 15
transgression 51, 241, 242–243
transistor-transistor logic (TTL) 204, 245
transmedia 118, 213
treasure 9, 13, 59, 148, 149, 154, 156
Triple-A games 11, 41, 99, 183, 278
Tuck, H. 205
Turing Test, The 212

turn-based games 11, 58, 111, 227
turn-by-turn *see* turn-based games
TV Gaming Display 203
Twitch 121

Uematsu, N. 112–113
Ultima 10
Ultima IV: Quest of the Avatar 280–286
Ultima series 280–286
Uncharted 2: Among Thieves 98
United States Supreme Court 249
Universal City Studios Inc. v. Nintendo Co., Ltd., 65
Universal Soldier (film) 167
Unreal Engine 117, 120
Unreal Tournament 71
Urban Dynamics (book) 234
Uston, K. 193–194

Valiant Hearts 274
Valley 212
values in games 100–102
Valve 209
Van Damme, J.C. 167–168
Vanderhoef, J. 35
variability: modular 181–182; organic 181–182
vector graphics *see* graphics
Vib-Ribbon 51
video game industry 2, 19, 35, 40, 63, 64, 67, 99, 104, 126, 148, 150, 162, 179, 180, 194, 203, 206–208, 248–249, 263, 286, 289; revenue streams 100
Video Whizball 14
Videogame Ratings Council 170
violence 21, 24, 30, 32, 44, 47–49, 57, 62, 71, 72–73, 124–126, 128, 142, 143, 166–167, 169–171
virtual production 297–298
virtual reality 54, 160, 162, 180, 221
visuality *see* cinema
Vogel, J. 167
VR *see* virtual reality

walking simulators (genre) 143
war game 44, 48, 227, 274

INDEX

War of the Worlds (novel) 246
Warcraft (franchise) 300, 303
Warcraft 300, 303
Warcraft II: Tides of Darkness 252–253
Warcraft: Orcs & Humans 58
warfare: representation 45–47, 49
Warner Communications 249
weapons 45, 47, 58, 60, 69–71, 88, 89, 96, 119, 135, 138, 154–155, 176, 219, 293, 301; bioweapons 218; Portal Gun 210, 213
western (genre): in other media 188; tropes 186
White, J. 3, 5
Wii Sports 55, 98, 286–292
Williams, K. 149, 151
Williams, R. 148, 150–152
Windows 95 CD Upgrade 225
Wing Commander 91
Wing Commander III: Heart of the Tiger 293–299
Winning Eleven 105
Wizard and the Princess, The 150

Wizard of Wor 66
Wizardry 58
Wizardry 58, 81
Wolfenstein 3D 69
Wolfenstein II: The New Colossus 49
Wood, C. 113
Word of Notch, The 163
World of Warcraft 60, 93, 96, 121, 182, 299–305
world: of the game 89–92, 222–224, 226
Wright, W. 233–234, 236–237

Xbox Game Studios 160, 163

YouTube 269; YouTuber 121

Zeigarnik effect 270
Zork 148, 305–312
Zu: Warriors from the Magic Mountain (film) 168
Zynga 99, 101

For Product Safety Concerns and Information please contact our EU representative GPSR@taylorandfrancis.com
Taylor & Francis Verlag GmbH, Kaufingerstraße 24, 80331 München, Germany

www.ingramcontent.com/pod-product-compliance
Lightning Source LLC
Chambersburg PA
CBHW071228230426
43668CB00011B/1350